The Race of Time
The Charles Lemert Reader

Edited with an Introductory Essay by
DANIEL CHAFFEE
AND SAM HAN

Paradigm Publishers
Boulder • London

Copyright © 2009 Paradigm Publishers

Published in the United States by Paradigm Publishers, 3360 Mitchell Lane, Suite E, Boulder, CO 80301 USA.
Paradigm Publishers is the trade name of Birkenkamp & Company, LLC,
Dean Birkenkamp, President and Publisher.

Library of Congress Cataloging-in-Publication Data

The race of time : the Charles Lemert reader / edited with an introductory essay by Daniel Chaffee and Sam Han.
    p. cm.
  Includes bibliographical references.
  ISBN 978-1-59451-645-0 (hard : alk. paper)
  1. Sociology. 2. Lemert, Charles C., 1937– I. Chaffee, Daniel. II. Han, Sam, 1984–
  HM585.R33 2009
  301.092—dc22

                                                                        2009025498

Printed and bound in the United States of America on acid-free paper that meets the standards of the American National Standard for Permanence of Paper for Printed Library Materials. Designed and Typeset by Straight Creek Bookmakers.

13 12 11 10 09 1 2 3 4 5

Contents

Foreword
THE WORLD ACCORDING TO CHARLES LEMERT

Anyone considering contemporary American sociology who began by looking around for a public intellectual who embodied the broad sweep of the discipline's conceptual trends and political currents would arguably do no better than closely reading the work of Charles Lemert. Lemert, whom Norman Denzin has called "the preeminent social theorist working in America today," has been a remarkably influential figure both in and beyond the academy. Multidisciplinary, astonishingly eclectic, politically astute, and without doubt the most passionate public speaker representing American sociology, his uniquely crafted social theory at once manages to reflect the imprint of, and triumphantly transcend, everything from neo-Marxism to globalization, Goffman to Giddens, poststructuralism to postmodernism. His concrete, conversational style of writing is legendary: he has, over many decades, enthralled students with readerly, engaged accounts of the latest theories from the Continent, the intersections of modern sociology and cultural studies, or the global transformations of contemporary capitalism. In his supple, sociological intelligence, stylish writing and commitment to progressive politics, he has managed the astonishing feat of combining modernity and postmodernity, identity and society, race and representation, utopia and realism.

In one sense, Lemert's sociological genius is all his own. Anyone who has spent as long as ten minutes in his company cannot help but be struck by his infectious zest for social life, his endless fascination for culture, tradition, and religion as well as his consuming interest in others. An intellectual free spirit and courageous nonconformist, Lemert's writing might arguably be treated as an instance of Freud's "polymorphously perverse" unconscious *in action*—as his writing wanders effortlessly from modernization to race, celebrity to biography, French sociology to postcolonialism. The fact that he makes all this look easy—indeed, his writing rarely falls short of the most radical sociological imagination, at once intellectually stimulating, sociologically engrossing, and politically committed—is, again, testament to the practiced arts of his sociological vocation. As Lemert has stressed time and again in his work, it is the mundane, repetitive, and routine nature of daily social life that gives to the structured, structuring order of modern institutions their solidity, strength, and durability—all of which serve to underscore the practiced arts of personal and professional life, the performance of our social scripts, and the political contours of our affective relations with others.

In another sense, however, Lemert's sociological gift is also a product of his time, his placement in the academy, and his intellectual debts. As a student of Talcott Parsons at Harvard, Lemert inherited a sharp, shrewd sense of the interweaving of the personal and the social in the production of institutional life. As a result of various contacts with Erving Goffman, he zoned in on the importance of the everyday— of practiced social performance—to social relations. As an acquaintance of Pierre Bourdieu during his years in Paris in the 1970s, he came to focus, in a rigorous and systematic fashion, on the centrality of habits to the reproduction of institutional social orders. And, as a friend of the American sociologist Alvin Gouldner, he came to be acutely alert to the social-historical contours of social crisis. None of these influences were straightforward, not unmediated by other intellectual currents. Lemert, more than most sociologists, developed and retains a powerful way of drawing from the most inspiring around him whilst integrating new insights into his own laboratory of social-historical thinking. In this sense, he has drawn from the constituted realm of social theory in the very act of reconstituting it in novel directions.

This remarkable blend of the idiosyncratic and the inherited, the constituting and constituted, is displayed time and again in the texts of this most wonderful collection edited by Daniel Chaffee and Sam Han. Consider, for example, Lemert's critique of postmodernism—which he developed initially in the 1990s in response to the modernity/postmodernity debate and then subsequently in a revised version in the early 2000s to deal anew with the issue of globalization. Unlike some rather more coy sociologists who have loosely affiliated themselves with the "postmodern turn" only to beat a hasty retreat when intellectual fashions changed, Lemert remains assuredly unafraid to designate some aspects of the global realities we inhabit today as postmodern through and through. As he ironically puts this (from the title of his deeply engaging book) "postmodernism is not what you think!" For Lemert, postmodernism is not just a theory; in point of fact it is a range of theories— social, political, cultural, aesthetic. But before the postmodern is calibrated as, or transformed into, "theory"—says Lemert—it is a *lived social reality*. What kind of reality? Postmodernism is certainly not cut from one cloth, and Lemert is astutely sensitive to the complex, contradictory ways in which postmodern cultural forms interweave with modernist social practices; the modern and postmodern know of no precise historical dividing line, and any attempt to impose one is sheer intellectualism. Viewed against the backdrop of conceptual approaches in which everything from MTV to Madonna to mobile phones were treated as postmodern, Lemert's deft-fingered dismantling of the opposition between modernity and postmodernity has been especially bracing. Let me draw this point out a little by situating Lemert's contribution to social theory within the wider frame of the debate over modernity and postmodernity.

Postmodernism has been routinely identified with political radicalism. From one angle, it is easy enough to see why this is so, for many of the leading theorists of postmodernity hail from that side of the political spectrum (such as Jean-François Lyotard, Jean Baudrillard, and Fredric Jameson). From another angle, it is much less obvious that postmodernism is itself a radical social and political concern. Indeed, the opposite might plausibly be argued. What has happened with the advent of so-called postmodern society is the collapse of modernist rationality, core community values, and ethical and moral foundations. The sociological message in this reading is that postmodernism, in fact, spells a repressive reorganization of everyday life within the ideological structures of the global capitalist economy itself. Thus the advent of postmodernism—with its dazzling globalization of social relations, its deconstruction of metaphysical foundations, its reification of technology, and its cult of consumer hedonism—fits hand-in-glove with the imperatives of a market logic in which everything goes but nothing much counts. Or, so the story goes.

Lemert's reflections on postmodernism, by contrast, underscore the extent to which this shift in cultural temper has been interwoven with that revolution in philosophical understanding generated by French poststructuralists from the late 1960s onward. The radical pluralism of postmodern social and philosophical thought is said to mirror the concern with difference, otherness, and heterogeneity evident in the work of poststructuralist thinkers as diverse as Foucault, Baudrillard, Derrida, Deleuze, Guattari, and Virilio. This connection between postmodernism and poststructuralism is perhaps nowhere better dramatized than in Lyotard's *The Postmodern Condition* (1984), in which the author boldly proclaimed that "the status of knowledge is altered as societies enter what is known as the postindustrial age and cultures enter what is known as the postmodern age." Affirming the need for postmodern multiperspectivism, Lyotard argued that the dominant narratives of modernity (reason, truth, justice, and emancipation) had lost their credibility. Whether this conceptual move from modernist certainty to postmodern ambivalence was a phenomenon born during the closing decades of the twentieth century is, as Lemert reminds us, debatable. "The Modern Age is being succeeded by a postmodern period." It was C. Wright Mills, not Lyotard, who wrote this.

Such is the general thrust of Lemert's approach to the modernity/postmodernity debate. His social theory contains, however, an even more important classificatory scheme, which needs to be briefly noted, as the scheme provides insight into how Lemert sociologically dissects the most complex theoretical edifices. Lemert seeks to challenge the dominant battle lines drawn between critical theory and structural sociology (with their emphasis on system, totality, universal emancipation) on the one hand and postmodernism (with its stress on deconstruction, particularism, and relativism) on the other. Postmodernism, says Lemert, cannot adequately be confined to either "micro"or "macro" perspectives. He instead attempts to develop new angles and classifications for comprehending postmodern social theory. "There are," writes Lemert, "good theories of

postmodernism and some bad ones." "Good theory"for Lemert necessarily under-
scores the point that postmodernism is radically heterogeneous; today's world is
awash with controversies and transformations. "Bad theory," by contrast, repeats
the binary opposition of modernism and postmodernism and sometimes carries
the pernicious suggestion that the former is defunct.

With great skill and verve, Lemert identifies three main discourses that make
up the modernity/postmodernity debate. First, radical postmodernism: a version
of social theory that considers modernism done with, the key figures of which are
Baudrillard and Debord. Second, radical modernism: a discourse that views modernity as pressing up against its own institutional limits, a discourse developed in
the writings of such diverse theorists as Habermas, Bourdieu, and Giddens. Third,
strategic postmodernism: a discourse that imagines alternative social futures by
rethinking and rewriting modernity itself, associated by Lemert with thinkers such
as Foucault, Lacan, and Derrida. Although I mention this scheme only in passing
(it is difficult to do justice to the complexities and nuances of Lemert's sociological
adventures into postmodernism), the point I seek to underline is that his discussion
of these approaches is sociologically bold. Lemert's figuration of the postmodern
is conceptually valuable primarily because he presses this transdisciplinary map of
postmodernism into a sociological outline of numerous new knowledge formations.
Feminism and postfeminism, dissident sexual minorities, the politics of race as well
as other forms of identity politics and forms of resistance to the modernist culture
of Euro-American values are analyzed as signs of a postmodernization of culture,
communications, and social conflict. Similarly, Lemert views postmodern forms of
popular culture and mass media as, in part, novel responses to the emotional fissures
and social dislocations of the late modern age.

In Lemert's analysis of postmodernism and indeed globalization, as throughout
the extracts in this collection, the marks of the sharpest kind of sociological critique
are evident: a capacity to situate social theories in the social-historical contexts in
which they arise; the finest assessment of how wider social things impact, intrude,
and rewrite the textures of our private and professional lives; and penetrating
discussion of how contemporary social processes are constantly interwoven with
a dynamic global narrative of advanced capitalism. In this sense alone, Lemert
presents sociology with a fresh challenge: if social theory is to engage both intellectually and practically with today's global realities, then it must be sufficiently
subtle, nuanced, and politically engaged to confront the immense opportunities
and deadly risks of our present social order. His uniquely crafted social theory—at
once conceptually scintillating and politically somber—is of such extraordinary
power precisely because he loops the private, biographical realm of the everyday to
the deadly structures that, if not contested, all too often produce a deathly kind of
negation. In the remarkable breadth and scope of the topics treated throughout this
collection—from religion and social knowledge to French structuralism to globalization and new individualisms—Lemert challenges, significantly and unexpectedly,
the enterprise of social theory itself.

~

I first "met" Charles Lemert through a text—as it happens, the text was *Social Things*. The year was 1997, the city San Francisco, where I was attending the American Sociological Association (ASA) meetings. It was the first time I had attended the meetings of the ASA, and truth be told was astonished at the lingering hold of an empirico or pseudoscientific version of sociology within many of the panels that I attended. At any rate, on the second day of the conference, I wound up at one of those panel sessions you just wish had been cancelled—the kind of session in which time appears to have ground to a halt. Mentally suffocated, I was determined to depart the mind-deadening session, and indeed made a bolt for the door, when one of the "papers" finally concluded. Twenty minutes later, I found myself in a city bookstore, which is where I stumbled upon *Social Things*. A candid assessment of the gains and losses of modern sociology, the book (then just published) was squarely pitched between individual experiences on the one hand and the power of social forces on the other. In the face of the new global realities of capitalism, Lemert offered the dramatic suggestion that routine, mundane, everyday social life is the key arena in which contemporary women and men explore personal, cultural, and political issues of our times through the "sociological imagination." The writing was brimming with energy, the sociology impassioned, the politics of it all urgent. The San Francisco ASA may have left me cold, but "finding" (in Winnicott's sense) Lemert's *Social Things* had been heartening.

A few years later, after I'd moved to the United Kingdom to take up a Research Chair in Bristol, I invited Charles Lemert to visit to give a series of public lectures. Arriving with his family, including young daughter Annie, Charles took the city by storm. His lectures were packed: students and staff from the city's two universities filled the lecture theaters to hear him speak on postmodernism, on globalization, on theory. Arguing that the academy was neglecting a whole range of vital political issues—evil, death, waste, morality—Lemert himself became a focus on intense intellectual debate in the most elegant of smaller UK cities. To that impact corresponded a tremendous influence he exerted upon my postgraduate students (he, literally, spent countless hours with them over two weeks talking about their doctoral research), and along the way managed to generate an idea for a book that the two of us would write. That book, *The New Individualism,* an extract of which appears in this collection, was concerned first and foremost with the dramatic reduction of our social lives as well as the raising of individualism to the second power within human experience in our age of intensive globalization.

Since that first meeting in the early 2000s, I have routinely met and worked with Charles Lemert (and continue to work with him, as his intellectual stamina appears to know no limit) in various countries (America, the United Kingdom, Ireland, Australia) and institutional contexts (Wesleyan, Kent, Flinders). There are, truth be told, only two other social theorists I personally know (Anthony Giddens and Zygmunt Bauman) who have embraced social theory as intrinsic to the practical and political tasks of daily social life with the level of intensity and commitment of Charles Lemert. His is a uniquely crafted social-theoretical angle on our times and of our lives in these times. This collection, edited by Chaffee and Han, is indeed the perfect introduction to Lemert's sociology.

Anthony Elliott
Adelaide, 2009

Introduction
LEMERT'S SOCIAL THEORY

Daniel Chaffee and Sam Han

Charles Lemert exists in the penumbra of sociology—at once operating inside and outside the discipline. His writing addresses contemporary social issues through engagement with theoretical issues such as postmodernism and globalization, but it is based on a sharp analysis of ontological, ethical, and epistemological issues at the heart of abiding and intractable social questions. Few figures writing in the social sciences today have the range and depth of knowledge of classical social thought. But his real genius is not in making sense of the theory of the day with a sound understanding of classical sociology, but in an abiding critique of sociology itself. He consistently argues that sociology is in a unique position to think about social ills and the possibility of social change yet cannot come to terms with itself.

Lemert is a rare thinker in an academic culture. A sociologist by label and practice, but not from his time as a minister or his studies at Harvard Divinity School, Lemert has held a unique place in modern U.S. sociology. On the one hand, he has been a part of mainstream academic sociological culture for more than thirty years, but on the other he has had one—very critical—foot outside the door precisely because of his abiding critique and support of a discipline that has always been torn between scientism and social ethics. The Enlightenment ideals of the modern project promised something that could not be delivered. Its motto was "Dare to know"—for modern practices, the principle of modern science and social thought is that knowledge stands on its own and is the source of liberation and freedom. The thinkers that have come to be understood as the founders of the sociological tradition—primarily Karl Marx, Max Weber, and Émile Durkheim—were all part of this Enlightenment ideal, but also aware of its shortcomings. In each of their ways, they were critical of the problems of the new social order—modern society.

Lemert holds that social theory is the work of coming to terms with the intractable social questions of the modern world—for instance, why is the world not better or different? He holds a couple of views about social theory that explain why he has never quite been a sociologist and why social theory is appropriate to the work of inscrutable social questions. First, social theory is distinct from sociological theory. Second, social theory is the attempt to imagine social things as competently as we can. Sociological theory and social theory can seem like one and the same, but for Lemert they could not be more different. Sociological theory is a theoretical grounding for academic sociological studies. Social theory is an attempt to grapple with the "inherent contradictory and absurd nature of reality" ("Sociological Theory and the Relativistic Paradigm," in this volume). In a recent book of the same name, Lemert calls this grappling "thinking the unthinkable" (Lemert 2007).

This brand of social theory arises from the unthinkable understanding that no knowledge to be had is disinterested, perhaps something that the founding fathers of sociology could not think themselves. Thus, Lemert has been known for bringing excluded thinkers into the U.S. sociological canon, including W. E. B. Du Bois, Charlotte Perkins Gilman, and Anna Julia Cooper; from excluded racial, economic, and gendered positions, they were all more willing in some ways to think about social problems.

Academic sociology has long grappled with the question of social knowledge. Indeed, Lemert writes extensively of Durkheim's work in distinguishing the study of sociology—social things as facts—from psychology (see the "Social Things" section in this volume). Indeed, since Durkheim's day, sociology has struggled with the problem of social things: At once they are glaringly obvious, but somehow obscure and difficult to label. This problem is compounded by attempts to find objective knowledge. To admit that knowledge is always politically interested is a difficult thing for academic sociology, but Lemert goes a step further in suggesting not only that it is "interested" but also that it arises from desire. His starting point here is the Freudian conception of the unconscious. Not only is knowledge of the social not sitting on the surface waiting to be apprehended but also it is perhaps sitting in the unconscious. Thus, sociology as an academic discipline is always informed—if not inspired—by social life and its myriad problems, and sociology is confused in its ability to label and respond to these problems because of its failure to see that knowledge is not always rational and waiting to be found.

Our aim in this Introduction is to contextualize the work of Charles Lemert within the ideoscape of U.S. sociology. Our goal is not to give a linear history or tell a biographical tale, but rather to situate his thinking and writing within and against the debates in which he participated. We are not attempting to give an entire overview of U.S. sociology or an entire overview of Lemert's corpus of work; rather, we mean to focus on his social theory of the inscrutable (or queer, unthinkable, aporetic). In so doing, we focus on debates in academic sociology that have been particularly intractable. We have chosen to focus our critical discussions of Lemert's work on the postmodernism and globalization debates. Even though Lemert became famous—if we can call it that—through his earlier work, it is the later work that is most striking in its critique of sociology and most promising in its desire to discover new sociologies for new social problems.

U.S. SOCIOLOGY

In the immediate postwar era, as had the United States geopolitically, sociology emerged among the human sciences as the biggest show in town. Its dominance, as George Steinmetz has detailed, was the result of an unholy alliance among the then-perfected mode of production, specifically Fordism, the state, and the discipline of sociology.

> An entirely new cast of characters entered the discipline from wartime and government agencies and from backgrounds in private industry, advertising agencies, and survey institutes. U.S. sociology's own view of itself in this period followed a narrative of steady progress from social meliorist beginnings toward scientific maturity. The main historical treatment of the field from the 1950s described the discipline as becoming ever more focused on "scientific method," which was identified with the quest to discover laws of behavior and a "preference for concrete, empirical work." (Steinmetz 2005: 117)

Though we do not share Steinmetz's view of prewar sociology as "social meliorist," we find prescient his observation that U.S. sociology developed its own narrative of progress to be coincident with the national narrative simultaneously being forged under the banner of building the American Century. Hence, as Steinmetz concludes, the regulatory regime of Fordism and its resonance with "U.S. sociology's positivist unconscious after World War II" promoted mainly positivist social research and, as most sociologists today would agree, quite successfully (Steinmetz 2005: 132). Hence, to this day, the doxa of U.S. sociology is methodological positivism. This is not to say that all who trained in sociology were universally methodological positivists but that even those who opposed it, in fact, recognized common definitions and boundaries of distinction, thus creating a methodological economy of prestige in which those who followed closer to a positivist research agenda were rewarded with symbolic and economic capital.

Whereas positivism slowly diffused into the field, sociology's eminent theorist still remained Talcott Parsons, whose AGIL paradigm (referred to more generally as structural functionalism) posited a general theory of action. Though not exactly an adventurous theorist, Parsons could not fairly be considered a positivist. Parsons aimed to construct a robust cross-disciplinary theory of action that could apply throughout the social sciences. This was to be done via severe categorization of what Parsons called the "social system." By framing sociality within a system,

Parsons would treat individuals as goal-oriented actors within various concentric systemic layers (the social system being the largest, within which existed the cultural system and so forth). At the core of the Parsons theoretical system was the concept of equilibrium, a conceptual remainder inherited from Durkheim. Just as the "social order" for Durkheim operated as that which would prevent mass anomie, equilibrium for Parsons was that which would limit deviance from the order of things.

Despite the rise of methodological positivism, Parsons's influence, at least among sociological theorists, was quite strong until at least the late 1960s. Of the various examples of his intellectual dominance, his engagement with classical social theory stands perhaps as his most easily identifiable influence on theory. With *The Structure of Social Action* (1967 [1937]), he drew critically from three thinkers: Émile Durkheim (his greatest influence), Max Weber, and Vilfredo Pareto. As the book gained status as a textbook for training in theory for sociologists, the Parsons three became the canon of sociological theory and did not face a serious challenge for the next thirty years. Then, in the 1960s, students of all kinds organized to demand the rewriting of syllabi to include Marx. For students who have studied sociology since the 1960s, this bygone canon is nearly unimaginable.

Thus, in the golden era of U.S. academic sociology, when Talcott Parsons was leading the discipline at one of the most prestigious academic institutions, so-called radicals were taking sociology in a very different direction. Politically, the 1960s could not have been more turbulent, with student protests rising up around the world, two examples of which are May 1968 in France and Students for a Democratic Society (SDS) and the civil rights movement in the United States. Academically, Herbert Marcuse, C. Wright Mills, and Alvin Gouldner, to name a few, were asking how things could be different and demanding a sociology more relevant and active in contemporary social issues. In a time of unprecedented economic prosperity, Marcuse suggested that people were unhappy consumers. Mills criticized academic sociology for being neither properly empirical nor philosophically robust. Gouldner explicitly announced the crisis that Mills and Marcuse had implicitly argued in their books.

THEORETICAL CRISIS

The radical students who spearheaded the movements of the 1960s gained considerable inspiration from key sociological texts: *The Sociological Imagination* (2000 [1959]), by C. Wright Mills; *One-Dimensional Man: Studies in the Ideologies of Advanced Industrial Society* (2006 [1964]), by Herbert Marcuse; and *The Coming Crisis of Western Sociology* (1970), by Alvin Gouldner. It is not surprising then that Tom Hayden, a young SDS leader at the University of Michigan–Ann Arbor, wrote his master's thesis on Mills (Hayden 2006). But beyond radical politics, these texts had distinct theoretical (or philosophical) dispositions that veered away from the dominant Parsonsian theoretical framework. Mills saw himself in the tradition of

German philosophy and American pragmatism. Marcuse, once a student of Martin Heidegger, was an associate of Max Horkheimer, the director of the Institute for Social Research at Frankfurt, otherwise known simply as the "Frankfurt School," which espoused a perspective referred to as "critical theory," a mixture of a decidedly philosophical Marxism along with borrowings from psychoanalysis and Weber. Gouldner, whose *The Coming Crisis* bookended the 1960s, was a self-described Weberian Marxist, whose earlier works were studies of bureaucracy and labor movements. Taken together, these books went against the grain of mainstream sociological theorizing, acting as a counterpoint to the restrictiveness of Parsons's structural functionalism and the greater methodological positivism that would soon overtake the entire field of study.

Mills's book, the earliest of the three published, was a harbinger of the coming troubles of academic sociology. In it, he took to task the two dominant factions of sociology—"grand theorists" and "empiricists." Undoubtedly, he had Parsons in mind for the former, and for the latter, he did not need to look any further than his colleagues at Columbia in the Bureau for Applied Research. He argued that, despite the superficial differences between them—that one was "theoretical" and the other "scientific"—they had one thing in common: a sociology detached from the everyday realities of most people. To the contrary, he argued that sociology should be defined by imagination, one able to connect the personal with the public. For those like Hayden who looked to sociology to understand social structures, Mills's book proved to be an important resource.

As many scholars of the 1960s have noted, Marcuse's work was a lightning rod for radical politics (see Douglas Kellner's Introduction to *One-Dimensional Man*). Written in the early 1960s, *One-Dimensional Man* argued persuasively that U.S. culture was increasingly homogenized and centralized, resulting in the dulling of critical human reason. Marcuse saw this as the most severe of potential political dangers, having himself been forced to flee his native Germany during the Nazi era. Without a critical capacity, Marcuse feared, Americans, much like some Europeans decades prior, would fall under the sway of fascism. In this way, with the degradation of critical reason, we were less free in advanced industrial society in spite of the nominally "advanced" state of that society.

Gouldner's *The Coming Crisis* came at the very end of the 1960s. The title of the book in some ways was misleading because he had already witnessed a crisis or a challenge to sociology while writing the book. He had witnessed a radical challenge to the canon, specifically for the entrance of Marx. (Today every undergraduate and graduate introductory theory class has Marx in it.) In other ways, Gouldner was throwing down the gauntlet. As was the case with his famous essay "Anti-Minotaur: The Myth of a Value-Free Sociology" (Gouldner 1962), *The Coming Crisis* took on the objectivism in U.S. sociology, which had held on to the false notion of the neutrality in research and scholarship. Gouldner, in effect, was not looking to revise sociology's canon, but simply to remove the aura of scientificity, what critical science studies scholars later on labeled "scientism." Though these three books cannot be representative of the entire spectrum of the challenge to sociology brought on by the radicalism of the 1960s, Mills, Marcuse, and Gouldner are figures that embody the spirit of the 1960s that spilled into the halls of sociology departments.

During these years, Lemert was outside of academic sociology, yet involved in the social issues of the day as a minister and seminarian. Like some other politically engaged Americans in the 1960s, he went on freedom rides through the U.S. South during the civil rights movement. As a minister in Needham, a suburb of Boston, he became aware of a crisis of suburban values, which became the topic of his Ph.D. dissertation. Through his interactions as a minister, theology became not only a convenient segue into social theory, but also a continually important impulse.

His desire for social change was never quite realized in the ministry. By his account, "I didn't last long as a preacher. I was good enough at it, but there was something wrong with the Christians" (Lemert 2006). His was an ironic comment about the contradiction of liberalism in people who on the surface are politically correct and care about social issues yet ignore large social issues, such as racism. At Parsons's Harvard, though not in sociology or his Department of Social Relations, Charles Lemert was making a move that many socially engaged individuals at the time were making: from social activism and religion into academia. In Gouldner's *The Coming Crisis,* a survey of U.S. sociologists found that 27 percent of them were either onetime clergy or had thought of joining the clergy (history has shown that many radicals, including Weathermen, eventually landed in academia).

The exchange between the ministry and academia was not limited to the influx of politically conscious individuals; it was also reflected in the faculty at Harvard who were interested in religion as a social foundation and in the social production of meaning. Although religion has always been an important point for social theory, from Marx's "opiate of the masses" to Durkheim's search for the social foundation of a civil religion, the study of religion and the social production of meaning was a prime focus at Harvard. Peter Berger's (1990 [1967]) "sacred canopy" and Thomas Luckmann's (1967) "invisible religion" are prime examples. In addition, Robert Bellah, famous for the phrase "American civil religion," was working on religion and social inclusion. But perhaps the most important influence was Lemert's Ph.D. supervisor, Harvey Cox, who had recently published *The Secular City: Secularization and Urbanization from a Theological Perspective* (Cox 1965). Unsurprisingly, given Cox as a supervisor, Lemert's Ph.D. thesis was about, according to him, the production of social meaning in the suburbs. (He finished his dissertation while a fellow at the Massachusetts Institute of Technology–Harvard Joint Center for Urban Studies; thus he also claims, "The dissertation was really about space.")

Lemert's first publication was clearly heavily indebted to his time at Harvard Divinity and wove together many of the themes that would come to be earmarks of his career: space, religion, and the construction of meaning. "Suburbs and *Steppenwolf*" (1971) was Lemert's answer to the "problem" of suburbia. Indeed, in the early 1970s, the suburbs, as an object of inquiry, were particularly interesting for sociologists. The basic premise, or "problem," was a Durkheimian one of social wholes and anomie: The suburbs were homogenized, excessively individualized, overly technocratic; and thus meaningful social interaction had been leeched out of everyday life. (See David Riesman's *The Lonely Crowd: A Study of the Changing American Nature* [1965 (1950)] or its modern equivalent, Robert Putnam's *Bowling Alone:The Collapse and Revival of American Community* [2000], for arguments about the loss of community in the suburbs.)

Arguing neither for new community-building nor for radical action, Lemert took a different tack in his critique, one that was to become typical of his style. Using Hermann Hesse's novel *Steppenwolf* (1927) as a critical metaphor, Lemert suggested that the suburbs should not abandon their strengths, namely, technology and education. But he argued that these were cerebral activities and should be balanced out by more sensuality—in other words, more dancing. Suburbs were a middle-class representation of the desire for freedom and peace, but instead of being liberated, suburbanites found themselves trapped by a "successful institutionalization of middle-class rationality" (Lemert 1971: 178). The suburbs were inextricably linked to the economy of the city but had become culturally—and for the most part racially—separated. The very people excluded by the single-mindedness of the technocratic, suburban elite—poor blacks, the working poor generally, and the people of the inner city—are those in the best position to help suburbanites get back in touch with morality and reconstruct community. This was the problem with the "nice" people of the suburbs: They had fallen victim to their own truncated, technocratic moral success. The moral order of the suburb held no place for the very real social exclusions, and thus no place for compassion, the building block of community.

For Lemert, the social problem was never attributable to a single social institution but rather was always endemic—and ironic. Hence, the problem of the suburbs was not social isolation per se (Durkheim's anomie, lack of integration into the social whole), but the active denial of the racial segregation promoted consciously and unconsciously by suburbanites. This was part of a general problem of modern consciousness that obfuscated difficult social differences. (See "The Uses of French Structuralism: Rethinking Vietnam" in this volume.) In addition, Lemert called into question the notion of social entities as things in themselves: The suburbs were not independent from the city and could not be thought of as economically or emotionally disconnected. There was also something troubling about race, something that could not quite be written off as "white fright." Lemert wrote that black leaders such as Malcolm X and Louis Farrakhan terrified white sensibilities because they upset the social order, disrupting the liberal ideal of one societal "we." (See "Dreaming in the Dark, November 26, 1997" in this volume.) Not only is the possibility of "a social" queered, but also the possibility of social change is made a moral one: Whose we? (See "Whose We? Dark Thoughts of the Universal Self" in this volume.)

After receiving a joint position in religion and sociology at Southern Illinois University–Carbondale, Lemert, through personal and professional circumstances, ended up in Paris in the summer of 1972, interviewing communist mayors. This was the first of many trips to Paris during the 1970s (several of them sponsored by

Pierre Bourdieu), where he spent a lot of time in the library reading French theory, including Henri Lefebvre's work on space, which had not yet been translated into English (Lefebvre 1991 [1974]). Even though Lemert's early work on French sociology was not a commercial success, it was a boost for his career in unlikely ways. Gouldner, then at Washington University in St. Louis, was just back from four years in Amsterdam, a kind of imposed exile for assaulting a student named Laud Humphries, whose dubious research practices in his study of gay sex in New York had led to a row between the two that ended with Gouldner physically assaulting the Ph.D. candidate. Upon Gouldner's return, other faculty members at Washington University were less than excited at his presence and Gouldner was semi-isolated. He had heard about Lemert's French work and invited him down.

On numerous occasions, Lemert has called Gouldner his "teacher." Though not his teacher by the strictest definitions, Gouldner shared with Lemert a common interest—as demonstrated in "Suburbs and *Steppenwolf*"—in a reflexively self-conscious theory. This was the core of *The Coming Crisis* and important to Lemert's theoretical trajectory. For both of them, theory was not simply a tool of critique or an addition to empirical sociology. Rather, theory needed to cut to the heart of social questions themselves and was always an implicitly political investigation. To have a self-conscious theory necessitated taking a long hard look at the politics of knowledge. Although sociology students today at liberal arts colleges may take for granted that sociology is about uncovering hidden social structures, this was not always the case. Feminists know this lesson all too well, having developed standpoint theory, which requires theory to state its basis *and* its own social position. Lemert has drawn upon this kind of standpoint theory, though not an essentialist one. W. E. B. Du Bois (1989 [1903]) used the metaphor of the "veil": The person inside the veil is hidden from view, but unlike the observer, can see on both sides. For Gouldner and Lemert, sociology could be much like the observer: unable to see those people and ideas excluded by its scientist assumptions.

Additionally, Gouldner impressed upon Lemert Marxism, which he had not yet encountered to a large degree. Although the heyday of McCarthyism in the U.S. academy had been long gone by the time Lemert was at Harvard, there was nevertheless a remnant of anticommunism, especially in sociology. Even Gouldner, who had grown up in the Bronx and studied at Columbia in the wake of 1960s-era prominent "New York intellectuals," who had been influenced greatly by Marxisms of all kinds, did much of his work on classical social theory on the much safer (politically speaking) Max Weber, after whom he named his chair at Washington University. Hence, the encounter with Gouldner was also Lemert's first serious engagement with Marxism. (The absence of Marx is quite clear in his first published articles, including "Suburbs and *Steppenwolf*.")

Not only did Gouldner draw Lemert into Marxist theory but he also drew him into theoretical academic circles—Lemert had been geographically isolated in southern Illinois. Through Gouldner, Lemert joined the editorial team of *Theory and Society,* a journal whose board bore the names of prominent social theorists such as Pierre Bourdieu, Randall Collins, Anthony Giddens, Martin Jay, and Robert Merton.

Above any "instruction," *Theory and Society* was Lemert's education in social theory, and his tenure there would shape much of his work to follow.

The group was mainly made up of sociologists, but not exclusively. There were historians (notably Martin Jay) and other social scientists interested in social and political thought. This rooted-in-sociology-but-open-to-other-disciplines dynamic of *Theory and Society* would influence the liminal status of Lemert's future writing in sociology. Moreover, as the brainchild of Gouldner, *Theory and Society* can be seen in retrospect as the actualization of Gouldner's critique in *The Coming Crisis*. It was a journal whose name suggested a subjugated sensibility in mainstream U.S. sociology at the time: To gain a critical perspective on society or social realities more broadly, theory was more than necessary; it needed to come first. Hence, the title was *Theory and Society*, not the other way around. This strong stance proved not to be convincing for the majority of sociologists and social scientists, who were moving toward positivistic quantitative methods in droves, devoid of theoretical logic. At this critical moment in the history of sociology, *Theory and Society* and *Telos* emerged as journals supported (through contributions) by U.S. social scientists interested in social thought, especially from Europe. *Telos* became one of the premier journals for German theory, gaining its notoriety for translations of texts by the likes of Theodor Adorno, Jürgen Habermas, Claus Offe, and others in the German tradition but also those such as Jean Baudrillard who had not been widely read by social scientists. And this was true for sociologists in particular, who had not been especially attuned to developments in Continental philosophy or sociology overseas. Hence, Lemert was situated in one of the few journals in the social sciences that drew from European as well as U.S. social-theoretical debates.

Lemert's blast of productivity and intellectual maturity of the late 1970s and early 1980s gave way to greater institutional recognition for him. By 1984, he had joined the theory section of the American Sociological Association (ASA) as a council member; he would eventually become chair in 1989. He would also leave Southern Illinois for Wesleyan University in Middletown, Connecticut, as chair of its sociology department. As chair of the theory section, Lemert edited *Intellectuals and Politics: Social Theory in a Changing World* (1991), which brought together perspectives on the role of the intellectual, politics, and social theory. This edited collection bore traces of Gouldner, who had first impressed upon Lemert the importance of thinking through these very themes in conjunction with one another. Additionally, it was symptomatic of what kind of mark Lemert would leave on sociology and social theory, always placing on equal footing the position of the intellectual, politics, and theory itself and exercising the reflexivity once called for by Gouldner and later proclaimed by his friend Bourdieu. From this position, Lemert entered key theoretical debates in 1990s sociology centered on epistemology, postmodernism, and the place of "theory" in the discipline.

STRUCTURALISM AND EPISTEMIC DEBATES

Though Lemert had read the philosophical canon as a theology student at Harvard, and French social theory during his time in Paris, he had not been in dialogue with social theorists of this caliber until he joined the *Theory and Society* cadre of scholars. In fact, prior to the publication of his first book, *Sociology and the Twilight of Man: Homocentrism and Discourse in Sociological Theory* (1979), Lemert was primarily a sociologist of religion. It was not until later that he became a prominent social theorist. As alluded to earlier, religion scholars develop a keen sense of social realities, and it comes as no surprise that sociologists of religion were responsible for shaping what in the United States at the time was the most significant epistemological contribution in post-Parsonsian social theory—social constructionism, which grew out of the phenomenological tradition of Alfred Schutz. Nevertheless, the work of Berger and Luckmann, individually and together, in social epistemology was unsurprising because as sociologists of religion they were dealing with intricate questions of cosmic proportions, as had Durkheim, who was not only a founding figure of social theory but also a sociologist of religion. In their now classic work *The Social Construction of Reality* (1966), Peter Berger and Thomas Luckmann argued that knowledge is constituted not by hard truths but by constructs developed in consciousness out of social interactions. It is, to put it rather simply, the theory of intersubjectivity passed on through Schutz from the master Edmund Husserl. But the phenomenological model, which Lemert referred to as "a kind of intuitive science of the private mind," was a contending theoretical model that incorporated, or misappropriated as some would argue, European philosophical elements. This is important to consider as social constructionism in the United States became the object of critique for U.S. theorists who had been reading with keen interest what was being branded as "French theory." (See Cussett [2008] for a great explication of the branding of postwar French philosophy in the United States.) As the United States followed the lead of Erving Goffman and Harold Garfinkel to ethnomethodology and an increasing focus on the individual, French theory tended toward structuralism and poststructuralism.

Lemert was one of those U.S. sociologists who had been interested in French structuralism, and *Sociology and the Twilight of Man* was nothing short of a sweeping poststructuralist-inspired critique of the dominant strains of the sociological theory of the day. In it, he took on social constructionism, ethnomethodology, critical theory, and functionalism. There his object was one he learned from Michel Foucault and Jacques Derrida, in particular, the Figure of Man, under which, he argued, these various seemingly disparate theoretical dispositions were unified. They all took "man" as both subject and object of knowledge, resulting in a mystical understanding of what man was—a rather ironic development seeing that sociology was a crucial part of what were once called the "human sciences." This, Lemert argued, was an inheritance of phenomenology, which of course was a parallel argument that Foucault and Derrida made in their critiques of structuralism. Though the book did not make him an instant success, it did contribute to his stature as chief intellectual "translator" of French theory for sociology. After *Sociology and the Twilight of Man* came a flurry of publications dealing with social theory and structuralism, including "Language, Structure, and Measurement: Structuralist Semiotics and Sociology" (1979) and the anthology *French Sociology: Rupture and Renewal since 1968* (1981).

POSTMODERNISM

Hence, in the 1990s, when sociology belatedly began its moment of reckoning with the consequences of this thing called "postmodernism," Lemert often contributed to those debates with a precision that would get at the crucial import of postmodernism without falling into a debate arguing for or against it. As was the case with the attacks on postmodernism in other disciplines, such as architecture, literary studies, and history, which had much earlier considered its importance, postmodernism's sociological detractors were polyphonous. Some claimed that postmodernism could not possibly be useful for sociology as it did not provide a clear research program, hence claiming that it was ascientific and, as such, simply "ideological." Others argued that a critique of modernity did too much damage to the nation-state, liberal rights, and cosmopolitan citizenship (Antonio 2000), which served as "identity pegs," as Erving Goffman once put it, for sociology's methodological and political identity. (More on this follows.) Yet there were others who were attempting to adopt a "postmodernist" agenda for sociology or, confusingly, were trying to formalize postmodern concepts for sociological theorizing (Allan and Turner 2000). And yet others argued for a much more reasoned approach to the critique of modernity (as postmodernism was mainly interpreted) and the use of modern concepts to that end (for example, Alexander 1991; Calhoun 1994), which was indeed a response to the rather empty yet oft-used criticism of postmodern theory as unnecessarily difficult to understand.

This kind of side-taking in debate, although clearly recognizable in the other disciplines that confronted postmodernism, was particularly intriguing for sociology because for the most part it was limited to sociologists who considered themselves theorists. Whereas the debates surrounding postmodernism in literary studies reached practitioners of "empirical" literary works as well as literary theorists, in contrast, postmodernism remained mostly a theoretical question for sociology because of the deep traditional divide between theory and empirical work in sociological research culture. We make these rather crudely put claims grounded on binaries in order to make a larger point regarding the place of the "postmodern challenge" in sociology; that is to say, it remained a debate that was relegated to "theory" as some sort of specialized subfield accessible only to self-fashioned "theorists." It is perhaps this central feature of sociology—the accepted separation of the practice of theory and the practice of empirical case studies—notwithstanding Robert K. Merton's (1968) notion of the "middle range" and Barney Glaser's (1967) "grounded theory," which barely have had much impact. Yet Lemert in his many writings on the subject would always argue that postmodernism was not so much a purely theoretical challenge to sociology as (and maybe, for some, terrifyingly) an ontological one.

One of the earliest documented confrontations with postmodernism in U.S. sociology was a symposium on postmodernism in the spring 1991 issue of *Sociological Theory,* the official journal of the theory section of the ASA, featuring a lead article by Steven Seidman as well as responses/interventions by many of the most prominent theorists in sociology at the time—Jeffrey C. Alexander, Robert Antonio, Charles Lemert, and Laurel Richardson. Here, as he did in many of his writings on the subject, we see Lemert not purely advocating on the question of postmodernism and sociology but rather elucidating a clarion call to renew sociology by perhaps taking it less seriously, that is, loosening its self-righteous boundaries of discipline. His contribution, "The End of Ideology, Really," began with a riff on a distinction Seidman attempted to make in his lead article between "social theory" and "sociological theory" in order to suggest that postmodernism, in so many ways, called for the end of an explicitly formal-scientific theory. This Seidman called "the postmodern hope." However, for Lemert, Seidman had too easily assumed a distinction that was widely accepted in the discipline. It was not necessarily the case, as Seidman argued, that "sociological" theorists (those who saw themselves as constructing a scientific theory testable by empirical science) often used that term in reference to their type. In fact, as Lemert pointed out, there was a bit of a semantic mess when it came to Seidman's offering a typological layout of "sociological" as opposed to "social" theory. As Lemert pointed out, "If sociological theory is truly dead from confusion and postmodern social theory alive to hope, then the differences between the two must be severe and definite. This surely is the point Seidman wants to make. Yet he seems to be making the case for a postmodern hope somehow able to do everything foundational theories do—just better" (Lemert 1991: 166).

This is one of the crucial points of Lemert's broad stance on the possibilities of postmodern sociology—if sociology were to take postmodernism seriously, it would no longer make any foundational claims. As he saw it, Seidman, Lemert's friend and intellectual ally, "understate[d] the intended confusion postmodern social theory creates to the same degree he overstates the unintended confusion sociological theory laments" in his attempt to jettison "sociological theory" (Lemert 1991: 167). Lemert expanded on this more systematically in *Postmodernism Is Not What You Think* (2005), a book whose title reflected the author's thesis. The title, as Lemert explained in his Preface, was meant to be a double entendre. It meant to suggest not only that "postmodernism" had been misconstrued but also that postmodernism was not a thing to be thought. Rather, as Jean-François Lyotard (1979) called it, postmodernism was a "condition," that is, a deep challenge to modernity and its corollary philosophy of modernism. In "The Uses of French Structuralism: Rethinking Vietnam" (in this volume), Lemert outlined what he believed to be a case for a postmodernist sociology, but one that avoided the pitfalls of too easily attempting to import postmodernism into sociological theorizing and methodology, so as to view postmodernism as a possible corrective to sociology's modernism. In point of fact, this approach, which he criticized in "The End of the Ideology, Really," would be attempting to "think" postmodernism in an instrumental sense. Lemert thus concluded that

> any attempt to develop a … postmodernist sociology entails a willingness to face this monstrosity of language. According to such a perspective [postmodernism], when language is taken seriously for what it is, the social world is seen in a particular way. It is no longer possible to view the world as internally and necessarily coherent. To take language seriously, as the structuralists do in their manner of writing, as

in their philosophy, is to decenter the world, to eviscerate it of grand organizing principles (God, natural law, truth, beauty, subjectivity, Man, etc.) that mask the most fundamental truth of human life, differences. (Lemert 2005: 106)

Yet Lemert acknowledged that this would require a lot of unlearning or, as Immanuel Wallerstein (2001) has recently called it, "unthinking" the basic assumptions of their sociological training. One such assumption, which pervades modernist culture, not to mention social science, is that of the opposition or dialectic between individual subject and social structure. In a commentary on "A Formalization of Postmodern Theory" by Ken Allan and Jonathan Turner, Lemert asked whether the formalization of postmodern theory for sociology was possible: "How is it possible to 'test' formal propositions about a possible postmodern world when those propositions so evidently apply, with comparable rigor, to classically modernist understandings of the modern world? Postmodern theory, if it makes sense at all, makes the claim that one of the decisive departures from the modern world is not the loss of the viable subject so much as the loss of the subject's ability to understand, even to explain, the world as a whole.... In other words, postmodern theories of a world without viable subjects are not tragedies but opportunities" (Lemert 2000: 397).

Lemert's approach to postmodernism displayed one of the key aspects of his work, his willingness to step outside of the disciplinary boundaries imposed by sociology. By doing so, Lemert demonstrated what he had been doing throughout his work, which was to have one foot in sociology and the other out. He described this task as the pursuit of a small-s sociology as opposed to a Capital-S Sociology. Thus, here he simultaneously explained and often defended postmodernism, not to achieve any ideological purpose but to clarify its own terms and to critique "totality," or what he called in his response to Allan and Turner modernity's penchant for the assumption of "final authority," albeit God or science. One illustrative example of this was the typology of critiques of modernity he offered in another chapter of *Postmodernism:* radical postmodernism (Baudrillard, Guy Debord, Lyotard), radical modernism (the Frankfurt School and Habermas), and strategic postmodernism (Jacques Lacan, Foucault, Derrida). According to Lemert,

> *Radical postmodernism* wages war on totality by moving beyond the real to the hyper-real. Radical modernism wages this war by radicalizing the most powerful critical weapons of modern culture to attack real totalizing effects. *Strategic postmodernism* neither gives up on nor overrates modernity's power. It wages war on totality by working within the modern, as modernity works within us. As modernity deceives us into ignoring painful differences, the last postmodernism seeks to subvert those deceptions by its own tricks. (Lemert 2005: 53)

The liminality of his theoretical corpus, however, was indeed a purposive decentering of sociological discourse for what he believed to be a more appropriate, and historical, analysis of the world, because worlds had certainly changed since the middle of the twentieth century. It is with the intent to write the "history of the present" (Foucault 1995: 30–31) that Lemert in "Social Theory at the Early End of a Short Century" (1994) called for the end of the postmodernism debate by agreeing on a single point—that the world now truly lacked a final authority. For Lemert, the "defense" of postmodernism only came out of a larger, more significant obligation to the great riddles of social theory. He believed that postmodernism and poststructuralism were necessary but not sufficient developments for considering the question "What is the world and how is it to be lived in by whomever, where?" (Lemert 1994: 146).

GLOBALIZATION

Following shortly on the heels of postmodernism, the globalization debates took over the social sciences with exponential rise. Some themes carried over: identity politics, the breaking apart of structural principles, and the general collapse of the world as it was known. Even though initially, at least academically, there were extensive debates as to whether "globalization" had taken place, culturally speaking, globalization was everywhere. One of the most striking features of globalization is its call to end modernist assumptions, which the postmodernism debate never convincingly did. Globalization, for whatever else it may be, brings social and cultural differences to the forefront, forcing a painful rethinking of previous assumptions about the world. Lemert writes, "Globalization, whether it turns out to be postmodern or not, is a social process in which the grotesque failures and social evils of the modern world cannot be easily painted over" ("If There Is a Global WE, Might We All Be Dispossessed?" in this volume).

Sociologically speaking, postmodernism dead-ended into the intractable positions of radical modernists (Anthony Giddens and Ulrich Beck, among others), those who held on to some modernist assumptions, and unabashed postmodernists (Baudrillard) for whom the world had entered a period of hyperreality. Perhaps more importantly, postmodernism as a critique of modernist ideals became an almost exclusively academic debate, whereas globalization is undeniably a prescient issue across the globe and across economic, political, and cultural concerns. Neither camp of the postmodern debate is able to sufficiently grapple with what has come to be called "global complexity."

For Lemert, a better way to address something like global complexity is by recognizing that the realities that modernist thinkers denied are coming back to the fore. The global world is one where differences are all too apparent. If social theory is to keep pace, it needs to focus on what the world is now, why that matters, and for whom—a theoretical, empirical, and ethical problem. Social theory of globalization should be doing several things, according to Lemert. The epistemological question of postmodernism is still pertinent in the fundamental question of how we apprehend the social reality of the world, and that question involves a serious consideration of the discourses and texts that few in sociology have been willing to do. (See "The Uses of French Structuralism: Rethinking Vietnam" in this volume.)

Past theoretical attempts to consider empirical data have been "pathetically retarded," according to Lemert. Thus, it is time to take into account the overwhelming data of the contemporary era, such as data about world migration. (See "If There Is a Global WE, Might We All Be Dispossessed?" in this volume.) A global reality marked by pressing differences creates new categories of people, not only those undertaking forced global migration for work but also those who are pulled out of their local contexts and cultures. Lemert argues that for everybody affected, globalization is about dispossession and nostalgia.

Globalization clearly marks the end of a unifying reality. Poststructuralism calls attention to the fact that the social reality we think we know might not be directly present. Similarly, Lemert points out that for most people one of the most striking empirical truths of globalization is that "the world, whatever it is, is no longer One and, being thus broken, there is no substantive protocol on the basis of which we can expect its reality to be validly discernible or reliably confirmed" (1994: 146). Even though there are many possible historical markers demarcating the beginning of globalization, Lemert in a sense marks it with the ironic, confusing end of a world order. He writes, "The American Century was always a theory of world order; the inference is that the cold war ended because certain deep cultural assumptions of the modern West have come abruptly to the end of their plausibility" (Lemert 1994: 141). It is the end of a unifying social reality, which means the end of a particular world, which is necessarily social. But the U.S. world order did not get broken apart by liberal hopes of multiculturalism. Lemert points out the inherent irony in the liberal multicultural dream. How is it that "multicultural" can refer to a single world? He writes, "If the world is multicultural, in any plausibly real sense, then the world is many worlds" ("Can Worlds Be Changed? Ethics and the Multicultural Dream," this volume).

For sociology, the question becomes "What is the nature of social entities?" Lemert asks, following Durkheim, how can the social whole—be it tribal, national, or global—maintain integrity in a global world? What is it even to speak of a global world? For if there is such a thing, then surely globes and worlds are different. The globe is the physical thing on which we stand. Worlds, however, are something else entirely. In his "sociology after the crisis," Lemert's (re)conception of sociology hinges in part on his argument that sociology is about theorizing difference. He critically asks, "Who am I if things social are different?" He writes, "Sociologies, it could be said, are stories people tell about what they have figured out about their experiences in social life" ("Sociology as Theories of Lost Worlds," in this volume). In so many words, "world" is a social and moral, not a geographical, space. Perhaps it is better to say that social realities occupy the space between the social worlds and the geographic reality onto which they project them.

Tied to the question of social worlds is the question of ethical worlds. This is one of the key characteristics of Lemert's social theory—that social theory is a moral theory. He writes, "If, as it is often said, ethics is the art of thinking through which *ought* applies to a given *is,* then ethics is always, implicitly or explicitly, social ethics—a variant, thus, of social theory" ("Can Worlds Be Changed? Ethics and the Multicultural Dream," this volume). The argument is provocative, but it shows that to hold a normative claim—an "ought"—one has to have a durable empirical conception of reality. Indeed, this was the basis of Durkheim's foundation of sociology, writing social facts as things. Durkheim sought to establish sociology not only as a scientific discipline, but as a possibility for restoring moral order in the modern world. Thus the question of modernity was a question of social and moral cohesion. In *Suicide: A Study in Sociology* (1997 [1897]), one of the formative disciplinary texts of sociology, Durkheim asserts the existence of social facts and the necessity of studying them as durable empirical entities in their own right. Suicide, Durkheim famously argues, is not about the individual so much as it is a social tragedy brought on by the inability of the social collective to provide stable and functional norms. Globalization, argues Lemert, upsets worlds, durable social conceptions of reality—thus making it all the more difficult to even understand where Durkheim's famous conscience collective might lie: "In a century well after Durkheim's, the inability of the larger social wholes to guide the lonely individual is all the more salient in proportion to the individual's inability to know what exactly a social whole might be.... At the beginning of the twenty-first century, not even the wine merchants of Burgundy can locate the definitive border where France ends and, say, northern California begins; nor, accordingly, from whence they might draw what moral aid they require" ("Durkheim's Ghosts in the Culture of Sociologies," this volume).

Globalization is about multiple realities and the fracturing of worlds. If social worlds have become fractured to the point where we do not know what the social groupings—or the conscience collective—might be, what should be the focus of sociology without durable empirical realities to study? If borders and boundaries are in fact diminishing, then how is somebody to be from somewhere? Lemert argues that this is not just a problem of the third world, or a strictly economic question, but a problem that challenges the global cultural and economic elite. If there is something like a global world, then it is one where people have been stripped of what they once thought a world to be, namely, a home. "Of all the possessions the loss of which would be most widely felt, the first would be home—and nowhere more so than in the modern world. If home is where a person is from, then not to be from anywhere in particular is to suffer a terrible fate in a culture that values the conquest of social space as much as modernity has" ("If There Is a Global WE, Might We All Be Dispossessed?" in this volume). The fracturing multiple realities are brought together in their dispossession. Granted, the dispossessions of globalization are "leaky as to analytic precision, uncertain as to the meaning of their global situation" ("If There Is a Global WE, Might We All Be Dispossessed?" in this volume). But dispossession at least provides a way to conceptualize the dismantling of social worlds and the possibility of a shared outlook, providing the grounds for change.

Dispossession is a question not only for the global poor and starving but also for the cultural and economic elite. And for all concerned, globalization can be deadly. For migrants and refugees, it is very clearly deadly, but it is also deadly for those at the upper end of the economic scale. Economic globals—the mobile power elite—are traveling more and more and becoming more detached from the worlds and moral systems they knew. Richard Sennett famously outlines the challenges of new capitalism for the personal and moral lives of the economic elite (Sennett 2000). The cultural elite, Lemert argues, stands out in the structures of global dispossession. The cultural elite comprises those who have the means to support themselves but have had their cultural worlds unsettled. The ideal type is Edward Said, an intellectual from a wealthy family who refused to overlook his Palestinian past. It is hard to think about social theory without embracing the exilic factors, the intellectual willingness to think against the prevailing ideas of the times. Social theory can thus provide an emotional disposition not only for living against the times—embracing the cultural uncertainty, rootlessness, and unsettling effects of globalization—but also for surviving globalization.

Looking at this same question of the emotional dispositions of globalization, Anthony Elliott and Charles Lemert in *The New Individualism* (2006) address some of the emotional costs of globalization. They reanalyze the concept of individualism for the connections of individual and society, arguing that globalization has changed society rapidly, leaving individuals scrambling to catch up. Older versions of individualism included the culturally duped individual of the Frankfurt School, controlled by ideology, and the isolated privatism of the 1950s American about whom Riesman wrote in *The Lonely Crowd*. The globalized individual is characterized by self-reflexivity. With a burgeoning amount of information and interconnected risk, the global new individual must think about her or his life in a new framework without a frame.

This belies the point, as Elliott and Lemert admit, that maybe there is not all that much new about the new individualism given that all the types share the same root, but they stress that what is new is the complex, difficult, and changing social reality that now faces people in global times. Thus, their analysis dives under economic explanations of globality and into the darker spaces of the affected psyches and the emotional responses to such a destabilized global world. The key changes of globalization have been the breaking of durable and cohesive social structures, leaving individuals both wealthy and poor in a privatized and deadly world of global violence, connected by a growing culture of "short-termism." Although globalization seems like a theoretical abstraction, individuals are paying a high price: suffering global epidemics such as HIV, rising income disparity between the rich and poor, and emotional privatization. Lemert and Elliott provide analysis of personal responses such as compulsive plastic surgery and self-help therapy addictions. However, they argue that aggression has been overlooked as a possible response to global problems. They write that some are able to survive by living aggressively. "They are men and women, and more children than you would suppose, who see and feel the self within, accept it for what it is, and use its aggressions and drives for attachment to others, with whom they remake themselves and what corners of the worlds they can" ("Surviving the New Individualism," this volume).

Elliott and Lemert bring the emotional costs and responses to a debate that has largely ignored individual problems and centered on economics, politics, and geography. The difficulty and the excitement of globalization are the radical shifts in the way in which life is lived—if one can get over the feelings of nostalgia for the old social order, one can begin to see the radical shifts not only as dispossession but also as a re-embedding and reconstruction of social actions. Globalization is not just about destruction and personal pathologies, but also about creative responses.

~

Throughout the recent theoretical debates in which Lemert has participated, he has held a consistent, if ironic, stance—at once critical, hopeful, and imbued with the aporia of social structures. In this book, we have divided his work into several analytic divisions (listed in the Table of Contents and hereafter in bold) that are both somewhat arbitrary and significant. They are only arbitrary in that the lines could have been drawn in other ways.

At the beginning of his career, Lemert was concerned more with epistemic questions, characterized in this volume as "**Rethinking Social Knowledge,**" the first section. Although it could be said that this concern is indeed an overarching theme in his work, more specifically at the beginning of his career he focused on broader cultural issues (suburbia), religious and relativistic paradigms, and their relationship to social knowledge, both sociological and practical. The chapters in this section reflect Lemert's engagement with relativism, to take on ideological commitments of academic sociology. "Cultural Multiplexity and Religious Poly-theism" applies a sociology of knowledge to the sociology of religion and "Sociologi-cal Theory and the Relativistic Paradigm" has in fact risen alongside sociological thought and, far from nihilistic, is useful for understanding the world in terms of complementarity.

How is it that "the social" can be defined, and once defined, how is sociology anything different from other social knowledge? In "**Social Things,**" the chapters track through some of Lemert's writings on Durkheim's sociology, specifically his stance on "the social" or the impossibility of "the social." Social things are made "real" by the coherent narratives that are told about them, including the construc-tion of "social worlds"—at once forceful and obscure. The worlds that structure the social are always disappearing, much as the specter of Durkheim haunts sociology. Far from a social constructionist perspective, both "Sociology as Theories of Lost Worlds" and "Durkheim's Ghosts in the Culture of Sociologies" seek to understand what a "world" is and the struggle to define it in global times. As Lemert insight-fully argues, Durkheim's "sociology meant to serve the moral needs of the world as he saw it" ("Sociology as Theories of Lost Worlds," in this volume). Social worlds are wrapped up in the moral ways in which we apprehend social groupings across the globe.

Social things being as they are—inscrutable—sociology is the worst except for all the others at grappling with things social. "**Critical Sociology**" illustrates, following from Gouldner's warnings, Lemert's hope of a critically self-reflexive aca-demic sociology. In "Sociology: Prometheus among the Sciences of Man," Lemert suggests that sociology is Promethean because it is able to borrow from so many interesting intellectual histories; it is better equipped but it is also thus hamstrung by debate. Though some attribute the "endless" debates to postmodernism, Lemert argues that to take postmodernism seriously is to realize that modernism held the false promise of the Enlightenment: progress. French structuralisms are a case in point: At one time they constituted a totalizing system, but with poststructuralist critique, the system revealed its inherent contradictions. But, importantly, to realize the contradictions is not to abandon the project. "The Uses of French Structuralism: Rethinking Vietnam" illustrates that a postmodern sociology is one that discursively and critically reflects on the assumptions of a discipline. "Against Capital-S Sociology," a review essay of Stephan Fuchs's *Against Essentialism* (2001), defends a postmodern willingness to work through social questions, and asks what the reality of social things is in the postmodern world.

The "**Dark Thoughts**" section contains two chapters from the book of the same name that begin to broach race, a subject to which Lemert had not devoted an entire volume. The first chapter, "Dreaming in the Dark, November 26, 1997," does not resemble the standard academic article. It is a meditation on a dream, a dark thought, so to speak, that he had in November 1997. The second, "The Race of Time," is an essay on W. E. B. Du Bois's *Black Reconstruction in America, 1860–1880* (1998 [1935]), in which Lemert uses Derrida's deconstruction to consider issues of temporality in Du Bois's historiography. In line with what David Theo Goldberg argues in *Racist Culture* (1993), Lemert suggests that race cannot be detached from Enlightenment thinking, which dominated the intellectual underpinnings of modernity. Dark thoughts, as opposed to enlightened thoughts, are a way of analyzing the social world against the grain, which Lemert, in a brilliant rhetorical move, suggests can best be found in the works of African U.S. scholars whose writings were ignored and even erased from the dominant intellectual history of social theory. Dark thoughts, therefore, are the realities that expose the underbelly of modernity—the heavy cost of progress—shadowed by the glow of modernity and effectively sent off on a ship of fools.

The "**Ethics and Identity**" section extends the themes found in the previous section, specifically around the question of multiculturalism and the demise of identity politics. In "Whose We? Dark Thoughts of the Universal Self, 1998," Lemert questions the implicit assumptions made not only by individuals but by academic sociologists about social groupings. His question is much more than a literary condemnation; it has significant social-theoretical consequences. Whenever scholars and theorists use "we," they assume a reference to and identification with a "society" in which this "we" is a category or means of inclusion—and, of course, exclusion. The markers usually assumed are more hidden than they seem to be. Hence, the question of identity is always an ethical one, an admission that the warriors of identity politics did not bother to ask. "Can Worlds Be Changed? Ethics and the Multicultural Dream" is a critique of the idea of universal human value in the face of modern social differences, most importantly race. Ethics is always social theory because it is a question of social divisions and differences, the analytic constructions at the heart of all normative questions.

The linkage of ethics and identity is especially important for Lemert because the discourse of globalization has been dominated by those who believe that we live in a world that is smaller and more connected. Yet, as Lemert contends, globalization, if anything, must be considered an explosion of worlds. By this he refers not only to the increasing levels of economic and social inequality but also to the impact of decolonization movements on contemporary geopolitics. And thus, for Lemert, it is best to describe what many scholars and journalists have called globalization as **"Globalized Worlds."** In this section, the lead chapter, "If There Is a Global WE, Might We All Be Dispossessed?" is a transitional piece from the previous section. In it, Lemert argues for a nuanced view of identity amid increasingly globalized realities, one he believes should be defined by the metaphor of "dispossession" or "exile." He extends this discussion in "Surviving the New Individualism," his most recent collaborative work with Anthony Elliott.

REFERENCES

Alexander, Jeffrey C. 1991. "Sociological Theory and the Claim to Reason: Why the End Is Not in Sight." *Sociological Theory* 9, no. 2: 147–153.

Allan, Kenneth, and Jonathan H. Turner. 2000. "A Formalization of Postmodern Theory." *Sociological Perspectives* 43, no. 3: 363–385.

Antonio, Robert J. 1991. "Postmodern Storytelling versus Pragmatic Truth-Seeking: The Discursive Bases of Social Theory." *Sociological Theory* 9, no. 2: 154–163.

———. 2000. "After Postmodernism: Reactionary Tribalism." *American Journal of Sociology* 106, no. 1 (July): 40–87.

Bellah, Robert. 1967. "Civil Religion in America." *Journal of the American Academcy of Arts and Sciences* 96, no. 1: 1–21.

Berger, Peter. 1990 [1967]. *The Sacred Canopy: Elements of a Sociological Theory of Religion.* New York: Anchor Books.

Berger, Peter, and Thomas Luckmann. 1966. *The Social Construction of Reality.* Garden City, NY: Doubleday.

Calhoun, Craig J. 1994. *Social Theory and the Politics of Identity.* Boston: Blackwell.

Cox, Harvey. 1965. *The Secular City: Secularization and Urbanization from a Theological Perspective.* New York: Macmillan.

Cussett, François. 2008. *French Theory: How Foucault, Derrida, Deleuze, and Company Transformed the Intellectual Life of the United States.* Translated by Jeff Fort. Minneapolis: University of Minnesota Press.

Du Bois, W. E. B. 1989 [1903]. *The Souls of Black Folk.* New York: Penguin.

———. 1998 [1935]. *Black Reconstruction in America, 1860–1880.* New York: Free Press.

Durkheim, Émile. 1997 [1897]. *Sociology: A Study in Sociology.* Translated by John Spaulding. New York: Free Press.

Foucault, Michel. 1995. *Discipline and Punish: The Birth of the Prison.* Translated by Alan Sheridan. New York: Random House.

Fuchs, Stephan. 2001. *Against Essentialism: A Theory of Culture and Society.* Cambridge, MA: Harvard University Press.

Glaser, Barney, and Anselm Strauss. 1967. *The Discovery of Grounded Theory: Strategies for Qualitative Research.* Piscataway, NJ: Transaction.

Goldberg, David Theo. 1993. *Racist Culture: Philosophy and the Politics of Meaning.* Oxford, UK: Blackwell.

Gouldner, Alvin W. 1962. "Anti-Minotaur: The Myth of a Value-Free Sociology." *Social Problems* 9, no. 3: 199–213.

———. 1970. *The Coming Crisis of Western Sociology.* New York: Basic Books.

Hayden, Tom. 2006. *Radical Nomad: C. Wright Mills and His Times.* Boulder, CO: Paradigm Publishers.

Lefebvre, Henri. 1991 [1974]. *The Production of Space.* Translated by Donald Nicholson-Smith. Oxford, UK: Blackwell.

Lemert, Charles. 1971. "Suburbs and *Steppenwolf.*" *Andover Newton Quarterly* 11, no. 4: 171–182.

———. 1979. "Language, Structure, and Measurement: Structuralist Semiotics and Sociology." *American Journal of Sociology* 84, no. 1: 929–957.

———. 1979. *Sociology and the Twilight of Man: Homocentrism and Discourse in Sociological Theory.* Carbondale: Southern Illinois University Press.

———. 1991. "End of Ideology, Really." *Sociological Theory* 9, no. 2: 164–172.

———. 1994. "Social Theory at the Early End of a Short Century." *Sociological Theory* 12, no. 2: 140–152.

———. 2000. "A Commentary on Allan and Turner: Sailing in Postmodern Winds—Formal Methods in Uncertain Worlds," *Sociological Perspectives* 43, no. 3: 387–397.

———. 2005. *Postmodernism Is Not What You Think.* 2nd ed. Boulder, CO: Paradigm Publishers.

———. 2006. Personal Interview with Daniel Chaffee and Sam Han. July 9, 2006.

———. 2007. *Thinking the Unthinkable: An Introduction to Social Theories.* Boulder, CO: Paradigm Publishers.

Lemert, Charles, ed. 1981. *French Sociology: Rupture and Renewal since 1968.* New York: Columbia University Press.

———. 1991. *Intellectuals and Politics: Social Theory in a Changing World.* London: Sage.

Luckmann, Thomas. 1967. *The Invisible Religion: The Problem of Religion in Modern Society.* Macmillan.

Lyotard, Jean-François. 1984 [1979]. *The Postmodern Condition: A Report on Knowledge.* Translated by Geoff Bennington and Brian Massumi. Minneapolis: University of Minnesota Press.

Marcuse, Herbert. 2006 [1964]. *One-Dimensional Man: Studies in the Ideology of Advanced Industrial Society.* New York: Routledge.

Merton, Robert K. 1968. *Social Theory and Social Structure.* New York: Free Press.

Mills, C. Wright. 2000 [1959]. *The Sociological Imagination.* Fortieth Anniversary Edition. New York: Oxford University Press.

Parsons, Talcott. 1967 [1937]. *The Structure of Social Action.* 2nd ed. New York: Free Press.

Putnam, Robert. 2000. *Bowling Alone: The Collapse and Revival of American Community.* New York: Simon and Schuster.

Richardson, Laurel. 1991. "Postmodern Social Theory: Representational Practices." *Sociological Theory* 9, no. 2 (Autumn): 173–179.

Riesman, David, Nathan Glazer, and Reuel Denney. 2001 [1950]. *The Lonely Crowd: A Study of the Changing American Nature.* New Haven, CT: Yale University Press.

Seidman, Steven. 1991. "The End of Sociological Theory: The Postmodern Hope." *Sociological Theory* 9, no. 2 (Autumn): 131–146.

Sennett, Richard. 2000. *The Corrosion of Character: The Personal Consequences of Work in the New Capitalism.* New York: Norton.

Steinmetz, George. 2005. "The Genealogy of a Positivist Haunting: Comparing Prewar and Postwar U.S. Sociology." *boundary 2* 32, no. 2: 109–135.

Wallerstein, Immanuel. 2001. *Unthinking Social Science.* Philadelphia, PA: Temple University Press.

Acknowledgments

Though thanks may not be exactly the appropriate sentiment, they are indeed due to Charles Lemert. As mentor and friend, he has offered unending support to us both. Our relationship with Charles began in his social theory seminar at Wesleyan University and continued through the founding of an advanced social theory seminar, which several years on continues to engage students in advanced discussions of social theory.

We should also like to thank Dean Birkenkamp, our editor at Paradigm Publishers, and the rest of the staff at Paradigm for their support and work for this project. Additionally, Ann Hopman at Paradigm has been incredibly helpful.

Thanks to various colleagues at Flinders University, Australia, and The Graduate Center, City University of New York, for their intellectual participation and engagement with this project, in particular Anthony Elliott, Eric Hsu, Mary Holmes, Patricia Ticineto Clough, and Jerry Watts.

And a special thanks to members of each of our families who have supported us: Jonathan Chaffee, Katy Chaffee, Tamara Waraschinski, Elias Chaffee (Daniel), Paul Han, and Khalia Frazier (Sam).

Lastly, the following presses and journals kindly allowed for reproduction: *boundary 2, Sociological Theory, Sociological Inquiry, Thesis Eleven,* Routledge Publishers, Cambridge University Press, and the ghost of *Social Compass.*

I

Rethinking Social Knowledge

1

Cultural Multiplexity and Religious Polytheism

Religious ideas are transmitted in cultural systems through which they are rooted in historically concrete social structures. If sociologists of religion could agree that their scientific community has an axiom, a statement of this sort would surely receive the honor. This paper will argue that—while we can and should continue to take for granted most of what is implied in this axial statement—there is need for further analysis of the matter of the rootedness of religious ideas in their historically specific social structures. In particular a consideration of the impact of modern social and cultural conditions on religious ideation is needed.

The independent variability of religious ideas; the causal correspondence between religious ideas and social structures; the persistence of the religious factor (or its equivalent)—these extensions of the above designated axiom are now elementary assumptions in the scientific study of religion. Indeed they are the common thread woven throughout the history of the discipline. Beginning with the classic defenses of the autonomy of religious ideas (Weber, Troeltsch), these assumptions have subsequently found their way into prominent theoretical statements in the major sociological schools; namely: functionalism and neofunctionalism (Parsons, Bellah, Geertz),[1] interactionism (e.g., Hugh Duncan),[2] and phenomenology (Berger, Luckmann).[3] All in all, the literature is well stocked with: replications of the Weber thesis,[4] discussions of the epiphenomenal problem,[5] measurements and analyses of the degree and nature of secularization in modern society,[6] empirical and quasi-empirical investigations of new religions and the religious dimension of social movements and institutions,[7] and programmatic recommendations for the operationalization of religious variables or the typologization of religious institutions.[8] While it could not be argued that there is nothing more to contribute along these lines, it can be shown that this entire body of literature reveals a common failure of nerve (to borrow again from Gilbert Murray). The failure stems, I would argue, from a reluctance to take with full seriousness a critical aspect of the discipline's axial assumption;

namely: the question of the extent to which the social and cultural configurations of a given epoch influence the nature of religious ideation peculiar to that epoch. The background for this failure appears to be an oversensitivity to lapsing back into a crude Marxian reductionism.

Whatever the cause (and I do not intend to explore this interesting question here), the evidence for the failure of nerve is clear. Directly stated, the failure is the apparent unwillingness to see that the traditional categories for the sociological analysis of religion are culture-bound. They derive from the thought world of traditional Judeo-Christian culture. Thus, their applicability to the complex modern situation must remain in doubt. Roland Robertson has diagnosed this problem:

> The category "religion" is one which has arisen in sociocultural contexts where the Judeo-Christian tradition has predominated. A great difficulty in the sociology of religion is the extent to which our basic conceptual apparatus is derived from the doctrines of Christian religions. The church-sect distinction developed initially in a sociological context by Weber and Troeltsch is the outstanding specific example of such a "Christian" conception. The ideas of religion and religiosity are products of basically Christian thinking because of the tensions expressed in Christian doctrine as between, on the one hand, social and terrestrial reality and, on the other, transcendent spiritual reality.[9]

Even more poignant an illustration is the unembarrassed ease with which Durkheim was able to introduce the category "church" into his definition of religion employed in the study of elementary religion among primitive cultures.[10]

Virtually all of the literature that influences thinking in the field is as "Christianized" as are the works of Weber, Troeltsch and Durkheim. In this respect avant-garde scholars such as Harvey Cox and Robert Bellah have not been appreciably more sensitive to the problem than their more traditional colleagues, Andrew Greeley, Dean Kelley, Charles Glock and Rodney Stark, and others. Cox, of course, employs Christianized categories quite intentionally.[11] Only slightly less intentional is Robert Bellah[12] whose definition of religion in one of his most formal scientific manuscripts is based quite directly upon the concept "ultimate concern," the invention of a Christian theologian, Paul Tillich. "Ultimacy" is clearly the type of religious idea that can flourish only in traditional western Judeo-Christian thinking with its emphasis upon a transcendent God and the supernatural/natural hierarchical cosmology. Thus, the apparent radicalism of Cox's studies of modern secular and festive man may be seen, from this point of view, as actually quite conservative. Likewise, Bellah's imaginative proposal of symbolic realism among multiplex modern selves loses considerable plausibility in the absence of a theoretically radical understanding of religion. Thus, with respect to the persistent influence of Judeo-Christian doctrine on social scientific categories, Cox and Bellah do not differ significantly from scholars such as Greeley, Lenski and Glock who assume a simple positive equation of "religion" with "church" in their studies of modern religion.

The only major exceptions to this failure are the important theoretical contributions of Peter Berger and Thomas Luckmann.[13] Their importance lies in providing the theoretical groundwork for an extra-Christian theory of religion while, at the same time, setting forth a viable explanation for the social foundations of religion. Regrettably there has been little advance beyond their introductory proposals. What is needed is a further specification of the precise structures of complex modern culture and analysis of religious ideation in the context of those structures. What follows is a contribution in this direction.

Specifically, I wish to take my strategy from the theoretical argument of Berger and Luckmann that the sociology of religion may be understood as a variant from of the sociology of knowledge.[14] In one respect, Berger and Luckmann have merely formalized an assumption that goes back to Durkheim and Weber. It is not at odds with the axial statement with which we began. However, little exact attention has been given to the comparative sociological study of religious ideas in traditional and complex modern sociocultural contexts. The following draws upon Bellah's work but goes beyond it in extending his analysis and then applying it to the general features of religious ideas in American theology during the past decade. Primary attention is given to the sociological analysis of the idea of monotheism. Secondly, the essay offers the analytic grounds and preliminary evidence for the possible emergence of a religious polytheism. Strictly speaking, the term "polytheism" must be used metaphorically. It refers to the softening of the monotheistic principle in the direction of allowing for the positive value of multiple "power centers" in the social-psychological foundations of modern religion.

MONOTHEISM AND CULTURAL MONOPLEXITY

The dominant religious idea of traditional, premodern Western civilization is the Judeo-Christian concept of monotheism. To this idea credit is given for the rise of Western historical consciousness. This familiar conclusion is well established in sociology by Weber,[15] Parsons,[16] Bellah;[17] in the history of religion by Eliade;[18] and in recent theology by thinkers such as H. Richard Niebuhr,[19] Harvey Cox,[20] and Richard Rubenstein.[21]

Corresponding to the religious idea of monotheism is the essentially monoplexic nature[22] of the traditional sociocultural system. Simply defined, monoplexic sociocultural systems are characterized by the fact that one system of values, ideas and beliefs orders and defines all of relevant reality. This is not to say that monoplexic cultures are devoid of ideational diversity. It merely means that one consistent system and mode of thought is seen to be so powerfully legitimate that other nomic perspectives are unable to compete.

These observations are quite elementary. However, what has been frequently overlooked is the important correlation between these sociocultural facts and the types of ideas (and knowledge in general) that correspond thereto. If we take a sociology of knowledge perspective, then we are compelled to conclude that the fit between ideas and specific cultural contexts is far tighter and more necessary than hitherto imagined. For example, we can take a step beyond Weber. Weber was, of course, quite right in observing the correlation between the rise of monotheism and the historical perspective contained in prophetic Judaism.[23] What he did not assert is that the monotheistic principle must be restricted only to monoplexic cultures such as traditional Israel, Rome, Greece, or Medieval Christianity. Stated more rhetorically, we can say that monotheism cannot be expected to survive the decline of traditionalism.

Karl Mannheim's study of the origins of modern thought[24] can be applied to this analysis. Mannheim relocated the beginning point for modern thought. He pushed it back beyond its customary place with Descartes to Luther. Referring to epistemology in general, Mannheim interpreted Luther as the first to introduce an authentic subjectivism into Western thinking. In contrast, the traditional Middle Ages were characterized by an epistemological objectivism which corresponded to the stable, integrated, relatively undifferentiated nature of the medieval world order. Luther's tandem doctrines of the "inner man" and "justification by faith alone" provided—for the first time—a legitimate locus for subjective knowledge. In Mannheim's words: "Protestantism rendered subjective a criterion which had hitherto been objective, thereby paralleling what modern epistemology was doing when it retreated from an objectively guaranteed order of existence to the individual subject."[25] This breakthrough on the level of ideas was possible only because of the breakdown of the traditional monoplexic social structure, said Mannheim:

> From a sociological point of view the decisive fact of modern times, in contrast with the situation during the Middle Ages, is that this monopoly of the ecclesiastical interpretation of the world which was held by the priestly caste is broken, and in the place of a closed and thoroughly organized stratum of intellectuals, a free intelligentsia has arisen. Its chief characteristic is that it is increasingly recruited from constantly varying social strata and life situations, and that its mode of thought is no longer subject to regulation by a caste-like organization.[26]

From Mannheim we have the basis for an historical analysis of the social foundations of religious ideas, namely: Traditional monoplexic social structures will support, on the cultural level, an objectivist epistemology which, in turn, anchors a monotheistic type of religious ideation. From this conclusion it is possible to draw—within an historical frame of reference—the general features of complex modern culture.

RELATIVISM AND MULTIPLEXIC CULTURE

Modern sociocultural structures may be characterized as multiplexic (following Bellah). The enormous variety of ideas, beliefs, values, and institutional options and demands of modern society must be seen as more than pluralistic. It is not simply a matter of differentiation, but rather of the type of variation in which thought and belief possibilities are virtually limitless. The consequence is reflected by what Robert

J. Lifton calls the protean self-process: "The protean style is characterized by flux and flow in the 'self-process'—a term preferable to others such as 'personality' and 'character' which suggest a certain fixity . . . Thus we see in the protean style an interminable series of experiments and explorations—some shallow, some profound—each of which may be readily abandoned in favor of still newer psychological quests."[27]

Accordingly, modern thought patterns are what Mannheim calls subjectivist. Thus, modern religious ideas, as formulated by theologians working within traditional Jewish and Christian contexts, may be expected to exhibit the influence of multiplexity in the form of an increasing attention to polytheistic possibilities.

To describe the modern civilizational complex as multiplexic is merely to extend an elemental law of classical social thought. It is well known that formal sociological theory arose with one denominator common to virtually every major school of thought. Durkheim, Weber, Toennies, Cooley, Maine, all organized their theories around a periodization of history in which traditional and modern societies were sharply dichotomized. The substantive categories varied (organic solidarity, rationalization, *gesellschaft,* secondary groups, and law), but the essential and constant conclusion was that modern society is increasingly differentiated and particular actors are increasingly atomized with respect to each other. I beg indulgence for the rehearsal of so obvious a fact. It bears repeating here only because, in my judgment, students of religion have insufficiently attended to its implication for the nature of modern religious ideation.

The linkage between the differentiated and atomized nature of modern social structures and the pluralistic quality of modern religious ideation must, for completeness' sake, be traced through the nature of modern knowledge systems in general. I return here to Mannheim. It is to Mannheim's credit that he described the development of modern thought in dynamic rather than the generally static structural terms of the classic dichotomous theorists. For Mannheim, the crucial social system variable in modern thought is horizontal and vertical mobility (as opposed to *structure*):

> It is primarily the intensification of social mobility which destroyed the earlier illusion, prevalent in a static society, that all things can change, but thought remains eternally the same. And what is more, the two forms of social mobility, horizontal and vertical, operate in different ways to reveal this multiplicity of styles of thought. Horizontal mobility (movement from one position to another or from one country to another without changing social status) shows us that different peoples think differently . . . [However] only when horizontal mobility is accompanied by intensive vertical mobility, i.e., rapid movement between strata in the sense of social ascent or decent, is the belief in the general and eternal validity of one's own thought forms shaken.[28]

Thus, exposure to alternative definitions of reality is the social prerequisite for the critical mentality (which Mannheim ultimately defined in terms of "evaluative ideology"). Simultaneously, the critical method of modern thought (as in Descartes,

Kant, Hume) is possible only in the presence of a subjectivist epistemology. And, to complete the circle, the subjectivist thought pattern is possible only when epistemological objectivism is broken-through which, in turn, is possible only when there are legitimate alternatives to the monoplexic hegemony of traditional civilizations.

The temptation to explore the highly interesting empirical and analytic adumbrations of this conclusion (especially Mannheim's concept of the historicist period) must be suppressed for the sake of the more immediate goal: the specific problem of the nature of contemporary religious knowledge.

ORIGINS OF A CHRISTIAN POLYTHEISM

A brief survey of trends and innovations in Christian theology in the past decade reveals a theme which may be interpreted as the possible beginnings of a polytheistic theology. Indeed the polytheism is only implicit. Yet, when analyzed from a sociological and historical perspective, these trends within the thought system of modern institutional religion may be seen as the natural outgrowth of a multiplexic sociocultural situation. Before considering the implicit polytheism itself, I wish to analyze its roots in both the subjectivist and relativistic thought forms of multiplexic culture.

Beginning with what H. Stuart Hughes labeled the generation of the 1890s (Freud, Weber, Pareto, Durkheim, Croce and others), we may see the decisive rise of the critical-subjectivist period. Hughes described it thus:

> The study of the society they gradually came to see as a vastly more complicated matter than one of merely fitting observed data into a structure of human thought that was presumed to be universal. Such a "fit," they recognized, was far from automatic: they saw themselves as removed by one further stage from the direct confrontation of their materials which earlier thinkers had taken for granted. In short, they found themselves inserting between the external data and the final intellectual product an intermediate stage of reflection on their own awareness of these data. The result was an enormous heightening of intellectual self consciousness—a wholesale reexamination of the presuppositions of social thought itself.[29]

The generation to which Hughes refers stopped short of the more radical critical attitude that followed. Freud, for example, systematically opened the element of the irrational in his anthropology but, in the end (in *Civilization and its Discontents* and elsewhere) opted for the rational: "The fateful question of the human species seems to me to be whether and to what extent their cultural development will succeed in mastering the disturbance of their communal life by the human instinct of aggression and self-destruction."

It was the succeeding generation of the 1920s and 1930s in which the more completely radical perspective appeared. Beginning with this period and continuing to the present time we may see an increasingly serious widespread movement toward the abandonment of the objectivist perspective and the extreme expression of the critical-subjectivistic mode of thought. This pattern appears in a remarkable number of inherently different fields of endeavor: physics, art, music, literature, drama. psychology and theology.[30] More specifically, I am referring to the emergence of relativism and the uncertainty principle in modern microphysics, of absurdism in literature and drama, surrealism in art, atonalism in music, radicalism in psychology and psychotherapy, and a whole host of inventions in theology (to which reference shall be made below in detail). It cannot be argued that in any of the disciplines (with the exception of physics) has the radical/subjectivistic spirit become the dominant or exclusive perspective. On the other hand, it cannot be denied that the new perspective is firmly entrenched in each of its respective disciplines and, furthermore, that its simultaneous appearance in so many different realms of work is of importance to intellectual and social history.

Of more immediate interest to our present topic is the striking evidence that this movement in the realm of ideas corresponds to the increasing multiplexification of the modern world. For example, in 1920, Werner Heisenberg—author of the famous uncertainty principle in physics—understood his world in the following manner:

> The end of the First World War had thrown Germany's youth into a great turmoil. The reins of power had fallen from the hands of a deeply disillusioned older generation, and the younger ones drew together in an attempt to blaze new paths.... It was here that I had my first conversation about the world of atoms ... The cocoon in which home and school protect the young in more peaceful times had burst open in the confusion of the times.... We discovered a new sense of freedom and did not think twice about offering views on even such subjects as called for much more basic information than any of us possessed.[31]

On the level of ideas the following themes appear: (1) The abandonment of traditional, linear modes of thought (Newtonianism in physics, realism in art and drama, the tonal scale in music, the sane/insane distinction in psychotherapy, and belief in One God in theology). (2) The substitution of relativizing modes of thought set in sharp contrast to the traditional form (relativity in physics, absurdism in drama and literature, discord in music, the affirmation of insanity in radical psychology, and the death of God in theology). (3) The "apotheosis of the platitude"[32] in which the unique event is seen as the clue to cosmic reality. Thus, in physics, the microparticle was explained by reference to the macrocosm of all space and time. In absurdist drama, the moment in the life of two clowns is the medium for a metaphysical statement about the absurdity of human existence in Beckett's *Waiting for Godot*. The perverse normalcy of the "insane" calls into question the nature of norms throughout social reality as in R.D. Laing. And the horror of Auschwitz is generalized into a criticism of Western historicism and traditional monotheistic religion in Richard Rubenstein.[33] More precisely, this element suggests that the absurd (the unknowable particle, the clown, the madman, the dead God) is the only clue to the meaning of the universe. This is close to Eugène Ionesco's version of 'pataphysics: "For 'pataphysics, all things are equal; the 'scientific' and the 'nonsensical' weigh alike in the scale of eternity, since both are arbitrary, both are absurd.... 'pataphysics rejects the search for truth (a 'generality') in favor of a voyage of discovery and an adventure into eternity—which, of course, is where we all live."[34]

These three themes—criticism, relativism, 'pataphysics—in the order of ideas may be seen as corollaries to the sociocultural facts of multiplexity—mobility, atomism, and the humanist rebellion against routinization. It is this tradition of thought so clearly unique to multiplexic culture that, for the sociologist of religion, suggests the foundation for the polytheistic urge in recent theological literature. I wish now to refer directly to that literature.

Within the last ten years theological literature has seen a decided shift away from attempts at theological objectivism (Barth, Tillich, Brunner). Theological discussion has been characterized by a high degree of speculation and innovation, very little of which has been in the objectivist mode of systematic theology. Three trends appear: the death-of-God movement, festivity/fantasy theology, and Christian henology. In each we find the themes of the wider intellectual ethos. Likewise, in each we see the imprint of multiplexity.

The death-of-God theologies of Altizer, Hamilton and others was, necessarily, the first to arise. Here we see the radical, subjectivist critique of theological objectivism. It is, therefore, easy to understand why Altizer relied so heavily on William Blake and Nietzsche and why Hamilton could write an essay entitled "Banished from the Land of Unity."[35] Richard Rubenstein, the Jewish theologian, illustrates the religious extension of the subjectivist and relativist principle:

> If there is a God of history, He is the ultimate author of Auschwitz. I am willing to believe in God in the Holy Nothingness Who is our source and our final destiny, but never again in a God of History.... What the death-of-God theologians depict is an indubitable cultural fact in our times: God is totally unavailable as a source of meaning or value. There is no vertical transcendence.[36]

In the death-of-God movement we see the expression, in the realm of religious ideas, of the stark antirationalist relativism of the larger intellectual and artistic movement to which we have just made reference.

Christian festivism, accordingly, is related to Ionesco's absurdist 'pataphysics. The festivity/fantasy theologies of figures like Harvey Cox and Sam Keen[37] introduce into religious ideas the constructive principle that the "peculiar" or the "lowly" is the clue to religious meaning. Fantasy, on the psychological level, and foolish festivity (clowning), on the sociopolitical level, are proposed as positive sources for theological understanding. See, for example, Cox:

> Fantasy like festivity reveals man's capacity to go beyond the empirical world of the here and now. But fantasy exceeds festivity. In it man not only relives and anticipates, he remakes the past and creates wholly new futures. Fantasy is a humus. Out of it man's ability to invent and innovate grows. Fantasy is the richest source of human

creativity. Theologically speaking, it is the image of the Creator God in man. Like God, man in fantasy creates whole words ex nihilo, out of nothing.[38]

It is important to note that Cox developed his thinking by returning in part to other contemporary absurdist theorists—John Cage, the composer, and Antoine Artaud, the dramatist.

The third theme is less explicitly developed. Its first formal statement is the Christian henology[39] found in Herbert Richardson's *Toward an American Theology* which is important particularly because it is written in direct response to multiplexic culture (what Richardson calls "The Sociotechnic Age"). It appears implicitly in Harvey Cox's description of the multiplicity of choices available to secularized Christian persons and in the creative possibilities of Christian fantasy. Bellah could well be added to this list because of the extent to which he is read seriously by nonsociological students of religion. His view of transcendence in "Transcendence in Contemporary Piety" as well as his famous, enthusiastic review of Norman O. Brown's concept of polymorphous perversity is of importance here.[40] Also, in the same vein Peter Berger's quasi-theological statement of the "signals of transcendence" may be added to the list.[41]

In many respects the most interesting example, for our purposes, is Richard R. Niebuhr's recent book *Experiential Religion*. Niebuhr is of special interest because—in contrast to Cox, Richardson, Bellah and Berger—he is not an avant garde theologian, neither by style nor substance. His primary sources through the years have been Calvin and Schleiermacher. Yet, Niebuhr begins with the fact of modern man as "radical man" whose life experience is characterized by a multiplicity of powers radiating into his concrete existence. God, accordingly, is described as the ultimate power behind these powers affecting radical man:

> God is principally the Summoner from habit to transcendental freedom. But more than that, he is the moral beauty lying beyond all known patterns, codes and laws, empowering men to venture into the unknown with the pioneer of faith. And one affection pervades the whole polarity of self and field of assailing and persuasive power. It is courageousness, a self-denying courage—and an invincible sense of being destined to share in the shaping and reshaping action of God-Ruling.[42]

This is a position strikingly similar to Herbert Richardson's henology, in spite of the dramatic differences in source and orientation between the two thinkers: "Henology does not affirm yet another conception of being alongside existing ontological options. Rather, it attempts to affirm that which is necessary to every ontology, namely: whatever being is said to be, it must be said to be one ... Thus henology can thereby both explain the legitimate claims of modern relativism and yet show the way beyond this cul-de-sac."[43] The important observation to be made here is that both Richardson and Niebuhr, while seeking a monotheistic position, find themselves compelled to define the traditional concept in positive relationship to multiplexic culture.

My interest here is not in the theological differentia as such, but in the importance of these movements—in their grand aspect—for an understanding of contemporary religious ideas. Thus, Christian atheism, festivism, and henology may be interpreted as movements within formal, church religion corresponding to the general features of the subjectivism of the complex modern thought world. The two taken together reflect the type of religious and secular ideation that may be expected in a multiplex sociocultural ethos.

CONCLUSION

Among the principal responsibilities of sociological analysis is the task of investigating ideas, movements and institutions that are hidden in what social actors take for granted. However, with respect to the prospect of increasing attention to relativistic themes and, specifically, to polytheistic possibilities in modern religious ideation, sociologists could well miss the implications of an important movement because of its own (unexamined) doctrinal perspective.

On the other hand, evidence for a Christian polytheism—or at least Christian henology—becomes obvious when the sociology of religion takes a sociology of knowledge approach both to its own ideological commitments and to the sociocultural forces at play in a multiplexic ethos.

NOTES

1. T. Parsons, "Introduction to Culture and the Social System," *Theories of Society,* vol. 2 (New York: Free Press, 1961), 963–993; R. Bellah, "Religious Evolution," *American Sociological Review* 29 (June): 358–374; C. Geertz, "Religion as a Cultural System," in *Anthropological Approaches to the Study of Religion,* ed. V. M. Banton (New York: Praeger, 1966).

2. H. D. Duncan, *Symbols in Society* (New York: Oxford University Press, 1968).

3. Peter Berger, *Sacred Canopy* (New York: Anchor, 1969); T. Luckmann, *Invisible Religion* (New York: Macmillan, 1967); P. Berger and T. Luckmann, *The Social Construction of Reality* (New York: Anchor, 1967).

4. For a review of recent literature see G. B. Bouma, "Beyond Lenski: A Critical Review of 'Protestant Ethic' Research," *Journal for the Scientific Study of Religion* 12 (1973): 141–156.

5. For an important, recent attempt to clarify the analytic issues surrounding this problem, see R. Robertson, *Sociological Interpretation of Religion* (New York: Schocken, 1970), 34–77.

6. The latest contributions here include Andrew Greeley, *Unsecular Man: The Persistence of Religion* (New York: Schocken, 1972); Dean Kelley, *Why Conservative Churches Are Growing* (New York: Harper and Row, 1972); Richard Fenn, "Toward a New Sociology of Religion," *Journal for the Scientific Study of Religion* 11 (1972): 16–32.

7. For example, J. Needleman, *New Religions* (New York: Doubleday, 1970); T. Robbins and D. Anthony, "Getting Straight with Meher Baba," *Journal for the Scientific Study of Religion* 11 (1972): 122–140.

8. See, for example, M. B. King and R. A. Hunt, "Measuring Religious Dimensions" (Dallas: Southern Methodist University Studies in Social Science No. 1, 1972); M. B. King and R. A. Hunt, "Measuring the Religious Variable," *Journal for the Scientific Study of Religion* 11 (1972): 240–251.

9. R. Robertson, *Sociological Interpretation of Religion,* 43.

10. É. Durkheim, *Elementary Forms of the Religious Life* (New York: Free Press, 1965), 62.

11. Harvey Cox, *The Secular City* (New York: Macmillan, 1965).

12. See Bellah, "Religious Evolution": "Religion [is] a set of symbolic forms and acts which relate man to the ultimate conditions of his existence." Bellah acknowledges the outright influence of Tillich on his thinking in his autobiographical statement on symbolic realism (ibid., 245).

13. P. Berger and T. Luckmann, *Social Construction of Reality*, 244.

14. Ibid.

15. Max Weber, *Sociology of Religion* (Boston: Beacon, 1963), 20–31, 138–150.

16. Talcott Parsons, "Christianity and Modern Industrial Society," in *Sociological Theory and Modern Society* by Talcott Parsons (New York: Free Press, 1967), 392.

17. Bellah, "Religious Evolution."

18. Mircea Eliade, *Cosmos and History* (New York: Harper, 1959).

19. H. Richard Niebuhr, *Radical Monotheism and Western Culture* (New York: Harper, 1943).

20. Cox, *The Secular City*, 17–38.

21. Richard Rubenstein, *After Auschwitz* (Indianapolis, IN: Bobbs-Merrill, 1966).

22. The terms "monoplexic" and "multiplexic" are based upon and derived from Bellah, "Religious Evolution."

23. Weber, *Sociology of Religion*.

24. Karl Mannheim, *Ideology and Utopia* (New York: Harcourt, Brace, 1936).

25. Ibid., 35.

26. Ibid., 11–12.

27. Robert J. Lifton, "Psychological Man in Revolution," in *Social Change and Human Behavior*, ed. G. V. Coelho and E. A. Rubenstein (Washington, DC: National Institute of Mental Health, 1972), 69–88.

28. Karl Mannheim, *Ideology and Utopia*, 7.

29. H. S. Hughes, *Consciousness and Society* (New York: Vintage, 1958), 16.

30. Elsewhere I have discussed these movements in greater detail. See "Sociological Theory and the Relativistic Paradigm" in this volume.

31. W. Heisenberg, *Physics and Beyond* (New York: Harper and Row, 1971), 1.

32. R. Coe, *Eugène Ionesco* (New York: Grove, 1961).

33. R. Rubenstein, *After Auschwitz*.

34. R. Coe, *Eugène Ionesco*, 8, 9.

35. T. J. J. Altizer and W. Hamilton, *Radical Theology and the Death of God* (Indianapolis, IN: Bobbs-Merrill, 1968).

36. R. Rubenstein, "Cox's Vision of the Secular City," in *Secular City Debate*, ed. Daniel Callahan (New York: Macmillan, 1966), 142–143.

37. H. Cox, *Feast of Fools* (Cambridge, MA: Harvard University Press, 1969); S. Keen, "Manifesto for a Dionysian Theology," *Cross-Currents* (Winter 1968–1969); also J. C. McClelland, *The Clown and the Crocodile* (London: Westminster, 1970).

38. Cox, *Feast of Fools*, 59.

39. Richardson defines henology in the following: "the development of the meta-sciences is dependent upon an explicit understanding of that unitizing principle which makes a multiplicity of category systems, modes of explanation, and methods possible. To understand this unitizing principle, and the complexity of the term 'unity,' is the task of henology." *Toward an American Theology* (New York: Harper and Row, 1967), 73. In this definition we see Richardson's struggle with the multiplicity-unity problem that is the substance of the polytheistic urge.

40. Bellah, *Beyond Belief*, 196–208, 230–236.

41. P. Berger, *A Rumor of Angels* (New York: Doubleday, 1969).

42. R. R. Niebuhr, *Experiential Religion* (New York: Harper and Row, 1972), 8–9.

43. H. Richardson, *Toward an American Theology* (New York: Harper and Row, 1967), 106.

2
Sociological Theory and the Relativistic Paradigm

I can still remember that as a child my mother could not get me away from the puppet shows in the Luxembourg Gardens. I could have stayed there spellbound for days on end. I didn't laugh, though. The spectacle of the guignol held me there, stupefied by the sight of these puppets who spoke, who moved, who bludgeoned each other. It was the spectacle of life itself which, strange, improbable, but truer than truth itself, was being presented to me in an infinitely simplified and caricatured form, as though to underline the grotesque and brutal truth.

—Eugène Ionesco

I wish to begin by asking the reader to consider the following social phenomena. The most powerful army in history is totally frustrated by ill-equipped guerrillas in the jungles of Vietnam. The world's two most successful communist states renounce their common international purposes and compete with each other for the favors of bourgeois civilization's most famous anticommunist crusader. The most sophisticated of all the natural sciences—microphysics—welcomes to its theoretical bosom such rationally bizarre notions as: complementarity, relativity, and indeterminacy. Sincere, believing Christians and Jews join hands with Nietzsche in proclaiming the death of God. History's most accomplished political technocrat, Richard Nixon, is unable to manage the most elemental technocratic tool, espionage. Bobby Seale runs for mayor of Oakland. The common theme in and of these phenomena is that they are absurd. They resist simple explanation by rational thought.

If the reader now finds him/herself thinking (positively or negatively) that he/she is facing another radical tract, then I have a basis for making my point. The above list need not be seen as rhetoric or caricature. It can be read as fact. While I will gladly admit to legitimate dispute over the nuance or connotation of the language by which they are described, there can be no serious dispute over the fact that the phenomena indicated have occurred. The only significant discussion can be over their meaning.

13

The temptation to reduce these facts to ideology may well reveal the limitations of the rationalist assumptions that govern most sociological theorizing. The point I wish to make is that sociological thinking, as it now stands, is not able to explain satisfactorily the meaning of these and similar social facts. They are manifestly not *simply* problems of "deviance," "status inconsistency," "false consciousness," "normative upgrading," "system dysfunction," "institutional breakdown," "rapid social change," and so forth. The strange, improbable and, often, grotesque nature of undeniably real phenomena in the modern world cannot be explained easily from within the thought world of extant sociological theory. Sociology lacks what Ionesco's puppet show (cited above) possessed. That is, the ability to portray "the spectacle of life itself ... strange, improbable, but truer than truth itself ... presented in an infinitely simplified and caricatured form, as though to underline the grotesque and brutal truth" (Coe, 1961:16).

Quickly, I should state that my purpose here is not to propose a radical sociological nihilism. I believe that positive, constructive sociological theory is both possible and necessary. At the same time I have profound doubts as to the adequacy of our present theories to the task of explaining the complex and often comic nature of the facts of modern society. This paper seeks to examine sociological theory in comparison with an important, competing theoretical system. By placing the two side by side, it is hoped that clues for a reconstruction of sociological thought might be suggested, even though the details of that enterprise must of necessity be postponed.

Recent studies (Friedrichs, 1972; Effrat, 1972; Douglas, 1971) have explicitly applied Thomas Kuhn's (1962) theory of scientific revolutions to sociology. Other studies appearing in the past decade (Gouldner, 1971; Cicourel, 1970; Berger and Luckmann, 1966; Young, 1971; Schroyer, 1970; Tiryakian, 1965; Denzin, 1969; Warshay, 1971; van den Berghe, 1963; Jay, 1973; Goodwin, 1971; among others) have investigated the status and prospects of the central, paradigmatic frames of reference in sociological theory. Following Friedrichs (1972), who was following Kuhn (1962), we may note that when normal science encounters anomalies there is a sharp increase in experimental speculation and self-examination. Kuhn says: "The proliferation of competing articulations, the willingness to try anything, the expression of explicit discontent, the recourse to philosophy and the debate over fundamentals, all these are symptoms of a transition from normal to extraordinary research" (1962:90). In general terms, this constitutes a reasonable description of the current state of sociological theory.

Friedrichs's important study makes it unnecessary for me to refer further to the internal condition of sociological theory. I wish instead to concentrate my attention upon sociology's external relationship over against the state of theory in other fields of contemporary intellectual and artistic endeavor.

In this regard, an important point must be made with respect to the history of the application of Kuhn's model. Kuhn's original essay (1962) referred only to the process of scientific revolutions within the natural sciences. As Friedrichs has pointed out (1972:xxvi), Kuhn himself subsequently acknowledged the appropriateness of its generalization to the social sciences (1970a, 1970b). There has been some effort in this direction in anthropology, economics, and political science, as Friedrichs has shown (1972:xxvi). However, efforts such as these focus entirely upon thought structures internal to the disciplinary tradition. None have considered the question of common paradigmatic themes external to any one discipline or among various intellectual fields. Ultimately, this possible extension of Kuhn's ideas would require a rigorous sociology of knowledge perspective. To look at common intellectual themes occurring within the same ethos requires a dual investigation of the themes themselves and their foundations in the social situation to which they are related. It is surprising that sociology of all fields has failed to do this. My purpose here is to explore this possibility. To this end, I will not work explicitly with the differentia of Kuhn's theory. Rather I wish to set aside even Kuhn's crucial argument to the revolutionary nature of paradigm shifts and, for the present, concentrate exclusively on the idea that paradigms exist at the level of the thought structures of a given ethos. While it is not possible to do so in this paper, eventually the full analysis will require a consideration of the structures of thought throughout the ethos in relation to the features of their possible social bases. My purpose here will be limited to an examination of one aspect of modern thought to show that a paradigm does exist and then to point out that sociology is unique among major intellectual disciplines in its apparent refusal to take seriously its existence.

THE RELATIVISTIC PARADIGM

There is a way of thinking about reality that is unique to the modern (or, more accurately put, late modern) world. Its uniqueness lies in the broad consensus among scientists, thinkers, and artists with respect to a new understanding of natural and human reality. The idea itself has existed in a variety of incarnations prior to the 20th century—in the flux of Heraclitus, the dreams of Ezekiel, the paintings of Bosch, the art and poetry of Blake, among many others. The uniqueness therefore is in the consensus, not in the idea itself. This is an important fact for sociological analysis. It forces us to think about the social conditions that have encouraged the new perspective.

Described most generally the perspective is one that views all reality—natural and human alike—as relative. Conversely, it is marked by a deeply held hostility to traditional epistemological objectivism (cf. Mannheim, 1936:55–108). The type of thinking to which I am referring can be seen in the maelstrom of intellectual and artistic movements, new ideas, and cults that have appeared in this century—relativity theory (physics), expressionism and cubism (art), dadaism (art, poetry, drama, music), atonalism and experimentalism (music), complementarity and indeterminacy principles (physics), the apotheosis of the schizophrenic (psychology), surrealism (art, literature), absurdism (drama and literature), Christian secularism and atheism (religion), the apotheosis of the comic (art, literature, drama, religion). With the exception of the revolutions in art and modern microphysics none of these can be said to constitute the dominant paradigm within their respective "disciplines." At the same time, it can be said that each represents a well-defined sphere of legitimate endeavor in their respective "fields." And, more importantly, the commonalities among these movements are sufficiently clear so that they may be taken together as a single perspective. In this connection, we must note that the process of bureaucratic differentiation by which we are inclined to isolate these movements into distinct disciplines, departments, or professions is a result of the institutionalization of the same traditional rationality against which the new perspective has intentionally positioned itself. Pablo Picasso, Eugène Ionesco, John Cage, Harvey Cox, Werner Heisenberg and R. D. Laing can be located in distinct "fields" in only the most artificial and purely functional way. The substantive products of their work demand attention across traditional institutional barriers.

Moreover, the relativistic paradigm is not easily analyzed in a systematic fashion for the simple reason that fundamental to the paradigm is the conviction that reality itself is not self-evident and orderly as traditional thought has presumed it to be. Relativism, in each of its forms, is critical of traditional rationality. It stands against Newtonianism, rationalism, realism, tonalism, objectivism. Thus it is suspicious of rationally generated "systematic" explanation. To understand it we must attempt to view it from our perspective within traditional thought, realizing that we are likely to distort but that this is the only means we have to understand it. The terms by which the elemental features of the paradigm may be described could be taken from any of its several manifestations. I will take them from the thought world of microphysics because here they are concisely stated and empirically well documented.

The three basic elements in the relativistic paradigm are: (1) complementarity, (2) indeterminacy, (3) relativity. These correspond precisely to the analytic phrases used by Coe (1961) to summarize Ionesco's absurdism: (1) "a world of infinite coincidence," (2) "the void at the center of things," (3) "the apotheosis of the platitude."

(I) *Complementarity*—In physics, complementarity asserts that electrons must be understood to have both the quality of waves and of particles. The result depends on the type of observation performed. This is an assertion based upon undeniable experimental evidence. It was first discovered to apply to light and, later, to matter. Complementarity was one of the several points at which microphysics overthrew the rationalism of the closed, orderly, observable Newtonian world. We can no longer know reality in the classical way. Heisenberg has said: "If two observational situations are in the relationship Bohr has called complementarity, then complete knowledge of one necessarily means incomplete knowledge of the other" (1971:121).

This discovery in physics is equivalent to the more radical antilogical absurdism in Ionesco. While the expression is more intentionally radical, its roots are the same, for Ionesco's principal philosophical influence is from Stéphane Lupasco, the philosophical proponent of the principle of contradiction (see Coe, 1961:25, 26). Moreover, Coe argues that Ionesco's use of contradiction is directly related to quantum physics' doctrine of complementarity:

> Microphysics suggested that certain forms of energy shared simultaneously the contradictory properties of waves and particles; quantum physics gave it to be understood

that the "logically" impossible could and did happen.... The exact significance of these ... discoveries, whether to the scientist or to the professional logician, is irrelevant; what matters here is the impression that they left upon the consciousness of the intellectual or artist. And this impression was one of a major revolution striking at the very foundations of logical thought, and backed by those who hitherto had been the stoutest pillars of rationalism: the scientists. (Coe, 1961:24)

Thus, for Ionesco—and absurdism in general—existence itself is merely given as pure fact. It has no inherent logic. It is absurd. Accordingly, artistic realism is seen as a form of classic rationalism and, from the absurdist point of view, is not only impossible but anathema. To use Coe's phrase, man lives in a world of infinite coincidence.

The artistic revolt against rationalism and its positive assertion of the principle of complementarity extends to art and music. In art, Picasso decisively left his classical period when he turned to Cubism which may be understood as complementarity with respect to artistic space. The Cubist movement broke up space (to use Katherine Kuh's phrase), then rearranged the parts so that differing perspectives—such as the front and back of an object—are simultaneously juxtaposed. Antonina Vallentin has said: "Cubist painters claimed that they were conveying a new vision of reality—reality as it really was in the multiplicity of its aspects, not fixed and monolithic as it appeared to the human eye" (1957:113). Cubism led naturally to the collage which was the classical artistic medium for expressing complementarity in the Dada, surrealistic and Pop art movements. Representational realism is replaced by a graphic portrayal of the contradictory complexity of a reality viewed as infinitely coincidental.

In music, the radical experimental musician John Cage employs complementarity in the sense that he rejects the classical forms of music based upon rational relationships among ordered tones. Cage, instead, sees the new music as a juxtaposing of noise (or sound) and silence. In Cage's music (as in Bohr's complementarity and Ionesco's antilogic) this juxtaposition of hitherto irreconcilable elements results in the undermining of the very heart of traditional "logical" epistemology, the subject-object dichotomy.

> For, when, after convincing oneself ignorantly that sound has, as its clearly defined opposite, silence, that since duration is the only characteristic of sound that is measurable in terms of silence, therefore any valid structure involving sounds and silences should be based, not as occidentally traditional, on frequency, but rightly on duration, one enters an anechoic chamber as silent as technologically possible in 1951, to discover that one hears two sounds of one's own unintentional making (nerve's systematic operation, blood's circulation), the situation one is clearly in is not objective (sound-silence), but rather subjective (sounds only), those intended and those others (so called *silence*) not intended. If, at this point, one says, "Yet! I do not discriminate between intention and nonintention," the splits, subject-object, art-life, etc., disappear, an identification has been made with the material, and actions are then those relevant to its nature. (Cage, 1939:14)

From this Cage draws the rationally absurd conclusion: "A sound accomplishes nothing; without it life would not last out the instant" (Cage, 1939:14).

In contemporary theology, the principle of complementarity is not developed as clearly nor as radically as in science and the arts. (This is due, we may assume, to the fact that while the idea has always been present in Western religious thought—as, for example, in the Christian doctrine of the trinity—it has only recently come to the fore as a dominant theme.) Since the early sixties, however, complementarity has surfaced. It is to be found in the absurdist conclusion of the death of God theologians that only when the death of God is acknowledged can modern man become fully religious. Similarly, it appears in the antilogic of Christian secularism such as Harvey Cox's ironic argument that the most central sacred tenets of Jewish and Christian faith are fulfilled in modern secular life (see Cox, 1965). In both cases, the problem with which theologians are struggling is the inherent contradiction between historical time and eternity. It poses the question: how can religious man simultaneously relate history and eternity, his traditional past and his experimentally open present? Cox's answer is juxtapositional theology.

> A method of juxtaposition in theology should begin with "radical theology" by recognizing that our present is one of discontinuity and *is* real, not simply transient. I should go even further than the radicals, however, by assuming that this experience of tension between past, present, and future is valuable, and not merely something to escape. It should assume that the contradiction we feel today between what is and what has been should not be overcome by finding some way to negate the tradition. The experience of discontinuity is also an authentic one. It is the very oddness, incredibility, and even at points weirdness of traditional faith that makes it interesting to us today.... Juxtaposition sees the disrelation between inherited symbol and present situation not as a lamentable conflict to be resolved but as a piquant cacophony to be preserved. (Cox, 1969:131, 2)

In modern psychological theory, the principle of complementarity is at approximately the same level of partial development as in theology and for the sane reasons. It is new. But it is present in a variety of forms (see Boyers and Orrill, 1971), in the work of David Cooper, Aaron Esterson, Gregory Bateson, Theodore Lidz, Thomas Szasz and—most of all—R. D. Laing, who has given it the most dramatic and intentional expression. Laing seeks to destroy the rationalist distinctions between experience and behavior, the inner life and the outer world, psychiatrist and patient, sane and insane. Stated philosophically, he too stands against the rational dichotomy between subject and object. Drawing heavily upon existentialist and phenomenological ideas, Laing juxtaposes being and nonbeing. Man "is enabling being to emerge from nonbeing" (1967: 42). Thus, the person's experience of relationship with another person juxtaposes the logically contradictory facts of the other's presence with his absence (negation):

> All experience is both active and passive, the unity of the given and the construed; and the construction one places on what is given can be positive or negative: it

is what one desires or fears or is prepared to accept, or it is not. The element of negation is in every relationship and every experience of relationship. The distinction between the absence of relationship and the experience of every relationship as an absence is the division between loneliness and perpetual solitude, between provisional hope or hopelessness and a permanent despair. (1967:37)

(2) *Indeterminacy*—The second element in the paradigm is closely related to the first. It may be seen as an (anti-) logical extension of the first. If complementarity reveals the antirational, absurd nature of reality, then indeterminacy specifies this fundamental assertion by describing—again, paradoxically—the content of the emptiness of reality which is there even though it cannot be there. Indeterminacy arises at the boundary between assumption and methodology. The assumption that reality is ultimately empty is the result of a positive method. Thus the distinction between method and assumption is obliviated. The result is not sheer nothingness, but a void that—in spite of its refusal to reveal itself—is the central feature of reality. The elliptical nature of these comments is clarified somewhat when one looks at the concrete applications of indeterminacy.

In physics, Heisenberg's indeterminacy followed from Bohr's complementarity (see Heisenberg, 1971:76–81). Together these ideas were the core of the new quantum physics which may be summarized crudely as the conclusion that the microparticles of which all matter is composed cannot be said to "exist" in any traditionally rational (Newtonian) static sense. Indeterminacy is based upon the method of observation. Its elemental fact is that the instrument of observation necessarily disturbs the observed particle. Thus, it cannot be known as such. P. W. Bridgman, the American physicist, has said that the physicist "has learned that the object of knowledge is not to be separated from the instrument of knowledge. We can no longer think of the object of knowledge as constituting a reality which is revealed to us by the instrument of knowledge, but the two together, object and instrument, constitute a whole so intimately knit that it is meaningless to talk of object and instrument separately" (March and Freeman, 1963:161). The implication is that the fundamental elements of nature are not really "there" in the traditional sense. They are indeterminate and can be known only as the scientist, in effect, creates them. Heisenberg has said: "The goal of scientific investigation is no longer a knowledge of atoms and their motions as such, independent of the formulation of our experimental investigations. Rather, we find ourselves, from the very beginning, involved in the give-and-take between nature and man, so that the customary division of the universe into subject and object—into internal and external world—leads us into difficulties" (March and Freeman, 1963:168).

In absurdist drama, the spirit of indeterminacy is captured in Coe's phrase "the void at the centre of things." Like Sartre in *No Exit* and Beckett in *Waiting for Godot*, Ionesco—throughout his drama—asserts the absurdity of life, typically framed in terms of its purest expression, death. "Death," notes Coe (1961:70), "is the one constant theme which gives unity to Ionesco's theatre; sooner or later, the cadaveric quality of words is transmitted to the living organism, and there are few among his major plays with neither corpse nor killer." As in physics, the indeterminate void at the center of reality must be seen in connection with the author's dramatic method. Thus, Ionesco's characters are "deliberately blurred in outline" and are "shifting and interchangeable" (Coe, 1961:77). More fundamentally we must note the absurdist's methodological attack on words. Antonin Artaud, the absurdist theorist, has said: "For I make it my principle that words do not mean everything and that by their nature and defining character, fixed once and for all, they arrest and paralyze thought instead of permitting it and fostering its development" (Artaud, 1958:110). However, also as in physics, this attack upon the rational method does not result in total emptiness. The void is there, but it leads to something positive (although admittedly in an ambiguous sense). "Beneath the poetry of texts, there is the actual poetry, without form and without text" (Artaud, 1958:78). The blurring of characters and the confusion of words that appear repeatedly in absurdist drama have the intended goal of confronting man with the absurd void, but also of pushing him through the void at least to the brink of the *possibility* of a reason beyond rationalism. "In one brief passage, Ionesco goes even further, and suggests that the very ubiquity, the very omnipotence, of the absurd contains its own denial, and that "maybe there is a reason, over and above *our* reason, for existing. Everything is so absurd, that even *that* is possible" (Coe, 1961:69).

In art, the foregoing is replicated. Contradiction leads to void, but the void transcends pure nothingness. Dadaism—best known for its art but also a widely based movement expressing itself in music, poetry, and drama—is perhaps the most extreme expression of the void. Tristan Tzara, in his "Dada Manifesto of 1918," said: "DADA MEANS NOTHING.... If you find it futile and don't want to waste your time on a word that means nothing...." Surrealism, the constructive corollary of Dadaism, is the clearest instance of this feature of the indeterminacy principle. For example: "Dalí added collage to his painting, using pasted photo engravings in order to accentuate the interplay of fact and fancy. By contrasting irrational content with unexpected realism, these artists made the impossible seem plausible.... They virtually caused the unreal to appear 'realer' than reality" (Kuh, 1965:70).

With respect to music, John Cage expresses indeterminacy through the central place he gives to *Silence* (the title of his best known book). Cage's compositions are indeterminant. They are open-ended. The performers compose as they perform. The conductor basically provides the "raw materials" which are the range of possible sounds and the scheduled duration of silences (Cage, 1939:36). The conductor merely keeps track of time (duration) for the performers. Thus, the restrictive rational organizing work of traditional composers and conductors is pushed to the background. The performers compose. They employ their sounds as methodological devices to make "meaningful" the void of silence. The performance is indeterminate. It is based upon silence. Yet it is creative. It requires participation. "This is a lecture on composition which is indeterminate with respect to its performance. That composition is necessarily experimental. An experimental action is one the outcome of which is not foreseen. Being unforeseen, the action is not concerned with its excuse. Like the land, like the air, it needs none. A performance of a composition which is indeterminate of its performance is necessarily unique. It cannot be repeated" (Cage, 1939:39). Thus, with Cage as with Ionesco and the others, the "void at the center of things" is an absurdly positive construction deriving from the "infinite coincidence of all things."

In theology, the most prominent expression of indeterminacy is the affirmation of the death of God. Here, the void created by the death of the rationalist God is the occasion for man's freedom to participate in humanity. For example, Thomas Altizer has said:

> Once the Christian has been liberated from all attachment to a celestial and transcendent Lord, and has died in Christ to the primordial reality of God, then he can say triumphantly: God is dead! Only the Christian can speak the liberating word of the death of God because only the Christian has died in Christ to the transcendent realm of the sacred and can realize in his own participation in the forward-moving body of Christ the victory of the self-negation of Spirit. (Altizer, 1966:111)

The death of God rejects the classic "methodologies" of traditional religion, the assent to Objective Truth characteristic of classical Roman Catholicism and the stern, moralistic activism of Calvinistic Protestantism. For example, the Jewish theologian, Richard Rubenstein, sees the torture and death of Auschwitz as the logical outcome of Western man's intense belief combined with a protestantized commitment to shape history. Hitler, while Catholic in background, was Protestant in practice. He was acting "morally" to shape history as would any good Calvinist. The methodological alternative posed in theology follows Ionesco in being radically antipolitical and antihistorical. Thus, a theology of festivity naturally followed the death of God movement. It is by festive participation in life itself ("saying yes to life"—the Nietzschean phrase used by Harvey Cox and Corita Kent) that one overcomes the absurd conclusions of history (Auschwitz) and participates in a reality that transcends the absurdity of rationally conceived and lived existence.

In the psychological theories of R. D. Laing (as we have already noted above) nonbeing and negation is at the center of being. It becomes for Laing the philosophical principle by which he redefines the normal. Normalcy is repressive. "What we call 'normal' is a product of repression, denial, splitting, projection, introjection and other forms of destructive action on experience ... It is radically estranged from the structure of being" (Laing, 1967:27). Accordingly, madness is seen as the personal method by which one may push through the absurdity of normalcy. The void is the nonbeing into which one descends in madness. Simultaneously, madness is the *method* through which one participates in the deeper reality.

> Schizophrenia is "itself a natural way of healing our own appalling state of alientation called normality." ... "Madness need not be all breakdown. It may also be breakthrough. It is potentially liberation and renewal as well as enslavement and existential death." It is not an illness to be treated, but a "voyage." Socially, madness may be a form in which "often though quite ordinary people, the light

begins to break through cracks in our all too closed minds." (Boyers and Orrill, 1971:137–138)

(3) *Relativity*—We come now to the very heart of the relativistic paradigm. Here we may consider the positive and constructive aspects of the paradigm. This is its "content." The relativity principle is, of course, close to complementarity and indeterminacy. However, it ranges well beyond these two by asserting that while all "things" are relative to each other it is still possible to describe a matrix in respect to which the parts of reality may be located. The most important feature of the matrix is that, being relative, it overthrows the rationalist distinctions between the "big" and the "small," the "greater" and the "lesser," the "higher" and the "lower," and so forth. In other words, while the principles of complementarity and indeterminacy rebel against the rationalist epistemological distinction between knowing subject and known object, the relativistic principle overthrows the rationalist ontological perspective that views the natural and human world in hierarchical terms. Relativity radically equalizes all things, persons, events, and facts in reality. All things become platitudinous and, simultaneously, the platitude reigns supreme. In Coe's phrase relativity involves the "apotheosis of the platitude." Let me illustrate.

With respect to physics, we need only state the most simplistic features of the general theory of relativity. It states that time and space cannot be taken as independent fixed referential systems. One cannot say that a given body is here or that a given event occurs at this specific time. We are unable to measure, in absolute terms, the whereness or whenness of bodies except by comparing them with each other. "The essential formulation of the principle turns out to be the following: It is not, as Newton assumed, empty space but the matter distributed through space that determines, at each instant and at each location, a definite physical reference system. This amounts to saying that the motion of a body is discernible by certain simple laws only when measured relative to all other matter in the universe" (March and Freeman, 1963:94, 5). This is to say that the "existence" in space-time of any particular body forces us to think of that body relative to all other things in reality. Thus, we cannot meaningfully speak of an absolute objective system of nature in which there is an "up" and a "down" or a "big" and a "small" except in relative terms. The most recent extension of this principle is the theory of conformal invariance, described here by John A. Wheeler:

> In the past five years one of the greatest developments in elementary particle physics has been so-called conformal invariance, the discovery that the equations of elementary particle physics possess a property that in effect is this: changing the scale in which you examine the phenomenon does not change the nature of the phenomenon. This strange feature of nature that permits us to subsume the very large and the very small under the same kind of equation is something we don't yet understand, but it raises in one's mind the perpetual question: can it be true that what we think of as the very small and what we think of as the very large are really not so different? (Helitzer, 1973:29, 30).

In absurdist drama relativity becomes the "apotheosis of the platitude." While in physics, bodies have no absolute, linear relationship with each other, likewise, in absurd drama words lose their absolute linear meaning. In a world where all words are relativized, then the platitude—the elementary particle of human verbal interaction—becomes all important. By "measuring it" over against the absurdity of all reality, the platitude becomes the key to whatever meaning there is in total reality. The philosophical background for this way of thinking is the College of 'Pataphysics to which Ionesco has affiliated himself (Coe, 1961:7–10). It derives from the classic absurdist writer, Alfred Jarry. Its basic assumptions are:

> 1. 'Pataphysics is the science of the realm beyond metaphysics; or, 'Pataphysics lies as far beyond metaphysics as metaphysics lies beyond physics—in one direction or another … 2. 'Pataphysics is the science of the particular, of laws governing exceptions. A return to the particular shows that every event determines a law, a particular law.… 'Pataphysics is pure science, lawless and therefore impossible to outlaw 3. 'Pataphysics is the science of imaginary solutions. In the realm of the particular, every event arises from an infinite number of causes. All solutions, therefore, to particular problems, all attributions of cause and effect, are based on arbitrary choice, another term for scientific imagination 4. For 'Pataphysics, all things are equal.… (Shattuck, 1960:27–29)

'Pataphysical thought, it may be seen, does not cower in the isolation of particulars from each other. Rather it employs positive imagination to frame the microparticles of human experience in macrocosmological terms. For example, Coe says of Ionesco: "By showing up the meaninglessness of conventional idiom, by shattering the hard crystallized phraseology of common speech, his achievement is to throw back into the melting pot all those individual elements of which rational language is composed; and from there, a whole vocabulary can then emerge anew, scoured of its accumulated patina of overtones and associations: the long-awaited raw material for a new generation of poets to work upon" (Coe, 1961:44, 5). In the absurdist 'pataphysical point of view the relativity principle becomes quite explicitly a strategy both for drama and for life in an absurd world.

> Life is, of course, absurd, and it is ludicrous to take it seriously. *Only the comic is serious.* The 'pataphysicalian, therefore remains entirely serious, attentive, imperturbable. He does not burst out laughing or curse when asked to fill out in quadruplicate a questionnaire on his political affiliations or sexual habits: on the contrary, he details a different and equally valid activity on each of the four sheets. His imperturbability gives him anonymity and the possibility of savoring the full 'pataphysicalal richness of life. (Shattuck, 1960:29; emphasis mine)

Thus, we see the emergence of the fully serious comic clown. In rationalist thought, the clown is a lowly creature, the circus a band of deviants whose only purpose is to entertain the normal. In the absurdist frame of reference the situation is equalized.

All men are clowns. The only choice is whether or not to take this fact seriously. The clown is the particular. The clown is the imaginary solution to the problem of the meaning of reality. The particular and the total are not different.

'Pataphysics had its direct influences on the world of art. The ideas of Jarry influenced Picasso during his early years in Paris (Blunt, 1969:8). More explicitly the Dadaists relied conclusively on radical ideas of not only Jarry but also Jacques Vaché, another of the early 'pataphysicalians (Grossman, 1971:19–36). Dore Ashton has said:

> The Dada legacy passed on to contemporary artists is expressed in the hybrids produced, for instance, by Claes Oldenburg. A replica of a shirt, painted to look wrinkled and soiled, is enlarged to fill indifferent spaces. It is an object that has no attached value. It is there: meaningless, absurd, but there. Similarly, in the "happenings" there is no organic development, but a series of confused events aimed at the articulation of chaos. The use of countless rags, broken crockery, tin cans, and other throwaway material is an obvious arrow pointing to a negative polemic. Painting, sculpture, the dance, music are thrown into a happening at random. This is not the divine fusion envisioned by the Wagnerites, but, rather, a diffusion which these young protagonists consider characteristic of existence. Apollinaire's burlesque, and even Dadaist criticism, are dropped out in this process of condensation, of stripping in reverse. By throwing everything in, the young happening artist reaches the same point as the purist, who throws everything out. (Ashton, 1969:185, 6)

Only the comic is serious. Thus, we see in modern art the importance of the clown in Picasso, Rouault, and Chagall. More profoundly, we see the expression of the same theme in the psychological counterpart of the comic, fantasy. In fantasy and dream, the boundary between fear and fun, nightmare and creative imagination is perfectly fluid. These themes are ever present in van Gogh, Picasso, Matisse, Miro, Lee, Oldenburg, and Dalí. We may take the threads presented by the clown, the dream, and fantasy and weave a gestalt that allows no absolutistic hierarchical view of the world. Modern art rejects uncritical attention to landscape and perspective. It starts with the broken-up bits and pieces—the particles—of existence and uses them to express the comic and fanciful, extrarational possibilities in this chaos.

The Dionysian mood that appears in drama and art is found equally in music and theology where it is affirmed in an even more positive fashion. With John Cage it appears in his intentional use of everyday life's particular noises for musical creativity: "Wherever we are, what we hear is mostly noise. When we ignore it, it disturbs us. When we listen to it, we find it fascinating. The sound of a truck at fifty miles per hour. Static between the stations. Rain. We want to capture and control these sounds, to use them not as sound effects but as musical instruments" (Cage, 1939:3).

Religious thinkers such as Sam Keen, Corita Kent, and Harvey Cox are in the same tradition. Cox, for example, has quite systematically sought to bring together the Dionysian themes of festivity and fantasy into a new formulation of religious thought. In his book *Feast of Fools* he emphasizes the role of festivity and fantasy in leveling the social world. "Unmasking the pretense of the powerful always makes their power seem less irresistible" (Cox, 1969:9). Cox also emphasizes the creative possibilities of this relativizing experience:

> Fantasy like festivity reveals man's capacity to go beyond the empirical world of the here and now. But fantasy exceeds festivity. In it man not only relives and antici-pates, he remakes the past and creates, wholly new futures. Fantasy is a humus. Out of it man's ability to invent and innovate grows. Fantasy is the richest source of human creativity. Theologically speaking, it is the image of the creator God in man. Like God, man in fantasy creates whole worlds *ex nihilo*, out of nothing. (Cox, 1969:59)

Finally, the psychology of R. D. Laing culminates in his belief in the Holy Fool. Madness and sanity are relativized with respect to each other. Even more, the mad are those with the greatest possibility for finding essential humanity. In the "normal" world the schizophrenic is feared and isolated. In Laing's ideal world, the schizophrenic, whose life is broken up into many chaotic experiences, is the one who is most likely to attain true, transcendent selfhood. He does so by journeying back to life's elementary particles.

> In this particular type of journey, the direction we have to take is back and in, because it was way back that we started to go down and out. They will say we are regressed and withdrawn and out of contact with them. True enough, we have a long, long way to go back to contact the reality we have lost contact with. And because they are humane, and concerned, and even love us, and are very frightened, they will try to cure us. They may succeed. But there is still hope that they will fail. (Laing, 1967:168)

SOCIOLOGICAL THEORY AND RELATIVISM

Recent studies of the state of sociological theory (Gouldner, 1971; Friedrichs, 1972; Warshay, 1971) perceive and predict increasingly theoretical pluralism. The absence of a single dominant paradigm seems self-evident even to the casual observer. This is especially so now that the influence of Parsons seems to be waning steadily. Friedrichs, for example, concludes his *Sociology of Sociology* with the following:

> With the growing realization that all specific conceptual and empirical activity within a science is dependent ultimately upon a larger "given" gestalt, scientific communities may themselves come to accept a fundamental pluralism as an appro-priate style for the life of the scientific mind just as much of the larger populace of the West has come to accept pluralism in civic and religious life as an appropriate

response to an awareness of the repetitive nature of revolutions in the history of the civic sphere. (1972:325)

The analysis I have presented of the relativistic paradigm requires us to pause before uncritically accepting theoretical pluralism as a necessity. We have seen that the relativistic paradigm, which has developed in exactly the same ethos and time period as has sociological theory, makes quite a different response to the pluralism of modern culture. Relativism has incorporated modern pluralism within itself. The result has been a remarkably consistent and integrated paradigm which has forged a single coherent perspective with a broad applicability to a number of methodologically diverse disciplines. Sociological theory, on the other hand, is responsible to a comparatively small range of methodological and topical considerations, yet has been unable to take the plurality of modern life into its thought structures. Simply stated: Both sociology and the relativistic paradigm have arisen in a plural ethos. Sociology appears to have been fragmented as a result. Relativism has transcended the pluralism and escaped fragmentation.

It is conceivable that what we are witnessing in contemporary sociological theory is not nearly so much pluralism as a property of structures similar to crystals in the natural world; that is, structures so highly bonded and ordered that when they encounter sufficient trauma they shatter. Apparent sociological pluralism may actually be the fragments of a common thought pattern shattered by a plural ethos.

We can appreciate this possibility only when we see the concept *paradigm* in its fullest possible sense. Kuhn's own definition has a number of elements, each existing at different levels. While he clearly allowed that the paradigm refers to "accepted examples of actual scientific practice—examples which include law, theory, application, and instrumentation together—private models from which spring particular coherent traditions of scientific research" (1962:10), he also included the world view of the scientist: "Therefore, at times of revolution, when the normal scientific tradition changes, the scientist's perception of his environment must be reeducated—in some familiar situation he must learn to see a new gestalt" (1962:111). The full understanding of a paradigm must, therefore, include a variety of features, ranging from the concrete ideas governing the practice of scientific research to the general way in which the scientist thinks about the world. I would argue that the conclusion that sociology is experiencing paradigmatic pluralism emphasizes the former to the exclusion of the latter. It is, so to speak, fixated at the level of various schools and subtraditions within the discipline, ignoring all the while the more general features of the sociological worldview.

When we look at the state of sociological theory at the level of general epistemic and ontic assumptions, the internal pluralism can be interpreted as a competition among schools within roughly the same theoretical orientation. This conclusion is supported all the more when one compares sociology—taken as a whole—with another paradigm that operates quite independently of sociology, namely relativism.

Following Trent Schroyer (1970), we may classify the major competing thought structures *within* sociological theory under three rubrics: strict science, hermeneutical science, and critical science.

Strict science thinks in naturalistic terms. It assumes the existence in nature of an inherent order that may be discovered by the rational capacities of the scientists. Strict science, therefore, includes positivists such as Lundberg and structural functionalists such as Parsons. The human is, in some crucial sense, subsumed under the natural. Its basic ideas are order, objectivism and rationality.

Hermeneutical science thinks of man as the order-producing agent. The natural and the human are differentiated. The emphasis is on man, primarily in his intersubjective relationships. Man is seen as a symbol-producing, meaning-seeking creature. Since Dilthey and Weber, hermeneutical science has appeared in symbolic interactionism (e.g., Mead, Blumer), phenomenological sociology (Schutz), ethnomethodology (e.g., Garfinkel, Cicourel), as well as in mixed forms of the above (e.g., Berger, Luckmann).

Critical science, according to Schroyer (1970:215), "is capable of analyzing the supposed and actual 'necessity' of historical modes of authority and that presupposes the interest of the emancipation of men from law-like patterns of 'nature' and history." While critical science distances itself from the naturalism of strict science and the historicism of hermeneutical science, it nonetheless retains certain of their common epistemic and ontic assumptions. It relies upon a rational analysis of sociohistoric conditions. It assumes sufficient order in reality so that intentional action in history is possible. It continues to assume that man is a meaning-seeking, symbol-making and freedom-needing creature. Since its classical origins in Marx, critical science has appeared in the work of the Frankfurt School (e.g., Habermas, Marcuse; cf. Jay, 1973).

The unity of these major subtraditions within sociology may be seen when they are compared, collectively, to the relativistic paradigm. All three—strict, hermeneutical, and critical science alike—share paradigmatic assumptions which relativism rejects. Sociological thought uniformly works from the assumption that reality is (1) continuous, (2) determinate, (3) objectively meaningful. Relativism, on the other hand, rejects all of these assumptions.

(1) While relativism views reality as inherently contradictory, all three sociological subtraditions see it as continuous. Strict sociology assumes the existence of continuous laws or structures in the natural and human worlds. To no less an extent, hermeneutic sociology assumes that man not only can produce order, but that he does. Order is merely historicized. The hermeneutical scientist, thus, investigates these orderings. He/she does not doubt that they exist. On the surface, critical sociology with its commitment to the dialecticity appears to accept the principle of contradiction. But dialecticity is different from complementarity in that the dialectic always moves toward a resolution, a new thesis. Relativism excludes any such urge toward resolution. Complementarity radically accepts the inherent contradictory and absurd nature of reality. Thus, while we may view the three subtraditions of sociology as a continuum of increasing relativization, none become fully relativistic. In sociology,

reality remains continuous. Thus, sociologists think in severely linear terms: Cause and effect, subjective meaning and objective reality, thesis and antithesis all are understood as exhibiting linear, continuous relationships.

(2) While relativism views reality as indeterminate, sociology views it as determinate. While sociology allows for intervening variables, dysfunction, conflict, the subconscious, false consciousness, and the like, it assumes fundamentally that social reality is knowable. Personalities, societies, cultures, classes, institutions and so forth are determinate realities. The scientist's rational capacity to know these determinate realities is not doubted. Strict sociology, therefore, measures and analyzes. Hermeneutical science "understands," observes, or reduces. Critical sociology analyzes critically. There is no doubt over essentially rational methodologies, because there is no doubt with respect to the determinate nature of social reality.

(3) While relativism equalizes reality by showing that all particulars are relative to each other and to the totality, sociology assumes the objectively meaningful nature of its particulars. In its most essential form meaning assumes the objective existence of hierarchical relationships, the most fundamental of which is the relationship between meaning itself and nonmeaning (chaos). Thus, strict sociology measures or analyzes relationships among persons according to their position in stratification systems or of institutions and functions with respect to their levels of generality. It assumes uncritically the validity of the hierarchical distinctions between social organization and social disorganization, between function and dysfunction, between the normal and the deviant. Hermeneutical sociology (in addition to sharing the hierarchies of strict sociology) assumes the existence of a hierarchy among the levels of language, culture or meaning produced by man. And critical sociology assumes a value differential between the bourgeois and proletarian classes or between capitalist managers and the free people. The relativist paradigm, on the other hand, rejects all such objective hierarchies. All things are equal. The particular is apotheosized.

CONCLUSION

I must repeat that my purpose has not been to recommend sociological nihilism. Nor have I been interested in judging between the relativistic and the sociological paradigm. My essential argument has been that we may see in the modern world a relativistic paradigm that has arisen side by side with the main currents of sociological thought. Relativism is a coherent way of thinking in terms of complementarity, indeterminacy and relativity. It could be dismissed as idiosyncratic were it not for the demonstrated fact that it is found among natural scientists, artists, dramatists, philosophers, and social scientists alike. Sociology could perhaps reject relativism were it only the creative and "speculative" product of writers and theologians. Such a dismissal is more difficult when it is found in the hard scientific work of microphysicists and the clinical evidence of psychologists.

When sociological theory is compared with the relativist paradigm, the alleged pluralism of contemporary theory is seen in a new light. On the level of "schools" and subtraditions it cannot be denied that there is theoretical pluralism within sociology. But when the full meaning of Kuhn's concept of paradigm is explored, we must extend the notion to include world view or general epistemic/ontic assumptions. When we consider the thought structures of classical and contemporary sociology in this regard, the pluralism thesis must be qualified. Theoretical pluralism does exist at the subtradition level in sociology. It does not exist to the same degree when one considers sociology's epistemic and ontic assumptions. The differences among strict, hermeneutical, and critical sociology do not appear conclusive from this broader point of view.

REFERENCES

Altizer, Thomas J. J. 1966. *The Gospel of Christian Atheism*. Philadelphia, PA: Westminster.

Artaud, Antonin. 1958. *The Theatre and Its Double*. New York: Grove.

Ashton, Dore. 1969. *A Reading of Modern Art*. Cleveland: Case Western Reserve University.

Berger, Peter, and Thomas Luckmann. 1969. *The Social Construction of Reality*. New York: Anchor.

Blunt, Anthony. 1969. *Picasso's "Guernica."* New York: Oxford University Press.

Boyers, Robert, and Robert Orrill, eds. 1971. *R. D. Laing and Anti-Psychiatry*. New York: Harper and Row.

Cage, John. 1939. *Silence*. Middletown, CT: Wesleyan University Press.

Cicourel, Aaron. 1970. "Basic and Normative Rules in the Negotiation of Status and Roles." In *Recent Sociology*, vol. 2, ed. Hans Peter Dreitzel. New York: Macmillan.

Coe, Richard. 1961. *Eugène Ionesco*. New York: Grove.

Cox, Harvey. 1965. *The Secular City*. New York: Macmillan.

———. 1969. *The Feast of Fools*. Cambridge, MA: Harvard University Press.

Denzin, Norman. 1969. "Symbolic Interactionism and Ethnomethodology: A Proposed Synthesis." *American Sociological Review* 34 (December): 922–934.

Douglas, Jack. 1971. "The Rhetoric of Science and the Origins of Statistical Social Thought: The Case of Durkheim's Suicide." In *The Phenomenon of Sociology*, Edward Tiryakian. New York: Appleton-Century-Crofts, 44–57.

Effrat, Andrew. 1972. "Power to the Paradigms: An Editorial Introduction." *Sociological Inquiry* 42, nos. 3–4: 3–33.

Esslin, Martin. 1961. *The Theatre of the Absurd*. New York: Anchor.

Friedrichs, Robert. 1972. *A Sociology of Sociology*. New York: Free Press.

Gamow, George. 1966. *Thirty Years That Shook Physics*. New York: Doubleday.

Goodwin, Glenn. 1971. "On Transcending the Absurd: An Inquiry in the Sociology of Meaning." *American Journal of Sociology* (March): 831–846.

Gouldner, Alvin. 1970. *The Coming Crisis of Western Sociology*. New York: Basic Books.

Grossman, Manuel. 1971. *Dada: Paradox, Mystification, and Ambiguity in European Literature*. New York: Pegasus.

Heisenberg, Werner. 1971. *Physics and Beyond*. New York: Harper and Row.

Helitzer, Florence. 1973. "The Princeton Galaxy." *Intellectual Digest* 3, no. 10: 25–32.

Ionesco, Eugène. 1960. Rhinoceros *and Other Plays*. New York: Grove.

———. 1964. *Notes and Counter-notes*. New York: Grove.

Jay, Martin. 1973. *The Dialectical Imagination: A History of the Frankfurt School and the Institute for Social Research, 1923–1950*. Boston: Little, Brown.

Kuh, Katherine. 1965. *Break-Up: The Core of Modern Art*. New York: Graphic Society.

Kuhn, Thomas. 1962. *The Structure of Scientific Revolutions*. Chicago: University of Chicago Press.

———. 1970a. *The Structure of Scientific Revolutions*. 2nd ed., enlarged. Chicago: University of Chicago Press.

———. 1970b. "Reflections on My Critics." In *Criticism and the Growth of Knowledge*, ed. Imre Lakatos and Alan Musgrave. Cambridge: Cambridge University Press.

Laing, R. D. 1967. *The Politics of Experience*. New York: Ballantine.

Mannheim, Karl. 1936. *Ideology and Utopia*. New York: Harvest.

March, Arthur, and Ira Freeman. 1963. *The New World of Physics*. New York: Vintage.

Parmelin, Helene. 1969. *Picasso Says ...* , translated by Christine Trollope. London: Allen & Unwin.

Read, Herbert. 1960. *Art Now*. Marston Mills, MA: Pitman.

Schroyer, Trent. 1970. "Toward a Critical Theory for Advanced Industrial Society." In *Recent Sociology*, vol. 2, ed. Hans Peter Drdtzel. New York: Macmillan.

Shattuck, Roger. 1960. "'Pataphysics Is the Only Science." *Evergreen Review* 4 (May–June): 24–33.

Tiryakian, Edward. 1965. "Existential Phenomenology and the Sociological Tradition." *American Sociological Review* 30 (October): 674–688.

Vallentin, Antonina. 1957. *Picasso*. New York: Doubleday.

Van den Berghe, Pierre. 1963. "Dialectic and Functionalism: Toward a Theoretical Synthesis." *American Sociological Review* 28 (October): 695–705.

Warshay, Leon. 1971. "The Current State of Sociology Theory: Diversity, Polarity, Empiricism, and Small Theories." *Sociological Quarterly* 12 (Winter): 23–45.

Wisse, Ruth. 1971. *The Schlemiel as Modern Hero*. Chicago, IL: University of Chicago Press.

Young, T. R. 1971. "The Politics of Sociology: Gouldner, Goffman, Garfinkel." *American Sociologist* 6 (November): 276–281.

II

Social Things

3
Sociology as Theories of Lost Worlds

"It all began with the first storyteller of the tribe." So said Italo Calvino speaking of men, storytelling, and the moral reponsibilities of daily life. He continued:

> Men were already exchanging articulate sounds, referring to the practical needs of their daily lives. Dialogue was already in existence, and so were the rules that it was forced to follow. This was the life of the tribe, a very complex set of rules on which every action and every situation had to be based. The number of words was limited, and, faced with the multiform world and its countless things, men defended themselves by inventing a finite number of sounds combined in various ways. Modes of behavior, customs, and gestures too were what they were and none other, constantly repeated while harvesting coconuts or scavenging for wild roots, while hunting lions or buffalo, marrying in order to create new bonds of relationship outside the clan, or at the first moments of life, or at death. And the more limited were the choices of phrase or behavior, the more complex the rules of language or custom were forced to become in order to master an ever-increasing variety of situations. The extreme poverty of ideas about the world then available to man was matched by a detailed all-embracing code of rules.[1]

Thus began practical sociology in an attempt to overcome an original poverty of ideas about the world.

Sociologies, having thus begun, are proper to an imaginary space between real worlds such they are and those lost sometime in a past. Sociologies, both practical and professional, were (but may no longer be) the struggle of men (in all the meanings of the word, acknowledged and suppressed) to rid themselves of the choking effect of rules. Certainly, from its first beginnings in modern culture, especially in the late nineteenth century, professional sociology has been similarly preoccupied with these dilemmas of the human condition.

Italo Calvino's remarks were first delivered as a talk in Turin, Italy, in 1967 just when European and North American cities were on the verge of the most massive, and widespread, political and cultural turmoil to break out since World War II. His words are the sociological observations of a man who, though not a professional sociologist, posed the right questions. Calvino, a writer, lived by the imagination. What allowed him, at a time of pending crises in the West, and without professional qualifications, to imagine so precisely the reality of sociology?

Twenty-five years later, in late 1992, on one of his last days as the forty-first president of the United States, George Herbert Walker Bush spoke at Texas A&M University. As retiring world leaders have every right to do, Mr. Bush told the story of his presidency. The speech was, in effect, an informal sociology of the world during his lifetime. Though less elegant in scope and style, Mr. Bush's speech was in its way like Calvino's. What appeared unusual about Bush's sociology, if I may continue to put it this way, was that it was the social theory of a lost world, of the world order that many had come to believe had passed away, or was, at least, in some difficult last stage of its life. In fact, President Bush's story, in being a passable sociology of his times, was a story many others could have told in their way:

> In thirty-six days I'll hand over the stewardship of this great nation, capping a career in public service that began fifty years ago in wartime skies over the Pacific. And our country won that great contest but entered an uneasy peace. You see, the fires of World War II cooled into a longer cold war, and one that froze the world into two opposing camps: on the one side, America and its allies—and on the other, the forces of freedom, thus, against an alien ideology that cast its shadow over every American.[2]

This story was not easily told. In these first lines Mr. Bush slipped on a badly tangled metaphor. From the fire of real war the world cooled into a cold that froze the opposing camps: "on the one side, America and its allies—and on the other, the forces of freedom"! At first, one supposes the confusion is nothing more than Mr. Bush's chronic trouble with spoken English. But the speech itself is about a confusing turn of events. Not many, however high or low their office, know how to tell it straight. How, indeed, does one account for the end of the Cold War without using the language of Cold War?

Though a president, Mr. Bush spoke with the difficulty most people experience when describing a changing world. In his case, it was hard to say which was the side of freedom—America and its allies? the dark alien ideology? The political facts of the collapse of the Soviet Union were, indeed, that the "forces of freedom" (Boris Yeltsin's standing against the tanks in the summer of 1991) had brought down the Communist Party. But, in the story as customarily told and known to Bush, Yeltsin had been, strictly speaking, in the other camp. The most essential principle of Cold

War social theory was that America was the force of freedom. To make narrative matters worse, Bush had then to explain how, precisely, this force for freedom, now exhibited on the other side, had come to assert itself out from under the dark shadows of an alien ideology. If such a force is real in human history, then—by its own logic—it must be either natural to all human creatures or, somehow, distinctly American. If the former, then the collapse of communism is readily explained. If the latter, then it is not. The elder Mr. Bush, the last of the cold warriors, obviously believed the latter. A few paragraphs after opening, he said: "My thesis is a simple one: Amid the triumph and the tumult of the recent past, one truth rings out more clearly than ever. America remains today what Lincoln said it was more than a century ago: the last best hope of Man on Earth." But, if America is indeed the world's last best hope, how could freedom have sprung robust in Moscow against the tanks in late August 1991? Bush was telling his story of a world that had just lost a long-standing claim to reality. But that world was already lost to reality by the time Bush gave his speech. It would be wrong, therefore, to hold it against him or anyone else who could not make complete sense of it. When telling the story of one's world anyone can come up against this problem. Whatever is, or was, real is seldom precisely comfortable within the terms of the story.

Sociologies, it could be said, are stories people tell about what they have figured out about their experiences in social life. This is the most basic sense in which sociology is always an act of the imagination.

What distinguishes a sociology from other endeavors to imagine the meaning of human life is that a sociology, whether practical or professional, intends to give special attention to the social. As a result, the first problem a sociology encounters is that the general object of its attentions is nearly impossible to define, mostly because it lacks a readily observable set of things to which a definition might refer. The social is different in this respect from, for example, that which serves as the object of specialized interest to a psychology. Even when psychologists disagree on the proper name for their defining field of objects—brain, learning, mind, behavior, cognition, human development, the unconscious—they are able to indicate some object more or less readily imaginable because it is felt to be palpably concrete. I may not understand much of what a professional psychology means to say about the biochemistry of brain physiology, but I have little trouble imagining what a brain is and what, in principle, its neurology might be about. Neither the word "social" nor its cognate, "society," inspires the same degree of confidence in the commonsense imagination. Ironically, this very fact makes the field of social life to which a sociology pays attention even more a reality reliant on the imagination. There are thinkers who consider this an inherent weakness of the enterprise, but such a view is ungenerous.[3] One cannot any more hold a sociology to account for the inherently uncertain nature of its object than an astrophysics for the far more impetuous uncertainty of its. No one ever actually sees those bright, distant, dead stars. A sociology, likewise, need not be embarrassed by the greater definiteness of other fields.

This is not to say that attempts to understand and describe society, or the social, are practices lacking a serious attitude toward reality. A very great deal of reality, social and otherwise, subsists mostly in the imagination (and some realities, such as the power of lost fathers, only exist there). Everyone knows, beyond much reasonable doubt, that there is a sphere of social things out there that affects human life in powerful ways. Whatever we may call them, these social things are usually considered more immediate forces than, say, those that owe to the alignment of stars warped in distant times and spaces. From this view, a sociology, while deficient in respect to its definiteness, is enriched by its association with important and powerful aspects of the human environment.

Society, one could say, is that layer of our environment which uneasily settles the area just beyond the limits of what humans are able to know with their ordinary senses. "Society," accordingly, is not anything we can feel, smell, touch, see, or hear—at least not directly. Yet, we can think it, talk about it, and use it—and its gross constituent parts—in order to explain the lives we and others lead. How and why, for example, such strange, but normal, social practices as breakfast? How, were we to figure it out, could breakfast make sense without the social arrangements we never see that bring some of us each day our daily bread?—to say nothing of those ancient rules lost in time that imposed the fast broken arbitrarily at dawn? In this still quite abstract sense, society is not, after all, that much different from, once again, the brain. For it is not, of course, the mass of brain tissue kept viable in saline solution that is definite to a psychology. Brain tissue can be the general object of a psychology only to the extent that psychologists imbue it with scientific significance by means of coherent talk about its (presumably causal) relations to learning or perception. So, society (however much less definite a thing it is) is a meaningful resource for explanation only when, through a series of sometimes complicated procedures, it is made to bear a relation to those phenomena ordinary persons can truly sense, directly.

A sociology is, perhaps, somewhat more like an economics that stipulates what is commonly called a "market" as the general name for its field of significant objects. Such a market is said to provide the nurturing environment in which prices rise and fall in some relation to the supply and demand, of and for, commodities. In this sense, an economist's "market" is little different from a sociologist's "society"— neither in itself is a particularly concrete thing; both, thereby, work primarily in the imagination.[4] Yet an economics, while lacking the advantages of a more concrete neurophysiology of the brain, still has the upper hand over a sociology. While the economist's market is unlike any real market in which, face-to-face, people negotiate prices for valuable goods, it is still a sphere of social life ordinarily encountered each day one pays the current price for red peppers or regular, unleaded fuel. By contrast, even though most people encounter, on the same daily basis, indications of the prestige others do or do not attribute to them, somehow such a societal mechanism is felt to be less concrete. A sociology is very well able to describe the relation between an individual's social status and the complicated system of statuses by which a society somehow determines who gets which status for how long and why. This system, additionally, can be discussed in relation to other socially structured things such as the structures defining occupations, incomes, values, and class differences. But none of these larger societal things is generally considered to be as directly related to ordinary life and experience as are the market structures determining prices. We are not soon likely to witness a segment of the evening television news reporting the daily composite index of social prestige rankings. We do, however, get precise, numerical, and regular reports on the cost-of-living index and stock market values of selected industrials, usually just before the sports scores and weather reports.

In many ways this is a surprising fact. The amount of prestige accorded us in society affects our lives every bit as much as do prices, and much more than the weather or football results. One day, suddenly, for no apparent reason, those whose opinions of us were taken for granted rise to greet us with surprising enthusiasm, or, they remain inexplicably silent upon our entry. Are not such measures of the daily rise or fall of one's prestige vitally important to the individual? Does not one's prestige determine in a most fundamental way one's ability to afford the costs of life? Is it not well known that the poor, having little prestige, pay more, not less, for their daily bread? Yet, such social things as prestige are usually not considered to be as real as economic things. Similarly, though all known theories of economic markets are every bit as reliant on the tutored imagination, a sociology is considered the less real or less concrete activity. In this respect, it is most like history, which has no definite field of objects (unless one wants to refer to time, which, by contrast, makes market and society seem as concrete as brain tissue). Histories, however, are seldom subjected to public scorn as are economic or social theories. It is probable that the public's willingness to allow histories this relative immunity from close scrutiny owes to a general recognition that we require a healthy supply of meaningful stories about our pasts.

Whatever may be the differences among the activities by which humans interpret their worlds to themselves, there is one important habit of nomenclature practiced commonly, if not universally. Many, if not all, types of human knowledge tend to use the same term to define those features of reality that most abstractly account for their better organized and evidently distinct spheres. With rare exception these are called *structures*. In some psychologies, the brain may be taken as the mass of structures in relation to which mental life is supposed to make sense. In most economic theories a market of some kind serves an analogous purpose. Thus, in a sociology, society is the imagined mass of structures without which a great deal of group life would make no sense. Much the same is said of the far less certainly structured relations in interstellar space-time that make qualified sense of what is usually called the universe.

When they are used to organize what is said about the meaning of social, natural, and most physical events, structures have the following qualities:

1. Structures endure over time.[5]
2. They are thought of as salient—that is, if not actually big, at least powerful in relation to that which they structure.
3. Their salience is commonly considered a consequence of their capacity to endure over time; thus, durability is a normal way of describing the reality of structures.
4. Yet, enduring structures are seldom directly observable in their entirety; and, they are never fully *present*.[6]
5. Structures, therefore, tend (usually if not always) to be products of the human imagination.[7]
6. Finally, as a corollary of the preceding, the reality of structures is always a discursive fact; that is, structures lack concrete significance until we say something about them—in talk, writing, or other forms of communication about the nature of such things in themselves.[8]

In short, among social things structures are never present—neither in time nor being. Neither markets nor societies nor anything of this kind is visible as such. The reality of social structures, insofar as it can be grasped, is in what is said about them.

Thus considered, sociologies are unavoidably theoretical. Being necessarily concerned with structures, sociologies are the activities whereby the structures of worlds lost to immediate consciousness are made tentatively real. Whatever evidence sociologies may refer to (no matter how technical or informal) makes sense only when someone tells it in some kind of a story. Even "s = 1/i" and other formal statements make scientific sense only when the story they condense is told.[9] Sociologies, thus, are much like histories, with one important difference. Historical imagination reconstructs the past. The structured worlds of which histories speak are lost in the sense that, even when a history is told for the purpose of criticizing or explaining the present (or giving direction to a future), the story (by agreement) is of that which transpired in a definite past time. Sociologies, by contrast, purport to tell the stories of social worlds as they are, presently. Among professional sociologists, this is the usual reason given for distinguishing between sociology and the two fields with which it shares the most in common, history and anthropology. But if one steps outside the circle of academic interests, it becomes plain that the distinction is not remarkable, for one fundamental and unavoidable reason.

All attempts to explain with reference to a structure are, necessarily, reconstructions of worlds that may or may not any longer be present. This is most especially true in astrophysics, where the described structural relations are often of worlds long since dead. It is obviously true of histories and anthropologies, but also of sociologies whose structures persist in present time as only the considered talk of those who imagine them. No socially structured thing can be observed as such in its present. Or, it might be said, sociologies seek to distinguish themselves from other forms of social knowledge by the not entirely unreasonable practice of thinking of their structures as structures-presenting-themselves in the present.[10] It is reasonable to think this way only with a sense of humor in the face of the ironic fact that there is no other way to think of enduring social structures.

Sociologies, for example, discuss the family as though it were a definite and stable structure. Yet, there is every reason to believe that the family most often talked about in discussions of such issues as family values is a structure that exists in the present at best precariously. In the United States, the two-parent-(of-different-genders)-plus-a-variable-number-of-children-but-no-other-kin-(not to mention: living-together-and-at-least-minimally-sheltered)-family is far from the norm. Whatever the kin structure in American society is, if there is one, it is unlike the imagined structure. It is possible, historically, that such a structure, if it ever was the family structure for industrialized societies, may actually have been normal for a very short time only in the years immediately following World War II. Today, among persons living in domestic units of some kind, scarcely half are in families of this sort, and the number is shrinking rapidly, especially among Blacks.[11] How many of today's domestic arrangements might be called a family without doing violence to what is normally meant by the term is another question still. In what sense, for example, is a typical lesbian-headed household with children an "American family"? What is to be made of the fact that one of the newest, most rapidly growing "family" units is the never-married, single householder? Are unsheltered families still families in the "American" sense? We have no certain way to determine just what exactly is the demographic average family form. This is so partly because demographers rely on census reports often taken years before the sociologists have anything to say about the trend in family structures.

More to the point, this is so for sociologies of all kinds, because their social worlds are like the astronomer's universe—at best, virtual realities; at worst, ones dead years before. In some cases a sociology describes a world that has been destroyed, literally, of which one of professional sociology's contemporary classics, *The Urban Villagers,* is an example. The working-class neighborhood of Boston studied in this book was literally destroyed during the research—lost, in effect, to urban "redevelopment."[12] In other cases, like attempts to interpret the structure of family in the recent modern world, the uncertainty of the world is a methodological condition. But, in all instances where people, for whatever purposes, purport to tell the story of a social world, their only real reference can be to the virtual world in the story, whatever else they may tell themselves or others. Sociologies, therefore, are always theories of possibly, even probably, lost worlds. For all intents and purposes, wherever this kind of talk about structures takes place, the world is at *least* lost to the story itself. Social reality, in this sense, is always in the story. Once President George H. W. Bush's discursive dilemmas were, in this respect, part of his normal sociology.

From the beginning even the best professional sociologists had to face, often against their wills, the perverse reality that all social worlds are lost. This is the way in which, in their earliest days, professional sociologies were attentive to practical ones.

Émile Durkheim (1858–1917) was the first professional sociologist, but not by any means the first sociologist. He was among the first to organize sociology as an academic field in the modern university. Practical sociology, in the sense of attempts to talk about the social world, was practiced throughout the modern era since at least the eighteenth century. But professional sociology did not come into being until quite late in modern times; not until after the modern research university was well organized in the United States and Europe beginning in the 1860s.[13] Though the first successfully institutionalized professional sociology was in the United States, at the University of Chicago in the 1890s, Durkheim's role in the organization of academic sociology was memorable because he provided the classic definition of the field. To this day, among academic sociologists, no definition of sociology's subject matter and object field is more compelling. In 1894, in *The Rules of Sociological Method,* a small book written for the express purpose of organizing the scientific foundations of sociology, Durkheim first stated his famous definition of a *social fact* as "(a) any way of acting, whether fixed or not, capable of exerting over the individual an external constraint; or (b) which is general over the whole of a given society whilst having an existence of its own, independent of individual manifestations."[14]

The striking feature of Durkheim's definition that caused it to be remembered must have been that it served practical and professional sociology equally well. Durkheim himself was quick to say that he invented the concept social fact, thus defined, because a distinctively social type of fact was necessary if there was to be an academic field by the name of sociology. Though the term "sociology" had been widely used in France since the days of Henri de Saint-Simon (1760–1825) and Auguste Comte (1798–1859), neither of Durkheim's predecessors thought of sociology as a field of academic specialization.[15] It was Durkheim, more than anyone in Europe, who dedicated himself to making sociology a formal university science.[16] His definition served this purpose well. For sociology to be an academic science it needed to claim a special kind of fact, one "having an existence of its own, independent of its individual manifestations."

Three years after *Rules,* in 1897, Durkheim's next major book, *Suicide,* was published. This book was written in order to demonstrate the power of this definition, thus the salience of sociology itself, as he had advertised it in *Rules.* By applying his sociology to a human phenomenon that in common sense one might think of as an irrational act of the individual, Durkheim made a brilliant tactical strike against those who would resist the idea of sociology's distinctive scientific value. *Suicide* succeeded. For many, it remains today a model of careful empirical study, clever theoretical analysis, and respected accounts, not just of suicide but of the tragic effects modern society can have on people. *Rules* and *Suicide,* along with Durkheim's first book, *Division of Labor in Society* (1893), established Durkheim's reputation, which he soon converted into a position of prominence in Paris, where he taught, wrote, and led the famous Durkheimian school of sociology until his death in 1917. Except for the University of Chicago's Department of Sociology, no other school of sociology at the time had achieved so much public and academic success as Durkheim's.

But, unlike other of the great social theorists of the classical age—Karl Marx (1818–1883), Max Weber (1864–1920), Sigmund Freud (1856–1939)—there was little about Durkheim's personality or personal style that might explain his enduring importance as a sociologist. Though he took a courageous public position against the military in the Dreyfus affair and was a public figure of note in Third Republic France, neither he nor his writings were of the sort that would excite public imagination. There is little among Durkheim's writings to compare with the memorable public lectures of Weber on science and politics in Munich in 1918 or with Marx's 1848 *Manifesto of the Communist Party* or with Freud's numerous popular lectures on psychoanalysis. Though Durkheim's ideas were widely known and debated in France, it is hard to say why, at least at first reading. The explanation of this anomaly of Durkheim's public success over the years lies less with Durkheim than with sociology itself.

A sociology will not endure for very long, nor rise to public notice, if it fails to capture something important in popular experience. A sociology need not *be* popular. But, to endure, it must make compelling sense *in* public, even if ordinary people (so-called) do not read it. The first volume of Marx's *Capital* (1867) was infinitely more technical than his and Engels's 1848 *Manifesto* yet, reading them, one can readily see the sense common to both and thus appreciate how even those without expert knowledge of political economy could read (that is, get the point of) *Capital*. There is no known instance of a professional sociology, no matter how technical, achieving a durable recognition without first expressing something powerful in the collective lives of those about whom it claims to speak.

A most famous instance of this rule in the post–World War II era was the sociology of Talcott Parsons (1902–1979). Parsons's writings are nearly impossible even for the trained eye to read, objects of scorn to many fellow sociologists (notably Mills and Gouldner), abstract beyond words. Yet, the sociology of Parsons dominated a great deal of social science through the 1940s, 1950s, and well into the 1960s. Even today, hardly anyone who comments on social thought or popular culture in that era fails to mention Parsons.[17] Why? Certainly, among other reasons, because Parsons's academic sociology in the 1950s expressed the popular social hope that— after a half-century of war, holocaust, and economic crises—perhaps America had finally discovered the moral key to a world without conflict. Durkheim's success in the pre–World War I period, and his lasting importance, owes to a similar reason. Durkheim, like Parsons after him, believed in the possibility of the conflict-free society. Both wrote professional sociologies that, while seldom read outside scientific circles, could be read in ways that seemed to ring true to what people in society felt and wished. Those who think professionally about society are also men and women who go somewhere at the end of the day to live however they live with whomever, and to read the daily news; even to worry as we all do. Whatever membrane separates professional social science from ordinary life is at best semipermeable, if not downright sievelike. This is especially true of sociologies of all kinds.

Even Durkheim, whose professional life among the cultural elite of Paris in his day was seemingly well sheltered, knew well enough the personal troubles of people in

France, Europe, and the modern world. At least, he had his own practical theory of those troubles. That theory, in its most elementary form, informed most of what he did, even the most technical of his scientific studies. Easily overlooked, Durkheim's practical sociology appears refracted already in the first part of his definition of a social fact as "[a] any way of acting … capable of exerting over the individual an external constraint." Like many modern people (in his day and ours), Durkheim felt society was a constraint on the individual. In this formal definition in his book on methodology, this belief is disguised—dressed up for presentation in his new science, which, he says at the end of *Rules*, ought to "renounce worldly success and take on the esoteric character which befits all science."[18] Yet, neither Durkheim himself nor his sociology ever renounced the world. His sociology meant to serve the moral needs of the world as he saw it. Even his idea of social fact served this mission.

The book Durkheim published in 1893, the year before *Rules*, was as much a moral philosophy as a sociology. Many years later, anyone reading *Division of Labor* would be justifiably surprised that a book like *Rules* could follow so closely. This earlier book was his first, full sociology of the modern world. In it, Durkheim expressed his interest in social facts constraining the individual, but, in contrast to the definition of the year following, those facts were here understood explicitly as *moral* facts. In *Division of Labor*, interestingly, moral facts are a subject of concern not because they limit the individual but, just the opposite, because they *fail* to constrain individuals sufficiently well:

> It has been said with justice that morality—and by that must be understood, not only moral doctrines, but customs—is going through a real crisis.… Profound changes have been produced in the structure of our societies in a very short time. … *Our faith has been troubled; tradition has lost its sway; individual judgment has been freed from collective judgment.* But, on the other hand, the functions which have been disrupted in the course of the upheaval have not had the time to adjust themselves to one another; the new life which has emerged so suddenly has not been able to be completely organized and, above all, it has not been organized in a way to satisfy the need for justice which has grown more ardent in our hearts. If this be so, the remedy for the evil is not to seek to resuscitate traditions and practices which, no longer responding to present conditions of society, can only live an artificial, false existence. What we must do to relieve this anomie is to discover the means for making the organs which are still wasting themselves in discordant movements harmoniously concur by introducing into their relations more justice by more and more extenuating the external inequalities which are the source of the evil.[19]

From the very earliest of his writings to the end, Durkheim's sociology played deceptively on a loose, but definite, relation between things moral and things social. This was not by chance. He was the child of generations of Jewish rabbis who became a founder of sociology at the cost of renouncing the moral tradition of his origins.

From his first great book, *Division of Labor*, to *Elementary Forms of the Religious Life* (1912), his last, Durkheim was preoccupied with the problem found in the contradiction in his famous definition of social facts. The distinct facts of sociology were distinct in Durkheim's mind because the conviction of their generality arose from his (the individual's) experience of their constraining power. The definition in *Rules* seems merely to answer the question "What is a social fact?" But on closer reading of the famous definition (p. 20) one notices that it is in two parts, separated and linked by an "or." One might think of this "or" as a simple organizing connective were it not for the evidence, earlier in the chapter, that the famous definition unites much more than the two analytic components of a formal definition.

The definition of social facts serves double duty. On the surface, in its formality, it defines a science. But, nestled in the not immediately obvious tension between its two parts, the definition hides Durkheim's lifelong attempt to figure out the complicated relation between the moral life and the science of his modern world.[20] The social fact of Durkheim's definition of social facts is that, try as he might, he could not resist the constraining power of his practical morality on his scientific sociology. Earlier in the chapter in *Rules,* before he formalizes his definition, Durkheim makes a statement that merits more attention. Here he speaks of social facts more discursively, appealing, it seems, to the reader's practical, moral concerns:

> As an industrialist nothing prevents me from working with the processes and methods of the previous century, but if I do I will most certainly ruin myself. Even when in fact I can struggle free from these rules and successfully break them, it is never without being forced to fight against them. Even if in the end they are overcome, they make their constraining power sufficiently felt in the resistance that they afford. There is no innovator, even a fortunate one, whose ventures do not encounter opposition of this kind.
>
> Here, then, is a category of facts which present very special characteristics: they consist of manners of acting, thinking and feeling external to the individual, which are invested with a coercive power by virtue of which they exercise control over him. Consequently, since they consist of representations and actions, they cannot be confused with organic phenomena, nor with psychical phenomena, which have no existence save in and through the individual consciousness. They constitute a new species and to them must be exclusively assigned the term *social.*[21]

In this somewhat less formal attitude, Durkheim reveals himself—though surely without wanting to. It is evident that the formal definition, which concludes the chapter, is meant to be the one referenced and used in the science he is intent on inventing. But this long passage leaks meanings that are evidently there though not fully intended. A science of social facts that will shape the future is drawn from an informal ethical judgment of the changed and changing social world. The question implied, but not asked in so many words, is that of the constraint imposed by social facts on individuals: Is it good, or not? The answer turns entirely on the dilemma posed by the opposing forces of his science and his morality.

When they serve as the necessary foundation of Durkheim's science the constraining facts are unequivocally good. But, when Durkheim seeks to illustrate in a looser, more rhetorical style, he comes to the example of the most salient figure in classic social theories of the modern world, the industrialist. Like Marx's Mr. Moneybags (in *Capital*) and Weber's capitalist entrepreneur (in *Protestant Ethic and the Spirit of Capitalism*), Durkheim's industrialist is the figure of, and for, that social individual who both made and now represents the modern world itself. Marx thought of him as the greedy owner of capital, and Weber considered him the ascetic entrepreneur caught eventually in the cage of his own calculations. But Durkheim saw him in the industrialist, as the cultural hero embodying the moral dilemma, and hope, of modern man. For all intents and purposes, Durkheim ignored the difference between the industrialist and, himself, the prototypical sociologist: "Even when in fact I can struggle free from these rules and successfully break them, it is never without being forced to fight against them." Marx's capitalist does not struggle, and Weber's entrepreneur does nothing, in the end, but struggle. But Durkheim's modern man (like Calvino's) struggles to break free from rules. Thus, when Durkheim frees himself from the formal rules in order to illustrate in common language the beneficent constraints of social facts in daily life, he comes quickly to modern man himself struggling to be free from the fact of those same constraints.

At first, this is not surprising. Among the great classical social theorists, Durkheim's Enlightenment inheritance was the least contested. He was the direct descendent not just of Comte and Saint-Simon but of Montesquieu and Rousseau.[22] Durkheim's modern man, quite naturally, would be expected to struggle against the constraining rules. The industrialized man's moral purpose is, precisely, to free himself from the "opposition" of prior rules. This is the constraining force that in science is a good but in moral life is at least a dilemma. He said, to recall, in *Division of Labor*: "Our faith has been troubled; tradition has lost its sway; individual judgment has been freed from collective judgment." One year before *Rules,* the opposition of traditional rules was good in the complicated sense that its loss frees modern man too much. In *Rules,* constraint was good in an entirely different sense, that of the unambivalent virtue of the facts upon which his sociology depended.

The contradiction nestled in Durkheim's definition of social facts springs from its lair to run wild in his other works, earlier and later—*Division of Labor* and *Suicide.* Each, it can be shown, is a book built on misrecognitions of the very facts upon which it relies. Each in its way is good sociology to the ironic extent that it exceeds, or refutes, Durkheim's formal definition of professional sociology. Neither can be explained fully by recourse to such standard interpretive methods as the author's scientific logic because the misrecognitions in each are less a matter of error than of the necessary contradictions of a moral theory of modern man.

Durkheim published the first of these two books, *Division of Labor,* one hundred years exactly before George H. W. Bush, upon leaving his presidency, told his contradictory story of the end of the modern era. Durkheim, writing earlier in that era, was in the same unwitting predicament as Bush. Neither was able to resist the constraining facts of the modern world. Each had his theory of a lost world, theories that similarly fell short of the reality of which each spoke. Thus, both suffered not the indignity of error but the ordinary conditions of doing sociology.

~

Surprisingly, one of the normal ways people of all kinds exercise their sociological imagination is by regularly reading and discussing the classics. In the simplest of terms a classic text is one from a prior lost world that, for any number of reasons, continues to promote discussion well after its time is past.

Each of Durkheim's major books is considered a classic among one or another group of social theorists. For this reason, the books are read and reread—often less to extract direct scientific information than to root subsequent social theory in some tradition, usually in order to explain to one's own world of fellow theorists just who one thinks he or she is. The classics people read and talk about become part of their public identities.[23] Thus, reading the classics is an inherently conserving activity in which readers situate themselves in some relation to a tradition without which they would become less in some way. As a result, it is not only possible but likely that subsequent readers of classics will overlook what they are not looking for in the first place. Since, in addition, the writers of classics are themselves identified with a tradition (even if it is the tradition they are in the process of inventing), they too will be predisposed to "miss" something. Inevitably (perhaps necessarily), the circulation of ideas, including social theories, flows in and around what is unsaid.[24]

Durkheim's *Rules* and *Suicide,* for examples, are reread by theorists looking for an origin to certain traditions of scientific sociology. Those who cherish them are seldom inclined to reread *Division of Labor* with the same loyalty. Those who read *Division of Labor* are somewhat, but not considerably, more inclined to read *Elementary Forms of the Religious Life,* which today is considered an important classic for the study of culture, generally not an important subject to those who identify themselves with *Rules*.[25] And so on. The same is so with all great classic writers and their books. Some read the young Marx, others the mature one. Some read Freud on sex, others his drive theory, others his interpretation of dreams. Some read *Hamlet,* others *Much Ado About Nothing.* What is there depends on what one reads, which, in turn, usually depends on what the authors read and said or did not say.

To read all of Durkheim's classic books is, therefore, to take the risk of being astonished by what one might have assumed was there somewhere but turns out to be missing. Durkheim, the most important definer of professional sociology, neglected to provide an explicit, general theory of society. Though quick to define sociology's facts, and sure in his diagnosis of the dilemmas of modern society, Durkheim says relatively little about the general structural object comprising those facts and that dilemma—society itself.

One might not notice Durkheim's omission were it not for the fact that other of the classic writers—Weber in particular, Marx in his way, even Freud—occupied themselves with the invention of a general and explicit theory of society. Some might say that the *Division of Labor in Society* was Durkheim's general theory of society. But his ideas on society in that book were either dropped or substantially revised almost immediately, even by the time he got to *Rules* the next year, certainly by the time of *Suicide* in 1897. It is true that *Suicide* is an implicit theory of the moral crisis of modern societies, and thus a continuation of the moral concerns of *Division of Labor*. But *Suicide,* as it turns out, is largely preoccupied with suicide rates, leaving to the imagination the general thing, society, that may under varying conditions be said to compel the act of self-murder. There is, however, something of a general theory of society in *Elementary Forms,* which is not entirely what it claims to be (a study of religion). *Elementary Forms* is at least as much a study of the social foundations of human knowledge. It is here, and only here, that the reader finds the thin outlines of a general theory of society, most memorably in the phrase that completes the logic of the definition of social facts: "Society is a reality *sui generis.*"[26] But what strikes most is the preemptory universality of the definition. It is drawn from analysis of the most elementary societies, applied therefrom to all others, including the modern—as if his studies of the 1890s describing the differences between traditional and modern societies no longer mattered. They did, of course. But still, there is something odd here in the fact that nearer the end of his life Durkheim, in his most bold and coherent book, could so readily think of society not just as the source of knowledge and culture but as the simple undifferentiated thing-in-itself for which the most elementary of totemic societies was a sufficient model.

How could he do this? Why was it necessary? The answers were already evident in his first book. In *Division of Labor* Durkheim first introduces his famous expression *collective conscience,* about which much is said because of its double meaning. Like the moral purposes nestled in his definition of facts, this expression enjoys a similar double play by virtue of the French term *conscience,* which covers the two meanings: moral conscience and consciousness—the former a moral quality, the latter a state of mind (in this case, a state of the collective mind). Thus: "The totality of beliefs and sentiments common to average citizens of the same society forms a determinate system which has its own life; one may call it the *collective* or *common conscience.*"[27]

After diagnosing the hidden in the definition of social facts in *Rules,* one is rightly suspicious of this definition in *Division of Labor.* Its first phrase is the language of the science to be defined (a rhetorical reversal of the pattern in *Rules*). Here Durkheim writes of the power of beliefs and sentiments *as though* the collective conscience were common to all societies without regard to their historical variations. As it turned out, it was not. This loss (his "loss of faith") is the moral theme of *Division of Labor.* The phrase, along with the suspicion it evokes, is entirely convenient to Durkheim's study of the differences between two historic forms of social organization that, in their differences, put at issue the status of the collective mind—most particularly, whether the collective mind, moral and conscious, is common. This, in fact, is the crisis of which Durkheim spoke at the end of the book, and the crisis best known by his most famous concept, *anomie.*

In *Division of Labor,* Durkheim's *society* occurs in two distinct forms: The traditional is mechanical; the modern is organic. By the former Durkheim meant to suggest the more elementary or primitive societies in which the social consciousness is common, simple, undifferentiated—hence, like mechanical parts, fixed in their relations or, in Calvino's words, defined by an "all-embracing code of rules." By the latter societal form, he meant modern societies in which the advanced state of the division of social labor creates a different type of collective life—one in which the solidarity among the parts is organic in the sense that various parts of biological bodies enrich the bodily whole by their different functional gifts. The idea of the modern society as organic is clearly meant to describe the reality of social differences arising when the original collective life with its powerful common conscience gives way to the modern division of social labor.

It could be said that Durkheim's *Division of Labor* is a social theory of social differences, which, in a sense, was the subject of all classic modern sociologies. In the culture of the late nineteenth century, social differences were principally understood as class differences with which European societies, especially France, had struggled politically throughout the century. Then, differences due to race, gender, sexual orientation, or colonial life were, for the most part, not thought through, certainly not as they are today. With Durkheim, thus, that the more mechanical societies of his day were almost exclusively nonwhite and non-European and were in many cases colonized goes without mention. When, at the end of *Division of Labor,* he bemoaned the loss of traditional faith, Durkheim clearly had in mind not the traditional life of the most elemental societies but Europe and France before the modern era, under the ancien régime. That the European dark ages might have come under the same, or different, social laws as the dark continents of Africa or Native America and aboriginal Australia (from which he drew his evidence in *Elementary Forms*) was not well considered. The dark past of *Division of Labor* was ancient Israel, but in *Elementary Forms* it was aboriginal Australia and North America.[28] The effect of an equation of false similarities is to erase the differences of race Durkheim does not see. Such blind spots in Durkheim's social vision were, like his doubled definition of social facts, less an error than a condition of his sociology.

Durkheim, thus, found himself in a most demanding, if not impossible, circumstance. He was required to explain social differences, the dominant structural fact of modern society, while under the moral constraint to explain away the evident reality of those differences. In other words, he was forced by the cultural logic of his times to resolve those differences, the reality of which he could not deny. His solution was to interpret class wars less as a social fact of modern life than as corruption of the modern division of labor.[29] Class divisions could not be a social fact, by his definition, because they most evidently disrupted that condition by which social facts were defined: the generality of constraining force. So long as there are class differences, the *sui generis* society cannot uniformly constrain its members. Durkheim, therefore, had to deal with differences of this kind, which he did with so much finesse that the reader might not at first detect the awkward moves required to protect the collective conscience in a divided society. For example:

> In sum, since mechanical solidarity progressively becomes enfeebled, life *properly social* must decrease or another solidarity must slowly come in to take the place of that which has gone. *The choice must be made.* In vain we shall contend that the collective conscience extends and grows stronger at the same time as that of

individuals.... *Social progress, however, does not consist in a continual dissolution.* On the contrary, the more we advance, the more profoundly do societies reveal the sentiment of self and of unity. *There must, then, be some other social link* which produces this result; *this cannot be other than that which comes from the division of labor.*

If, moreover, one recalls that even where it is most resistant, mechanical solidarity does not link men with the force as the division of labor, and that, moreover, it leaves outside its scope the major part of phenomena actually social, it will become still more evident that social solidarity tends to become exclusively organic. *It is the division of labor which, more and more, fills the role that was formerly filled by the common conscience.* It is the principal bond of social aggregates of the higher types.[30]

In this summary of the argument of *Division of Labor* it is apparent that Durkheim's moral vision—that is, the practical demands of his sociology—overwhelms his science.

Durkheim must, now, account for the salient differences structured into modern life without the very term by which society is defined, collective conscience. Thus, he must say what he must not have wanted to say, namely: that the division of labor "must" be that which the common conscience once was; or, roughly: that common social life in modern society is founded, somehow, in the nature of differences. This *must* be so because "social progress does not consist in continual dissolution."

But what is to be made of this "must"? Everything! It is the necessary term that accounts for that which is missing. If there are social facts, there *must* be society. If social progress, there *must* be something to take the place of the collective conscience. Since modern society is divided (and the conscience cannot be truly common), that division of labor must now be the source of society. Durkheim's "must" poses as a logical corollary when, everyone knows, it is more a conjecture.[31] His "must" is the link to what one must turn to when evidence and reason are exhausted. *"Le coeur a ses raisons que la raison ne connait point"* (The heart has reasons which reason knows nothing of).[32] Durkheim's "must" stands at the limit of social facts. It is the clue to contradictions hidden away in an otherwise calm, progressive sociology. When, at the end, in *Elementary Forms,* Durkheim returns to the collective conscience, he returns in order to explain knowledge itself. There, in the book that drew its reasons from the logic of the most elementary social forms—the aboriginals of Australia and North America—that is, those societies that could not reasonably be said to be the traditional of Europe. In this last great book, Durkheim atributes all knowledge, including the proud and hopeful knowledge of modern man, to society. Society is the collective force from which derive the collective representations, which in turn account for the categories of human knowledge. But this neat formula relies on a prior refusal to see what is plain to see. This formulaic society, a *sui generis* reality, was most real not among his own European fathers but among those whose racial as well as social differences from white Europe were so evident that one failed to speak of them only when preoccupied by some greater moral task, such as inventing sociology in order to save modern progress.

It is apparent that in summing up his grand theory of knowledge, Durkheim, though unable to speak of them, still harbored dark thoughts about the unity of collective life, thoughts that were, again, displaced: "In summing up, then, we *must* say that society is not at all the illogical or a-logical, incoherent and fantastic being which it has too often been considered. Quite to the contrary, the collective consciousness is the highest form of the *psychic life,* since it is the consciousness of the consciousness."[33] But Durkheim, one can see, is too deeply implicated to extricate himself at the last. If society is the "highest form of psychic life," then is it not also "fantastic"? Durkheim's society is, in fact, a product of the "psychic life," thus of the imagination.[34]

Durkheim's sociology was a theory of lost—hence fantastic—worlds. He would have been horrified to contemplate that he of all people could not outrun so base and seemingly psychological a fantasy. It was against just this that he had wished to found his sociology. Durkheim had, however, set for himself, and sociology, an impossible task. Societies, though real in their effects, are also imaginary. Yet, in denying this fact, and much else, Durkheim was nothing less than a modern man—modern culture being that which struggles inconclusively with social differences. Having broken with the rules of the first men, moderns like Émile Durkheim and George Bush, the elder, find it difficult to tell their stories.

NOTES

1. Italo Calvino, "Cybernetics and Ghosts," in *The Uses of Literature,* trans. Patrick Creagh (New York: Harcourt, Brace, Jovanovich, 1982), 3.

2. George Bush, "America: The Last Best Hope for Man on Earth," *Vital Speeches of the Day* 59 (January 15, 1993): 194–197. The speech was delivered on December 15, 1992. It is the policy of *Vital Speeches* not to edit the material it prints. Thus the words quoted are relatively close to Bush's own as he spoke them.

3. "An occasional thoughtless thinker asserts that science is a free creation of the human spirit." George Homans, *The Nature of Social Science* (New York: Harcourt, Brace, 1967), 7. The author of this line is one of a long line of sociologists who consider it thoughtless to construe science as free and human. Against this are social scientists who would agree with Susan Krieger, *The Mirror Dance* (Temple University Press, 1991), 52: "A good feminist, like a good social scientist, ... should try to give others space to speak in their own words and style."

4. For an excellent discussion of just how imaginary a "market" can be, see Charles Smith, *Auctions* (New York: Free Press, 1989).

5. A classic discussion of the first three qualities of social structures is Fernand Braudel, *The Mediterranean and the Mediterranean World in the Age of Philip II* (New York: Harper, 1972 [1949]). Compare Immanuel Wallerstein, *Modern World-System,* 3 vols. (New York: Academic Press, 1974, 1980, 1989). On structures in space and time see Anthony Giddens, *The Constitution of Society* (Berkeley: University of California Press, 1984), esp. ch. 3.

6. The classic discussions of the problem of presence are the early writings of Jacques Derrida: *Speech and Other Phenomena* (Chicago, IL: Northwestern University Press, 1973); *Of Grammatology* (Baltimore, MD: Johns Hopkins University Press, 1974); *Writing and Difference* (Chicago, IL: University of Chicago, 1969).

7. An important recent discussion of imagination and the structure of the modern world is Benedict Anderson, *Imagined Communities* (London: Verso, 1983).

8. Some important recent discussions of this principle are Fredric Jameson, *The Political Unconscious* (Ithaca, NY: Cornell University Press, 1981), esp. ch. 1; Hayden White, *Metahistory* (Baltimore, MD: Johns Hopkins University Press, 1973); Dierdre Boden and Don H. Zimmerman, *Talk and Social Structures* (London: Polity, 1990); Erving Goffman, *Interaction Ritual* (New York: Doubleday, 1967).

9. This is the general version of Durkheim's formula for egoistic suicide: "Suicide varies inversely with the degree of integration of [religious, domestic, or political] society." See Émile Durkheim, *Suicide* (New York: Free Press, 1951 [1897]), 208. The entire story of this famous book, to say nothing of Durkheim's idea of sociology and modern society, is suggested by and entailed in "s = 1/i."

10. Jameson *(Political Unconscious)* is particularly astute on this point. Also, Anderson's *Imagined Communities* shows how the nation-state, a most essential structure of the modern world, came to be in this way.

11. According to a 1994 U.S. Department of Census report, *The Diverse Living Arrangements of Children, 1991,* only 25.9 percent of Black children and 50.8 percent of all children live in nuclear families comprising both biological parents and full brothers and/or sisters. Between 1970 and 1992, the number of children living with mothers and without fathers (of any kind) has doubled. In 1992, more than half of all Black children lived with mothers only. Between 1970 and 1992, the number of children living with unmarried couples has increased nearly 600 percent, and one of the fastest-growing domestic units is single people who have never married. For data, see *Statistical Abstracts of the United States, 1993,* 54–65. For discussions from various points of view, see Judith Stacey, *Brave New Families* (New York: Basic Books, 1988); Kath Weston, *Families We Choose: Gays, Lesbians, Kinship* (New York: Columbia University Press, 1991); Barrie Thorne and Marilyn Yalom, eds., *Rethinking the Family* (Boston: Northeastern University Press, 1992).

12. Herbert Gans, *The Urban Villagers* (New York: Free Press, 1982 [1962]). For years, sociology students have read of Gans's lost neighborhood as though it were real, which it is, even though it did not survive to see the book published.

13. Lawrence Veysey, *The Emergence of the American University* (Chicago, IL: University of Chicago Press, 1965). In France, see Terrence N. Clark, *Prophets and Patrons: The French University and the Emergence of the Social Sciences* (Cambridge, MA: Harvard University Press, 1973). Compare to the German case: Fritz Ringer, *The Decline of the German Mandarins* (Cambridge, MA: Harvard University Press, 1969). For the University of Chicago, where sociology was first fully institutionalized, see Martin Bulmer, *The Chicago School of Sociology* (Chicago, IL: University of Chicago Press, 1984).

14. Émile Durkheim, *The Rules of Sociological Method,* ed. Steven Lukes, trans. W. D. Hall (New York: Free Press, 1982 [1894]), 59. Emphasis added.

15. Both Saint-Simon and Comte thought of sociology more as a general social philosophy of modern science than as a scientific field in the academic sense. There is an important disagreement over which of the two was the first to use the term and, thus, who was the real father of sociology. Lewis Coser, *Masters of Sociological Thought* (New York: Harcourt, Brace, Jovanovich, 1977, 3) argues for Comte. Alvin Gouldner, "Introduction," in Émile Durkheim, *Socialism,* trans. Charlotte Sattler (New York: Collier Books, 1958), p. ix, favors Saint-Simon. Gouldner (p. ix) adds that the traditional inclination to view Comte as the true forefather of sociology arises from a desire to suppress knowledge of Saint-Simon's influence on socialism and Marx, thus to discourage the tendency to confuse sociology with socialism.

16. Clark, *Prophets and Patrons;* Charles Lemert, ed., *French Sociology: Rupture and Renewal since 1968* (New York: Columbia University Press, 1981), especially the chapter by Victor Karady; Steven Lukes, *Émile Durkheim: His Life and Work* (New York: Penguin, 1973); Dominick LaCapra, *Émile Durkheim: Sociologist and Philosopher* (Chicago, IL: University of Chicago Press, 1972). See also articles in the special issues of *Revue française de Sociologie,* vols. 17 (1976) and 20 (1979), both edited by Philippe Besnard. See also Philippe Besnard, *The Sociological Domain: The Durkheimians and the Founding of French Sociology* (Cambridge: Cambridge University Press, 1983).

17. For example, John Patrick Diggins, *Proud Decades: America in War and Peace, 1941–1960* (New York: Norton, 1988), 248–249. Feminism, in particular, takes Parsons seriously in this way; see, for example, Winifred Breines, *Young, White, and Miserable* (Boston: Beacon, 1992), ch. 1.

18. Durkheim, *Rules,* 163.

19. Émile Durkheim, *Division of Labor in Society,* trans. George Simpson (New York: Free Press, 1964 [1893]), 409. Emphasis added.

20. For example, Durkheim's "Professional Ethics," in *Professional Ethics and Civic Morals,* trans. Cornelia Brookfield (New York: Routledge, 1992), one of his many essays on ethics, begins: "The science of morals and rights should be based on the study of moral and juridical facts" (1).

21. Durkheim, *Rules,* 51–52.

22. Émile Durkheim, *Montesquieu and Rousseau: Forerunners of Sociology,* trans. Ralph Manheim (Ann Arbor: University of Michigan Press, 1960).

23. Though neither would put it just this way, see Jeffrey Alexander, "The Centrality of the Classics," in Anthony Giddens and Jonathan Turner, eds., *Social Theory* (Palo Alto, CA: Stanford University Press, 1987); and Calvino, *Uses of Literature,* ch. 2, "Why Read the Classics?" Also, there are instances, especially among certain professional sociologists, where the refusal to be known as one who reads any classic is an appropriated identity.

24. Foucault, most significantly in later years, developed the idea of the unthinkable and the unsayable with more or less evident reference to its classic sources, which include Marx, Freud, Hegel, and Nietzsche. See Michel Foucault, *The Order of Things* (New York: Vintage, 1970), 322–328.

25. Among those who take Durkheim's *Elementary Forms* as their classic are Claude Lévi-Strauss; see, for example, *The Scope of Anthropology,* trans. Sherry Ortner Paul and Robert A. Paul (New York: Jonathan Cape, 1967); and Michel de Certeau, *The Practice of Everyday Life,* trans. Steven F. Randall (Berkeley: University of California Press), ch. 5. Those who take Durkheim's *Suicide* as their classic include Arthur Stinchcombe, *Constructing Social Theories* (Berkeley: University of California Press, 1968), 15–18; and James Coleman, *Foundations of Social Theory* (Cambridge, MA: Harvard University Press, 1990), 13. Sociologically, the former two have very little in common with the latter two.

26. Émile Durkheim, *Elementary Forms of the Religious Life,* trans. Joseph Swain (New York: Free Press, 1965 [1912]), 29.

27. Ibid., 79.

28. On the odd juxtaposition of primitives and others see Marianna Torgovnick, *Gone Primitive: Savage Intellectuals, Modern Lives* (Chicago, IL: University of Chicago Press, 1990), esp. chs. 1 and 11, where the Jew and the primitive in Durkheim's successor, Lévi-Strauss, are discussed.

29. See Book 2 of Durkheim's *Division of Labor.*

30. Durkheim, *Division of Labor,* 1964, 173. Emphasis added.

31. In French, the crucial phrase "There must, then, be [some other social link]" is *Il faut donc bien.* The English "must" translates the French idiom *il faut.* The French, literally, "It is necessary that," is, in effect, a more forceful locution, consistent with colloquial and logical language in which the speaker wants to say "this *must* follow or else everything else makes little sense."

32. Blaise Pascal, *Pensées,* section 4.

33. Durkheim, *Elementary Forms,* 492. Emphasis added. Compare Durkheim and Marcel Mauss, *Primitive Classification,* trans. Rodney Needham (Chicago, IL: University of Chicago Press, 1963).

34. To speak of the sociological imagination in this sense is not necessarily to reduce social things to the psychological. One such alternative use of the imaginary is Jacques Lacan's *Écrits,* trans. Alan Sheridan (New York: Norton, 1977), among many others, including those works indebted to Lacan.

4
Durkeim's Ghosts
in the Culture of Sociologies

Durkeim's claim on the minds of generations of social thinkers owes, as these things often do, to an ever heightening sensibility to the concerns he addressed in his time. The industrial and social conflicts that shocked his generation in the waning years of the nineteenth century have, in the early twenty-first century, passed on, but not away. Perturbations interior to a national community have not so much disappeared as been caught up in a jumble of global conflicts. As a result, it is no longer possible to look for the cause of social disorders where Durkeim did—in the entrails of an encompassing Society defined implicitly by a territorial polity covering a purportedly distinct national culture.

Whether global conflicts are more or less severe than those of early industrial nation-states is an open question. But they are more pervasive—normal enough to require ever more explosive outbursts of violence to keep media attention focused; or, if not more pervasive, then more visible. Durkeim's generation saw what it saw of the wider world through glasses dimmed by the blush of European colonial domination. In the comparison, the unsettlements in Europe in Durkeim's day—even those leading up to the Great War which ended the innocence of his generation—seem local and passing. Today's troubles may be different in degree, perhaps modified in kind, but they are similar enough to render Durkeim's definition of the crisis, if not his solutions, disconcertingly apt to a much different time.

It may be that the dead stir up dread because they are not dead enough. Legion are they who prefer their dead to stay put as are, say, Comte and Spencer who haven't budged in years. We visit them, if at all, as curiosities. Then there are ones like Durkeim and Marx, who are far from ready for the wax museum. The living dead, when they are not a comfort (as, remarkably, they can be), disturb the hold people like to have over their own times and places. Yet, they haunt variously according to their several natures.

Durkeim disturbs for reasons different from the others. Marx and Freud are two contrary examples of theorists from another time, who, while living, wrote convincingly of ghosts haunting Europe and of uncanny visitations from the Unconscious, which may be why, while dead, they will not quit the scene even when hunted down by detractors. They exposed themselves to attack on the critical flank of their daring theories of modernity's dishonest social veneer. Though differently, to be sure, Marx and Freud believed as Weber and Durkeim could not: that to understand modern societies of the industrial age it was necessary to begin from the assumption that the appearances of the new technological wonders were false representations of the underlying realities. For them, the facts of modern matters are haunted by hidden and contrary forces—the mode of production in Marx's case, the Unconscious in Freud's.

Durkeim, in this one respect, was more like Weber. Each struggled, in his way, to explain the new world as it presented itself. Neither could quite believe that what met the eye was as far as it was from the whole truth. Weber, however, and unlike Durkeim, had the stronger inkling that something inscrutably perverse was wrong on the surface of social things. Still, unlike Marx and Freud, the best Weber could do was to describe the enigma where the others insisted that the perversities of modern life were, in truth, interpretative guides to the underlying and contrary realities. In the end, Weber could do little more than bemoan the facts that cut both ways at once—modern rationality enhanced human freedom, while at the same time trapping the modern in the iron cage of rational efficiency.

Durkeim, at least in the early empirical studies, notably *Suicide,* was barely skeptical at all—a character trait lacking in Durkeim to the extent that it was prominent among the other three. For Durkeim, the social facts he took as social things in and of themselves were drawn up in numerical rates he had culled from Europe's dusty archives. This—the naive move of an ambitious younger man—led him down the slope of scientific trouble greased by the all-too-comfortable slippage from reality to gathered data to fact to analytical stabs at the truth. The others held fast to a higher, if equally vulnerable, ground.

Marx and Freud, by developing their reconstructive sciences of material and emotional netherworlds, complicated the logic of daily life at some embarrassment to their methodological boasts in the triumph of the aggravated revolution and the patient therapy of the talking cure. Weber, by setting forth the grand interpretative method of understanding, was in his way the more daring of the lot, though at the cost that accompanies even so astute an appeal to the intersubjective: that of freezing modern man in his tracks, the lost soul cut off from the traditions, looking foolishly for the charismatic prophet. By contrast, one could make the case that Durkeim's caution, though it cost him dearly on the political side, left him the option he chose, however unwittingly, of revisiting the scientific side to supply the traction his early theories lacked.

Still, none of them would come to life today were it not for one or another nod to the finitude of social life—its politics and sciences included most especially. With or without a theory of ghosts, all were consumed by the past. They were at the head of the short list of survivors from a generation preoccupied with the lost past—a preoccupation without which what today we call the social sciences might not have come into being in their present form. Sociology, in its earliest days, was nothing if not a running commentary on the fate of traditional values in the caldron of modern times. It was precisely the question of human values that united all the European men, if not others. The quest for values in a valueless world led to the classic European experiments with four of the essential methods still at work in social theory and sociology. Marx's foundational value of the elementary labor process as a transcending critical tool, Weber's intersubjective value as the probative method of the ideal typical, Freud's imputation of scientific and therapeutic value to the chaos of dream talk, Durkeim's imbrication of social values upon the isolated individual— these were the subtly hidden, but evident, concerns that moved the European men of classic social theory. Each was an attempt to measure the continuity of the new modes of social order against what was to them a dead or dying past.

Durkeim led both academic and social movements promoting the reform of science and of the educational system in France. He believed, and many agreed, that the science he conveyed could heal the discord in and among over-individualized moderns. While controversial in his day, this aspect of Durkeim's life work seems a bit pathetic today—and no more so than when imagined as a solution to the divisions in the wider global spheres. Still, in surprising ways, Durkeim's ideas stand among the living dead—even when, in some aspects, their enduring viability courses along a thin vein oblique to the heart of much social theory.

The surprise is palpable because Durkeim, more than the others, was the one forced by his times as by the mistakes of his early method to change course later in his work. Without getting onto the line Louis Althusser made famous in regard to Marx—whether there were two of him, the one young and the other mature, from which we get the question of whether there can be two anyones other than Jesus and Wittgenstein—it is fair to say that, though all purportedly great thinkers change their minds to some degree, few changed theirs as much as Durkeim did his.

Though it could hardly be said that Durkeim was the most intellectually courageous of the four, when compared to standard fare in that or this day, he was in his own fine way. And no more so than in the notable change of emphasis he came to in the last years of his life and work—a change all the more difficult to make because those were the years of his public life when his ideas were most exposed to scrutiny for his work as the leader of a school of social thought but even more as the leader of a movement to reform the foundations and practices of public education in France.

It is too easy to complain, as some do, that Durkeim was the conservative among the founding fathers. The merit of the plaint is barely sufficient to the lie it covers. By contrast to, say, Marx or even contemporaries in the European Diaspora—writers like W. E. B. Du Bois and Charlotte Perkins Gilman in the United States—Durkeim was among those more comfortable against the odds of social facts. But when measured against garden variety social thinkers, he was far from hide bound. Otherwise, he would not haunt. The method of the early years, which may have required the change of heart and mind in the later years, turned on a concept that has enjoyed a robust staying power—a power that outruns, in many ways, its generator.

The concept, of course, is his most famous: *anomie*—the state of mental confusion caused by the absence of workable norms for the conduct of daily life. A century later, the exact conditions for which Durkeim invented the concept have passed. Still, *anomie* reminds that, whatever else might be among the necessary functions of the larger social things, the group, however massive (even global), must provide some effective grade of social regulation. When individuals are left without guidance by the group, the anomic state of mind undermines the benefits of individual liberty, leading to confusion of which suicides, as horrifying as they are, are not the most terrible of social tragedies, as survivors of ethnic wars and terrorist attacks in our time will testify.

In a century well after Durkeim's, the inability of the larger social wholes to guide the lonely individual is all the more salient in proportion to the individual's inability to know what exactly a social whole might be. At the end of the nineteenth century, even when one was, as Durkeim, a member of a stigmatized minority, a Frenchman had little trouble imagining France as somehow the name for a society capable of ministering to his need for protections of various kinds. Durkeim, with Zola, was on the winning side of the Dreyfus Affair. But, at the beginning of the twenty-first century, not even the wine merchants of Burgundy can locate the definitive border where France ends and, say, northern California begins; nor, accordingly, from whence they might draw what moral aid they require.

Just the same, the writings that gave rise to the concept anomie resist easy reading today because they come to us through time's digressions. Durkeim's key word was dated already at the very moment it was revived for future use. In the case of anomie, it was not Durkeim's writings of the 1890s that lend it value today, but that of a single essay written in the late 1930s. Robert K. Merton's "Social Structure and Anomie" (1938) fortified the concept by embodying it with a more robust theory of social structures—notably, a theory of structures that turned on the failure of societies to provide the means by which social protections could be gotten: jobs. Merton had the advantage, not just of time, but of the perspective of the Great Depression of the 1930s.

By introducing the income-producing job as the institutionally normal means by which the individual achieves the cultural goal of social recognition, Merton killed with one stone the two birds that eluded Durkeim. The one was Durkeim's unrequited confidence in the norms of a national culture as glue sufficiently fast to hold unsettled social structures in place. Merton bolstered this flimsy idea with the material bond of economic structures. In the same shot, Merton set to rest Durkeim's over-wrought theory of the social as the near-exclusive dominating force in the lives of individuals. He shored up the social by buttressing the individual with a moral power of its own—that of adapting to the anomic bewilderments structural failure produces. The repair was passive, to be sure, but fungible enough to purchase a theory stronger than Durkeim's original.

By diverting the blame for social deviation toward the social, Merton thus relieved the individual of responsibility for a failure of moral nerve. If the moral whole is to demand cultural achievement of a certain kind, it must provide the means. In the case of the market-driven, capitalist democracies the means were those generated in the labor market. Whether in the 1890s, or the 1930s, not to mention the 2000s, even in the more advanced societies, such as they are, there never were, nor ever will be, income-producing jobs for all sufficient unto the goal of the decent life, much less the successful one. With this recognition, Merton allowed for meaningful responses to anomic confusion less severe than self-slaughter—in particular the time-honored one of innovation: walking the straight and narrow by crooked means. Merton's anomie of the 1930s stands up to the global miseries of the 2000s better than Durkheim's original in the 1890s, making him, incongruously, the latter-day giant upon whose shoulders the original stands.

In more ways than this celebrated one, Durkheim's ideas continue to haunt social thought today. Even those who harbor a prejudice against the very idea of reading the classics can be found among the great number of those who appreciate that ideas, as such, survive for the good when they are passed down as exemplars of good practical work. Such was the endowment of Durkheim's unquestionably prudent definition of scientific sociology. Still today, all the objections notwithstanding, it would be hard to come up with a definition of sociology that improves on Durkheim's; or one alluded to more often even by those whose sympathies for its author are as tepid as their acquaintance with its source.

The genius of Durkheim's approach was that he defined sociology not as a philosophy but according to its method. In the memorably succinct words of his preface to *Suicide:* "Sociological method as we practice it rests wholly on the basic principle that social facts must be studied as things, that is, as realities external to the individual." To whatever extent the definition may have been a rhetorical move to separate sociology from the prevailing individualisms and psychologies of his day, it remains a monument to what is easily forgotten: There are things in these worlds that are social through-and-through; and not, thereby, susceptible to distillation or reduction into any other sort of reality. By stipulating sociology as a method of the social as a thing unto itself, he avoided the philosophical burden of having to elaborate an ontology of social things. Had he done otherwise—as by training he was more than well equipped to do—Durkheim would have surely lost in open debate with the psychologizing philosophers of that day, a lesson no doubt learned from the fabulous success of his *normalien* schoolmate, Henri Bergson. Thus, after a clumsy attempt to stipulate the protocols of his method in *Rules of Sociological Method* (1894), Durkheim made his point in *Suicide* (1897), a masterpiece that bore a conspicuous subtitle: *A study in sociology.*

Suicide was Durkheim's own occasion to kill two birds with a single shot. The one was defense of his definition of a field so new in 1897 as to require the precise language of the subtitle to distinguish it as a study from the pre-existing sociologies of Auguste Comte, among others, which were not studies of any real thing in particular. In *Suicide,* Durkheim was establishing an empirical social science. Such a task was not original to him, but, notwithstanding the institutional barriers he could not overcome in his day, sociology today is a university discipline in part because Durkeim was one of those who put it to a definition serviceable enough to justify the enterprise in the research university. At the same time, Durkeim's method of sociological study was and is consistently much more majestic than many of the enterprises that, in subsequent years, would make ill-informed appeals to *Suicide,* in particular, as a classic textbook for what all-too-sadly is misidentified as quantitative sociology.

One of the pities of professional sociology is the way so many of its adherents divide themselves and each other into rival camps—one quantitative, the other qualitative—as if any serious empirical research into social things could ever forswear one or the other. At the very least, Durkeim did not. When he engaged himself in the quantitative study of suicide rates, for example, he did so because of his prior concern with the quality of modern life, which concern required the interpretative tools necessary to tenderize his very hard data. By the standards of subsequent generations, Durkeim's technical method is a model of intellectual style. By defining the field as one of empirical study he allowed himself room to engage the philosophical controversies of the day, while simultaneously advertising the new discipline as science, yes, but also much more—ultimately, as an informed palliative for modern society's then most acutely painful crisis: How, in practical terms, can the social whole—whether tribal, national, or global—maintain even the minimally necessary degree of integrity so as to hold the straining members at peace, if not exactly in harmony?

In 1903, the year after satisfying the traditional French sacred pilgrimage from provincial birth to a spot in the Parisian lights, Durkeim published, with his nephew Marcel Mauss, the long and famous essay on knowledge and science, *Primitive Classifications.* For the decade that led from there to *Elementary Forms* in 1912, he worked on many fronts, but none more consistently than the interwoven themes: knowledge, education, and religious culture. Taken as a whole, the subjects led to a book not so much about religion as about what we today so innocently call "culture." These writings of the decade from *Primitive Classifications* in 1903 to *Elementary Forms* in 1912 were, in effect, the first thoroughly systematic *and* enduring study of the cultural logics by which socially bound people represent themselves to themselves—the logic of *collective representations.*

No other term in the Durkeimian vocabulary, not even the more famous *anomie,* gathers together so many of the strands of the intellectual patrimony he left the generations to come. In these latter days, when culture is widely taken as applicable to everything under the sun—from the newest turn in social theory to the necessary conclusion to which material realities are forced when the worlds are bound so tightly (or is it loosely?) by the thread of telecommunications—Durkeim's elegantly precise *collective representations* does the work of a thousand variations on its weaker cognates.

What more exact way could there be to describe the intended effect of the over-conceptualized sociology of culture than Durkeim's original? The collective representation is precisely the form by which a culture, as the concept has come to be applied in social science, does the work of expressing the collective self-identity of those who gather in the name of a local culture—of, that is, as Durkeim himself put it at the very end of *Elementary Forms:* "the consciousness of consciousness." Here, of course, he was redefining the foundational Cartesian principle in sociological terms. By replacing the individual *cogito ergo sum* with consciousness of the collective whole, he sought to buttress the foundations of knowing with the mortar of social life.

At the end of Durkeim's last major work, he summarizes the high purpose of the sociology he began to define in the 1890s as very much more than an academic field—as, in fact, the proper subject of knowledge reflecting upon itself:

> In summing up, then, we must say that society is not at all the illogical or a-logical, incoherent and fantastic being which it has too often been considered. Quite on the contrary, the collective consciousness is the highest form of the psychic life, since it is the consciousness of the consciousness. Being placed outside of and above individual and local contingencies, it sees things only in their permanent and essential aspects, which it crystallizes into communicable ideas. At the same time, it sees farther; at every moment of time, it embraces all known reality; that is why it alone can furnish the mind with the moulds which are applicable to the totality of all things and which make it possible to think of them.

The logic of collective representation is the logic of logic—the foundation of all thought in social as distinct from mental life.

Durkeim's idea, with all of its talk of essences and permanencies, would appear to be old-fashioned epistemological foundationalism. To be sure, the categories of modern philosophy, most of all those of Kant, were very much on Durkeim's mind. Yet, his sociological solution to the neo-classical question of how the mind knows was one that got around problems philosophy did not begin to get to until Nietzschean ideas blossomed late in the century of Durkeim's death when Richard Rorty among others shattered the philosophical mirror by thrusting a stake to the heart of metaphysical realism. Not even the traditions of Kantian idealism of practical knowledge or the American pragmatism issuing from William James and the Metaphysical Club—both working in full force at the time Durkeim was rethinking his theory of knowledge—dared to slay the vampire of Being as such that sucked the life out of any possible empirical sociology of historical forms.

What even pragmatism in America and neo-Kantian idealism in Europe lacked was an ironic sense of practical knowledge—of, that is, the principle that truth claims made in reference to purportedly real worlds do not require the *a priori* of Truth as a naturally occurring entailment of the real things in and of themselves. Kant invented the robust modern notion of practical knowledge apart from knowledge—certain of the things themselves as an idealized state of Being outside of, but corresponding to, the categories of mind. Pragmatism, though an independent philosophical tradition, had the effect of supplying the moral nerve Kant shrank from—that the final test of the truth of real things was in the practical pudding. Durkeim was far from a pragmatist as pragmatism came to be after his American contemporary William James. Yet, the effect of his achievement in these later works was comparable while serving the different purposes he intended from the beginning—those of establishing a sociology not of knowledge but of knowing—one that would stand the test all sociologies must pass: of being a workable ethic of knowing in which the practical consequence of knowledge of social things issues from the same social things to which it applies. Though little remarked upon, this was a bold, if half-witting, move on Durkeim's part and one that exceeded even the subtleties of any and all theories of the double hermeneutic.

Durkeim meant to define and develop a sociology that would serve two gods—the modern science of social things, the modern social ethic of the good society. He knew very well that sociology, the science, could not retreat into the culture of academic categories. He knew just as well that there would be no sociology worthy of its moral purposes without a theory of knowledge of its own kind that could, at the very least, come to terms with the categories of social knowing—by being, that is, a recognizable source of plausible truth claims in regard to social categories or classes as distinct from metaphysical Being or beings.

Durkeim had begun in the 1890s defining sociology as a method, thus to avoid the trap of philosophical dead ends. Yet, his first venture in *Rules* and *Suicide* veered too far in the direction of a technology of facts and was, thereby, insufficient to a theory of social facts for which is required a technique that accounts equally for the constitution as for the collection of facts. Did he know this? Did he recant the early and innocent elementary form of his science? Not exactly; at least not in so many words. What he did, however, was to instigate a series of individual and collective works that consumed the years of his fully adult life in Paris, where his prominence allowed him to form the group of brilliant scholars who adumbrated the details of Durkeimian sociology; while also teaching teachers who would reform the French educational system in terms that would, in principle, remake the secular French national consciousness by means of the cultural tool of transmitting the high culture that would serve as the collective representation of a moral France able to ameliorate the pain of uneven social divisions of labor. It was a collective labor that required, all at once, an adequate representation of social things, but also of science, hence also of the social foundations of knowledge. The plan bore all the traces of the Enlightenment project, as of the philosophical traditions of the nineteenth century. But, in being a moral sociology—being, in pragmatic effect, a sociology as social ethics—Durkeim's sociology as it came to be in the latter works was, in the words he used to describe the representations of the *conscience collective:* a "communicable idea" able "to embrace all known reality" thus to "furnish the mind with the moulds which are applicable to the totality of all things" thus to "make it possible to think of them."

Had these later works not been offered to a reading public familiar with Durkeim's early empirical writings, they might have been taken as little more than a backhanded entry into the classically nineteenth century debates over idealism and realism. *Elementary Forms* would have seemed to be a mere social epistemology founded in an ontology of social spheres—somewhat the problem Weber's hermeneutic method suffered. Here, the key intervening text is, again, *Primitive Classifications* where, with Mauss, Durkeim gives good, if insufficient, evidence that, when thinking is thought as a social thing, Class replaces Being as the point of departure.

The difference is an important one—for Durkeim and for the social thought that would creep up under the shadow of the second of his ghosts. The one fatal flaw in Durkeim's *Suicide* was a classic one—that of assuming a direct and uncomplicated correspondence between facts and the social things they were assumed to represent. In his effort to lay sociology out upon a methodological bed unadorned by philosophical controversy, Durkeim began with an assumption that he believed was methodological when in fact it had to be philosophical: "Sociological method as we practice it rests wholly on the basic principle that social facts must be studied as things, that is, as realities external to the individual." He would have kept within the limits he imposed on himself had he been more disciplined in studying social facts as if they were things external to the individual. In fact he studied his facts as things in themselves, thus slipping unawares under the cover of Kant's partial solution to the dilemma of a post-metaphysical practical knowledge; hence, the striking rhetorical structure of *Suicide*.

Given Durkeim's aspiration to found sociology on the method of social facts as things in themselves, it is evident that the outcome of *Suicide* would not do. This may be why, over the fifteen years following 1897, his thinking underwent a change slight in appearance only. The difference is not in the axial theme of the primacy of the social over the psychological—but in the method itself. By 1912, in *Elementary Forms,* he drops all pretense of inventing a new method designed to tease out the social from a field of empirical things. In its stead is the classically French ethnological method of secondary analysis of field reports of the more elementary forms of social order. Since Montesquieu, at least, the French paved the way for what became modern ethnography, which was originally and literally the writing of a people's social forms—where the facts derive less from their numerical freshness than from their comparative logic; and where the data are precisely the collective representations of social forms. In other words, the purposes of the study cannot be achieved without a theory of the consciousness of consciousness, of knowledge as knowing from the social inside of such things.

Durkeim may have had little choice but to give up the methodological convictions in *Suicide.* At least this is what he did, presumably because he wished to complete the sociological project in *Suicide.* If we may engage our own method of sympathetic speculation, it seems that he could not possibly have been entirely satisfied with the early results which left his new science so exposed to the criticism of being little more than just what he intended it not to be—a thin science that pursued the empirical status of social things on the grounds of a synthetic *a priori* of types stipulated not by the evidence but by the mental categories of social logic. Whether or not some archivist will ever determine (if one has not already) what Durkeim may have privately thought of his dilemma, we can rest assured that a departure so striking as that of *Elementary Forms* from *Suicide* was taken only in the complete expectation that it would be noticed—indeed in the wish that it would be.

Modern social theory can only be grateful that Durkeim took the step, whether or not he knew what he was doing. It became the move that led to what some call cultural studies, others call cultural sociology, and still others call post-structuralism—none meaning quite the same thing. As indefinite as the labels may be, what all the early twenty-first-century variants of the social study of cultures have in common is a genetic filiation from and against the structuralism of Claude Lévi-Strauss whose cultural method stands at the crossroads of two of Durkeim's contemporaries, neither of whose relation with Durkeim was as direct as one would suppose, given the obvious similarities of thought.

The one was Lucien Lévy-Bruhl, Durkeim's younger colleague at the Sorbonne, whose *How Natives Think* in 1910 posed one of the questions Durkeim was dealing with in *Elementary Forms*. In the search for an account of the social origins of knowledge in the elementary forms of religion, Durkeim was necessarily asking one of the pivotal questions of modern social science: If there can be a science of social moderns must we conclude that the social traditionals, being without a science, were thereby unable to think as moderns do, thus unable to progress toward fully enlightened humanity? Durkeim's answer, like Lévy-Bruhl's, anticipated Lévi-Strauss's: No, on the contrary, it is their sciences that are different, not their humanities. Thinking, hence science, derives from a common aspect of all forms of social life: the social order itself.

The other largely unmediated line from Durkeim's time to ours is that from the notoriously anonymous Swiss linguist, Ferdinand de Saussure, whose theory of language as a social arbitrary is so acutely Durkeimian as to be painful to the absence of evidence of a direct relation. The Saussurian principle that would surface in the structural anthropology of Lévi-Strauss had at its heart the primacy of the arbitrary social contract. If, as Saussure claimed, the linguistic sign bore no evident relation to the thing it signified, then, as Lévi-Strauss would say, the cultural myth was similarly not an expression of social things themselves but of the mental state that only the collective life can nurture, then it stands to reason that the collective representation is at the foundation of social thinking itself. Or linking the two aspects, as Durkeim did with the idea of collective representations: *Social things can be thought only by social things because thought itself is social in nature.*

This is the remarkable difference between Durkeim's idealism of the social subject and Weber's of the hermeneutic circle. In the German line the knowing subject uses subjecthood as the instrument of interpretation of social things. In Durkeim's line, the subject knows because, and only because, he is a social thing. In other words, what Durkeim achieved—innocently in relation to the Germans; and knowingly in relation to his earlier experiment at, in effect, a sociological transcendence of Descartes by way of Rousseau—was not so much to eradicate the subject, as is sometimes thought, but to locate the subject amid social things. This could only happen with an implicit theory of culture as collective representations—as, in effect, a theory of discourse as not the expression of intersubjective truth but as the primary surface of intelligible social encounter with the collective—an encounter that can only be thought by way of consciousness of collective consciousness, which is to say: by life within the representations of bounded social life. This is the move Durkeim stumbled upon early when he slipped a particular social thing, suicide, under the discursive form of its representation, suicide *rates*. But the statistical rate would not do the work he intended of inserting the action of individuals, even the extreme action of self-slaughter, into the realm of social things. In short, the final solution was to replace beings with classes, where classifications are mental categories that enjoy a necessarily duplicitous and doubled relation to social reality: *social classes,* in all the usual, including formal sociological, senses of the word *class.* Classes—high, low, or middle, and all their finer distinctions—constitute the scale of social differences where science and injustice meet. They are the practical means of classification of all things, including social ones, into some scheme whereby the time, place, and totality of their relations to each allow for the very possibility of their causal relations.

Durkeim was, thereby, the first sociological constructionist—which accomplishment relied upon an implicit semiotics of the systems of social meanings classified according to the syntax of their logical possibilities. This, in turn, opened the door to Lévi-Strauss's full-blown semiotics of cultural meanings in the 1940s, which required, even as it anticipated, the so-called post-structuralism of the 1960s, which in its turn entailed a series of cultural and social studies of the 1970s and 1980s, which led to some of the more conspicuous features of the current situation.

Looking back from a century's long retrospect, it is shocking to see how Durkeim's thinking in his later years so thoroughly defined the terms of debates that rage in our time. What boggles is the list of issues at stake in another millennium that can be traced back to the ghosts of the other Durkeim, including but not limited to: the troubling idea that knowledge is socially constructed; the crisis unsettling the principles of representation (political as well as scientific); the not entirely false turn to language; the disturbing instability of analytic categories; the unavoidable uncertainty of foundations to modern knowledge; the ruthless arbitrariness of social as well as cultural categories; the moral liquidity associated with relativity of forms of truth; the evident indefiniteness of the Subject in moral action as well as scientific knowledge; the clever idea of a new science of literary tropes; among others.

It is not that Durkeim himself is responsible for all this. Indeed, a man so thoroughly and righteously cautious as he was could not have been expected even to dream of such things. Yet, it may well be that his scientific caution is what led him to correct the slippages of his early method of social facts as statistical representations by substituting a comparative method of collective representations of social forms. Which correction may be interpreted less as a maturation of his thinking, more as a resolution of an internal contradiction that has always been at the heart of empirical social research—one that Durkeim, more than any of his contemporaries (with the possible exception of Freud) realized had to be gotten around. His getting around it appears only superficially as a change of heart and method. Under it all, it was—to use the figure of speech—his own coming to terms with the haunting suspicion that he had not gotten the social fact thing right the first time. It is therefore Durkeim's own cautious restlessness that conjured up the two ghosts of subsequent sociology—that of the heroic dream of social things as a quantifiable utopia of facts; and that of the ironic joke that social things are facts insusceptible to representation by any foreign language, not even the pure discourse of formal arithmetic.

Far from being merely the first serious formalizer of an expressly sociological method, and thus the one to expose earlier sociological positivisms as little more than regurgitations of Comte's half-baked cult of science, Durkeim was in the end as much a skeptic as a believer in progressive science. For it was he alone—and he more than the outspoken skeptics of his time, Weber and Freud—who doubted in the end that facts are positive occurrences waiting only to be captured, or alternatively to be caught unawares by a hermeneutic trick. In the turn from the positive facts of self-slaughter to the inscrutability of collective representations Durkeim fulfilled the foundational principle of sociology as a method for the study of social things in the only way it can be fulfilled. That is: by granting the social thing its due as truly a member of its own class of things which class is not ultimately reducible to any other, nor plastic to representation by direct or formal languages.

To put it otherwise, Durkeim knew, without ever saying so, that social things are never fully present or visibly positive to the naked eye. Social facts are like none others more than astronomical ones. As the light by which stellar space-time is measured represents a long-dead body of mass and density long since gone from the measurable surface of universal things, so too the light of collectively represented social forms is the attenuated reflection of long-dead structures whose form can never, ever, be measured in their own space-time. There is always a death behind facts of these kinds.

The younger, if not young, Émile Durkeim of the 1890s seemed to believe, as young men do, that deaths are real only insofar as they are transposed into facts. He could thus write of the suicide as if death were a cold, hard fact. But, as everyone who has faced the dead knows, death is never merely a fact of this kind. For the living, the beloved dead, however and whenever they died, continue to live on. One wants never to believe the fact of their absence. Their deaths are (in the famous word) always *deferred*. Or, one might say: the fact of death is always unclosed for the living. If so, then it must follow that social facts are those facts so preoccupied with how the living sustain their relations with others that they, too, are ghosts ever open to revision. And this was what Durkeim unwittingly was trying to avoid saying in his social theory of knowledge in *Elementary Forms*. If, in the end, facts are known by the social categories of life with others, then, since others do in fact change their collective mind, knowledge itself is always a struggle to hold on to the elusive dead. If so, if even possible, then is not sociology a study not of social facts as such but of their loss to present time? Did not Durkeim measure the facts of anomic sufferers in his data against their loss of the moral body religion once provided? And did he not, later in his days, push the envelope of sociological measurement not forward to the purified technology of statistical significance but backward into the infinite regress of the elementary social form of social knowledge itself? What members of social groups cherish, whether or not they have the collective language to say it, are the dead structures of their possibilities.

All social science is gnostic—a secret code to wisdom passed down by the apparitions of realities that present themselves under the guise of fact. They are made to appear as if they were, if not quite hard, at least erect members of a representative body of truths, when in truth they are limp digits that depend for their potency on the fast hands that shake them to life.

Hence, the upsetting, and to some appalling, turn of events at a certain moment in the history of the twentieth century—a moment conspicuously different from its surface appearance, one in which the affluence of a postwar recovery covered the decrepitude of the European Diasporic culture of confidence.

That moment was just after World War Two. The place was, for the most part, Paris. And the reason was, in a word, the exhaustion of the Western powers after a good half-century of political turmoil, war, depression, and loss of faith in their own promises. As John Maynard Keynes, Georg Lukács, and Reinhold Niebuhr, among many others, said early in the decades after World War One had devastated the political dogmas of classical, nineteenth-century liberalism, we can no longer take the moral individual at face value. He (so to speak) is not, as history had then already proven, the motor force of human Progress. Hence, the interregnum of new deals and state-directed monetary policies that prepared the historical ground for another war. As Immanuel Wallerstein describes it, the interregnum was actually a truce amid one continuous war of the first half of the twentieth century between the United States and Germany for control of the world order. Still, the despair of the wars, and much else, and the failure of the classic version of the liberal ethic of free markets and enlightened individuals, helped prepare for the appeal of structuralism in France and elsewhere in Europe (not to mention in American academic sociology, with Talcott Parsons and Merton) after World War Two. The French, in particular, among others on the European continent (and in contrast to the British and the Americans), could resist German occupation only as courageous individuals in small clandestine groups, underground. To rid the surface of the earth of Nazi evil quite naturally was to open the intellectual skies to the idea that the truth of human things is in the visible structures, waiting to be seen, or (better) interpreted. Hence, too, the hermeneutic impulse that in France took the surprising quasi-scientific version of a structural semiotics of cultural forms.

This is the time and place where something began. Structuralism, henceforth, developed for a while, then prompted a reaction that came to be known as post-structuralism. Though at considerable odds in certain ways, the one could not have held forth without the other and in many instances the relations between structuralism and its alter were incestuous. Roland Barthes, a founder of structural semiotics, was also, later in his all-too-short life, a figure in the post-structural movement in *Mai '68*. Louis Althusser, than whom few were more the scientizing Marxist, was among Michel Foucault's teachers, as he was a colleague of Jacques Derrida. And Derrida cut his eye-teeth, first, on the interpretation of Husserl, an oblique source of the post-structural, who led, in some small way, to his famous 1966 essay on the decentering of human sciences which turn on a most appreciative criticism of Lévi-Strauss's structural logo-centrism. To the extent that structuralism was, as has been said over and over again, a reaction to the subjectivism of post-war existentialism— the philosophical thread of the Resistance experience; then, to the same extent, post-structuralism was only superficially a reaction to structuralist objectivism. Both movements were, in some very fundamental way, a coming to terms with the impossibility of liberal-modern culture, which had not very well endured the wars of the twentieth century (save in a bastardized form in the United States where the ideology of liberal consensus had its very short day before the Red Scare took away its breath).

The impossibility of liberal culture is a hard notion. One that is far from being widely accepted. One against which the resistance is scrupulous, if unevenly informed. But it is also a notion that had been a long time coming. It was in fact a concern that occupied Durkeim and his generation in Europe—and concerned him to such an extent that one of the reasons for his turn to culture was a proper and abiding concern over the liberal culture he believed so strongly could save the modern social order. In the end, sadly, it is possible that the impossibility of the liberal moral bond killed Durkeim.

Émile Durkeim died in Paris in 1917, at the height of his adult powers, just when, it happens, the Great War was breaking the heart of the European Diaspora. Ghosts arise from unsettled haves—from deaths that trouble the living because they come too inexplicably soon. Those who die young may not always be good, but whatever they are, they leave behind an untold story. Ghosts are the apparitions of the Unclosed because they remind the living that they really don't know all the answers. The better part of a century after Durkeim's death amid war in Europe, many well settled in the better positions of the house Europe built are spooked by reveries of their nineteenth-century ancestors who promised so much and delivered so little.

Durkeim died of a heart broken by the death of his son who was lost in the war and who, like all sons who die in such a service, are for their survivors the nightmares of what could have been. In his youth, Durkeim trusted, as could only a man raised on faith, that the Good Society would repair itself, even on the wounds of industrial conflict. This he believed so very well that he invented his version of scientific sociology that was to be both the true and the good of the Good Society. Yet, as could only a man of faith, nurtured in a Jewish village in the provinces of an anti-Semitic nation, Durkeim's faith was always cut with vinegar. He knew that faith in the social was as much a risk as was the modern idea that a good enough science could both tell *and* establish the truth of social things. Hence, from this young Durkeim came the ghost of a scientific positivism so foolish that not even Comte, himself no minor fool, could have conjured up such a one.

To the extent that ghosts are the spirits of the Unclosed, they always come in twos. We, who have actually seen ghosts, first think the apparitions are a case of double vision. We reach in the dark for our glasses only to find that the doubling remains. This is as it must be if we are being spooked by whatever came to an unnatural end. The end that fell upon the one lost is very, very real. In fact, it takes on a life of its own. In the case of Durkeim's empirical sociology the presence was, as it must be in these matters, the presence of an absence. Durkeim, thus, had to see (so to speak) that social facts could not produce a moral order sufficient to ward off the *anomie* that led to self-destruction. By 1914, France and the rest of Europe, soon to be joined by its North American Diaspora, had already embarked on the path of self-destruction.

The ghosts of Émile Durkeim are so much more upsetting than their author would have ever dreamt or wished them to be. That is very often the way with ghosts, especially those that rise from the bodies of writing. Durkeim, the man, was a serious and sober man of science. As such he left behind the written record of his own attempt to come to terms with the ghosts that required sociology be what it has become—a science of sorts; a social ethic no less; a politics of social change; a monument to the lost past of human values. In so many remarkable ways Durkeim's ghosts were more honest than those more often thought to have been the radical thinkers. Marx, who was certainly the better writer and the more brilliant thinker, was a bit too old hat. He held too strongly to the axiom that, though perverse, the world could be made to revert to its better being. Weber, who was certainly the more subtle scholar, was too troubled by his own ghosts ever to face as thoroughly as Durkeim did the ones in his own method. Freud, who was the more successful in advancing his program for the treatment of social and psychological ills, was unable, or unwilling, to offer up very much more of a social criticism than that the civilization was discontented due to its own interior instincts for violence.

Durkeim was, almost certainly, the lesser of these founding fathers of classical Europe in one or more aspects. But when it comes to haunting, he stands up very well, perhaps in the long run even better. In the long run, Durkeim's struggle to get from the study of suicide to a full theory of social knowledge yielded up a disposition to rework the social form by the only method available—that of taking the cultural as the more or less only but still good enough representation of the structures of social things. To say, thus, that the truth, such as it is, is a social thing unsettles the hope that the social order is both real and good, even if not entirely good enough to be true. Still, the thought was the bracing inspiration of the other ghost of social theory.

Because sociology, at least, and very likely all cultural forms, cannot avoid the haunts it would be rid of, it fell unto hard times well before it realized. The slippage, however, was not so much a tragedy as an ironic comedy of errors whereby the field fell, oddly, back onto the historical conditions of its emergence in Durkeim's time, thus back into the practical soup from which its science draws the breath of what human value it has. Academic sociology's first generation in the 1890s at Chicago was a motley crew of schoolteachers, philosophers, newspapermen, clubwomen, clergy, political troublemakers, and the like. Before there was a professionalized academic sociology, there was not much that was more organized than Marx's writings. Still the generation of the 1890s, with the possible exception of Weber, and the partial exception of Durkeim, had no other pool from which to draw the students who would become academic sociologists. They drew what they could, especially in Chicago, from the streets and poorhouses, and the schuls and churches, where reformers were at work.

When asked why sociology is always different from other of the social sciences—always in spite of itself more unruly and uneven—the answer is because of our ghosts. They are the ghosts of the practical sociologies that come before sociology proper—the spirits of those who came to the field from the streets and back alleys. Durkeim differed only by having experienced a childhood in the rural past already fading as the urban centers overtook the villages that, for more than a few millennia, were the true glue of moral societies surrounded by agricultural fields.

The word *culture* derives, over those same millennia, through many languages as, first, "the place wherein a local god is worshipped" to "the more literal field of horti- and agri-culture enterprise," to the scientific field wherein cultures are the intended breeding grounds of microbes, to the capital-C Culture of the early ethnologists and ethnographers to whom Durkeim turned, late in life, to plant the truth of his sociological method in a well-cultured field, which, in this day, many (Bourdieu most poetically) take as the *champ* in which the practice of sociological habits takes place.

Culture is not a subfield. It is the field itself, without which there is nothing we can know. Durkeim was the first to recognize this fact of our life, which is why he haunts us in so many ways.

NOTE

"Durkeim's Ghosts in the Culture of Sociologies" in *Durkeim's Ghosts: Cultural Logics and Social Things* (Cambridge, UK: Cambridge University Press, 2006), pp. 8–28.

III

Critical Sociology

5
Sociology
Prometheus among the Sciences of Man

Prometheus, like most Greek legendary heroes, had two, unreconciled fates. He was, first, the titan chosen by the gods to create Man. He did this work well, but was outflanked by a sneaky brother and fellow titan, Epimetheus, who had already given the animals the natural gifts of strength, courage, and speed. Prometheus's Man was thereby disadvantaged among earthly creatures. So Prometheus, emboldened by competition with his brother, challenged the gods. He stole fire from the heavens as his gift to Man.

Zeus, threatened by Prometheus's challenge to his power, visited a double punishment. The jealous god used Pandora to unleash upon earth disease, spite, envy, and revenge thus forever dampening Man's power. Still unappeased, Zeus had Prometheus chained atop Mount Caucasus, there to be forever scorched by the sun and picked at by vultures.

Prometheus took this fate well. It was presumably his satisfaction in having well created and well endowed Man that allowed him to endure a gruesome torture without visible agony. This was his second fate.

Sociology suffers a similar double fate. More than any other of the social sciences, sociology invented Man as an object of scientific discourse.[1] Further, it has led the others in stealing fire from the classic academic gods, the arts and sciences. Sociology's willingness to borrow, steal, explore, and experiment with the ideas of others distinguishes it among the social sciences. None other has been so reckless to the point of making itself an object of not infrequent derision. None has so risked its success as a science to maintain its power as a general intellectual enterprise. This boldness is sociology's first fate.

But its daring, like Prometheus's, has enchained sociology to a seeming eternity of internal philosophical bitterness and external exposure to the vulture Science picking at its entrails. The bitterness is sociology's chaotic philosophical pluralism. The vulture is, in truth, the ideal of science which tortures sociology by never letting go, always picking at its guts, its passion for Man. Hence a second fate which, again in Promethean fashion, sociology endures well probably because of an inner certainty that it does some things no one else can or will.

To understand how sociology came to this end we must examine its origins and subsequent development.

THE INSTITUTIONAL ORIGINS OF SOCIOLOGY

Sociology was not created *ex nihilo*. Its institutional history as an academic discipline began decisively in the 1890s. Like all the social sciences that emerged in the nineteenth century, sociology had a long prehistory. Ideas that were later appropriated by the discipline are assumed to have anticipated it. One compelling argument is that the first sociological impulses can be found in the tragic outlook of the Greeks.[2] It is a common belief that the first prefigurements of sociology were the early social philosophies of Hobbes, Rousseau, Machiavelli, and Locke.[3] Durkeim was not altogether chauvinistic in claiming Montesquieu's *The Spirit of Laws* as the first sociological textbook.[4] And one could scarcely argue against the view that sociology owes a considerable debt to those who invented its name and proclaimed its importance to the modern world, Saint-Simon and Comte; and to those who, without claiming a title for their labors, did the first modern sociological field work, de Tocqueville, Quetelet, Le Play and others.[5]

Yet, none of these early sources, nor any of the others that could be listed, were sociology. Sociology, as we know it, is and always has been a discipline.[6] Its character and its fate are, thereby, bound tightly to the modern University, and all those apparatuses important to university-based academics—scholarly journals, learned societies, textbooks.

Sociology's early relationship to the University was not universally harmonious.[7] In England, the University kept sociology out until after the Second World War. In Germany, the relationship was more openly bitter and confused. Weber resigned his university appointment due to illness. Simmel never kept a regular professorship in the University. Among the enduring giants of classical German sociology, only Toennies held an academic appointment at Kiel. In Germany early sociology grew through the German Sociological Society (founded in 1910 by Weber, Toennies, and Simmel) and the general social science journal *Archiv fuer Sozialwissenschaft* (edited, for a time, by Weber and Sombart, among others). In France, thanks largely to the prestige and early success of Durkeim and his circle, sociology held a tangible, if not prominent place in the University from the early years of the century. But, even here, the first undergraduate degree in sociology was not offered until 1958 and only thereafter, in the decade of the 1960s, did sociology blossom as a universally legitimate discipline. Throughout Europe (including Italy) sociology struggled in its relationship to academia until the years of economic prosperity and social change following the Second War.

Only in America did sociology find its way early and decisively into the University, principally due to the sponsorship of the University of Chicago which established a Department of Sociology in 1893, the year after its own founding. Albion Small was the first chairman of that department, the first editor of the *American Journal of Sociology,* and cofounder of the American Sociological Society. The early Columbia school, under Franklin Giddings, enjoyed a good, if more modest, early success, while programs at Brown (under Lester Ward) and at Yale (under William Graham Sumner) faltered after early promise. Just the same, and notwithstanding the long predominance of the Chicago School, sociology was widely institutionalized in American colleges and universities well before the turn of the century.[8]

Sociology's relationship to the University was, in the early period, uneven. Its history in Europe was different from the United States. In Europe, it struggled to get into the University. In America, it never knew another real home. In both places, the condition of admission, whether easy or hard won, was the same. Sociology was required to think of itself as a science. And this fate thrust sociology into its Promethean bind.

Science is not sociology's natural character, but an imposed form that works to restrict an original passion. Passion, fire, humanism, romanticism, faith—words like these must be used to describe sociology's other, suppressed fate. Prometheus, the fire thief and creator of Man, lies behind, and is the explanation for, the sufferer bound to Mount Caucasus. Allegories are tricky, but here they work because the other side of sociology is the side open to a world outside the University. And, in the beginning, this world (for sociology at least) was a world of contradictions—promise and misery, hope and suffering. It was the new, industrial world at the turn of the century; the world that required in the human sciences a clear vision of and commitment to Man; a world which, to those who tried to heal and explain it, simultaneously called upon one's sense of passion for its good, compassion for its pain, and faithful vision for its promises. There is no simple way to characterize the antipode to science in sociology. Some have tried. But such reductions as "critical," "romanticism," "humanism"—left to themselves—lead naturally to a growing chain of qualifiers.[9] This other side of sociology, at least in the early years, cannot be reduced because, first, it is the foot sociology kept planted outside the categorizing world of academia and, second, in different places that foot found different soil. With Durkheim it was a combination of Jewish culture and Dreyfusard liberalism. With Weber it was a fusion of ancient Protestant confusion and contemporary post-Bismarckian liberalism filtered through a dramatic family conflict in Weber's tormented mind between loyalty to mother and to father.[10] In the Chicago School it was, more directly, the generations of ministers, journalists, and social reformers that stood behind the founding of scientific sociology in America.

So, passion, fire, humanism—metaphors are opposed to the Science of the modern University in which sociology sought a home. The story of sociology is the story of its learning to live with these two fates, and its telling begins with the enduring successes of the classical period, Weber, Durkheim, and Chicago.

THE CLASSICAL ERA: WEBER, DURKEIM, CHICAGO

Sociology's classical era dates from 1893, the founding of the Chicago department, to 1935, the year in which the predominance of Chicago sociology was successfully challenged by the disestablishment of its *American Journal of Sociology* as the official journal of the American Sociology Society.[11] In between lies all the grand originating moments of the discipline: Durkeim's publication of the modern manifesto of sociology, *Rules of Sociological Method* (1895), and, three years later, his founding of French sociology's original scientific journal, *L'Année sociologique*; Weber's publication of his best known work, *The Protestant Ethic* (1905); the founding of the German Sociological Society (1921) and, in the years before the First World War, the meeting of Weber's famous and incomparable Heidelberg circle;[12] and Park and Burgess's classical textbook, *Introduction to the Science of Sociology* (1921), and the years in which the four giants of American sociology led the American Sociological Society (Lester Ward, 1906–1907; William Graham Sumner, 1908–1909; Franklin Giddings, 1910–1911; Albion Small, 1912–1913). It was a period bounded, symbolically, by the death in 1883 of the nineteenth-century sociological giant University sociology could never scientize, Karl Marx; and, on the other end, by the publication of the first textbook of sociology's postwar golden age, Talcott Parsons's *The Structure of Social Action* (1937).

The heritage of the classical period is two individuals (Weber and Durkeim) and a tradition (Chicago). But it should be understood that the individuals were, in fact, traditions. The writings of Weber and Durkeim, combined with their lasting influence through the impressive circles they gathered to themselves, served the equivalent function to the more secure institutional path of the Chicagoans. The result was the same. Weber, Durkeim, and Chicago are, by a long shot, the classical sources still read today. They shaped modern, postwar sociology.[13] And they embodied sociology's double fate.

Max Weber, the theoretical Minotaur. This was Alvin Gouldner's way of describing Weber's theoretical (and emotional) cleavage between classicism and romanticism, science and humanism.[14] More than anyone else, the titan of German sociology embodies (and led the way to) sociology's double fate. For Weber, science was a near religious calling which instills in the scientist (including the sociologist) the passion necessary to endure the "tens of thousands of quite trivial computations," the drudgery in which scientific truth is found. The unremitting final condition of scientific truth is that no matter how hard one works, good works may not issue in great ideas, yet ideas will never occur without that hard work. Ideas are a gift of grace. "Ideas occur to us when they please, not when it pleases us."[15] The scientist's double bind is classically religious (actually Lutheran). Hard work is a necessary but never sufficient path to truth. Only passionate devotion allows him to endure. This is the cleft Weber: called and passionate, but ultimately limited by truth's inscrutability. The double bind is itself doubled. One relies on passions for motivation and endurance, but must be ever mindful of passion's danger. Passion may tempt the scientist to compromise objectivity; hence Weber's famous commandment: thou shalt remain value-free.

In every superficial respect Durkeim—the cool, purposeful, Parisian academic and public servant—was the very opposite of Weber. Where Weber's passions nearly tore him apart during a long period of mental illness and, through his career, in the deep ambivalence of his theoretical writings, Durkeim's passions, personal and theoretical, were kept in tight control. Lewis Coser aptly describes him as a "man made of whole cloth," one who "did not waver from his allegiance to a cosmopolitan liberal civilization in which the pursuit of science was meant to serve the enlightenment and guidance of the whole of humanity."[16] As a teenager he settled accounts with the long line of rabbis which proceeded him. He decided not to follow his father into the rabbinate and immediately embarked on the life trajectory which, then as now, is typical of successful, cosmopolitan French. He was a brilliant student in his provincial secondary school, transferred to the prestigious high school in Paris (*Lycée Louis-le-Grand*), eventually gained admission to the elite *École Normale Supérieure* (where he studied with Henri Bergson, Jean Jaures, among other future luminaries), and, like most of its graduates, taught in various provincial lycées for several years. After periods of further study in France and Germany, he was appointed to a post at Bordeaux. At the callow age of 29 he was invited to offer the university's first course in social science. He became full professor within a decade, and was enormously productive. In 1902 he fulfilled the dream of all aspiring French academics—a professorship in Paris (at the Sorbonne in Durkeim's case). In the ambience of *fin de siècle* Paris and the exuberance of Third République liberal culture, Durkeim established the first chair in sociology in the French university system, directed the famous journal he had founded (*L'Année sociologique*), was active in public life, made sociology a legitimate topic of conversation, became famous himself, and influenced the course of modern French education by introducing his sociological ideas on moral education into the curriculum at the École Normale.[17]

Durkeim's career path was cool and that cool partly explains his greater success, relative to Weber, in establishing sociology in his society's university system. As we shall see, the extra scientific passions survived, but when it came to the science of society they were strictly suppressed. Durkeim's *Rules of Sociological Method,* a programmatic tract designed to announce and define a positive sociological method, is an arid, spiceless, passionless little text that today baffles students for saying so little. But today's readers, like modern readers of Weber's pronouncements on value freedom, seldom understand the book's context. The condition for establishing sociology was to distinguish its field from that of other disciplines, to define, as Foucault might have put it, an epistemological space for sociology. Thus, the first rule of sociological method was: avoid philosophy. "But the role of sociology," said Durkeim, "must consist precisely in liberating us from all parties. This will be done not so much by opposing one doctrine to other doctrines, but by causing those minds confronted with these questions to develop a special attitude, one that science alone can give through direct contact with things."[18] The first purpose of *Rules,* thereby, was to distinguish sociology from philosophy, ideology, and other social sciences (especially psychology).

Unfortunately, whenever a practical project governs so profoundly a scientific program the burdens of the former exert distorting pressures on the latter. Durkeim's formula for sociology seemed clean enough; it was: *Sociology can be a science only if it has its own field of facts. That field is social facts. Social facts are the moral pressure of social things [his well known conscience collective] on human behavior. Social things cannot be reduced. They are not, least of all, psychological things.* As an abstract formula it sounds proper and workable. Why not? But the underlying distortions appeared as soon as Durkeim set the method to work. *Suicide,* his justly famous empirical study and the showcase for his method, is organically flawed by the distorting effect of practical ambition on his rules. The trees of this brilliant exercise in logic and statistics draw attention away from the bizarre shape of the forest. Durkeim was so intent on demonstrating that suicide is a moral and social thing that he claimed it is not, therefore, a personal or psychological thing. To secure this common sense improbability he made the incredible error of equating suicide, the social thing, with suicide rates, the statistical thing. "We must not forget that what we are studying is the social suicide-rate."[19] Here is Durkeim's naive positivism and, because he stated it with so much cool, generations of subsequent sociologists overlooked his error, and for good reason. It was a natural way to make the semblance of science.[20] Of course, Durkeim had no alternative. The condition for making suicide a social thing is to make it a statistical rate. But this sly confusion of scientific things with social things entails two indefensible claims: suicide is not really a social thing (but a rate); there can be no individual suicides (since rates cover social things).

No liberal man with his passions up front would ever claim that individuals don't kill themselves merely because individual deaths can't generate rates. But Durkeim did. This consequence of Durkeim's attempt to make a science governs his puny theory of the social individual. In effect, there is no viable, individual agent in society for Durkeim. Between the social force of society (the conscience collective) and raw animal passions, there is nothing.[21] Human passion as a component in forceful individual action is unthinkable.

If Weber is the embodiment of sociology's early Promethean double fate, Durkeim is the prefiguration of the schizoid manner in which subsequent, maturing sociology would have to manage this contradiction. Weber struggled with it. Durkeim was more truly Prometheus. He accepted (even gladly) the chains of science, gaining strength in his public life from the fires of liberal passion.

The Chicago School offered still a third way around the double fate. The Chicago tradition, from the beginning, neither struggled with nor segregated its liberal passions and its science. Like the tides each had a natural time. To be sure, Chicago sociology, as we've seen, began as a university discipline, and was vitally concerned to demonstrate its status as a science. But the science question, though vexing, probed less voraciously at the American viscera. Perhaps this was so because the god Science was more fully appeased in Chicago. The University of Chicago was a remarkably vigorous and progressive institution that granted sociology a virtual carte blanche:

a Ph.D. granting graduate department in 1893, sponsorship of the *American Journal of Sociology* (still housed at Chicago), and, indirectly (through its subsidy of an outstanding faculty), presidents and other leaders of the American Sociological Society. The University reflected the dynamism of America's new, frontier city, and sociology benefited from this association, as well as the more remote, but surely powerful, influence of that hallmark American virtue: pragmatism.[22] The Americans, at Chicago (as elsewhere), though familiar with and frequently trained by European social thinkers, bore little of the urgent obligation to stake out philosophical positions against the dominant thinkers of the day.[23] What Simmel, Weber, or Spencer thought mattered only if it was useful. The Americans could ignore them, if they wished. In these ways, the Chicagoans enjoyed a freedom which surely made them less anxious about the face they put on their sociology. Across the United States, sociology emerged as a teaching subject deeply married to very undisciplined topics like social ethics, social welfare, social reform, and even theology.[24] Likewise, at Chicago—the place of its birth as a formal university discipline—one worried little about the social origins of its professors, or the liberal sometimes laughably unscientific character of its research work. Though many of the early Chicago faculty were traditional academics, many were not originally. Albion Small was trained as a minister. Robert Park had been a journalist. Ellsworth Paris served as a missionary in Africa. Louis Wirth was a social worker. No surprise that early M.A. theses and Ph.D. dissertations in the sociology department included such titles as "The Influence of Modern Social Relations upon Ethical Concepts," "Social Policy of Chicago Churches," "Attempt of Chicago to Meet the Positive Needs of the Community," "Garbage Problems in Chicago," "A Study of the Stock Yards Community at Chicago."[25]

The Chicago School of the 1920s produced two enduring traditions of empirical social research, urban ecology and social psychology. The foundational idea of the urban ecology movement at Chicago was that the city is organized into natural areas which, in Park's words, "are the products of forces that are constantly at work to effect an orderly distribution of populations and functions within the urban complex."[26] The best that can be said for the urban ecology idea is that it surely wins the gold medal for benign ideas that survived a long time. For this very reason, the idea suited Chicago's purposes perfectly. Though the social ecology work was the most scientizing of the School's two classic contributions, it scientized loosely. In substance, the idea of urban zones merely organized, classified, and softly formalized empirical research Chicagoans had been doing, would have done anyhow, and are still doing. It allowed them to deploy sociology in their natural urban laboratory, Chicago, and thus to keep faith with the University and still not abandon the social pathos that it held dear.

Chicago's social psychology was a fortuitous result of friendship and network over the early years. John Dewey, George Herbert Mead, and Charles Cooley (at the University of Michigan) shaped the original ideas that Mead's student Herbert Blumer would eventually codify under the name by which we recognize it, symbolic interactionism. After Dewey left Chicago, hundreds of students followed Mead's lectures on social behaviorism. They learned from Mead a social philosophy that was, in most respects, the easy theoretical solution to sociology's Promethean double bind. Mead held that social Man was, indeed, a liberated, symbol-using, meaning-generating being yet, at the same time, he was a creature bound to respond to stimuli external to himself (hence, Mead's behaviorism). Thus was created a theoretical microworld of locally creative men, responding imaginatively to transcendent, external symbolic stimuli. Chicago sociology has always given good, frequently exciting, accounts of the meaningful and symbolic interaction of individuals in microsettings. But it has never dared to ask the big question: What if the ultimate source of meaning is systematic distortion visited by the macroworld of interest motivated, class-based institutions, the State, the Corporate world, the Ruling Class, or any social big thing? Chicago social theory, from Mead through Blumer to Erving Goffman and the ethnomethodologists, ironically gained disciplinary respectability by a subtle modesty that allowed it to be, in what it did, outrageous.

Symbolic interactionism, Chicago's most distinctive theoretical tradition, entered into a seedy covenant with the University for which it has never been judged because its empirical descriptions of the underdog world, of the mentally ill, of the hidden dynamics of medical practices, and urban suffering were so compelling and so sensitive. Chicago limited itself, theoretically and empirically, to the underworld and backstages in which are hidden the terrible secrets and raw passions of modern, urban society. It simultaneously ceded to others within the University (including their social ecological colleagues) responsibility for the macro questions. We covenant, they said, to use our fire only in this small world, if you grant us right of place in the disciplines. Like all compromises there have been costs and benefits. On the benefit side, Chicago sociology, more than any other (including Weber's and Durkeim's), has been enormously productive, largely because it has been left alone. On the cost side, Chicago sociology was limited not only in theoretical scope but place of residence. Clearly, such sociology could only work in universities liberal and brash enough, like the original University of Chicago, to accept the deal. Thus, Chicago sociology has succeeded only at Chicago, Berkeley, and other outposts of the California system (especially San Diego, Santa Barbara). Where it sought other homes, at Iowa, Illinois, or Pennsylvania, for instance, it was either changed, or isolated.[27] Chicago sociology never had its day in the traditionally prestigious American universities. Columbia and Harvard, the great postwar departments, actively ignored the Chicagoans. Today the department at the University of Chicago is arguably the most prestigious there is. But the original Chicago spirit has long since migrated to California.

So, what Chicago sociology accomplished was to provide early American sociology with several generations of safe haven and university legitimacy, to say nothing of training most of its scholars, maintaining its journal, and putting the discipline on the map. When, after the Second War, sociology entered the world of big science, refusing to compromise the scientific ideal, it broke decisively with Chicago. Thus, in 1935 the American Sociological Society's rejection of the *American Journal of Sociology* as its sponsored journal was the beginning of the end of Chicago's supremacy.

ORIGINAL SOCIOLOGY AND MAN

Before turning to contemporary sociology, I must clean up the mess any allegory, like the Promethean, inevitably leaves. The telling of sociology's early story is actually two stories in one. Both tolerate the Promethean allegory well, but one part of the text I have allowed to stand as metaphor: the claim that sociology created Man. This is messy, so let me come clean. I mean Man as a specific object of social thought and, thus, I mean it technically, as much as figuratively. Man, as an object of thought, arose, after Kant, with the dramatic modern splitting of natural, pure reason from social, practical reason. This, of course, is a formulation which I owe to Foucault. In his archaeology of the human sciences, *The Order of Things,* and elsewhere, Foucault claimed that the social sciences were products of the nineteenth-century liberal, bourgeois interest.[28] Nineteenth-century humanism was a convenience of the capitalist class. Epistemological categories are, in Foucault's writings, modes of permissible discourse shaped by the forces of social power. Consequently, the categories of knowledge most convenient to nascent capitalism were those which defined man as (a) finite in the face of nature, and, nonetheless, (b) potent, as subjective consciousness, in the realm of human history. Though Foucault never said it in so many words, this neat formula allowed the two requisites of modern, capitalist knowledge: that it combine formidable sanctions requiring humility (better to control the limits of knowledge) with superficially gentle permission for the powerful to deploy knowledge freely (better to shape society in the form of bourgeois sensibilities, while using it to limit the play of the lower classes).

High and late nineteenth-century liberalism was as different from the classical liberal assumptions of the utilitarians as the factories of Manchester after 1860 were from the public markets of the Massif Central in the 1780s. The passions of late liberal Man are those of Man freed from the awful metaphysical burden of obedience to and responsibility for natural, cosmic, transcendent truth. Man, thus, is free to think and act within his own history, a history created (in Hobsbawm's phrase)[29] by the dual revolution in politics in France and in capitalist industry in Britain. This, surely, is what Auguste Comte, in his tendentious way, was trying to get at. And, even more certainly, this is what Comte's heirs in sociology believed.

The faith of industrial liberalism is ironic. Man is limited. Because he is limited, he is free to make history. This belief made sociology possible insofar as the very idea of society, in the modern sense, is a product of the complexities of civil society. Therefore, just as this liberal ideal made sociology possible, so sociology made Man in its own liberal image.

Weber, Durkeim, and the Chicagoans were three regional articulations of this liberal faith. Each saw social science as a product of the finitude of knowledge. For Weber, the scientist awaited an inscrutable Idea. For Durkeim, moral society itself took on a nature-like objectivity against which man was a shrunken cipher, overwhelmed by animal passion. For Chicago, at the other extreme, the social complex was totally Other, and human freedom was modestly confined to the microworld of families, gaming tables, back wards, and neighborhoods. But this is one side of the formula. At the same time, each also gave place to the potency of historical man—subjective meaning in Weber, liberal statesmanship and public service in Durkeim, and an overblown dedication to the passionate underlife of Chicago. In each, human passions stood firmly in significant relationship to an Other which defined its limits. Of course, in sociology, as in liberalism generally, the ultimate limit on passion was, and is, Science, an over-reading, too confident rationality.

SOCIOLOGY BOUND: 1935 TO THE PRESENT

America's island character explains both the freedom enjoyed by the Chicago sociologists and the fact that, in 1935 (while Europe, having not recovered from one world war, was preparing for another) the American sociological community was sufficiently developed and undisturbed that the anti-Chicago coup could take place. In Europe sociology groped between the great wars. The struggles of Weber and Durkeim to make it acceptable to university culture continued to be frustrated. After the Second War sociology had acquired its modern character, the face of which was distinctively American. When, in the fifties and sixties, European sociology experienced its long sought after popularity, its institutional shape followed the American lead. University based teaching programs were organized. American empirical techniques were imported. Europeans, in an exceptional reversal of roles, made ritual pilgrimages to learn American ideas and methods.[30]

In the United States remarkably little of substance carried over from the classical period. Save for Chicago social ecology and symbolic interaction, little endured. No one today reads Park and Burgess, Giddings, and Ward—except out of historical curiosity. What did survive was form, not substance. The Chicago university model was the most important, but the beginnings of an important Columbia school were in evidence. In both places, the decisive technical change was the rapid growth, in appeal and sophistication, of quantitative methods (but this factor was less important than the former). It must not be overlooked that the University is not the only place for intellectual work on problems of modern society. Political parties, trade unions, churches, journalism, the secular world of letters, the life of the unattached writer—these alternative institutional homes had been natural to presociological social theorists (Marx being the conclusive example) and, to this day, they are still convenient to Europeans in many intellectual domains. If not rejected, these alternatives were at least by-passed largely due to the classical conviction that sociology ought to be a university-based science. It was in the United States that this fate was finally determined.

After the war sociology felt few pangs of conscience for leaving the world and entering the cloistered, scientific university. It need not be said that the prevailing mood in the fifties and sixties was faith in science and technology to solve the problems of the world. Thus, sociology could split topic and resource. The topic of its teaching and research was indeed the world—of social change, of unrest, of affluence, of new suburbs, of crime, of racial injustice. Its resource had become the tools of modern science, refined to suit the special purposes of social research. In the postwar period survey research, statistical techniques, theory construction methods, field work were all formalized. Even the apparently "qualitative" methods were transformed into sometimes surprisingly methodologically self-conscious activities like ethnomethodology.[31] Everyone worried about methods, and the underlying, uniting impulse was to establish scientific credentials for the sociological enterprise. All the while, the world was calling sociology for help in rebuilding a broken, now rapidly changing world. Sociology had it both ways, now totally with impunity. Free to be science; called to serve the world. Students, government officials, politicians, the corporate world, the military establishment sought sociological advice. The discipline was popular and, for an all too brief moment, affluent in students, teaching posts, and research funds. In the United States, Marxists, liberals, and the politically neutered enjoyed without discrimination the research and career advantages of great universities and their establishment research centers, like the Bureau of Applied Research at Columbia, the Institute for Social Research at Michigan, the National Opinion Research Center at Chicago. And in Europe in the sixties, emergent sociological stars frequently bore the complex burden of appealing simultaneously to radical (largely working class) students, centrist governments, and the universal demands of the international (meaning, American) sociological community. More than a few had their lives changed by the impossible choice of which side of the barricades in the flawed revolutionary moments of 1968.[32] But these are the inconvenient costs of affluence, an affluence that soon ran dry.

Sociology's moment of disciplinary affluence lasted from the immediate postwar years through the late sixties.[33] Its symbolic original moment was 1937 when Talcott Parsons published *The Structure of Social Action,* the massive, little read, two volume book which set the agenda for Parsons's dominance as theoretician, organizer, and teacher. This, at least, is the common faith. It should be added that the year following, 1938, Robert Merton published the first of many highly influential articles, "Social Structure and Anomie." If Parsons, in *Structure of Social Action,* reworked Weber and Durkeim (and others from the classical period) to set modern sociology on its theoretical course, then Merton's "Social Structure and Anomie" was but the first of many articles which, less self-consciously, took the classical heritage as a resource for modern empirical social research. This essay and those that followed were collected and published (first in 1949) as *Social Theory and Social Structure,* which stands, alongside Parsons's *Structure,* as *locus classicus* of the age of sociological affluence. Though they were by no means in total agreement (in spite of the fact that Merton took courses from Parsons at Harvard and remained a loyal friend through his life), the two took different intellectual courses (undoubtedly, in part, a case of the slightly younger giant seizing the opening left by the older). Parsons was the theoretician; Merton the "middle range" thinker who looked everywhere for potential researchable topics, Parsons's book has been the more heralded. Merton's surely has been the more important insofar as it, like Park and Burgess's 1921 classic, led graduate students to their dissertations and mature sociologists to their life's research.

As much as their writings and more than their professional service (both were presidents of the American Sociological Association; Parsons in 1949; Merton in 1957), these two men shaped contemporary sociology by their teaching. Parsons gathered the Harvard School into the famous Social Relations experiment (an institutionalized version of his general theory), while Merton, with Paul Lazarsfeld, was central to the nearly as famous Columbia School of which the Bureau of Applied Social Research is the symbol of its crucial difference from Parsons's more theoretical approach. It would be imprudent to list and impossible to overstate the importance of the names of students of these two.[34] Through the 1960s virtually no one of substance in American sociology was not affiliated (as colleague, student, or student of a student) with the Harvard or Columbia schools. By contrast, the Chicago tradition was in dispersion and even it felt obliged to respond to the dominant positions taught by Parsons and Merton.

Naturally, the teaching reflected an outlook. Just as Merton's life-long commitment to leading others to empirical research is reflected in the clear research-oriented conceptualizing in *Social Theory and Social Structure,* so the breadth of Parsons's influences are foreshadowed in the gargantuan scope of *Structure of Social Action*. Parsons's general theory of action attempted, after 1937, a bold reshaping of the wisdom of classical sociology (especially that of Weber and Durkeim) into a fully modern, formal, empirically testable general theory of society. Social action was, therein, taken as an instance of action systems generally for which natural models (physiological, then cybernetic) served as Parsons's theoretical beginning points. Thus, social systems were those bordered on the one hand by biological systems and, on the other, by personality systems. Social action was, thus, governed by cultural patterns, but pushed by adaptive energy deriving from man's biological nature. The details of the scheme are, today, little read, but it has made its mark. The division of the world of socially relevant actions into biological, cultural, sociological, and psychological (with the economic and political taken, implicitly, as aspects of sociology), when shorn of its theoretical glamour, is of course nothing less than a way of both cataloguing the social sciences and of strategically situating sociology among the disciplines. It should be said that Merton's tripartite division—culture, social structure, personality—is a more modest version of a similar world view. Whatever the lasting merit of the two theoretical positions they each served to codify sociology's place in the University. Social scientists think in terms of these divisions partly because they grew up in colleges so divided and partly because Parsons and Merton (and their students) reflected those divisions in their scientific work. That the world may not be a mirror of the University is an idea yet to be considered. Parsons and Merton can hardly be blamed for enforcing such an institutional straightjacket on academia. They simply did, and did well, the work begun in the classical era. They established sociology's place in the University, both by giving it a discernible scientific form and by teaching the legitimacy (indeed the indispensable importance) of sociology's centrality to the University. It is no accident, therefore, that Parsons was both an academic organizer (in his leadership of the Social Relations experiment at Harvard) and that education was foremost among his life-long empirical interests. Nor is it coincidental that Merton is founder and to this day the acknowledged leader of a subdiscipline, the social scientific study of science. To them sociology owes its sense of place and the University now owes its unavoidable obligation to make place for the one *general* social science.

Unfortunately the foundation was laid in sand. By the middle sixties sociology's scientific imperium came under attack. Though Merton remained relatively immune to direct personal attack, Parsons became the object of scrupulous and principled (if occasionally overdetermined) assaults. He was criticized for being too abstract, writing too opaquely, caring too little for social change, being too establishment, *inter alia.* The critical voices were heard by students of an emerging generation of social theorists who had been schooled in the civil rights and anti-war movements before they had read Parsons and Merton. The sixties started a rush of students to courses in sociology and of graduates of the social turmoil to sociology doctoral programs. In Europe and the United States these were even seen as encouraging signs. It appeared as though sociology would thrive for years to come as the growth market in the University. One could well endure a bit of rowdiness on campus and pluralism within sociology as long as the students were interested (and preoccupied). In the years around 1968 in American sociology (as in European social theory in Germany and especially, France), new theoretical ideas burst forth in volcanic proportions. In the same years when, outside the social sciences, Derrida, Barthes, Habermas, and Foucault were coming into their own, in sociology one encountered books on every conceivable sort of new sociology: phenomenological, existential, critical, systems theoretical, theory constructionist, conflict-oriented, ethnomethodological, symbolic interactionist (yes, Blumer's major book did not appear until 1969). Everyone, quite naturally, began immediately to reread Thomas Kuhn's *Structure of Scientific Revolutions* for a clue to all these new paradigms, and an explanation for the breakup of the preceding structural functionalist one. There was absolutely no reason to doubt that sociology was doing anything other than redirecting itself and, in the process, discovering what came to be considered its natural form, pluralism.

It didn't turn out that way. The explosion in the late sixties went the way of all good fireworks. By 1980 sociology majors in American colleges and universities had declined 52% from a high of thirty-one thousand in 1979,[35] academic positions for promising sociologists disappeared, departments began to shrink, and the government turned a deaf ear to pleas for research funds. In the late sixties and early seventies sociology had been living off borrowed capital. The prestige of the discipline in the previous generation carried it into and partly through a period of crisis, but that prestige could not solve sociology's original problem, that of its double fate. Sociology may or may not have taken the wrong option in entering the University, but the blindness with which, especially during its affluent era, it committed itself to Science was, in hindsight, surely a mistake. It is one thing to promise, another to come through. Sociology, after the war, promised to supply solutions for society's needs and, on this condition, it was welcomed and well fed. But when the answers did not come, or, at least, did not work, the hosts began to wonder what they had gotten into. The symbol of sociology's failure to deliver is James Coleman (surely today one of the most respected of its practitioners). In 1966, Coleman supplied the comprehensive data upon which the Great Society's busing and educational reform policies were built. Today he is a leading revisionist critic of busing. Likewise, students were delighted to taste the pleasures of sociology's decidedly vocational subjects when there were jobs aplenty, but less so when they had to worry about employment. When governments withdraw funding and students withhold attendance, no academic discipline can remain untouched.

What broke the promise of sociology's scientific promise was not something inherently wrong with sociology. It was something wrong with its alliances. Sociology had forgotten that, for it, science was, literally, a discipline. Discipline binds and limits, even if for some noble purpose. But ascetic disciplines are the antithesis of human passions. Universities always and forever have had, will have, and should have trouble with the passions. Sociology had then to pay the price for having ignored its other fate, that of carrying fire to Man.

SOCIOLOGY HEREAFTER

Sociology has lost itself to science and the University. But this does not mean that sociology cannot have a relationship to science or place in the University. What it must learn to do is to abandon its quite understandable desire to escape the double fate. Surely its choice of a life with science was, given the circumstances, the wiser course. There is no reason to believe that sociology would have been truer to itself had it chosen the course of identification with human passions (had it, in America, chosen to remain in the prophetic tradition of the social gospel and social reform movements that were so prominent in its heritage).

But now allegory fails. The Promethean figure, having served well to this point, leaves the impression that the alternatives are few: either science or passion; or as alternative to these alternatives live with the Promethean dialectic—chained but proud, scientist but rebel. So, since allegories are meant for telling stories and, by the same token, are not meant to diagnose real, present circumstances, I excuse Prometheus in order to draw my conclusion.

Sociology needs to look in two directions: at itself to determine what it can and cannot be, given where and what it is; and at its institutional home to determine its place, given what it can be.

What sociology is, as an intellectual activity, is a product of its historical origins and its inherent nature. Sociology, as we have seen, began in the nineteenth century. It is, therefore, quintessentially modern. There was no sociology prior to the emergence of the modern, liberal democratic state. There could not have been. The collapse of absolutism and the appearance of civil society and the ideal of liberated, autonomous political Man were the necessary preconditions to an activity the central questions of which have always been, *mutatis mutandis,* how do individuals remain free in community? How does community remain orderly so that individuals are free? Sociology is indeed a product of the dual revolutions. The modern state and the modern economy are equally sociology's preconditions and this means that it is as indebted to capitalism as it is to political liberalism. The proof of the claim is that not only has sociology not existed prior to these revolutions, it does not exist in regions which these revolutions have not claimed. Eastern bloc sociology, like instant coffee, is interesting only when it is not compared to the real thing.

In other words, sociology came to be because a new form of social life posed an immutable puzzle. How do free individuals keep order? There is no known answer to this question. The fact that, relatively speaking, they have kept order is as much a puzzle. And, the further, though arguable, fact that they have kept order mostly through domination and unfairness is surprising only because it leads to still another puzzle of liberal societies. Why is it that, apparently, they can be free only with some presumably tolerable unfreedom, which unfreedom contradicts their reason for being. Social theorists from Hobbes to Habermas rightly consider the legitimation crisis the central question.[36] Sociology is unique because it is the one nineteenth-century discipline that has taken these questions as its reason for being. What outsiders frequently take to be sociology's philosophical flakiness is nothing more than its laudable refusal to let go of our society's original puzzle.

This does not say that sociology is nothing more than social philosophy. Sociology arose when and how it did because it participated, if unwittingly, in the rejection of metaphysics. Liberal, civil societies do not lend themselves to interpretation through questions of being, essence, or, even, truth. Hegel was the last metaphysician, which is why sociologists have made use of him only after he was inverted by Marx. Sociology is, therefore, an empirical activity, and this explains its affinity for the sciences. Modern society, since the nineteenth century, wanted the order/freedom puzzle resolved in concrete terms. And sociology attempted to comply by paying attention to the central specifics. Durkheim's *Suicide* is fundamentally a book about the collapse of moral order in modern societies. Weber's *Protestant Ethic* is an essay on the cultural origins of modernity's confining over-commitment to rationality (what he called the iron cage). Chicago's twin fascination with urban environments and the social psychology of human freedom led to a series of studies of the plight of the poor, the deranged, the criminal, or the ill rejected by mass, modern society. Sociology has always been at its best when describing, in specific terms, the concrete ways in which individuals can and do struggle (and fail to struggle) with the modern puzzle: being unfree in a theoretically free society. Conversely, it is at its worst when it attempts to generate scientific laws about the nature of things. Durkheim's *Suicide* and Weber's *Protestant Ethic* are utterly compelling as well described ethical statements and puny as scientific arguments or methods.

The real double bind of sociology is that it is, indeed, the most general of the social sciences, but its generality is attained only when it keeps faith with the ethical nature of its primordial question. As a general science it falters, in part because it lacks a proper, assigned domain of empirical investigation. Its rival social sciences—economics, psychology, politics—will always out-scientize sociology because they enjoy the tremendous advantage of having an undisputed empirical territory within which they are free to announce the general laws of markets, minds, and voting. Parsons tried, as we have seen, to stipulate a domain for sociology but he failed, partly because he tried to do it abstractly, and partly because the social system is not a real thing, but a mystery.

Modern society is ultimately unintelligible. Where the order problem really troubles is when it confronts the question of macrostructures. (Microstructures and micro orders are no problem, as the Chicago tradition has repeatedly demonstrated.) Macrostructures—be they social systems, class structures, forms of political domination, world economies—are inherent mysteries, at least through the eyes of science. Macrostructures can never be observed. They are, by definition, imputed patterns comprised of artful pictures based on numerous little observations. One cannot paint society's pictures by numbers.[37] Ultimately, the structured nature of orderly (or disorderly) modern society can only be painted imaginatively. In this respect good sociology is good literature, in particular, good fiction, as Marx first demonstrated. Thus sociology will always be closer kin to the one social "science" that is most marginal to science and most loyal in the arts, history.

Therefore, what sociology can be is a marvelous bastard—the illegitimate child of science, nurtured by a primordial, ethical question. Sociology is the artful concrete accounting of inherently ethical questions.

For this very reason its place in the University should be guaranteed. The University, after all, is culpable for its part in the duplicitous alliance sociology made with it. If sociology fooled itself, and its host institution, by falsely claiming to be science, the University, on its side, entered freely, and no doubt greedily, into the marriage. Since most marriages begin on false assumptions, there is no reason why this one cannot follow the lead of most enduring marriages. There is after all nothing dishonorable about discovering, in mature life, the foolishness of youthful dreams, then building a new, second life based on the reality of whom the partners have actually come to be. So what if sociology failed to be the science, and the University failed to pay the bills? We should not lose sight of the fact that the University is nearly as troubled today as are certain of its disciplines, like sociology. The University will never, nor should it, give up its prior commitment to science. But, one hardly need say, science itself has learned the limits of its rationality. The most intellectually vibrant areas of intellectual debate today include those over the risks science has taken in nuclear physics, in biomedical experimentation, in bioengineering, and in the technologies of war and fuel. And these are deeply ethical debates which quickly lead the debate to the sort of questions sociology has always asked. The University surely has a place for the one social discipline that seeks knowledge, frequently in scientifically sensitive ways, to the general questions of Man's moral fate: How do we survive in a world that has outrun itself?

NOTES

1. This idea is developed at length in Charles Lemert, *Sociology and the Twilight of Man: Homocentrism and Discourse in Sociological Theory* (Carbondale: Southern Illinois University Press, 1979). The concept *man* is discussed in the present chapter.

2. Alvin W. Gouldner, *Enter Plato: Classical Greece and the Origins of Western Social Theory* (New York: Basic Books, 1965).

3. These are among the presociological writings anthologized in the section "Historical and Analytical Foundations" of an ambitious attempt to collect samples of all major sociological writings: *Theories of Society: Foundations of Modern Sociological Theory,* ed. Talcott Parsons, Edward Shils, Kaspar D. Naegele, and Jesse R. Pitts, 2 vols. (New York: Free Press, 1961).

4. Émile Durkeim, *Montesquieu and Rousseau: Forerunners of Sociology* (Ann Arbor: University of Michigan Press, 1965), 1.

5. On the prehistory of sociological research see Bernard Lécuyer and Anthony R. Oberschall, "Sociology: Early History of Social Research," in *International Encyclopedia of the Social Sciences,* vol. 15, ed. David L. Sills (New York: Macmillan/Free Press, 1958), 36–53. Compare Terry N. Clark, *Prophets and Patrons: The French University and the Emergence of the Social Sciences* (Cambridge, MA: Harvard University Press, 1973), Part II.

6. The term *discipline* is used here in Foucault's sense. See Charles Lemert and Garth Gillan, *Michel Foucault: Social Theory and Transgression* (New York: Columbia University Press, 1982).

7. For a brief review of sociology's development including its relationship to the University (and a good bibliography on these topics) see Albert J. Reiss, Jr., "Sociology: The Field," in *International Encyclopedia of the Social Sciences,* vol. 15, ed. David L. Sills (New York: Macmillan/Free Press, 1958), 1–23. For a discussion of France see *French Sociology,* ed. Charles Lemert (New York: Columbia University Press, 1981), chap. 1; and on Italy see Diana Pinto, "Sociology, Politics, and Society in Postwar Italy, 1950–1980," *Theory and Society* 10 (September 1981): 671–705. See also essays on national sociologies in *Twentieth Century Sociology,* ed. Georges Guwitch and Wilbur Moore (New York: Philosophical Library, 1945).

8. On Chicago sociology see Robert E. L. Faris, *Chicago Sociology: 1920–1932* (Chicago, IL: University of Chicago Press, 1967). And on early American sociology see Howard W. Odum, *American Sociology: The Story of Sociology in the United States through 1950* (New York: Longmans, Green, 1951), and a special issue on early American sociology of the *American Journal of Sociology* 50 (May 1945). For a truly deep background, before the Chicago era, see L. L. Bernard and Jessie Bernard, *Origins of American Sociology* (New York: Russell and Russell, 1965).

9. The sociologist who tried to sort out these oppositions is Alvin W. Gouldner. For a discussion of the problem in his work see Charles Lemert and Paul Piccone, "Gouldner's Theoretical Method and Reflexive Sociology," *Theory and Society* 11 (November 1982): 733–748.

10. See Lewis Coser's essay on Weber in Lewis Coser, *Masters of Sociological Thought* (New York: Harcourt, Brace, Jovanovich, 1971). Coser cites the standard biographies of Weber including that of Weber's widow, Marianne Weber.

11. The most recent discussion of the challenge to the Chicago School is Patricia Madoo Lengermann, "The Founding of the *American Sociological Review:* The Anatomy of a Rebellion," *American Sociological Review* 44 (April 1979): 185–198.

12. The group included Ernst Troeltsch, Simmel, Michels, Sombart, Wilhelm Windelband, Heinrich Richert, Karl Jaspers, Ernst Bloch, and Georg Lukacs.

13. Chicago continues today, transformed, as an independent sociological tradition. Weber and Durkeim were, in a fashion, institutionalized in the work of Talcott Parsons (discussed below). There is currently both a Weberian revival (especially among education specialists) and a very active Durkeimian studies group in Paris that includes Europeans and Americans.

14. Alvin W. Gouldner, "Anti-Minotaur: The Myth of Value-Free Sociology," in *For Sociology* (New York: Basic Books, 1973). Originally published in *Social Problems* (Winter 1962).

15. Max Weber, "Science as a Vocation," in *From Max Weber,* ed. H. H. Gerth and C. Wright Mills (New York: Oxford University Press, 1958).

16. Lewis Coser, "Émile Durkeim," in *Masters of Sociological Thought,* 149.

17. The standard biography of Durkeim is Steven Lukes, *Émile Durkeim: His Life and Work* (London: Penguin, 1973). For a discussion of Durkeim's influence on public education, see Roger Geiger, "Durkeimian Sociology under Attack: The Controversy over Sociology in the Écoles Normales Primaries," in *The Sociological Domain: The Durkheimians and the Founding of French Sociology,* ed.

Philippe Besnard (Cambridge: Cambridge University Press, 1983). The same volume includes many important essays on the influence of Durkeim and the Durkeimians.

18. Émile Durkeim, *The Rules of Sociological Method* (New York: Free Press, 1982), 159–161.

19. Émile Durkeim, *Suicide* (New York: Free Press, 1951), 147.

20. The problem of confusing the language of sociology (including statistical discourse) with real social things is discussed in various connections in Lemert, *Sociology and the Twilight of Man.*

21. Durkeim's view of the individual and passions is found, most explicitly, in a controversial essay, "The Dualism of Human Nature and Its Social Conditions," in *Essays on Sociology and Philosophy*, ed. Kurt H. Wolff (New York: Harper and Row, 1964), 325–340.

22. Faris describes both Chicago and the University of Chicago in the earliest years in Faris, *Chicago Sociology: 1920–1932*, chap. 2.

23. On the European influences on early American sociology see Odum, *American Sociology*, chap. 2.

24. L. L. Bernard, "The Teaching of Sociology in the United States in the Last Fifty Years," *American Journal of Sociology* 50 (May 1945): 534–548.

25. Faris, *Chicago Sociology: 1920–1932*, 10–11.

26. Cited by Faris, *Chicago Sociology, 1920–1932*, 60.

27. The school at Iowa took a more formalizing approach under Manfred Kuhn. At Illinois, Denzin, a major successor to Blumer as codifier of the movement, works in isolation, as did Erving Goffman (though by choice) at the University of Pennsylvania.

28. Compare Lemert and Gillan, *Michel Foucault,* chaps. 2 and 3.

29. E. J. Hobsbawm, *The Age of Revolution* (New York: Mentor Books, 1961), xv.

30. For a discussion of the French case see Lemert, *French Sociology*, chap. 1, and for the French and Italian cases compared, see Diana Pinto, "Sociology as a Cultural Phenomenon in France and Italy: 1950–1972," Ph.D. thesis, Harvard University, 1977.

31. Lewis Coser, "Presidential Address: Two Methods in Search of a Substance," *American Sociological Review* 40 (December 1975): 691–700.

32. For a discussion of the impact of 1968 in France and among its scholars see Raymond Boudon, "The French University since 1968," in Lemert, *French Sociology*, chap. 10.

33. The standard history of (and critique of) American sociology's affluent era is Alvin W. Gouldner, *The Coming Crisis of Western Sociology* (New York: Basic Books, 1970).

34. For hints of the magnitude of their influence see Talcott Parsons's own list of his students in Parsons, "On Building Social System Theory: A Personal History," *Daedalus* 99 (Fall 1970): 833; and see the contributors to the Merton festschrift, ed. Lewis Coser, *The Idea of Social Structure* (New York: Harcourt, Brace, Jovanovich, 1976).

35. Data supplied by the executive offices of the American Sociological Association.

36. Habermas has rekindled interest in this question, which originally was posed in sociology by Weber, among others. Jürgen Habermas, *Legitimation Crisis* (Boston: Beacon, 1975).

37. The structure problem is far too complex to discuss here. The impossibility of treating it scientifically is discussed in Charles Lemert, "Language, Structure, and Measurement: Structuralist Semiotics and Sociology," *American Journal of Sociology* 84 (January 1979): 929–957. It is worth noting that structure was the major theoretical preoccupation of both Parsons and Merton, and today it remains central to the work of the dominant theoretical sociologist, Anthony Giddens. See Giddens, *The Constitution of Society* (Berkeley: University of California Press, 1986).

6
The Uses of French Structuralism
REMEMBERING VIETNAM

If the world changed in recent times, when did it begin to change? A good case could be made for the American war in Vietnam as, if not the absolute beginning, the unmistakable sign that something new was up. When a great and global power fools itself so well over so long a time, then it is near impossible for anyone on the outside to call it out. The truth dawns, when it does, only when the power gets itself into trouble its self-deceptions cannot manage. Vietnam haunts because, as among the last of the decolonizing movements that began in India in 1947, it represents in ways that cannot be denied the extent to which the structure of global things has changed. One of the reasons so many loathe the theoretical traditions that devolved from French structuralisms is that they represent the decentered reality of global structures. They are in effect the Vietnam of modern culture.

At first, as structuralism pure and simple, the movement appeared as a formalism that seemed to reduce the human sciences to pitiful abstractions[1]—Lévi-Strauss's universal binary oppositions, Althusser's scientific Marx, Barthes's zero-degree writing and formalistic semiology.[2] At a second moment, between roughly 1966 and 1970, poststructuralism burst on the scene, incorporating strange Nietzschean and psychoanalytic concepts. The target was different, yet it retained clear affinities with the structuralism it attacked. Then, a decade or so later in the 1970s, postmodernism gathered force from numerous sources, presenting still another target both different from and continuous with the earlier structuralisms. It is difficult to take accurate interpretive aim at such a thing that is simultaneously different and the same.

To make matters even worse, the thing itself is, seemingly, intentionally obscure. It challenges what many believe to be true. Michel Foucault understood quite well the problems his interpreters faced: "I understand the unease of all such people. They have probably found it difficult enough to recognize that their history, their economics, their social practices, the language *(langue)* they speak, the mythology of their ancestors, even the stories that they were told in their childhood, are governed by rules that are not all given to their consciousness."[3] This is an important reason why no school of poststructuralist thought has fully developed in sociology. It is too much an affront to our habits of thought.

Structuralism was a departure from the strong theories of the subject of which, in France, postwar existentialism and phenomenology were the dominant cases. In the introduction to *The Raw and the Cooked* Lévi-Strauss says: "By pursuing conditions where systems of truth become mutually convertible and can therefore be simultaneously admissible for several subjects, the ensemble of these conditions acquires the character of an object endowed by a reality proper to itself and independent of any subject."[4] At first reading, structuralism's attack on subjectivist thought seemed conveniently within the limits of modernism. Early structuralism had all the appearances of an objectivist swing against subjectivist extremes. There was, however, much more to the story.

Poststructuralism was born along with, and as part of, structuralism. Derrida, speaking in 1966 at Johns Hopkins to the first major international conference on structuralism, began with words that recognized the duality and duplicity of structuralism:

> Perhaps something has occurred in the history of the concept of structure that could be called an "event," if this word did not entail a meaning which it is precisely the function of structural—or structuralist—thought to reduce or to suspect. Let us speak of an "event" nevertheless and use quotation marks to serve as a precaution. What would this event be then? Its exterior form would be that of a rupture and a redoubling.[5]

The words are opaque. They announce an event that ends events. They claim that the idea of structure had come to a point that would end both structure and event, yet they would remain in quotation marks, redoubled beyond this rupture.

For those not committed to its language and program, poststructuralism seemed (and seems) a stupid play with words. But from within it uses its language seriously, to liberate the play of words and ideas. Derrida announced a shift in Western thought. For this purpose he required the prior existence of structuralism, just as structuralism entailed, in Derrida's view, poststructuralism. The "post" in poststructuralism was a tactical joke, a playfully serious trick. Structure, Derrida went on to say, had served to limit and confine modern thought. "Event"—the concept structuralism sought to eliminate—was the false alternative, the artificial hope for emancipation from this confinement. Event was, after all, the code word of existentialism—and a cognate to other subjectivist ideals—the ideally free subject, consciousness, rational choice, subjectively intended meaning, the essential nature of "Man," and so on.

Structuralism, insofar as it led to poststructuralism, was its own gravedigger. These two awkwardly bound perspectives attacked the formative conviction of modernist thought, that the world could be viewed through the lenses of the subject-object dichotomy. Structuralism, with all its first appearances of objectivism, was the beginning of the end for objectivism and subjectivism. At least this was the claim of Derrida and others who were central to the poststructuralist movement in the late sixties and through the seventies—Foucault, Lacan, Kristeva, Barthes, among others.

But this claim required a still subsequent movement, postmodernism. If October 21, 1966, the date of Derrida's talk to the Johns Hopkins conference, was the beginning of poststructuralism, then with equal daring one might accept Charles Jencks's statement that postmodernism began with the death of modernist architecture at 3:32 p.m., July 15, 1972—the moment at which the Pruitt-Igoe housing project in St. Louis was destroyed.[6] Both dates are of course symbolic, expressing only the unique feature of the departure. Thus, if Derrida's talk identified poststructuralism as the end of the structuring of thought in the human sciences, postmodernism extended that principle to the end of structure in modern culture, beginning with the point at which culture and the built environment intersect, architecture. "The post-modern world heralds the collapse and the unfeasibility of the grand, centralized systems with which one once attempted to explain everything."[7] Pruitt-Igoe, therefore, is a convenient symbol. This massive housing project in St. Louis represented modernist architecture's arrogant belief that by building the biggest and best public housing planners and architects could eradicate poverty and human misery. To have recognized, and destroyed, the symbol of that idea was to admit the failure of modernist architecture, and by implication modernity itself. If this is too oblique a symbol, social theorists may take 1979 as the better inaugural date for postmodernism, the year of publication of two frequently cited texts, Jean-François Lyotard's *The Postmodern Condition* and Richard Rorty's *Philosophy and the Mirror of Nature.*

Lyotard began with a statement consistent with Derrida's in 1966. "Our working hypothesis is that the status of knowledge is altered as societies enter what is known as the postindustrial age and cultures enter what is known as the postmodern age."[8] Rorty states that the "therapeutic" aim of his book is "to undermine the reader's confidence ... in 'knowledge' as something about which there ought to be a 'theory' and which has foundations."[9] His view is comparable to Lyotard's that the conditions of knowledge have fundamentally changed because in the postmodern era knowledge, most especially "scientific knowledge, is a form of discourse."[10] These assertions built upon ideas that had developed in the preceding two decades. They were, therefore, consistent with Derrida's definition of the poststructuralist event within structuralism: "This was the moment," according to Derrida, "when language invaded the universal problematic, the moment when, in the absence of a center or origin, everything became discourse."[11]

One way or another, everything in the three structuralisms comes back to language, or more accurately, to a specific commitment to the idea that language is necessarily the central consideration in all attempts to know, act, and live. Though there are substantial disagreements within the structuralist line, all three movements—structuralism, poststructuralism, and postmodernism—intend to replace modernist principles of positive knowledge in the sciences, the social sciences, and philosophy with a new approach based on language. This conviction distinguishes this line of thought from others, like Habermas's, that similarly accept the importance of language.[12]

As the movement took each redoubled step, its language became more and more obscure. In the original structuralist phase the writings were difficult but not obscure. Lévi-Strauss's "Structural Study of Myth" and Barthes's "Elements of Semiology," like much of Althusser in this period, were hard to read, but readable. But when poststructuralism emerged full blown in the late 1960s, the writings became more and more resistant to normal reading. One leaves many of these texts with a barely liminal comprehension. One gets something, but what one cannot be sure. Critics frequently complain about this aspect of French social-theoretical writings. It is important, however, to understand that it is intended. The effect is sought as a matter of principle.

I propose, as an example, the first phrase of Derrida's 1966 statement: "*Perhaps something has occurred in the history of the concept of structure.*" The reader senses (though perhaps not consciously) that the first, surprisingly conditional word, "perhaps," serves a tactical purpose. It both brings Derrida's readers in and keeps them at bay. On the one hand, Derrida addressed his remarks to a largely American audience in Baltimore. The "perhaps" seeks out their relative unfamiliarity with his subject and the French style. It says: I won't quite insist on the following. Yet, on the other hand, what follows is very much an insistence: an event has occurred in the history of the concept structure. Derrida is proclaiming prophetically, insisting. The juxtaposition of the "perhaps" opens a space between his utterance and his readers. He wants the event to proclaim itself. This, we learn a few paragraphs later on, is the space in which language can play out its effects and announce itself. This is why some feel they don't quite understand or can't quite "get" the line of argument.

Derrida's argument is that this event was "*the moment when language invaded the universal problematic, … the moment when … [a] … everything became discourse … [b] … a system in which the central signified … [c] … is never absolutely present outside a system of differences.*"[13] The three ellipses (marked [a], [b], [c]) mark places where Derrida imposes significant qualifications. When the material is excluded, as above, the argument is relatively neat. But in each of these places Derrida's actual text presents material that strains the reading by introducing qualifications which make a philosophical statement, namely:

[a] "*in the absence of a center or origin,*"
[b] "*provided we can agree on this word [discourse]—that is to say,*"
[c] "*the original signifier.*"

Each qualifying phrase contradicts a reader's attempt to understand the event Derrida announces as a positive, factual moment in history. The first, [a], and the third, [c], introduce philosophical claims that cannot be proven, and each is so sweeping as to be beyond argument. The absent center, for example, refers to the assumption that prior to poststructuralism all traditional thought, including modernism, relied on a restrictive, transcendent principle. This, of course, is less a point of fact than of interpretation. Even as a point of interpretation it would have been hard to argue convincingly in 1966 that this was the essential nature of modernist thought. It is hard enough to argue the point today. The second qualification, [b], "*provided we can agree*" on the meaning of the term "*discourse,*" is both an acknowledgment of the strangeness of his idea to his readers and an expression of his now famous principle of deconstruction that we must use familiar language to express the totally unfamiliar.

The overall effect of the passage is to subject the reader to an insistence triply qualified, presented in the guise of an argument. It is not an argument that one can "follow" along a direct line of clear and distinct logical understanding. It is not a statement open to logical or empirical verification, but an invitation to enter a different, postmodern (that is, in 1966, poststructural) language within which one finds that everything is language. The argument which is not an argument is found only in a series of juxtaposed, different elements—conditional "perhaps" proclamation, structuralism/end of structuralism, poststructuralism/continuity of structuralism, argument/insistence. One wants to ask, what does Derrida mean? To which he would reply, if he were to reply at all: I am playing, seriously. "Play is the disruption of presence," he says near the end of the text.[14] All attempts to be clear are based on the philosophical presumption that meaning and reality can be present to consciousness. To "make clear" is to reflect or, in Rorty's term, to mirror nature. These are attempts to get around language which exists, so to speak, on its own terms.

Poststructuralism and postmodernism, though in different degrees and ways, each seek to destroy the ideal of pure, meaningful communication between subjects as a corollary to the disruption of the metaphysical distinction between subjects and objects. This is the way in which language invades the universal problematic. Language is assumed to be that one social thing that, when it is made the center of things, disrupts everything, including the possibility of a center of things. Language looks to the future. Thus Derrida ends this essay with a hesitant, fearful anticipation of a liberating birth, cloaked in a language one understands, barely:

> I employ these words, I admit, with a glance toward operations of childbirth—but also a glance toward those who, in a society from which I do not exclude myself, turn their eyes away when faced by the as yet unnameable which is proclaiming itself and which can do so whenever a birth is in the offing, only under species of a non-species, in the formless, mute, infant, and terrifying form of monstrosity.[15]

Any attempt to develop a poststructuralist, or postmodernist, sociology entails a willingness to face this monstrosity of language. According to such a perspective, when language is taken seriously for what it is, the social world is seen in a particular way. It is no longer possible to view the world as internally and necessarily coherent. To take language seriously, as the structuralisms do in their manner of writing as in their philosophy, is to decenter the world, to eviscerate it of grand organizing principles (God, natural law, truth, beauty, subjectivity, Man, etc.) that mask the most fundamental truth of human life, differences. Those who have followed developments in postmodernist feminist theory and literary theory realize that this conviction is filled with political intent.

> Aware that women writers inevitably engage a literary history and system of conventions shaped primarily by men, feminist critics now often strive to elucidate the acts of revision, appropriation and subversion that constitute a female text.[16]
>
> Scores of people are killed every day in the name of differences ascribed only to race. This slaughter demands the gesture in which the contributors to this volume are collectively engaged: to deconstruct, if you will, the ideas of difference inscribed in the trope of race, to explicate discourse itself in order to reveal the hidden relations of power and knowledge inherent in popular and academic usages of "race."[17]

Modernism is taken as the centered, hierarchical, Europeanized, dominant world against which the principle of difference is thrust to assert the realities of those whose daily lives are marked by the experience of difference—women, nonwhites, working class, the third world.

The question for sociology is what is it about language that permits such a long excursion from Lévi-Strauss's rediscovery of linguistics in the fifties to today's politics of difference? And what are the prospects in this for sociology?

Against philosophies of the Center (modernism in particular), poststructuralism introduced an intellectual politics based on the now famous concept of decentering. It is not always understood that decentering is less a philosophy, or a rival concept to those of modernism, than a practice. This is, in part, the point of poststructuralism's unsettling approach to writing.

From one point of view, decentering is a reasonably precise philosophical concept conveying Derrida's and Foucault's original attacks on centered philosophies, most especially phenomenology's extreme subjectivist philosophy of consciousness. This is the sense most accurately associated with the postmodernist rejection of Enlightenment theories of knowledge. From another point of view, decentering suggests a broad political opposition to all traditional and modern social forms, philosophy included, in which structures serve to inhibit social freedom. It is advisable, therefore, to think of poststructuralism and postmodernism as first and foremost forms of knowledge derived from a political practice. This attitude conveys not only poststructuralism's attempt to overcome philosophy for political purposes but also its claim that discourse and writing must be taken as the subject-matter and the means of intellectual work.

Such an interpretation of decentering makes a heavy demand on sociologists accustomed to viewing politics as something totally other than science, or, at most, that to which sociologists contribute expertise. Poststructuralism claims that intellectual work is political, and it does so with reference to concepts most sociologists would consider anything but political—text and discourse.

Roland Barthes defines the Text as "that *social* space that leaves no language safe or untouched, that allows no enunciative subject to hold the position of judge, teacher, analyst, confessor, or decoder. The theory of the Text can only coincide with the activity of writing."[18] This statement is linked to the claim that decentering is an ongoing intellectual practice deriving from the theoretical decision to interpret the Text in relation to other texts, rather than in relation to its author. For Barthes this involves the distinction between the work and the Text:

> The work is concrete, occupying a portion of book-space (in a library, for example); the Text, on the other hand, is a methodological field.... This opposition recalls the distinction proposed by Lacan between "reality" and the "real"; the one is displayed, the other demonstrated. In the same way, the work can be seen in bookstores, in card catalogues, and on course lists, while the Text reveals itself, articulates itself according to and against certain rules. While the work is held in the hand, the text is held in language.[19]

The work, therefore, is seen as the unit of modernist writing in which writing is a transitive activity—the production of literary objects by subjects, authors. Thus, the privileging of the Text over the work is another instance of the philosophical side of decentering, here the rejection of the purportedly modernist belief that the social world is inhabited by self-conscious subjects who project meaning into their works. It is a rejection of subjectivism as a cryptometaphysics.

This move replaces the original modernist couplet—*subject* (author)/*object* (work)—with something else which itself has the appearance of a couplet—*practices* (writing)/(intertextual) field. But the relationship of text to its intertextual field is active, creative, and practical. Practices/field has the form but not the substance of a conceptual dichotomy. It looks the same but is different—postdichotomous. Texts are products of intransitive writing, they are outside the subject-object dichotomy. "The Text cannot be thought of as a defined object."[20] It is, as noted, a methodological field, while the work is a concrete object. Texts are, therefore, play in a forever open and open-ended field which they produce and by which they are produced, and in which they must be interpreted.

The important thing to keep in mind is that poststructuralists view this reorientation as a general social-theoretical move. Though they remain close to the language of text and discourse, poststructuralists situate their views with respect to a theory of society. The critique of the subject-author is an instance of opposition to all forms of social domination. Much of Foucault's writing on various topics, from *The Order of Things* to *The History of Sexuality,* is in opposition to dominations represented by the engendered, Europeanized humanism which, in another context, is characterized by the term patriarchy.[21] The link between a general social theory and the problem of the author is apparent in Foucault's "What Is an Author?":

> We are accustomed ... to saying that the author is a general creator of a work in which he deposits with infinite wealth and generosity, an inexhaustible world of significations. We are used to thinking that the author is so different from other men, and so transcendent with regard to all languages, that as soon as he speaks

meanings begin to proliferate.... The truth is quite contrary ... the author does not precede the works, he is a certain fundamental principle by which, in our culture, one limits, excludes, and chooses.... The author is the ideological figure by which one marks the manner in which we fear the proliferation of meanings.[22]

In this respect, poststructuralism is a social theory articulated within concrete studies of literary, historical, and philosophical questions.

Poststructuralism is very much a product of the political and social events leading to and ensuing from May 1968 in Paris. Foucault's sexual politics, Lacan's engendering of psychoanalysis, Kristeva and Irigaray's feminist theories, Derrida's politics of difference, Deleuze and Guattari's schizoanalytic politics all are rooted, one way or another, in the late-sixties revolutionary politics that challenged the world-centered ambitions of postwar Gaullism. If, at that same moment, left intellectuals in the United States sought a coherent New Left alternative to both Old Left Marxism and Johnson-Humphrey liberalism, French intellectuals searched for an alternative that rejected traditional communist and socialist party politics and was post-Marxist without being anti-Marxist. In the one joint programmatic statement of the poststructuralist movement, when Foucault, Barthes, Derrida, Sollers, and Kristeva allowed and caused their separate projects to be joined in an edition of *Tel Quel* titled "Théorie d'ensemble" (published not incidentally in the early autumn of 1968), these politics were quite explicit. The introduction stated that their joint project was, in part, "to articulate a politics logically bound to a dynamically non-representative writing, that is to say: analysis of the confusion created by this position, explication of their social and economic character, construction of the relations of this writing with historical materialism and dialectical materialism."[23] It would be a stretch to consider this a social theory in the usual sense, but that theory is there.

In more sociological terms, the implication of this attitude toward writing as an intellectual practice is that action is oriented to an open field of play that lacks inherent, limiting rules. Rules become resources in Giddens's sense; limits are social arbitraries serving only to define the possibilities of transgression in Foucault's sense; the field defines the conditions and terms of practices in Bourdieu's sense. The structured field is viewed as open, that is, characterized by differences, absence, play. Hence the various descriptive terms one associates with this line of thought: discursive formation (Foucault), intertextuality (Barthes), *la langue* (Saussure), *champ* (Bourdieu). To these sometimes implicit visions of a field of play are juxtaposed the correlative notions that describe intransitive actions: practices, writing, speaking, habitus.[24]

On first examination, this would appear to be an interesting theoretical model in the form: *Think of social action as intransitive practices in a dynamically open field of play.* But it would not be a sufficient interpretation of poststructuralist thinking. Models, in its view, are modernist attempts to mirror the social world. Models depend on the assumption that the social (or natural) world can be represented, that is, "presented again" in the language of knowledge. Poststructuralism, implicitly, and postmodernism, explicitly, reject the Enlightenment ideas that knowledge is an autonomous and constituting feature of social life. There are no poststructuralist models. "Let us wage a war on totality; let us be witnesses to the unpresentable; let us activate the differences and save the honor of the name."[25] Postmodernist knowledge, such as it is, is the consequence, not a representation, of action in a field of play.

Therefore, what is at stake in a possible postmodern sociology is a willingness to move sociology away from its historic role as a discipline, a social science, a type of knowledge, and toward a more politically self-conscious practice that is neither traditionally Marxist nor liberal. Postmodern knowledge entails a postmodern politics. Like the strange space Derrida sought to open and use in the first words of "Structure, Sign, and Play," a poststructuralist sociology would have to be willing to tolerate the idea of working in a confusing, different social space that is neither epistemological nor political, but both yet neither—a very different idea of knowledge.

A poststructuralist or postmodernist approach to the concept of "reality" would be pragmatic. What do we intend by it? And can we get around it in order to enhance our ability to know and discuss? Can, therefore, the theory of Texts, including discursive texts, get us around the problems sociology, and other sciences, usually solve with reference to ideas like "empirical reality"?

The prospect of such an alternative depends on the plausibility of four assumptions already presented, explicitly or implicitly:

1. that theory is an inherently discursive activity;
2. that the empirical reality in relation to which theoretical texts are discursive is without exception textual;
3. that empirical texts depend on this relationship to theoretical texts for their intellectual or scientific value; and
4. that in certain, if not all, cases a discursive interpretation yields more, not less, adequate understanding.

Assumption 1 was stipulated in the above discussion. Assumptions 2 and 3 require further discussion. Assumption 4 is best considered with reference to a case study.

Theoretical statements mediate the "reality" contained in empirical texts— answers to questionnaires, performed rituals and observed behaviors (usually inscribed on film or tape or in notebooks), letters, corporate reports, transcripts, interviews, archives, census tracts. It is far from clear that there are any data "purer" (that is, "more real") than these. And none of these is anything but textual in the two senses poststructuralism employs. First, they are literally inscribed on one medium or another and are never used for analysis without being thus written. Secondly, they are useful for knowledge only to the extent that they exist in an intertextual field— with other empirical texts of the same sort, with other empirical texts of a different kind, and, most of all, with the theoretical texts out of which sense is made of them. It hardly need be said that raw data, in whatever form, are useless until they are situated with respect to theoretical statements. Theoretical statements, regardless of the "school" or methodological style in which they are expressed (scientific, humanistic, qualitative, ethnographic, etc.), are never made without a relationship to empirical data or an empirical reference, however abstract. Parsons's most abstract theory of the AGIL paradigm requires a great number of assumptions about the reality of the social world, such as a willingness to believe that societies are patterned, that culture is an effective control over society, that societies need integrative mechanisms like laws. None of these beliefs, however arguable, is held without reference to a wealth of empirical references. These references when held by a reader are necessary to the sense of Parsons's theory. They arise from the many empirical texts—ranging from survey results to everyday life conversations and everything in between—that inform a reader's ability to read. Similarly, such texts are also written, whether consciously or not, as an intervention in the field of existing texts sociologists variously consider germane to their work. It is not at all clear why one needs the idea of an empirical foundation existing beyond such an intertextual field.

Of the four assumptions, 4 is the sternest test of the prospects of a postmodern sociology. In the end, it is hardly worth the while to try something with so many inherent difficulties if there are no anticipated advantages over what we have now. So, then, what are the advantages? A question I propose to answer with reference to a case of undeniable, but still uncertain, reality.

Important as it is to American, and global, history the reality of the war in Vietnam is far from certain. For the majority of those who attempt to interpret it, their most vivid impressions come not from direct experience but from a strange conglomeration of texts—the memorial on the Mall in Washington, films, firsthand accounts of speakers, friends, or relatives, novels, Neil Sheehan's *New Yorker* articles and prize-winning book, college and high school courses, rhetorical allusions by politicians, archives, microfilm and microfiche, and so on. Is it an accident that the most searing film account, if not the roulette scene in *The Deer Hunter,* is *Apocalypse Now,* a montage of craziness and dream-like irreality in which the viewer is made to feel that nothing real was there? Was Vietnam after all nothing more than a repetition of a classic Conradian narrative—a crazed voyage through an exotic jungle in search of an unattainable insane kingdom in the heart of darkness? One wants to argue that this is a fiction and that the reality is still there. Reviews of each serious Vietnam film center on the question: Did this one, *Platoon* perhaps, finally capture the reality of the war?

It is possible that the search for the reality of social things is the true Conradian search. Where would one look for the reality of Vietnam? Are recollections of veterans or POWs more real than *Apocalypse Now*? Are the *Pentagon Papers*? Are Neil Sheehan's articles? Are Stanley Karnow's history and PBS documentary? Is that finer reality still buried in an archive somewhere? And cannot these questions be asked of most complex social-historical events?

In pursuit of a postmodern sociology, what can then be said about the empirical reality of a series of events like the war in Vietnam? I propose that we ignore, for the moment, our sociological thirst for reality, and consider it simply and straightforwardly as though it were, for all intents and purposes, a monstrous but plausibly discursive text. In this respect we should have to entertain the proposition that the war itself was discursive, a global inscription in which the United States sought to mediate its own sense of the irreality of world history.[26]

In the years following World War II, the United States quickly encountered an intolerable set of contradictions. On the one hand, the United States emerged from the world war as the greatest military and industrial power in history. On the other hand, as early as 1947, the year of George Kennan's famous long telegram enunciating the policy of containment, the Soviet Union was taken seriously, as well it should have been, as a rival power. The United States suffered the contradiction of being the supreme world power, but one of two supreme powers, hence not supreme. The McCarthy blight, in the early fifties, was a flawed attempt to mediate this contradiction by turning inward with the unreal insistence that anyone and everyone could be communist, and cause of America's loss of world potency. In 1954 Joseph McCarthy was censured by the United States Senate. In the same year Dienbienphu fell. In 1955 Eisenhower approved direct military aid to the Saigon government, thus beginning the US presence in Southeast Asia.

Was that presence, and the war that ensued, an attempt to resolve, discursively, the contradiction that McCarthyism failed to resolve? The answer lies in an analysis of the specific texts which articulate the theory that governed American war policy.

The decisive event that led directly to war was President Lyndon Johnson's decision in the first few days of February 1965 to escalate the bombing in North Vietnam. The previous summer, Johnson and his advisers invented an incident in the Gulf of Tonkin as cause to push through Congress the resolution that gave him virtually unchecked authority to engage in war. His defeat of Barry Goldwater in the November 1964 election added substantially to the mandate he claimed both for foreign policy leadership and the pursuit of his plans of a Great Society at home. In 1965 Johnson submitted 63 pieces of social legislation, a domestic program that exceeded even Roosevelt's for its ambition and commitment to America's disadvantaged. Few, if any, American presidents possessed so extensive a social vision. Yet that vision is easily forgotten because it was dreamt along with a view of America's world position that led to Vietnam.

On February 5, 1965, the Vietcong attacked an American installation at Pleiku, killing nine, and wounding a hundred American advisers. Johnson responded immediately by authorizing "Operation Flaming Dart," air raids against the North carefully selected because Soviet Prime Minister Aleksi Kosygin was then visiting Hanoi. The question before Johnson was, will the air strikes be expanded and the American engagement enlarged?

At the same time, on February 6 and 7, Johnson's adviser McGeorge Bundy, en route home from Vietnam, completed the draft of a memorandum that confirmed an earlier (January 27) report that the situation in Vietnam was deteriorating. Bundy's February 7 memorandum coined the ironic and highly discursive phrase, "sustained reprisal." This evidently duplicitous phrase came to justify and be the name for Johnson's evolving war policy. The memorandum argued that a policy of reprisals against the North would eventually "improve the situation in the South" by demonstrating to Hanoi the military resolve of the United States. The policy decision came quickly. On February 24, 1965, Johnson ordered Operation Rolling Thunder, sustained air raids on the North which by year's end totaled 55,000 sorties.

Like George Kennan's famous long telegram twenty years earlier that invented the equally discursive concept of containment, Bundy's sustained reprisal memorandum defined Johnson's fatal policy. By December 1965, 200,000 troops had replaced the 20,000 or so advisers in Vietnam at the beginning of the year. And by 1968 Johnson's presidency and his Great Society program would be in ruins, and the direction of American foreign and domestic policies would be, it now seems, irreversibly altered.

Bundy's February 7 memorandum did not cause the war. Texts don't cause anything in the usual sense. They are practices in an intertextual field. Their significance relies on their relationship to that field. It is easy to see both the discursive nature of the Bundy text and its crucial place in an intertextual field that included Johnson's own statements, the preceding generation's dilemma over America's contradictory world position, and subsequent interpretations of the war itself.

As Godfrey Hodgson points out,[27] Bundy's phrase, sustained reprisal, is a subtly double-sided notion that suits a former dean of Harvard College. Operation Rolling Thunder and all that went with it was surely "sustained" but in the dramatic escalation that followed the very meaning of "reprisal" was subverted. The supposed reprisal for Pleiku (and more remotely the nonexistent Tonkin incident) became initiative. The restraint suggested by the term reprisal was confounded by the reality of devastation that came to pass. Though the Pentagon wanted even more, the reality of over 500,000 troops and countless air sorties in the North and South altered, as we now know, the map of Southeast Asia, just as it altered the terrain of American political and moral conscience. In some very specific sense, "sustained reprisal" literally rewrote the reality of American life as it rewrote the geopolitical fate of Indochina.

Again, one must resist the temptation to say that Bundy's memo caused all this. It was not a cause, but a crucial discursive text that provided the theory which encouraged American desires to have it all—to be supreme abroad, while being a Great Society at home. The text's meaning is lodged in this more complex field, and its discursive value was that it both revealed and masked (to-ed and fro-ed so to speak) the reality of the policy's appeal to the best and brightest who advised Johnson and to Johnson himself. Johnson's famous complex about his Harvardian advisers did not prevent him from sharing their theory. He could not himself utter the language of a Harvard dean, but he could understand it. His own public statement announcing Flaming Dart used quite a different, and richer, metaphor: "We have kept our guns over the mantel and our shells in the cupboard for a long time.... I can't ask our American soldiers out there to fight with one hand tied behind their backs."[28] This Alamo metaphor from Johnson's Texas frontier background conveyed the same meaning as did "sustained reprisal." It lacked only the (to him) noxious qualities of a more Harvardian abstraction. He saw himself, as Doris Kearns's biography shows, as a tough, virile man of peace, defending America against an aggressor. "Rolling Thunder," to Johnson, was an act of peace, an instance of what William Gibson rightly calls doublethink.[29] But as discourse it has the same attributes as "sustained reprisal"—a play with words that plays with reality, simultaneously constituting and deconstituting the reality of the words and the world. And both figures of speech take their place alongside the war's most famous expression of doublethink, "We had to destroy the village in order to save it."

Doublethink is the discursive form required when there is no plausible reality on the ground to support the actions in the air of a contradictory theory of the world. This is not to say that nothing happened on the ground of Vietnam, that no one died. It does say, however, that we have no interpretive access to that reality, in large part because those who lived and died in the jungles did so because of the real irreality of a series of highly theoretical texts. The war was whatever reality it was because of a theoretical field in which sustained reprisal and Johnson's Alamo figure stood side by side, without prejudice to all the contradictions they contained.

This intertextual field in which the war in Vietnam was constituted stretches along several axes—horizontally across the differences of language between Johnson and Bundy, and vertically from their gross theory of the world to the irreality experienced by men and women on the ground. Bundy's abstract theory was not of a different order from the account of combatants. Hundreds of first-hand accounts by veterans describe the bizarre incongruence between hours spent when nothing happened, a fleeting and often unseen enemy, and eerie nothingness punctuated by death—of buddies, of the enemy, of people who looked like but were not enemy, of old women and children, and eventually of fragged soldiers. Foot soldiers lost all sense of the reality of normal distinctions—between war and just walking around, between enemy and ally, between combatant and civilian. "We knew," said Specialist Fourth Class Charles Strong, "where the North Vietnamese were, but we knew that if we got into it, they would probably have wiped a big portion of the company out. We were really dropped there to find the North Vietnamese, and here we was hiding from them. Running because we was hungry. We were so far up in the hills that the place was so thick you didn't have to pull guard at night."[30] This collapse of reality on the ground is perfectly well explained by the irreality of the theoretical policy that invoked the war. Some might think this destroys the material reality of jungles, death, and Vietnam. But does it? Is it not certain that our men would never find the enemy, or recognize them when they found them, when the war itself had little to do with anything real? After all, Bundy and Johnson could have learned from Dienbienphu that this was to be a war with enemies that could not be found. They ignored this lesson because they were creating another, textual reality having more to do with the Alamo and postwar fear of communism than anything actually on the ground in Vietnam.

From Hamburger Hill to Johnson's situation room the reality of Vietnam was created, then breached, then re-created in countless texts. What after all truly went on there? Where was there? And what is the meaningful distinction among the realities written in journals of American and Vietcong combatants, Johnson's memoirs, Bundy's memorandum, the Pentagon Papers, *Apocalypse Now,* the heartwrenching V-shaped memorial on the Mall, deaths which rewrote family histories, defoliation which rewrote the ecology of Southeast Asia, a military failure that rewrote the political geography of Vietnam? How could there be a study, including a sociological study, of Vietnam based on anything but these texts? Nothing else is out there, not now, and in an eerie sense not then.

It is certainly not by chance that one of the earliest successful works of post-modern sociology is about Vietnam. William Gibson's *The Perfect War* argues that war in Vietnam was an extensive elaboration of the codes contained in late liberal technocracy of which the Johnson administration was the epiphany. He demonstrates, to take one example, that the bombing around which the war was built was nothing more than an elaborate code for communications with Hanoi. The message was: "We want peace. We are resolved. You stop and we will too." Yet the message had no receiver to whom it made sense. In fact, the air raids on Hanoi's oil storage facilities were based on a certifiable denial of reality. The manifest purpose of these bombings was, Gibson shows, to communicate American resolve by destroying the bulk of Hanoi's oil reserves supporting infiltration of the South. By July 1965, when sorties reached more than 10,000 a month, almost 70 percent of the North's oil reserves had, in fact, been destroyed. Yet the actual daily need for petroleum fuel in the North was an amount that could be carried in 15 pickup trucks. The 30 percent reserve not destroyed was more than enough. This reality was knowable by the simplest of intelligence reports. But the bombing continued, directed in part by Secretary of Defense Robert McNamara who, as a younger man, had directed a study demonstrating that allied bombing missions in World War II had similarly little effect on the course of that war. What did the bombings mean? Their sense had nothing at all to do with an external reality. They were the necessary utterance dictated by a theoretical war policy code.

Gibson ends his book with a statement in which he means every word in a strict poststructuralist, even postmodern, sense. He says, referring to the irrelevance of a distinction between his sociological text on the war and the fated experiences of men and women who lived the war's irreality: "In this *corpus* men and women live and die; the stories of their lives and their deaths have their truths beyond in*corp*oration in any theoretical arguments."[31] In a world where reality is constituted in and by means of texts, everything is theoretical in some sense, because everything is discursive and, in situations where this is the case, what other reality is there?

And what event in world history was more disastrously a theory than Vietnam and all its entailments and permutations? Vietnam haunts because only now, generations later, have the structural changes wrought by globalization forced a discursive hand. Even the dimmest of believers in the modern way cannot any longer refuse to come to terms with the changing terms of global politics. Vietnam was not the first sign of the change. But we may be forced to remember it because it was the first that refused to go away.

NOTES

1. Raymond Boudon, *The Uses of Structuralism* (Portsmouth, NH: Heinemann, 1971).
2. Claude Lévi-Strauss, *Structural Anthropology I* (New York: Anchor, 1970), especially the famous essay "The Structural Study of Myth." Louis Althusser, *For Marx* (New York: Vintage, 1970). Roland Barthes, *Writing Degree Zero and Elements of Semiology* (Boston: Beacon, 1970).
3. Michel Foucault, *The Archaeology of Knowledge* (New York: Pantheon, 1972), 210–211.

4. Lévi-Strauss, "Overture to *Le Cru et le cuit*," in *Structuralism,* ed. Jacques Ehrmann (New York: Anchor, 1970), 44–45.

5. Jacques Derrida, "Structure, Sign, and Play in the Discourse of the Human Sciences," in Derrida, *Writing and Difference* (Chicago, IL: University of Chicago Press, 1978), 278. This famous essay first appeared in English in the collection of talks given at the 1966 Johns Hopkins conference on structuralism, reprinted in *The Structuralist Controversy,* ed. Richard Macksey and Eugenio Donato (Baltimore: Johns Hopkins University Press, 1971).

6. Charles Jencks, *The Language of Post-Modern Architecture* (New York: Rizzoli, 1977), 9.

7. Paolo Portoghesi, *After Modern Architecture* (New York: Rizzoli, 1980), 106.

8. Jean-François Lyotard, *The Postmodern Condition* (Minneapolis: University of Minnesota Press, 1984).

9. Richard Rorty, *Philosophy and the Mirror of Nature* (Princeton, NJ: Princeton University Press, 1979), 7.

10. Lyotard, *Postmodern Condition,* 3.

11. Derrida, "Structure, Sign, and Play," 280.

12. See Rorty, "Habermas and Lyotard on Postmodernity," in *Habermas and Modernity,* ed. Richard Bernstein (Cambridge: MIT Press, 1985). See also Fredric Jameson's foreword to Lyotard's *Postmodern Condition.*

13. Derrida, "Structure, Sign, and Play," 280.

14. Ibid., 292.

15. Ibid., 293.

16. Elizabeth Abel, ed., *Writing and Sexual Difference* (Chicago, IL: University of Chicago Press, 1980), 2.

17. Henry Louis Gates, ed., *"Race," Writing, and Difference* (Chicago, IL: University of Chicago Press, 1985), 6.

18. Barthes, "From Work to Text," in *Textual Strategies,* ed. Josue V. Harari (Ithaca, NY: Cornell University Press, 1979), 81 (emphasis in original).

19. Ibid., 74–75.

20. Ibid., 74.

21. Foucault's attacks on the logocentric and anthropocentric basis of modernism are explicit, if not as well known as Derrida's. See Charles Lemert and Garth Gillan, *Michel Foucault: Social Theory as Transgression* (New York: Columbia University Press, 1979).

22. Foucault, "What Is an Author?" in *Textual Strategies,* ed. Josue V. Harari (Ithaca, NY: Cornell University Press, 1979), 158–159.

23. *Théorie d'ensemble,* a special issue of *Tel Quel* (Paris: Éditions de Seuil/Collection Tel Quel, 1968).

24. For *champ,* see Bourdieu, *Outline of a Theory of Practice* (Cambridge: Cambridge University Press, 1977), among other places. For "structuration," see in particular Giddens, *The Constitution of Society* (Berkeley: University of California Press, 1984). For "discursive practices," see especially Foucault, *Archaeology of Knowledge.* For "intertextuality," see Barthes, "From Work to Text," among other places.

25. Lyotard, *Postmodern Condition,* 82.

26. Sources for the following are Mike Gravel, ed., *The Pentagon Papers,* vols. 1–4 (Boston: Beacon, 1971); Doris Kearns, *Lyndon Johnson and the American Dream* (New York: Harper and Row, 1976); William Gibson, *The Perfect War* (New York: Atlantic Monthly Press, 1986); and Stanley Karnow, *Vietnam: A History* (New York: Penguin, 1983).

27. Hodgson, *American in Our Time* (New York: Vintage, 1976), 229.

28. Kearns, *Lyndon Johnson,* 261.

29. Gibson, *Perfect War.*

30. Wallace Terry, *Bloods* (New York: Ballantine, 1984), 55.

31. Gibson, *Perfect War,* 476.

7
Against Capital-S Sociology

For the longest while, at least over the course of the century just past, a substantial group of very intelligent men (and increasingly, of late, women) have taken upon themselves the most excellent vocation of advancing the cause of something they call, unqualifiedly, "Sociology." It would be hard, indeed, to dispute that their cause is a good one. With or without the strong capital S, sociology (or, if you prefer, Sociology) is an honorable and vitally important human activity. In this respect, proponents of Sociology are entirely beyond reproach.

Still, as associates of this good cause know very well, questions have been raised, if not about them as individuals, about their practices. At the defiant extreme of opposition, one question asked is, roughly: Where do these jokers get off taking their very local men's-club understanding of sociology as though it were a Sociology in the sense of a "singular, properly disciplined, and open-membership professional guild"? The question is defiant because it is posed out of chronic irritation arising from years of exclusion, real and imagined. Fortunately, there is a more temperate version of the question, which is, roughly: If there is a Sociology, as obviously there is in some real sense, then should it, or can it, represent the very great number of actually existing sociologies? As a sign of how things have changed in recent years, the classic source of the more temperate version of the question was Alvin Gouldner, who, in his day, was anything but temperate. Gouldner was first among equals in a movement that took on steam in the late 1960s—a concerted effort to rethink Sociology as sociologies (or, in the quaint phrase of that day, as a multiple-paradigm science).

Curiouser still, in contrast to *Against Essentialism,* the book of present attentions, Gouldner expressed his renegade view in—among other places—a book he called *For Sociology* (1973). This was a bit of a joke on Louis Althusser's at-the-time well-read book, *For Marx* (1965). What I can say is that I did have them in mind, but sadly so, when I chose the title "Against Sociology" for this little essay. The sadness descends from the fact of life today that one can only be for something by first being against what would be called, in a now quaint word of this day, its "other."

In *Against Essentialism,* Stephan Fuchs offers a clever, intelligent, and robust defense of the deep structural properties of capital-S Sociology. Those who share Professor Fuchs's vision of capital-S Sociology will adore this book. They have sought and needed such a one for a long time now. Finally, it is here. If it serves them well, then it will serve all sociologies no less well. The only fear is that, like so many other ambitious and important books, it could be well praised and oft cited, but little read. The writing is quite good, occasionally hilarious, sometimes irritatingly apodictic, but always direct and learned. It is not, I have found, the kind of book one takes to the beach or keeps by the bed. It demands wide-awake, upright reading. Those willing to pay the price will reap its rewards.

Against Essentialism deserves mention in a distinguished company of books that, over the years, have tried to care for Sociology, the science, as Fuchs does. Sociology is constantly redefining itself, but never more urgently than during and since the turmoil of the 1960s. Hence, the special place of Gouldner's later writings, beginning with *Coming Crisis of Western Sociology* (1970) and *For Sociology* (1973) and including the great works of the end of his life (Antonio 2002). Gouldner aimed to rethink Sociology's *within* from a critical Marxist *without.* Somewhat later, Randy Collins did much the same, though without more than a shadow of Marxism behind his already mature commitments to the explanatory *within* of Sociology. His *Conflict Sociology* (1975) is an important but, today, largely neglected work. Collins, it hardly need be said, is of a younger generation than Gouldner's (though for a while Collins was a close associate of his in the founding of the magazine *Theory and Society*). Still, in the phrase Althusser himself helped to popularize, they were caught in the same "conjuncture"—the events that Immanuel Wallerstein aptly calls "the revolution of 1968." Wallerstein, closer in age and training to Gouldner's generation, deserves a mention in this all-too-brief history because his own challenge to capital-S Sociology appeared the year before Collins's *Conflict Sociology* and, unlike the works of this era by Gouldner and Collins, initiated an enduring change in Sociology by refusing to play its game. From (and since) the first volume of *The Modern World System* (1974), Wallerstein's work has had the effect of starting a new field of analysis that cuts across the official disciplines.

These three, among others, illustrate the three obvious ways by which any field like Sociology can be rethought—from without (as Gouldner did), from within (Collins), and by starting over (Wallerstein). None is analytically distinct from the others. All three ways overlap. All exhibit a loyalty to sociology, at least, and usually also to Sociology. The 1970s were, it seems, the era of stock-taking, during which these alternatives established themselves as deeper, more serious attempts to save sociology in ways that were not superficially (and passingly) experimental.

If *Against Essentialism* was written self-consciously with reference to works of this kind, it was not so much any of these (though Collins's and Jon Turner's witnesses on the value of explanatory sociology are clearly important) as it was postwar German social thought. Not, decidedly, Habermas, but Niklas Luhmann, who may well have been, if not one of Fuchs's teachers, a mentor. Luhmann's rethinking of systems theory in Sociology (including his hostility to Habermas's quasitranscendental critical theory) is the principal ghost that haunts *Against Essentialism*. One cannot turn a page of the book without sensing the hammer's head ready to strike the hardening steel of very tough ideas: *Care for Sociology; forget the imitators. Think networks; forget actors. Think variation; get rid of essences; und so weiter.* Every *for* comes with its *against,* never more strikingly than in my favorite chapter, "How to Sociologize with a Hammer," where Fuchs ranges far and wide beyond the resources of Sociology, rejecting what he considers junk, forging what he considers useful into Sociology's *within.* For myself, I agree at many points with Fuchs's critique of essentialism, even though I think the *outsider-within* position offers the better leverage. There is much to admire in Fuchs's *insider-without* approach, even when it goes too far or hammers too harshly. In any case, Fuchs offers his own amalgam of the three ways of the 1970s and deserves consideration in the company of those who led the way, which is a company, not of the like-minded, but of the similarly intended.

Readers will wonder about the book's title. To be *against essentialism* is to risk association with a good many of the extra-Sociological sociologies of culture, race, gender, sex and sexuality, postcolonial and identity politics, and much else. Given that the various closet sociologies are the principal source of the critique of essentialism about which one hears so much today, one must ask: What is Fuchs up to? What's the trick? These lowercase-s sociologies are, at least in part, that against which Fuchs directs his *Against Essentialism*. But, like him, they (whatever one thinks of them) are against essentialism. They are also, however, the very pretender sociologies that capital-S Sociology resents and dismisses by some generalizing phrase like *merely postmodern.* Fuchs makes it more than plain that he, too, is against the merely postmodern. Still, the genius of his book is that he discharges these other sociologies while also criticizing essentialism as it occurs in capital-S Sociology. I am not the least persuaded by his complaints against the merely postmodern (mostly because they are usually dismissed out of hand). But you have to respect the man's bravado.

Essentialism, the metaphysical concept, goes back at least to Aristotle. To hold, as this philosophical position does, that things have essences is to hold many things at once. In metaphysics, essentialism is the view that behind the being of objects there are essential categories. Today, analytic philosophy often calls these "natural kinds" (Fuchs 2001:122). Any naturally occurring woman, as she walks the street, is real only insofar as she is an instance of Woman, the natural kind. In premodern metaphysics (before Locke and Hume, then Kant; that is, not Heidegger), essentialism was a powerful philosophical position because, in cultures themselves inclined toward enduring and universal ideas, it was a ready principle from which everything necessary to metaphysics could be derived. Ontologically, if Being comprises essences, then the reality of particular things is a predicate of nothing less than the essential categories. If this, then epistemology, ethics, and aesthetics are all investigations into the essential nature of Being itself. Hence, traditionally, realism was a philosophy of essences for the most part. What opposition there was came in the form of various nominalisms (that the reality of particulars resides solely in their names). Still, in metaphysics, even certain nominalisms, anticipating Leibniz, took the position that the names applied to essences, including individual essences. Just the same, nominalism was a classical form of the skepticism that blossomed in the modern era.

In modern philosophy, since at least Locke's *Essay on Human Understanding* (1689), the realism controversy developed as an argument between empiricism and rationalism. Herein lay the persuasive power of Kant's formulation a century later. Modern philosophy, at least as it passed down into sociology, began with Kant's famous *Critique of Practical Reason* (1788), where he developed to a considerable satisfaction the possibility of reason in the absence of proofs for the existence of the *ding an sich* (the thing itself). Kant threw out pure reason in order to salvage reason itself—this by locating it in the *a posteriori* mental categories, thus permitting practical reason to do the work that essentializing forms of pure reason attributed to the categories as *a priori* essences.

Whether or not one cares one way or the other about the philosophical issues, even a most cursory history easily demonstrates their importance to Sociology. Without Kant, no Hegel; therefore, no Marx and, *mutatis mutandis,* neither Weber nor Durkheim (but possibly Chicago). Capital-S Sociology, in its main classical dispensations, has been inclined toward realism and empiricism, but also toward an essentialism of practical reason. Where there were exceptions—as in Simmel, the gloomy side of Weber, the early Marx, the later Durkheim, and so on—the exceptions were generally swallowed up by one or another essentialism. From *Protestant Ethic* (1904–1905) on, Weber held that the three types of authority and social order were essentially distinct (hence, his despair and the peculiar attitude toward the charismatic type). From *German Ideology* (1845–1846) on, Marx held the elementary labor process as the essential formula whereby ownership determined the modes of the production, even under despotism, where ownership was, at best, a figure of speech. The Durkheim of *Elementary Forms* (1912), the first serious argument for the idea that mental categories are actually socially constructed, went too far by suggesting that all societies construct them essentially the same way.

Sociological essentialisms are, thus, an excellent illustration of the limitations of essentialisms of all kinds. Whereas philosophical essentialisms tend to underestimate (or otherwise ignore) human freedom, essentialisms in Sociology (even when they are not structuralisms) tend to overestimate central tendencies at the expense of variance, thereby crippling its ability to generate empirically robust theories of social differences. This is why capital-S Sociology has been among the objects of criticism (not to mention derision) thrown down by various closet sociologies. Conversely, Sociology has dismissed each and all variants of the merely postmodern, including those (like various feminisms) that very often share capital-S Sociology's objections to theories even remotely French. Of these, none is more striking and persistent than feminism in Sociology (Alway 1995; cf. Thorne and Stacey 1985). The sad story of Sociology's resistance to feminisms could just as well be retold as the tale of its long marriage to methodological essentialism.

If women, in their particulate occurrences, are taken to be instances of a natural kind, then Sociology enjoys the convenience of taking gender as the sufficient variable unto a Sociology of Womankind. This operation works, however, if—and only if—gender is essentialized (even if as a nominal) as the covering concept for variations in the category of which women are proper members. Not incidentally, gender must also be stipulated a dichotomous variable, a move that benefits Sociology more than women in that it disallows (on technical grounds) the ever more probable likelihood that gender is better understood as continuous, probably contingent, certainly local (though not necessarily constructed), and surely not an essence (Butler 1990; cf. Fuchs 2001:67–68, inter alia). Hence, a particular woman is Sociologically interesting as a token of the gender type, considered dichotomously, as a digital—as, that is, the other to the one and only essential type, of which the standard measure is its deviation from the norm of Maleness (Goffman 1963:128–29). Though, to be sure, there are technical as well as principled attempts to get around this problem, it remains. Sociology understands variation as inherently measurable according to valid and reliable standards able to lend numerical weight to variables; the real variance will be artificially limited and differences ruled out (literally, measured away). Hence, also, the risk some feminisms take of reverting to a counteressentialism of the capital-O Other. Essentialisms—whether Sociological or sociological, whether Feminist or feminist, whether Homosexual or queer, and so on—are everywhere in any thinking enterprise that concerns itself with purportedly real social things. The question to ask of essentialisms is, therefore: Wherein subsists the reality of particular things, including social ones? If asked, always, in reference to real or purportedly real social things, such as women, such a question allows practical and routine inquiry to determine how and which truths (if any) can be distinguished in respect to which real variations.

Stephan Fuchs understands all this very well, and with uncommon philosophical sophistication. He begins, therefore, as a Sociologist must, with Sociology's interest in the real (p. 2):

> My major question is how cultures and observers do their work … I am more interested in differences between modes of relating to the world, not constants or universals. If there are constants, this is because they are being held constant by an observer. When this happens, essences appear, along with things-in-themselves or natural kinds. Essences prosper in the deep core of cultures, where they house that which they cannot even consider, let alone deconstruct. The literature has many different terms for this core, including paradigm, tacit knowledge, practices, ethnomethods, common sense, and pretheoretical understanding.

It is important to understand that statements like this one launch a book that is in fact a program, if not a prolegomenon, and that the book itself is, in effect, a series of enunciations stipulating a Sociology that *ought* to be (as distinct from being that Sociology itself). This is fair, I think. Fuchs believes, as he says, that Sociology can be "a great science" (p. 6). This is why he is *against essentialisms,* since to be for them (whether knowingly or not) is to make it impossible to be *for Sociology* as he understands it.

The key to Sociology is the observer, by which Fuchs means neither the mind of some individual observer nor the mythical observer of Sociological ethnography—the one who heroically struggles with his own disinterestedness while trying to get closer to the real social things (pp. 43–47). Fuchs's observer is actually not a person at all, but a position in a network. "In the beginning, there were networks" (p. 337). This is the first of 25 wonderfully instructive theses with which Fuchs ends the book (pp. 337–39). Another of his theses bears on the idea of a network: "Persons do not act, much less act rationally. 'Action' is how some observers make sense of some events. Personhood is an institution" (p. 338; or, in the text, p. 104):

> The basic antiessentialist premise is that "action" and "behavior," "persons" and "things," "nature" and "society," "science" and "humanism," and the other dichotomies are indeed not opposite poles of Being, separated by an unbridgeable essentialist gap. Rather, they are social devices of description and explanation that co-vary with other sociological variables, such as the status of observers, the conditions of observing, and the degree to which an observed system has been rendered predictable through normal science.

Passages like this one (of which there are many) are likely to drive the reader nuts. In one breath Fuchs says things that sound very *nouveau* (such as, forget the dichotomies because they make for essences), while in the next he is quite *ancien* (such as, submit observations to the judgments of normal science).

What is going on here? What is going on is that Fuchs is offering a most original reformulation of both systems and network theories in which the emphasis is less on the feedback loops or pathways resolving system tensions than on the "systems of relations wherein differences can matter" (p. 11). Those of us raised on Talcott Parsons and other earlier versions of systems analysis can hardly imagine such a statement. Again, you go a bit crazy. The things he says are neither quite what one was taught nor what one reads today. Are not the merely postmoderns the ones preoccupied with differences? Is not the emphasis on relations and differences the very contrary of a coherent science?

Whatever may be the debilitating effects of essentialism, does not an overriding emphasis on differences make empirical research technically unwieldy, if not impossible?

If social reality is nothing but relations, do we not lapse into a world of observers observing observations in a plentitude of variation? The answer Fuchs would give is (like much of what he says) a loud and didactic NO, of course not!

Antiessentialist realism (to which Fuchs devotes an entire chapter) is precisely about variance. "Realism increases as the result of many interacting variables … when a culture is grounded in routine machines, tools, and instruments" (p. 330). One can only say "Two cheers for Fuchs!" It is as plain as day that the difficulty Sociology has had in becoming the Science it aspires to be is that so much of its technical competence has been devoted to the control of measurement errors in the name of isolating causal pathways attributable to variables removed from routine operations.

The technical progress Sociology has made in this respect must be admired. But, the progress has been at the expense of explanations of real and abiding social differences in favor of clear and distinct working variables. The problem is not the practical work itself, but in the thinking that inspires it and issues from it. If you cook your data with enough catsup, you'll have a dish tasty to the kids who want familiar tastes. But if you want your data to taste like something real, you'll have to find a way to mix the tastes so that none is diminished. The best stews are not familiar, but an unusual combination of the strangely complex. The real world is a stew of this kind, not an extruded snack. Overdone data create the appearance of a capital-S Science, but they are not Sociology, which, if it is to be both antiessentialist and real, must allow for the social reality of irrevocable variance and difference.

Still, I give Fuchs only two cheers, deeply felt though they are. In the end, it seems to me that the *Againsts* from which he distinguishes his *Fors* are too needlessly many and too crankily dismissed. The result is that the book's defense of Sociology too often consumes without digesting the actual variance in the network of observers of this real, actually existing, world, such as it may be, ontologically speaking.

Some of us are, in effect, against capital-S Sociology precisely because we consider sociology so very important. The trouble with capital-S Sociology is only partly its not-very-well-thought-through essentialism. The even more troubling aspect of disciplinary Sociology is that it has become so needlessly defensive. There is a difference between a carefully worked through against and defensiveness. Again Fuchs is a marvel. He is not defensive in the usual obsequious manner. But he is by his offhanded treatment of that which he opposes; for example: "There is nothing new in postmodernism; its central topics—for example, the death of the Subject, antifoundationalism, or the critique of representation—can be recovered from the classics, without all the philosophical essentialism [sic!] of postmodernist critiques" (p. 3). The merely postmodern is far from the only baby thrown out with the bath water. So too are ethnomethodology, constructivism, capital-S Science, capital-C Culture, the Double Hermeneutic, and certainly deconstruction, among others.

Stephan Fuchs is such a trustworthy guide to the ideas he favors that it is a shame not to be able to trust his dismissals, of which the most notorious is his earlier essay on deconstruction (Fuchs and Ward 1994a). It is not that it is worthless—hardly that. But it does raise doubts about the method. Here he (apologies to Steven Ward) quotes not quite one line from Derrida (and that not from the principal source of Derrida's early thinking on the subject). All the rest is from secondary commentators. Then when he is called on his interpretation of Derrida (Agger 1994), he responds that the trouble with Agger is that "he has nothing at all to say about the substance of our argument" (Fuchs and Ward 1994b:506), when what Agger was saying was that Fuchs had nothing to say about the substance of Derrida's argument. You might have thought that in the passage of time, this sort of wise-guy dismissal would have softened somewhat. But no, and apart from the book, we see it again in 2001 in a review so nasty as to make your hair stand on end (Fuchs 2002), beginning with the title "To Whom It May Concern." Well, for one, it concerns me quite a lot when we speak to each other that way. We guys do this sort of thing to each other all the time. But isn't there a limit somewhere? Of course there is, and the limit is to be found in the desiderata of Fuchs's own book.

If, in the beginning, there are networks, and if networks nest observations, and, given that Sociology (like some but not all networks) must observe itself, then, by extension, observations of Sociology may (if not must) take place in some network other than formally organized disciplinary Sociology itself. Fuchs allows for—indeed, he insists on—the necessity of observations of networks from within. I agree unreservedly with his critique of the transcendental observing Subject. Self-observation is indeed one of the important ways the networks underlying cultures and sciences "care" for themselves (p. 42). Sociology cannot be disinterested, he says (pp. 42, 339), because like other network-embedded cultures, its business is this self-caring. This notion of cultures as caring for themselves is easily the most disarmingly tender thought in the whole book. If Fuchs means it, then he must care for what he means, and this leads to complications having to do with the self-referential nature of systems and networks. They may observe others. But, in caring for themselves, how do they avoid self-involvement? At one point, Fuchs says self-caring is to avoid being "careless" (p. 42), but in the end (p. 339) he clearly also means "caring" in the more tender sense. You cannot speak of caring as a virtue of cultures without facing up to the entailments of the figure you chose, even if (and especially if) you mean only to avoid being "careless."

To dismiss too handily, or too nastily, is at least careless. It is also not to care about the network. In Sociology, as in other social networks, there may be capital criminals who do not deserve to be cared for. But we must be as cautious in these executions as in all others. The reason for this caution is, of course, that to kill too readily is to be care-less about the network and one's own interests in keeping it going. If you doubt this, ask yourself if you'd choose to live in Texas—or, for that matter, in a capital-S Sociology that executes its own, or those at least seeking to be wise to its ways. More likely than not, if you had a choice, you'd look for some other network to live in, because you understand very well that anyone is at some risk in most networks, any number of which come with a hangman looking for work.

Where Fuchs's hammer builds him a gallows is, precisely, in his rejection of resources among the lowercase-s sociologies—in particular, feminism. Of all the traditions of thought that have taken capital-S Sociology seriously without necessarily being merely postmodern, feminism leads the list. It is true that a great deal of feminist sociology draws on thinking outside *the* Network. But, since at least the earliest writings of Dorothy Smith (1974) in the 1970s, sociological feminism has taken seriously the questions Fuchs puts at the center of Sociology. The first, if not only, point of standpoint feminism is precisely that one observes the world, not as persons, but from positions in networks. Hence, what women see is different from what men see—not because they are smarter, but because their experiences are shaped by different networks. Neither Smith nor any other feminist theorist has used *network* as Fuchs does. But they mean much the same sort of thing—up to a point. The point, among others, is chiefly that standpoint feminists want to avoid "objectified knowledge," which they very often consider a result of the prevailing "relations of ruling" (Smith 1974:14–18), which, in real social networks, are still today, generally speaking, relations ruled by men. There is an important difference between standpoint (and other) feminisms and what Fuchs wants to achieve for Sociology. He believes that a science (lowercase-s) is possible for Sociology, even if the S in Sociology's science is only implied. It is true that, by and large, most feminisms reject the authority of the disciplines, even when they are important players in their fields, as they are in Sociology.

What, more specifically, might Fuchs and those who will be enchanted by his book have to gain from giving up their defensive dismissals of other networks? There is one example from *Against Essentialism* that is particularly striking. The book is about culture, to be sure. But if there is one concept that is just as difficult to tame as *culture,* and also one without which it is hard to make sense of culture, it is *power.* Fuchs recognizes this: "Power is the juice that flows through the networks, without ever being concentrated in a single source or reservoir" (p. 260). Still, save for a few pages here and there, he has little to say about how that juice may flow differently in different networks, some of which surely are less well electrified than others. One cannot fairly expect Fuchs to take the feminist position on networks, their cultures, and their juice. But somewhere it might occur that there are real classes of persons whose networks have insufficient power to see the light of day; that, having less power, they might have a different—perhaps even a more acute—ability to observe in networks from which they are excluded, not to mention those in which they are proper members. This is precisely the point of standpoint feminism—a point as old as Hegel's master-slave doctrine. Women and slaves, among others of relatively underjuiced networks, may be forced to use their lack of power to sharpen their observing cultures. In either case, you can be sure that they know differently and certainly know what they know on the basis of an ability to do precisely what Fuchs wants from his Sociology—to know relations, not essences, in order to understand differences and variances.

Another feminist who has been at once indifferent to the merely postmodern and loyal to Sociology very well illustrates this alternative. For some time now, Patricia Hill Collins (1990) has attempted to rework the sociology of feminist standpoints. Among her most challenging ideas is one borrowed from outside Sociology, the matrix of domination (Collins 1990:221–38). Though the influence of Weber is apparent (domination), the possibilities of the matrix figure for network theory are not nearly as clear. The network metaphor tends, at best, toward the two-dimensional. Fuchs clearly wants to go well beyond the feedback-loop and pathway thinking of earlier systems and network theories. He wants, in short, a multidimensional view of networks as being capable of generating different observations. What better figure than the matrix, which (whether taken from mathematics or the movies) is, by its nature, multidimensional? Of course, this is not about figures of speech. Still, it is about getting sociology done properly, and one can hardly get it done without a more robust theory of power than what one finds in *Against Essentialism*. Some networks have juice. Others have the juice cut off when the powers decide to enforce a curfew. Collins proposes a solution. You cannot have a sociological theory of culture or knowledge with a theory of power because it is at least likely that what one knows, for better or worse, is a function not of juice but of learning to live without it. Fuchs seems to believe that the entailment of his first thesis ("In the beginning, there were networks") is that everyone lives in some or another network and that all networks are at least similar, if not the same. This may not be essentialism, but neither is it a robust theory of variance and social differences.

One might wonder if, as Fuchs admits, Sociology's network is different from some others in being required to observe itself, then in what does this difference subsist? Collins would say (and here she would agree with Smith and others) that, apart from Sociology, there are sociologies in networks in which observations are made by the "outsider-within" (Collins 1998:3–78, inter alia; cf. Smith 1974:21–24). Fuchs recognizes this possibility (pp. 35–40), but he resolves its tensions in favor of his own insider-without, where the without is highly circumspect. He grants that the outside observer has a different angle, but it is not an angle (especially not in the case of Sociology) from which he can accomplish real science, which is always facing variances that must not be covered by essentializing ideas. In short, much like the short shrift he gives to real outsiders, whatever their relations to the network of Sociology. Fuchs may well have limited himself needlessly.

REFERENCES

Agger, Ben. 1994. "Derrida for Sociology? A Comment on Fuchs and Ward." *American Sociological Review* 59: 501–505.

Alway, Joan. 1995. "The Trouble with Gender: Tales of the Still-Missing Feminist Revolution in Sociological Theory." *Sociological Theory* 13: 209–228.

Antonio, Robert. 2002. "For Social Theory: Alvin Gouldner's Last Project." Paper presented at the meeting of the American Sociological Association, Chicago, Illinois.

Butler, Judith. 1990. *Gender Trouble.* New York: Routledge.

Collins, Patricia Hill. 1990. *Black Feminist Thought.* Boston: Unwin Hyman.

———. 1998. *Fighting Words.* Minneapolis: University of Minnesota Press.

Fuchs, Stephan. 2001. *Against Essentialism: A Theory of Culture and Society.* Cambridge, MA: Harvard University Press.

———. 2002. "To Whom It May Concern: A Review Essay on *Making Social Science Matter.*" *Sociological Theory* 20: 131–133.

Fuchs, Stephan, and Steven Ward. 1994a. "What Is Deconstruction? Where and When Does It Take Place? Making Facts in Science, Building Cases in Law." *American Sociological Review* 59: 481–500.

———. 1994b. "Sociology and Paradoxes of Deconstruction: A Reply to Agger." *American Sociological Review* 59: 505–510.

Goffman, Erving. 1963. *Stigma.* New York: Simon and Schuster.

Gouldner, Alvin Ward. 1994. *For Sociology: Renewal and Critique in Sociology Today.* New York: Basic Books.

Luhmann, Niklas. 1994. "'What Is the Case?' and 'What Lies Behind It?': The Two Sociologies and the Theory of Society." *Sociological Theory* 12: 126–139.

Smith, Dorothy. 1974. "The Disjuncture between Sociology and Women's Experience." *Sociological Inquiry* 44: 1–13. Reprinted in *The Conceptual Practices of Power: A Feminist Sociology of Knowledge*. Boston, MA: Northeastern University Press, 1990.

Thorne, Barrie, and Judith Stacey. 1985. "The Missing Feminist Revolution in Sociology." *Social Problems* 32: 301–317.

IV

Dark Thoughts

8
Dreaming in the Dark, November 26, 1997

More often than not, dreaming is done in the dark. If the psychoanalysts and other sages of the human tribe are to be believed, dreams also come from a dark place—the unconscious, perhaps; or the spirit world of dead ancestors. But what is one to make of dark—racially dark—dreams?

Early in the morning of November 26, 1997, I had such a dream. Here it is, with slight revision, as I recorded what I could remember of it soon after waking:

Joyce Mueller! She still looked young as when she taught me to jitterbug, if that is what it was, in the early summer of 1952. I can feel her breasts through the cashmere as if it were yesterday. In the dream she was two years younger. A reversal! That one time, she made me feel like a little, little boy. The dream had us in a group. We were going out. I was in heaven. We came to a palace. It was Minister Farrakhan's. But it was in Harlem, not Chicago. It was a second floor dance hall, not the landscaped and guarded palace in South Side Chicago.

We climbed the stairs. I was invited to enter. Then I noticed that Joyce and her group were gone. The dance floor was empty, but the large hall was filled with feeling. The Fruit of Islam, always ready, kept themselves at a discreet distance. I saw Minister Farrakhan across the room, surrounded by followers. His own head was on the body of Martin. People came and went. I looked for the bathroom. I saw a sign that read "White Women." I was appalled. I left in indignation, but loitered about on the street below on a public square from which I could see the well-lit palace ballroom through floor-to-ceiling windows. Veiled women, under command, threw my belongings out the window to the street below. I immediately regretted that I had left. I wanted to go back up and protest by using the "Colored Men's" bathroom. And so I did. But the bathroom was merely a closet from which I could see the women's bathroom. Both were unadorned, plain, but clean. Once inside, it was clear to me that they were not segregated as I had thought.

I left again. I stood around on the street again, looking up. I saw the Minister's guards at the windows. They were dressed, not in their usual black suits and white shirts, but in outfits like those worn by gymnasts. One leaped feet first from the window above to the street. He landed a perfect 10. Feet planted, arms raised. Once again my belongings were being thrown from the window. He caught them as they fell. I felt rejected. But when they landed I saw that the things tossed out were religious objects. One was a candelabrum—perhaps a menorah.

The Minister himself then came down to join the crowd that had gathered on the street. He and I walked together, arm in arm. We talked intimately. We liked each other. We knew we did. But we said nothing of this. He hinted even less than I. But I knew. I wanted to tell him that I had once visited his place in Chicago and had taken a picture of it after one of the Fruit of Islam gave me permission. I really had wanted to tell him this, but there was no time. We were talking too much about important things. The dream ended just as I began to imagine myself replacing Ben Chavis as his advisor for the next Million Man March. I had begun to scheme how I would get him to drop from his speech all that ridiculous stuff about "the number 19."

Where does such a dream come from?

One idea about dreams is that they are the wishes and desires of the dreamer, and thus have little to do with the people who appear in them. Yet, the people who come into our dreams are real in their way. Joyce Mueller was. Minister Farrakhan is. So too is Ben Chavis. In our dreams they tend to get all mixed up with each other. Joyce Mueller became Minister Farrakhan who, in turn, was occupying Malcolm X's mosque while living in Martin Luther King's body. Who was the object of desire? Was it Joyce Mueller, or other white women whose bathroom repelled me? Or black men whose plumbing turned out to be just as plain as that of the white women? Was the desire sexual? Or racial? Or what? Or was it the desire to beat out other men for the affections of the real Man? Ben Chavis, before he became Chavis Muhammad and a Muslim minister, had been an ordained Christian minister in the same denomination to which I am ordained. Was he the one who did what I never could?

The questions never end. But dreams do, usually just when they have done the work of expressing the wishes one cannot bear in conscious life—often when they come to the point of expressing what one cannot bear to imagine in either life. How close did I really want to be to Minister Farrakhan, who may have had a hand in killing Malcolm X, yet whose speech in 1995 at the Million Man March was, I thought, wonderful—except for all that business about the number 19, which I feared was not good for the cause. *Whose We?*

The thing about dreams is that, for their brief duration, they can eliminate altogether any and all *Whose We?* problems. There is no We in a dream, at least not in its latent contents. In them we are walking arm-in-arm with ourselves—or, rather, with our innermost, momentarily unrestrained, wishes to join a We for which we are neither qualified nor prepared. This is the power behind all "I Have a Dream" speeches. When uttered in public, at the right moment, by the right person, they draw all those willing to march back down deep into their dreams in the dark.

There is a catch, however. Just as some few can call others back into their dreams beyond the *Whose We?*—so others can do the opposite. Malcolm X was so terrifying in his day, as Minister Farrakhan has been since, because they speak, in their better moments, of the American nightmare that there is not, and ought not be, any such thing as a societal We. Such a nightmare is the American white man's darkest thought. It may well be as dark for all white colonizers in the European Diaspora. In fact, there is no We in America, any more than there is in the world. And of all the ways by which the human We is divided, drawn and quartered, the analytic cut upon the skin—the racial cut—is the most visible.

One dreamer draws us back into the dark before there was any cut, to when there is only one undivided We of our most primitive wishes to be at one with the breasts at hand. Yet, the risk of that good, primitive dreaming in the dark is that the censoring self will not wake us up in time. Then along comes a Malcolm or Louis, or whoever, to bring on the nightmares. Number 19!—whatever that might mean.

Most of my dreams are about houses that are not quite homes. I grew up in houses like that. In my dreams these houses are always off—just like my darkest feelings about myself. They are unsettled at their foundation. They may have long winding corridors that go nowhere. They may be perched unevenly beside a river, ready to fall.

But there is one house dream that was different. I had it many years ago—before the habit of writing my dreams down. Yet, I can remember its crucial details just as well as I remember that night in 1952 when I felt Joyce Mueller's blossoming breasts touch my heart forever. It is unusual that anyone remembers a dream so well, and can repeat it from memory:

> I was in the basement of the house my father built in 1941 before he went to war. It was, I should say, the house in which Florence had lived with us before she bought her own at 54 York Street, downtown. In the dream I was looking around in the basement for something or someone. The space was clean but barren, lighted just enough to see my way around. Otherwise, the basement was dark as basements can be. I was looking for something. The light came from a room.
>
> I was drawn to that room. I felt the pull. Its door was ajar. I went to it. I felt guilt, but I could not stop. Inside, I found a most beautiful scene. A fine wooden table, Victorian and well polished, was covered with a lace cloth—perhaps even a veil. On the table was a burning lamp. The scene made me feel warm, welcome, alive. I was the only person in that dream.

Now I ask, which kind of dark dream was this?

In real life, my biological mother, whom I think of as the birth mother, always set a hurricane lamp at the window on a table where she would sit to drink her last cups of coffee. Its glass shade was a deep, dark red. It was usually on when I came home as a kid. It must have been burning when I came back from that dance with

Joyce Mueller. When my mother died I took that lamp. It sits beside me now. It is the first light seen when anyone comes up the hill to our home.

Dreams, whether those of a shaman or a psychoanalyst, are always condensations, displacements, and reversals of the stories we wish to tell ourselves in the dark. Was this dream of the lamp a dream of my wishes that my birth mother could be—could have been—what my other mother was in fact? And was it empty of any human form because the lit lamp was the reversal of those affections—the ones I had wanted so much in the upper floors of the house and could only find in the basement? The room in which the lamp on the table was dreamed was the room in which Florence had slept when she lived with us. I do not recall ever going into it wide awake. But I was able to dream it more than a half century later.

How many little boys and girls have dreams of their other mothers whose affection fills in for the ones withheld by the mothers other to the other mothers? And how many of those other mothers are colored people? Do we dream of them always in code—condensed, displaced, reversed? If we do, is it not then that dreaming in the dark is the vain attempt to calm the soul's aching for the ones whom one was never permitted to love as they loved us? If so—if only a tiny bit so—then it must be that these dreams we create by ourselves are always filled with the social imagination of those upon whom we trusted for our very lives.

Is it possible that white people everywhere dream in and of the darkness that holds steady the uneven foundations of their wobbly houses and uncertain selves?

9

The Race of Time

DECONSTRUCTION, DU BOIS, AND
RECONSTRUCTION, 1935–1873

Presentism is the sin of holding persons native to an earlier time accountable to the standards of a present time. Those blamed in the first place are usually dead, or otherwise indisposed. They cannot defend themselves. Yet they are accused. There are many examples. One could say, for example, that by today's standards Charlotte Perkins Gilman was at best a feminist essentialist, at worst a racist. Or it is possible to blame Anna Julia Cooper, one of her generation's most brilliantly timeless thinkers, for her failure to touch upon sex. And even W. E. B. Du Bois, than whom none among those in his several time zones was more prescient, could be accused of insufficiency with regard to women. He was a feminist in his way, but by present standards he was not a good enough one.

The thing about presentism is that it turns complaint upon the complainer. The deficiency of the one held to standards not of their time is converted into a criticism of the critic for his own failure to keep historical time in order. Yet presentism is not an entirely silly complaint. People do have to watch out for mistakes made in respect to rules they could not possibly have understood.

Still presentism may not be either the only or the worst failure of this kind. Though seldom remarked upon, it is readily apparent that there is a sin similar in its confusion of times, but different in the direction of the confusion. If *presentism* is the fault of holding the long, recently, or soon-to-be dead responsible for the manners of present company, then X is the error of failing to grant the real or virtual dead credit for having understood present manners *better* than present company. Since *pastism* is more monstrous a term even than *presentism,* why not call it, simply, X? The difference between X and *presentism* turns on the distinction made ever so delicately by the *Book of Common Prayer*—that between sins of omission and those of commission. Presentism, thereby, is the sin of committing a faulty attribution of omission to the dead who, at the time they were living, could not have known the rules they failed to obey. By contrast, X would be an active neglect by the living of the achievements of the dead—a commission exercised upon the refusal to grant that others knew the rules before they did. Within full-bodied analytic culture one might expect the X to be filled with something like "culpably feasible ignorance of the present-promise of past deeds." Since this won't do, let us call it X.

As it turns out, X is a good term with a history of its own. It was the X in Jacques Derrida's early writings on erasure that may have started the argument in the first place. His idea was that all could never be said and done. This he derived from the erasing X that he drew through most of the sacred ideals of the modern West—the primacy of voice, the privileging of articulate consciousness, the presumption of present meaning, the moral authority of the Self, the principles of the Center, and so on. The most notorious of Derrida's X's was in an essay that appeared in *Théorie d'ensemble,* the 1968 collective manifesto of the then new French social theory. There he explained his very squirrelly concept, *différance,* with the following remarkable statement: "Or si la différance est (je mets aussi le 'est' sous rature) ce qui rend possible la présentation de l'étant-présent, elle ne se présente jamais comme telle."[1] To make a long story short, Derrida meant to say that when we come upon certain crucial words like "is" (perhaps the most crucial and duplicitous of all words), we must think twice. To say "is" is to suggest that some or another (material or immaterial) subject "is" in the present time of the statement uttered. "Derrida is still alive." The man is present in the present time. Were "Derrida" to be a fictional character, as his detractors seem to suppose, the effect would be the same. The reader is asked to think of him, whoever he is, as present.

Whenever "is" is uttered, problems abound. The first of which is with "Being" itself—chief among those words about which Derrida (borrowing here with reservations from Heidegger) thinks we must think twice. When we utter "is," we are committing an ontology of sorts. It is impossible to utter the word "is" without implying a judgment about Being. Derrida was saying, in effect: Always and ever, put such words "under erasure" (*sous rature*) because nothing is ever present as such. This is a loose translation, but looseness is the famous point of the concept *différance*. Everything we say and think is loose—open to suspicion. Even, and especially, speaking itself is at best loosely related to one's *vouloir-dire*—to whatever one "means to say," to meaning itself. When some one or some thing "is said to exist"—that is: is meant to be thought of as "present"—Derrida means for us to draw the implication that such ones or things are, in fact, never truly present at the moment of the saying. There is, in effect, no "being present."[2]

As shocking as it may be to some, Derrida's experiments with X's as a way of managing the uncertainty of Being in human affairs is actually a Nietzschean commitment to writing philosophy with an eye to sociology. The famous *"La différance"* essay could not have appeared at a more poignant historical moment, 1968. This text was a short version of his earlier criticism of Husserl's philosophy of the voice as present meaning, *Speech and Phenomena* (1967). That in turn followed Derrida's two influential essays of 1966, "Structure, Sign and Play in the Discourse of the

Human Sciences" and "Freud and the Scene of Writing."[3] It was not by accident that the latter two turned on the problem of the unconscious in social life. "Structure, Sign and Play" attacked the unifying ideals of modern culture, including the human sciences. This famous essay, said to be the beginning of deconstruction in America, displaced the modern world's cultural Center by drawing an objection to Lévi-Strauss's structural anthropology. Structuralism, said Derrida, reclined too easily upon the hidden potency of the linguistic sign in order to fulfill the analytic ambitions of modern thought by reuniting nature and culture. "Freud and the Scene of Writing," with its astonishing recovery of Freud's metaphor of the child's magic writing pad, accounted for the absence of the unconscious itself in its tenuous presentations in dreams. Psychoanalysis deferred the meanings uncovered by the anthropological signifier.[4] Still, in both—the absence of nature in culture and of the unconscious in conscious life—Derrida called attention to the slips and tricks whereby the modern West meant to organize the world in its presence. Across and between the lines of these writings is the visual darkness of the colonial world from which he came and of which he refuses to speak.[5] The decentering of Western thought is the deferred effect of the political economy of the global decentering wrought by the decolonizing movements that were at their most acute in 1968. Hence, the irony: everything said in the *de*-mode is still meant to be a construction.

In short, *deconstruction is reconstruction with a difference.* It is not an analytic method so much as an attitude. It is a rewriting of the history of thought—and, by implication, of history itself—by the trick of using the language of thought to turn thinking—and history—on their sides, if not on their ears. Since, and before, those crucial essays and books around 1968, everything Derrida himself has done has been a relentless rewriting of Western thought from within its language. This is deconstruction, a word that has entered popular culture to odd, disturbing effect. I once heard a television announcer of an American football game say, "Let me deconstruct the New York Jets defense for you." What he was in fact saying when he used the word deconstruction was, "Let me tell you the meaning of what just happened on the field." That's what American football announcers do, accompanied by video playbacks. Hence, he was actually offering not a deconstruction but a garden-variety reconstruction—a vain attempt to bring events back into the present. (Only those who know American football will know just how vain the offer.) Deconstruction would have been, "Let us figure out what did not go on on the field and never could have and how this absence—these events that were not present, and never could have been—are the reason everything that did go on on the field was as it was."[6] Deconstruction is an aggression against any form of historical thinking, including all of History's selfish ontologizings—of its pretenses to make meanings present in order to organize the world in which they transpire. In the long course of modern culture, there are many versions of this deception, but the ideals of History, and of the progressive Subject, are as good as any for it.

Deconstruction, one might say, allows the meanings that would otherwise be said to remain in their naturally loose state of deferral—of being always at a remove from any attempt to capture and organize them, of being never present.

Deconstruction thus acknowledges the race of time. The time of modern culture is historical time in which everything depends on the possibility of running the past through the present in order to promise a "better" future that could ever "be." Modern time is, thus, time out of place. It refuses to account for the possibility that the present is nothing at all because all of its meanings are always somewhere else— waiting to be said, heard, written, acted upon.

The present races so fast as to be virtually always somewhere else. The question that could, therefore, be asked is, What does the race of time have to do with the time of race?

There could be no better source for an answer to such a question than W. E. B. Du Bois. In the present, early millennium, Du Bois is being brought into the present with a vengeance. Yet, many of those who attempt to make him present might be looking in the wrong place.[7]

Souls of Black Folk is, unquestionably, a fine work of literature, as it is an excellent source of social theories of the double consciousness, of the talented tenth, of the Veil and the color line, and of race theory in general. As great as it may be, *Souls* is not Du Bois's most important work. That distinction must fall either to his earliest important book, *The Philadelphia Negro* (1899), or to the much later *Black Reconstruction* (1935). Where *Souls* inspires and suggests new ways of thinking, *Philadelphia Negro* works through the factual account of the turn of the century urban Negro. Yet, to the same degree that *Souls* was instantaneously famous, *Philadelphia Negro* was largely ignored (as it still is) by the sociologists for whom it stands, by more than a decade, as the first important example of urban ethnography in America. The trouble with great ethnographies is that it is difficult to go back to them when they describe neighborhoods in the distant past.

Black Reconstruction—a work that offers both the literary pleasures of *Souls* and the scholarly detail of *Philadelphia Negro*—may well be Du Bois's greatest book. *Black Reconstruction* thinks race through in more enduringly substantial ways than does the famous essay at the beginning of *Souls,* which is oddly indefinite on the nature and upbeat on the prospects of the doubly conscious American Negro. Plus which, *Black Reconstruction*'s evidence is global (hence, relatively timeless) where *Philadelphia Negro*'s is local (hence, considerably time-bound). Still, it is not *Black Reconstruction*'s special literary and empirical effects that recommend it to readers in a new century. That distinction resolves upon its service as a meditation on the off-center time of race—of which Du Bois's book is surely the first and most important. Ever so cautiously, one might even describe *Black Reconstruction* as an early work in the prehistory of deconstruction. Between Nietzsche's *Genealogy of Morals* (1887) and Derrida's *Edmund Husserl's Origins of Geometry* (1962) and *Speech and Phenomena* (1967), few works come more quickly to mind for their reworking of the displacement of power upon so terrible an absence of human possibility. In any case, *Black Reconstruction* deserves very high regard because it, at least, approximates the work of sociological deconstruction that both Nietzsche and Derrida implied but never executed.[8] *Black Reconstruction* moves the critique of modernity's double-edged presentism beyond philosophy (where it has been well-served) into the empirical deferrals of social history—which itself has been struggling since Henry Adams to understand its own confusion with the present.[9]

By whatever name, *Black Reconstruction* is a study of the race of time founded upon an investigation of the time of race. To understand the book is to expose one's sense of historical time to the very uncertainty it is meant to overcome. Where the time of modern Progress is meant to order, the time of Du Bois's thinking—and of his subject—in *Black Reconstruction* is the time of suspense, if not disorder.

From the first, one must wonder why this book, and why then? On the surface, the answer seems simple. The origins of the book may have been as early as 1929 when the *Encyclopedia Britannica* rejected Du Bois's invited essay on the American Negro. The encyclopedia editor recognized the excellence of the essay, but objected to one, seemingly temperate, statement of fact with respect to Reconstruction: "White historians have ascribed the faults and failures of Reconstruction to Negro ignorance and corruption. But the Negro insists that it was Negro loyalty and the Negro vote alone that restored the South to the Union; established the new democracy, both for white and black; and instituted the public schools."[10] The refusal by the world's most prestigious encyclopedia to print even so deliberate a remark reveals the extent to which racist dark thoughts pervade liberal culture.

But the motivation for *Black Reconstruction* may have been the publication, also in 1929, of an overtly racist interpretation of Reconstruction. *The Tragic Era,* by Claude G. Bowers, was the book that prompted Anna Julia Cooper to urge Du Bois to an answer.[11] Du Bois hardly needed urging. He had already, and some time before, staked out his claims against the prevailing (and white) scholarly and popular opinion that the failure of Reconstruction was due to the cultural and political insufficiencies of the freedman, not of the American system itself. As early as 1909, at the meetings of the American Historical Association, Du Bois had presented "Reconstruction and Its Benefits" before the establishment of American historians. His audience on that occasion included the leader of the one school of thought he and other reasonable scholars had most reason to fear.

William Archibald Dunning of Columbia University had not only published (in 1907) the most influential of liberal but still anti-Negro interpretations of Reconstruction (*Reconstruction, Political and Economic: 1865–1877*), but he was the leader of a school of historians who advanced the same old white Southern thesis—that it was the Negro who had failed Reconstruction, not the other way around.[12] The position of the Dunning School was, in short, that the white South was prepared, after the Civil War, to enter the work of rebuilding the South and its union with the North, but that the freed Negro's lack of education and general unreadiness and unwillingness to assume worldly responsibilities caused its failure.[13] The line between the Columbia position and overt racism was as fine as the analytic scruple that caused the *Encyclopedia Britannica* editor to refuse Du Bois's 1929 essay. But it was visible enough.

In 1910, in Du Bois's published version of the AHA paper, he chose to emphasize just exactly those qualities the establishment felt were lacking among freed

Negroes—thirst for learning, civic duty, political responsibility.[14] Some (notably David Levering Lewis) see this article as the "germinal essay for what would become *Black Reconstruction*.[15] Certainly, the 1910 paper is written in the prodigiously documented style of the 1935 book. But the earlier paper lacked the theoretical lift of the later book. It was too much Du Bois, the social scientist, responding to an opposing thesis. It lacked just exactly what made the book so distinctive—scholarship turned to propagandizing ends.

Between 1910 and 1935 Du Bois had spent a full quarter-century as editor of *The Crisis,* the foremost (if contested) organ of public communications for the National Association for the Advancement of Colored People (the NAACP). In 1934, he left the organization he had helped found in 1910. He was fed up with those in the NAACP (and especially Walter F. White) who sought to trim his sails as the de facto spokesman for the movement and the Association. Though Du Bois had returned to Atlanta University in 1934, which gave him time to work on *Black Reconstruction,* it is hardly likely that Du Bois would have cast overboard the sustained political work of his mature life. In 1935 he was 68 years old. He was, no doubt, glad to return to his scientific work. But, the record of his life's work, before and after 1934, is clear. He would permit no silencing of his voice on behalf of the American Negro—at least not until he did so voluntarily by giving up, at the very end, on America herself.

If there was an early outline for *Black Reconstruction* it was not the 1909–10 paper but a still earlier work—the 1901 *Atlantic Monthly* essay "The Freedman's Bureau" (which appeared as "Of the Dawn of Freedom," in *Souls* in 1903). A more beautifully composed and succinctly stated history of Reconstruction there could hardly be. Yet, its high literary values make no exception to his already-then theoretical conviction that the failure of Reconstruction turned on a systematic failure of the nation to extend civil and economic justice to the Negro.[16] This essay, written at the turn of the century when Du Bois was barely thirty, lacked the bracing sense of economic and political reality of *Black Reconstruction,* written during the Great Depression when he was in his late sixties. Still, its broad conviction that cultural or moral failure is always also a fault of the political economy is already evident (as it was, to be sure, in the 1909–10 response to Dunning).

Du Bois's 1935 book, thus, confounds attempts to understand Du Bois in his own time. There is no question that *Black Reconstruction* deserves its reputation as the earliest of his major works most obviously influenced by Marxism. Du Bois, like most others, changed his mind as time went by. Yet, his basic ideas were evident from the beginning. Those who doubt that *Souls* (1903) was already a political-economy of race in the making might submit their doubts to *Philadelphia Negro* (1899). It is hard to say when and where he began to think as he thought in *Black Reconstruction.* It is not difficult at all to conclude that this was his most mature work—the coming out of ideas that were long a-brewing, the coming together of his scientific and political work, the coming to fruition of what turned out to be his last major book written under the already attenuating sway of the nationalism central to the double consciousness of the *American* Negro.[17]

Du Bois was well aware of his place in history. He was, in this and other ways, self-conscious. Yet, he seldom stood on ceremony. He was more than ready to take himself out of a present that ill-served his own, sometimes out of place, sense of historical progress. This, precisely, is what he did in 1934 when he quit the NAACP after so many years. He quit on principle. But which principle and, again, why then? Some may be surprised to learn that the principle was whether or not there were situations in which the NAACP would tolerate racial segregation. Du Bois took the position that there were. Walter White, then in the early years of his own twenty-five years' service as Executive Secretary to the NAACP, claimed that the organization never did and never could condone it. White, an intellectual in his own right,[18] should not have taken up the debate with Du Bois, who surely knew the facts better. But Du Bois did not enjoy White's support by the majority of NAACP's Board. As from the beginning of the organization, those of more traditional values wanted Du Bois to toe the organizational line, whatever it was. The dispute over segregation philosophy in 1934 was pretext for White's move against the editor of *The Crisis,* which led to Du Bois's resignation. Judging from his statements at the time, Du Bois was not fooled. Still, he joined the argument, if only to demonstrate his superior adherence to principle.

The Board's position was that Du Bois was wrong to condone segregation even for strategic reasons. At issue was his May 1934 editorial in *Crisis,* "Segregation," which called for real politics.[19] He began, "The thinking colored people of the United States must stop being stampeded by the word segregation." In effect, Du Bois's argument was the one that would reappear in *Black Reconstruction.* The American Negro must not allow an overdetermined race consciousness to blind him to the class consciousness necessary for "his economic emancipation through voluntary determined cooperative effort"—including, importantly, cooperative effort with sympathetic whites of the working class even when they demanded social segregation. This was 1934 (but think of what satisfaction the argument would have given Booker T. Washington, dead since 1915). White, representing the Board's position, claimed that Du Bois had contradicted the NAACP's official position. They demanded his compliance. The Board sought to vet all such statements by Du Bois before they were printed in *The Crisis.* You can imagine! They knew of course what he would say. They were forcing his hand. The dispute continued heatedly through the early summer until Du Bois insisted upon his resignation, effective July 1. The outcome was never in doubt. Still, he relished the debate. Du Bois's initial reply came early that year, January 17, 1934.[20] He sneered that White hardly knew what he was talking about. The Board had in fact "advocated and strongly advocated a segregated Negro officer's camp after we found that we were not allowed to enter the regular officer's camp during the war." The subtext of the sneer must have been that during the war White was a young, recent graduate of Atlanta University where Du Bois had taught before joining the NAACP. (In later retorts, Du Bois gave other, later examples.) The January letter challenges White and the Board to prove him wrong. But the defiance is mostly part of the game. Du Bois knows he is right. He knows what moves are being made against him. He is ready for the fight; even more, he is clear on the principle.

Du Bois concludes the January 17 letter with a telling distinction of principle, which may have everything to do with different times along which he and the organization he helped found were traveling. Just after issuing the challenge that White prove him wrong (and knowing that it cannot be done), Du Bois addresses the issue of principle: "Of course in my editorial and in your letter, it is manifest that we are not both speaking always of the same thing. I am using segregation in the broad sense of separate racial effort caused by outer social repulsions, whether those repulsions are a matter of law or custom or mere desire. You are using the word segregation simply as applying to compulsory separations." Though it would seem to be at worst a fine theoretical distinction, or at best a choice of tactics (as it was), Du Bois's remark is also calling attention to a difference in the racial times that in 1934 segregated him from the organization to which he had devoted so much. In his final letter of resignation (June 26, 1934), he describes those differences—and they have everything to do with economic crisis then at hand:

> I firmly believe that the National Association for the Advancement of Colored People faces the most grueling of tests which come to an old organization: founded in a day when a negative program of protest was imperative and effective; it succeeded so well that the program seemed perfect and unlimited. Suddenly, by World War and chaos, we are called to formulate a positive program of construction and inspiration. We have been thus far unable to comply.
>
> Today this organization, which has been great and effective for nearly a quarter of a century, finds itself in a time of crisis and change, without a program, without effective organization, without executive officers who have either the ability or disposition to guide [it] in the right direction.
>
> These are harsh and arresting charges. I make them deliberately, and after long thought, earnest effort, and with infinite writhing of the spirit. To the very best of my ability, and every ounce of my strength, I have since the beginning of the Great Depression, tried to work inside the organization for its realignment and readjustment to new duties. I have been almost completely unsuccessful.

Du Bois means to say that his opponents in the NAACP are living in another time—and that the time the American Negro must live in is the time of the Great Depression in which positive programs of economic development must come first, before all else—even before stands against segregation that could put Negroes out of work, income, or housing.[21] The new time required a political economy of racial history—not a theory so much as a practice and a program.

What was the time of *Black Reconstruction*? Was it the biographical time of its author who had come to the end of the line with NAACP integrationism? Or, more broadly, was it the time of the history of the American Negro who, having moved from country to city, and served in the Great War, then faced his own choice between racial and economic goals? Or, more broadly still, was it the global time of economic change and the political adjustments required by the rise of industrial capitalism?

In 1931 Du Bois received the first of the small grants that supported his research for *Black Reconstruction*. This was in the second year of the Great Depression. In 1932 he was at work on the book. His research began. This was the worst year of the Depression.[22] In the United States eleven million were unemployed—nearly twenty percent of the work force. Industrial production was half of what it had been in 1929. National income fell by thirty-eight percent in the same three years. The economic crisis was global. Shipbuilding, coal production, steel manufacture declined sickeningly. Farm prices collapsed. Industrial and farm workers alike were out of work, and income. Among industrial powers, the United States and Germany were the hardest hit. In 1933, Franklin D. Roosevelt became president of the United States, just weeks after Adolf Hitler became chancellor of the German Republic. The die was cast. A second world war would follow upon the economic crisis which in turn followed, in part, the economic and political uncertainties unresolved by the Great War. In 1934 Du Bois broke with the NAACP. He was in Atlanta, working primarily on the book. By the time of its publication in 1935, nothing anyone did or thought, anywhere, was done out of the time of the Great Depression. The Twenties were long gone. No more parties—not at Gatsby's at West Egg, nor at the Redfields' in Harlem.[23]

Still, why a book on Reconstruction in the American South, a story which had come to an end six decades before, in 1877, when Du Bois was still a schoolboy in Massachusetts? Why at such a remove in time did Du Bois turn his attention to what became, by any measure, the most sustained, and demanding, scholarly work of his life[24]—but on a topic seemingly so out of time with the Great Depression that had crystallized his stern coming to odds with official NAACP principles?

The answer is clearer than meets the eye. Anyone thinking deeply about Black America during the Great Depression could hardly not have been led back, sooner or later, to the Long Depression that began in 1873. In Du Bois's case, it was sooner—and for good reason. The Long Depression began with the panic of 1873 and continued episodically for a quarter century until the recovery of 1896 that lent so much hope to the turn of the century.

For whites, the Long Depression meant, in E. J. Hobsbawm's phrase, the bust of the boom that had driven the Age of Capital, the end of the longest period of economic expansion in the early history of industrial capitalism.[25] Between the run on the banks in 1873 and 1878 when ten thousand business failed, half the nation's iron producers also failed, as did half of its railroads, leading in turn to the collapse of industries and business that had risen with these heavy industrial enterprises.[26] It meant also an interruption of the migration of white labor from Europe that would not recover until the 1880s. Everyone was caught up in the crisis. But blacks suffered differently.

For blacks freed after Emancipation in 1863, the Long Depression meant the end of Reconstruction. Though the end did not come until the compromise of 1877, it was foretold by the collapse of the Freedmen's Savings and Trust in 1874, brought on by the panic of the previous year. The ultimate collapse of Reconstruction as an effort to support the economic, political, and educational development of freed blacks came as a direct political result of the economic crisis. Though the Republicans had wavered in their support of Reconstruction since Lincoln's assassination in 1865, they remained the party most friendly to Southern blacks. But the economic crisis diverted the attentions of the Northern whites, and led to the rise of the Southern Democrats. By a quirk of American electoral laws, in 1877 a Republican, Rutherford B. Hayes, eventually won the presidency after losing the popular vote. This famous compromise was the exchange of votes in the U.S. Congress required for certification of Hayes as president for the abandonment of Reconstruction in key Southern states. At that point, Reconstruction came to an end, to be replaced by the restoration of white dominance throughout the South.

The Civil War and Reconstruction have been called, by some, the Second American Revolution. Du Bois called Reconstruction the Second Civil War. North and South, blacks and whites, suffered through the Long Depression—but the crisis and its consequences returned them to their separate historical times. Freed men and women in the South were thrown back to feudal conditions made more severe by the crippling effects of war upon an agrarian system that had lost its most valuable commodity—enslaved labor. The white South was itself divided between the poor whites forced to compete with freedmen in an unstable labor market, and the propertied class that rose from the ashes to reassert its domination. Hence the arrangement—described first by Du Bois, and recently by David Roediger—of the racial wage. Poor whites were granted the racial privilege of their whiteness in compensation for their misery in the economic system.[27] The Reconstruction, so-called, of the American republic, and of its war-ravaged South always meant something different to whites than to blacks. With the collapse of Reconstruction as a national goal, the principals in the Southern drama were returned, if not to the exact structural positions that prevailed before the War, at least to their respective historical times. It would be another full century until late in the 1970s before the American South would significantly shed the vestiges of its feudal past. For the long duration of that century, the South remained more or less bound to the feudal conditions from which the planters profited, the white worker survived with the modest privilege of his racial status, and the black worker suffered unspeakable human and economic misery.

Here was the reason necessary and sufficient to *Black Reconstruction*. The Long Depression of 1873 darkened the prospects of the first and second generation of freed people in the United States, just as the Great Depression of 1929 crushed the hopes of the third and fourth generations.[28] For Du Bois, the social historian of the American Negro, the reversion of times was utterly apparent—1929 brought back 1873, which in turn brought forward the burdens of the feudal past. For him it must also have brought up the bond in memory between his childhood among the first and second generations of post-Emancipation blacks and his "new duties" (as he put it in the 1934 letter of resignation) to the third and fourth generations. For a man of his political and scientific sensibilities, writing in 1934, there could have been no more obvious way to reason.

Du Bois was, in effect, writing out of his time back into the displaced time of the Reconstruction in American history that was, for the American Negro, a deferral of black hopes that turned out to be a deferral of national hopes, even global ones. No event in American history, and few in global history, more starkly uncovered the dark thoughts veiled by the bright promises of modernity, of capitalism, and of democracy. Slavery is evil. Reversion to its time, however displaced, is the darkest thought imaginable. By 1934, the darkness loomed again—a darkness familiar to blacks, surprising but still familiar to poor whites, and terrifying to the white propertied class. And this, precisely, is the point Du Bois makes at the beginning of *Black Reconstruction.*

> Here is the real modern labor problem. Here is the kernel of the problem of Religion and Democracy, of Humanity. Words and futile gestures avail nothing. Out of the exploitation of the dark proletariat comes the Surplus Value filched from human beasts which, cultured lands, the Machine and harnessed Power veil and conceal. The emancipation of man is the emancipation of labor and the emancipation of labor is the freeing of that majority of workers who are yellow, brown and black.[29]

The labor problem is inseparably a racial problem—and both are a global problem.

The disjointed times of colored peoples and white ones always had curved uncertainly toward each other—coming together in times of economic crisis, coming apart in better times. The crisis of the Great Depression was worldwide. Du Bois meant to address it by reverting to the crisis of the Long Depression of the previous century where the times, once again, stood still, reverted, and took up their segregated paths. *Black Reconstruction* both was and was not a book on a specific period in American history. It was every bit as much a working out of the loose uncertainties of modernity. Behind the page upon page of thick description in the book, this principle breathes life into the sad truth of historical fact.

Black Reconstruction is the story of three characters of the Old South. They can neither abide nor escape each other. In the end, they survive—each broken or otherwise cut off from his desires. Evil invites sympathy. Good stirs the higher spirits. None, however, can outrun his times. The tale cuts quickly to its tragic chase. No elaborate prologue or introduction. It begins with the story's lead character, the black worker who, though local to the American South, stands at the heart of world civilization. "Easily the most dramatic episode in American history was the sudden move to free four million black slaves in an effort to stop a great civil war, to end forty years of bitter controversy, and to appease the moral sense of civilization."[30] The slave is introduced with dignity for what he was, a worker. Du Bois does not waste words on sentiment for the victim. The black worker is the soul of the South, the energy of progress, and the soul of civilization. Du Bois does not waver on this. It is his answer to Bowers and the Dunning School, to all of ignorant hostility.

Reconstruction was doomed by forces superior to its better intentions. The white worker, powerless before these forces, nonetheless was the one who promoted, almost unwittingly, Reconstruction's failure and the second civil war of racial-based hatred that ensued. Again, the action is driven, not directed. After the War the planter needed the black worker more desperately than before. The freed people needed the work, land, and opportunity that, even under the Northern military administrators, were still mostly in the hands of the planters. This "rekindled" the "old enmity and jealousy of the poor whites against any combination of the white employer and the black laborer which would again exclude the poor white."[31] The planter, caught by his need of labor, nonetheless had to withhold "sympathy and cooperation with the black laborer."[32] The War had weakened both his social and his economic position, forcing him back into the unholy alliance with the white worker. Thus the black worker, even while he had the support of the Freedman's Bureau and the North, was left in the Southern lurch—his labor bound over in due course to a new system of economic slavery.

In the time of white history, Reconstruction was an interregnum of rule by ignorant, undisciplined blacks who destroyed their own chances. This was the view Du Bois was countering. But he countered it not so much by the sort of direct challenge he had put to Walter White in 1934 but by telling the story as it was. That story was not one of an interregnum so much as of a continuation of civil war in the South that began upon the deferrals of the good North and began almost as soon as the first had ended. In the story he is telling, the black worker must face continued abuse at the hands of the white worker and the planter who, in the short run of the next full century, won out over the confused generosities of even the better white folk of the North.

The time of Reconstruction was not forward, but backward. Even so, Du Bois was not without hope, as he wrote in the depths of the Great Depression, looking back. "Looking Forward" (chapter 7) is the part of the story that comes visible only by looking backward from the time of the Great Depression when the crisis of labor was more at the heart of world democracy than at any time before, or since. The difference in the end between Lincoln and the planters—even Washington and Jefferson—was that he was not a planter. Hence, "Looking Forward" begins with the line linking Lincoln with Christ, and Garrison, and even Johnson.[33] These were all working men. Du Bois surely understood that the white worker, even the white worker of the industrial North, saw the time of progress differently from the black worker. In many ways that is his point. Johnson, the white worker who became the lackey of the planters he hated, was different, but not utterly different, from Lincoln, the white worker become moral leader who could not put an end to planter greed. Du Bois did not forgive them, but he understood them sympathetically. And because he did, he was able even when writing backward to the failures of Reconstruction to draw from its story what threads of hope there were. What is so astonishing about Du Bois, the often arrogant and ultimately disdainful critic of American ways, is that he had held out such determined hope, even as the innocence of the time of *Souls* gave way to the realities of the time of the 1930s, and after.

"Looking Forward," like "Looking Backward," is written in black time. Just as the "backward" was the constant time of violence and slavery, the "forward" time was not the defeat of progress. Black time is the reverse of white time. What progress there was—and there was progress—was displaced not upon near promise but upon things to come that were already growing. And this is where Du Bois's book comes full bloom as a story in global history.

The 1860s were the high water mark of early industrial capitalism. In the United States, as in Europe, the capital benefits of the world colonial system were sunk deep into heavy industry. Coal, steel, and railroads were the foundations of the factory system of which Marx wrote in *Capital,* the first edition of which appeared in 1867 just as the American Reconstruction was beginning its downward slide into economic greed. Coal, steel, and the railroads were also precisely those industries that, along with the banks and small business, had begun their sickening long decline in 1873. Still, Du Bois understood that the future of the black and white worker lay with industrial democracy—as he was to put it later in his final word on Johnson and the Blindspot in America: "The only power to curtail the rising empire of finance in the United States was industrial democracy—votes and intelligence in the hands of the laboring class, black and white, North and South."[34]

So it is that "Looking Forward" is the chapter that unites the underlying themes of Du Bois's story. *Black Reconstruction* is told from 1934 back to 1873; hence, from the time of full-blown industrial crisis back to the first great crisis of industrial capitalism. Another reason one might even dare to think of Du Bois as Derridian before the fact is that he realized that industrial democracy had no precise origin. He realized that its beginnings in the 1860s were really a play upon the structuring work of the nearly four centuries of world building of the European Diaspora and its foundational colonial system. And he realized that this system, in turn, was a displacement of the West's dark pretenses of progress out of the primitive and colored past. How could he not have? But Du Bois also understood, most clearly in *Black Reconstruction,* that this color line was ever and always a long attenuated line through the laboring class as between the labor class and the propertied. The racial wage that bought off the white worker was not just another exchange *within* the capitalist system of surplus values. It was *the* exchange upon which everything else depended.

Put starkly, for Du Bois the race of progressive time was the time of race. There was, in his mind, no being-present when it comes to a system based on capital and exploitation. But there was exploitation—whether that of capital applied directly to human laborers in the feudal slave system, or the more analytic capital affixed to abstract human labor power in the factory system. Du Bois used Marx's ideas to be sure, as in *Souls* he used William James, perhaps, to reinvent the double consciousness. But he always *used* the thoughts of others to his own unique—arrogant, if you prefer—intellectual and political purposes. *Black Reconstruction* may be Marxist, in the sense that anyone writing in the 1930s with a genuine interest in industrial democracy would have written with Marx in mind. But Du Bois's book is not Marxism. Marx framed the continuities between the modes of production along the historical line of ownership of production's means. Hence, the transubstantiation of the feudal serf, or slave, was for Marx a change in the structure of ownership, from which came the transformation in the mode of production. Ownership, however, even when Marx discussed it in the early manuscripts like *German Ideology* and those of 1844, is an analytic concept borrowed from the political economists, from the ideology of modern, liberal thought. Du Bois borrows too, and surely his borrowing includes from Marx among other liberals; but Du Bois comes to very different conclusions, conclusions that in their way are those for which Marx was striving but never quite achieved.

Du Bois made no effort to iron out the history of labor's exploitation onto the flat plane of purposive history. He was the historian who disavowed History. The path between the backward and forward of the story in *Black Reconstruction* was not of a common, or even parallel, relation of ownership to labor. It was that, true; but more. The path was rather that through the worker himself—the black and white workers, upon whose backs *both* the system of feudal agriculture and modern industry depended. Marx valued the worker, for whom everything that matters mattered. But Marx's worker was, from the first of his explicit writings on the elementary labor process, never truly in history. His disavowal of the early modern method of projecting history back to an origin prior to history was more a rhetorical move than an accomplishment. For Marx, History was the history of the fall of free labor before the varieties of ownership. For which the proof was in the dream of the classless society as the redemption of History.

Du Bois thought about History and history in very different terms. He dreamt of no final utopia. He never gave the least thought to History with an Origin in Paradise. For Du Bois there was no History. Only histories—narrative accounts of hopes wrought against the record of oppression of the worker. Hope was founded, therefore, on the prospects of industrial democracy. In 1934, near the worst of the Great Depression, he could not have held this hope too firmly. But he held it—and not as a matter of principle (his principles led to action)—but as a matter of hard-won experience with the reality of work that was always racial. Marx, we might say, never more fully revealed his debt to the very liberal culture he claimed to abjure than in his famous inability to see the darkness of labor. Both the black and the white worker were bound in the subaltern system that industrial capitalism had, in the 1860s, perfected to its own ends. Neither truly saw the vision of paradise regained, because both in their segregated ways understood that the working class will forever be pushed, to the extent workers permit, back into the darkness. Liberal History claims there is only progressively more light. Du Bois's history, with its tenacious readiness to see the reversals—the forwards and backwards—of historical time, was always a story of the play of darkness upon the light.

This is the story of *Black Reconstruction*—clear and compelling, yet remarkably ignored save by specialists in the field of American history. When a great book is so avidly not read by those who need it most, this must be because it tells a truth they do not want to hear, least of all understand. This was the kind of truth Du Bois told near the end of his story (but just one-third through the book itself) when he wrote "Looking Forward." The forward of the new class of working men, white and black, was the forward of the struggle that was so salient in the 1930s, but already dawning as the Civil War ended—and as the Long Depression put a global pinch in industrial capitalism itself. It was the struggle between the possible decency of industrial democracy and the "American Assumption," which was the assumption of industrial capitalism that "wealth is mainly the result of its owner's effort and that any average worker can by thrift become a capitalist."[35]

The three tragic characters of Reconstruction were trapped in futility of massive proportions. The Civil War, though a dramatic event in the American republic, was ultimately but a salient variation on a global struggle. Though in the 1860s the European Diaspora would hold its exploitative grip on the colored people of its colonies from whom it stole its resources and labor power, by the time of the 1930s that grip would begin to slip—in part because of the Great War, in part because of economic distractions, and in part because of the uncertain rise of labor as a fellow sufferer in what progress there was to be had.[36] Still, Du Bois realized that the key to what reconstruction there might have been was the same as the key to the Civil War—the black and white worker. Not the planter. Not the great Liberator himself. Not the liberal North. But the worker. The tragedy fell upon them all because, even as early as 1864, when Reconstruction was first taking its fatal shape, and certainly by the crisis of 1873, it was plain for all who *could* see its history that the action would never be solely in the hands of the worker—black or white, Southern or Northern, African and Asian or those in the European Diaspora of the global North.

"Looking Forward," thus, is the story of dying old men of the North who were better, in their ways, than even Lincoln. Thaddeus Stevens of Vermont in the Congress and Charles Sumner of Massachusetts in the Senate carried forth the radical Republican vision of Reconstruction. But neither lived to see even the first fruits of their righteous demands. Stevens died in 1868, just before Sumner fell out of favor (he died in 1874). The vision they inspired won some gains of no minor importance. The Thirteenth, Fourteenth, and Fifteenth Amendments to the Constitution established basic rights and protections for the freedpeople of the South. Even though the South, with its Black Codes, and political leverage on the North, managed to outrun the rule of law, these protections eventually caught up with justice itself. It took a full century for even these fundamentals of justice to become the true law of the land. None of the best Northerners saw this day. Lincoln could not even imagine it. Stevens and Sumner died long before—their gains wiped out by Andrew Johnson and the others who sided with the planters for one final century more. Du Bois saw this history clearly, which is why he vested what hope he had—then as in the 1930s—in the worker.

Black Reconstruction tells its story in less than half its heft. If Du Bois erred in composition, he erred as a man late in his seventh decade might. (Not even he could foresee the three full decades left to him.) He wrote the book quickly, revising to the end. Under such deadlines as he imposed on himself, he probably could not step back to see that *Black Reconstruction* was really two books at once, if not three. After chapter 9, "The Price of Disaster," which ends on page 381 of a book of 737 pages (just shy of one-half), Du Bois offers five detailed chapters on the nature of the successes and failures of Reconstruction in the various regions of the South and the Border. These are, in themselves, brilliant for their historical nuance. He analyzes the different times and fates of Reconstruction according to the social and economic differences of the states. The black majority in South Carolina suffered a different outcome from the black majorities in Mississippi and Louisiana than did the black minorities in the rest of the South and the Border States. These accounts are worth reading in themselves. They extend by fine detail the narrative of the first nine chapters. But they could have stood on their own—at least for those whose primary interest is the question with which I began. Why this book—and why then?

The problem in reading *Black Reconstruction* is not its length and heft, nor its varieties of parts, but its defiance of our usual ideals of History—hence of our orientations in time. The time of race is, as Du Bois thought, the time of truths that are never present, even though they, in their absence, are always there. It is possible that the most widely known line ever written by Du Bois is his remark at the beginning of *Souls*. "The problem of the twentieth century is the problem of the color line." The appeal of the figure of the color line rests on its defiance of progress. As years, or decades, in the century now over passed on their way, the color line remained as it was at century's start, giving the figure an ever growing force. As the century ended, the color line remained in fact, if not in form, as it was in 1903. The reason for this cannot be found in *Souls,* but it can be teased from *Black Reconstruction.*

Even at the dawn of the twenty-first century—when the industrial system has fallen away, when work itself is transformed, when labor is put more on the margins of economic life—the twisted logic of racial time remains. The passing over into a new millennium, the passing away of an older economic system, the passing into public view of new (including racial) assertions of what were once Weak-We peoples—these are the marks of the new time in which the question ought to be asked: Can the world be understood under the intoxicating sign of History's Progress? Or must we think of it, and live in it, under the sober sign of time that races by only to revert, reverse, and revise itself?

NOTES

1. Jacques Derrida, *"La Différence"*: *Théorie d'ensemble* (Paris: Éditions de Seuil/Collection Tel Quel, 1968); reprinted in *Marges de la Philosophie* (Paris: Éditions de Minuit, 1972), 6.

2. Hence, to say "Derrida is still alive" is to mean to say what truly cannot be said: that he is "present" in the current time. This, of course, is a foolish saying because the "being-present" to me of anyone, including Derrida (in whose presence I have never knowingly been, not once), is always at a distance. However thin or thick that distancing space is—whether passable in an instant or in the duration necessary to cross an ocean or more—the alleged presence of another is always, and necessarily, deferred. Hence, *différance.* It is impossible, thus, to speak of "being-present" without meaning to discuss the simultaneity of time's space. Even if "Derrida" is a fictional character, meant to be thought of as currently alive in the time of my reading about him, he cannot be, at any negotiable present, here with me. Hence, further, the irony that fictional characters stand a better, but still futile, chance of being-present. Even if a nonfictional Derrida were, at the moment, "here" in the sense of "in my vicinity," he would not likely be present to or with me. Imagine, if you will, that he were "here" in the sense of being in my vicinity, perhaps "at" my home. Were he, he would not be here, where I "am." I am in my study, writing. He might be elsewhere in my vicinity, perhaps chatting with my twenty-month-old daughter, who, at present, is in her room. They would have some important things to discuss. Both are exiles of a sort. Plus which, at her not-quite-verbal stage, Anna speaks somewhat in the loose manner

that Derrida would respect. She is capable of uttering open-ended phrases without verbs. "Dad-dy, I … uhn … up." This can mean any number of things. Its precise meaning is determined by accompanying gestures of various kinds (pointings, arm wavings, hand takings, and the like). She may mean, "I want to be up on your lap" (+ arm waving). Or, "I want to be upstairs listening to music" (+ hand taking). Or, "I want my tricycle to be up in the family room" (+ pointing). "Dad-dy, I … uhn … up." (Or, sometimes: "I … uhn … Dad-dy … up." Pronounced: "Aah. uhn. Daay-dee. up.") You see how the omission of variants of the verb "to be" reflects a late primary process suspicion of the fixedness of things in Being. She is putting an "X" through her "Is"-es. Anyhow, were Derrida "here," he might be chatting with Anna since I am writing at the moment. He would be "here" only in a loose, even metaphoric sense. But suppose a friend (say, Patricia Clough) were to call. I, speaking loosely, would likely say: "Patricia, you won't believe it, but Derrida is here." This would not be accurate since he would actually be only in the vicinity, not immediately here. Patricia might say, however, "If he is, let me speak to him." Since he is reputed to be a very obliging man, Derrida would surely come to the phone if told that Patricia wants to speak—that is, to "be"—with him. Still, she would have to wait some few minutes for him to come to the phone. (Anna does not readily allow people she likes to leave her presence.) When and if, in due time, Derrida came to my study to pick up the phone, he would still not be "present" to Patricia as they spoke. He would not even be literally present to me were he to hang up the phone and say, perhaps, *"Alors, Charles, comment-ça va?"* Even that question, which is intended to have the effect of putting the two of us in the same presence, does not achieve its purpose. No saying, no writing, no utterance can put us where we are meant to "be" when the intention is that of "being-present." Even in speech between two currently living face-to-face characters, there is always a pause, even when the respondent has a reply at the ready. I know. This is tedious. One must wait too long for its "meaning." But what are we to do, if we are to talk about that which can never truly be spoken about in so many words? We must, in short, put an X through words we are forced to use. (If not "must," then at least we "ought" in the loose ethical sense of the word.) We ought, that is, to speak as if we were writing. Writing (including, one supposes, Anna's context-bound gestures) is the only form of utterance in which we can see the X's, or the silent *"e"* in *différence*—or the deferrals across space of the desire to be present with all those others, close and remote, with whom we can never be present.

3. "Structure, Sign, and Play in the Discourse of the Human Sciences," in *Writing and Difference,* trans. Alan Bass (Chicago, IL: University of Chicago Press, 1978), 278–294, was originally a lecture delivered on October 21, 1966, at the International Colloquium on Critical Languages and the Sciences of Man at Johns Hopkins University in Baltimore. "Freud and the Scene of Writing," in *Writing and Difference,* 196–231, was originally a lecture at the Institut de Psychanalyse, Paris; whereafter it appeared first in France in *Tel Quel* 26 (1966). See also Derrida, *Speech and Phenomena,* trans. David Allison (1967; reprinted, Evanston, IL: Northwestern University Press, 1973). Also from these two years, *Of Grammatology,* trans. Gayatri Chakravorty Spivak (1967, reprinted, Baltimore, MD: Johns Hopkins University Press, 1974).

4. Derrida was not the only one to contemplate the odd, if different, juxtaposition of psychoanalysis. Foucault took a similar liberty in his concluding comments to *Les mots et les choses* (Paris: Éditions Gallimard, 1966).

5. See Christopher Norris, *Derrida* (Cambridge, MA: Harvard University Press, 1987), 11–17.

6. In a strange footnote of reality upon text, the principal architect of the New York Jets' football team defense, Bill Belichick, resigned on January 4, 2000, the day after his mentor Bill Parcells resigned as head coach in order, it seems, to give Belichick the head coach job. Parcells wanted, perhaps, to prevent Belichick from taking a job with another team whose owner tried, three years before, to prevent Parcells from leaving his team to coach the Jets. No one knows why Belichick resigned on his first day on the job. Some think it was so that he could get out from under the pressure of his mentor, Parcells. Others think it was to take the job Parcells had left with the other team. In any case, whatever it was, in fact, going on on that particular field of dreams was never, and never could be, completely present and can only be supposed—which, it turns out, is the principal purpose of sports talk radio in the United States.

7. With rare exceptions, writings on Du Bois refer narrowly to *Souls*. For example, Hazel Carby, *Race Men* (Cambridge, MA: Harvard University Press, 1998), 9–44; Paul Gilroy, *The Black Atlantic: Modernity and the Double Consciousness* (Cambridge, MA: Harvard University Press, 1993), 111–145. Even the sweeping commentary on Du Bois's politics by Adolph Reed, *W. E. B. Du Bois and American Political Thought* (New York: Oxford University Press, 1997), makes no reference to *Black Reconstruction*, while offering a detailed exposition of *Souls*.

8. I realize the extreme nature of this claim. Still, it bears consideration if only because Derrida's relation to Nietzsche turns importantly (if not exclusively) on the idea that the only positive science of social things is one that issues from a study of absences. Derrida's contribution to social thought thus turns on his discovery of a middle passage between Saussure and Freud that makes Nietzsche's sociology of morals thinkable as a social theory—that allows language to serve at once as the medium and object of social studies. Curiously, save for Gilles Deleuze and of course Michel Foucault, few others attempted anything like an explicitly sociological investigation. When they did, as in the famous case of Roland Barthes's early semiological researches, they took an aggressively structuralist line, making them vulnerable to the criticism Derrida directed at Lévi-Strauss. Even Foucault suffered an odd sort of structuralist lapse in works like *Les mots et les choses* (1966), which in a fashion broke the developing line from *Naissance de la clinque* (1963) to *Surveillir et punir* (1975). In any case, the test of the claim lies not in the avowal of a philosophical affinity (Foucault was famous for his disavowals), but in the disavowal of a positive metaphysics, which certainly is what Du Bois did.

9. Henry Adams was himself repulsed by what was present at the end of the nineteenth century, which did not keep him from writing about the new industrial order with respect to what it was bringing into history in relation to what it was destroying. See, especially, Adams, "The Dynamo and the Virgin," *The Education of Henry Adams* (1906/1918; reprinted, New York: Modern Library, 1931), 379–390. Adams's memoir was, in fact, a medium for his final, general social theory of history, which is stated explicitly in the book's concluding chapters.

10. W. E. B. Du Bois, *Black Reconstruction in America, 1860–1880* (1934; reprinted, New York: Atheneum, 1992), 713. On background to the writing of this book, see David Levering Lewis's "Introduction," Du Bois, *Black Reconstruction,* vii–xvii).

11. Ann Julia Cooper, letter of December 31, 1929, to Du Bois, in *The Voice of Anna Julia Cooper,* edited by Charles Lemert and Esme Bhan (Lanham, MD: Rowman and Littlefield, 1997), 336. Lewis, "Introduction," ix, reminds us that Cooper was one among many (notably, James Weldon Johnson) who urged Du Bois to respond.

12. On the 1909 AHA paper, see Lewis, "Introduction," vii.

13. For a summary of the Dunning position, see Eric Foner, *Reconstruction: America's Unfinished Revolution: 1863–1877* (New York: Harper and Row, 1988), xix–xx.

14. "Reconstruction and Its Benefits," in *Writings by W. E. B. Du Bois in Periodicals Edited by Others,* vol. 2, ed. Herbert Aptheker (Millwood, NY: Kraus-Thomson, 1982), 6–22.

15. Lewis, "Introduction," vii.

16. W. E. B. Du Bois, *Souls of Black Folk* (1903; reprinted, New York: Bantam Books, 1989), 10–29 (especially 28–29).

17. Discussed more thoroughly in "The Color Line: W. E. B. Du Bois, 1903," in Charles Lemert, *Dark Thoughts: Race and the Eclipse of Society* (New York: Routledge), 169–192.

18. Walter F. White (1893–1955) graduated from Atlanta University in 1916. Two years later he served as assistant to James Weldon Johnson, executive secretary of the NAACP. During the 1920s he published two novels and won a Guggenheim in 1926, which supported research for a major study of lynching. He succeeded Johnson in 1931.

19. "Segregation," *Crisis* 41 (January 1934), reprinted in *Writings in Periodicals Edited by W. E. B. Du Bois: Selections from* The Crisis, vol. 2, ed. Herbert Aptheker (Millwood, NY: Krauss-Thomson, 1983), 727. Compare the editorial written in the midst of the crisis with the board, "Segregation," ibid., 755.

20. Du Bois to Walter White, January 17, 1934, *The Correspondence of W. E B. Du Bois,* vol. 1, *Selections, 1877–1934,* ed. Herbert Aptheker (Amherst: University of Massachusetts Press, 1973),

475. For the following see also Du Bois to Board of Directors of the NAACP, May 21, 1934, and to the board, June 26, 1934, ibid., 478–480.

21. The reprise of the January "Segregation" editorial in the May issue of the *Crisis* refers specifically to his support of a government-funded but segregated housing project that would provide homes for 5,000 Negroes.

22. Facts following are from J. M. Roberts, *Twentieth Century: The History of the World, 1901–2000* (New York: Viking, 1999), 339–345; and Martin Gilbert, *A History of the Twentieth Century, 1900–1933,* vol. 1 (New York: William Morrow, 1997), 808–828.

23. References are to two of the greatest novels of the 1920s, F. Scott Fitzgerald's *The Great Gatsby* and Nella Larsen's *Passing.*

24. The book is twice as long as *Philadelphia Negro* (1899; reprinted, New York: Schocken, 1967), which, in spite of massive detail, was completed in half the time. The fourth of Du Bois's major scholarly works (as distinct from general histories, essays, collections, fictions, and memoirs) was the doctoral dissertation *The Suppression of the African Slave-Trade to the United States of America, 1638–1870* (1898; reprinted, New York: Russell and Russell, 1965), which was broader in temporal scope but narrower in historical focus (and, still, shorter by a factor of three).

25. E. J. Hobsbawm, *The Age of Capital, 1848–1875* (New York: Mentor Books, 1979), 27–47. See also Foner, *Reconstruction,* 512–563.

26. Foner, *Reconstruction,* 512.

27. David Roediger, *The Wages of Whiteness' Race and the Making of the American Working Class* (London: Verso, 1991); and Du Bois, *Black Reconstruction,* 700.

28. The connection is drawn with wonderful precision by Jeffrey Kerr-Ritchie, *Freedpeople in the Tobacco South: Virginia, 1860–1990* (Chapel Hill: University of North Carolina Press, 1999), 248.

29. *Black Reconstruction,* 16.

30. Ibid., 3.

31. Ibid., 351.

32. Ibid.

33. Ibid., 182.

34. Ibid., 377.

35. Ibid., 183.

36. On the slip, if not decline, of empire in the 1930s, see Eric Hobsbawm, *The Age Extremes: A History of the World, 1914–1991* (New York: Vintage, 1994), 194–222; compare Roberts, *Twentieth Century,* 271–338.

V

Ethics and Identity

10

Whose We?

Dark Thoughts
of the Universal Self, 1998

As the sun set on that odd millennium, the world was faced with dark thoughts long denied. Something particularly strange was happening. It was more and more difficult to tell who was who—or, more precisely, who belonged to whom. People were claiming rights and memberships, not to mention actual relations, with brash imagination. It was then that the old skin and blood game took on new meaning. Not even the most revered were exempt.

Late in 1998, DNA tests confirmed with reasonable "certainty" that Easton Hemings, the fifth child of Sally Hemings, was fathered by Thomas Jefferson. This kind of thing had long been rumored. As time passed, the Founding Father was best known in the popular imagination for three things: author of the Declaration of Independence, slaveholder, and father of a child or children by one of his slaves, Sally Hemings.[1] Plainly, two of the three were dark thoughts in more ways than one. The three together were darker still.

Why these thoughts were as dark as they were was never entirely clear.

Everyone supposed, or should have, that Thomas Jefferson had had sexual relations with Sally Hemings. For years people had heard tell of his leaving her early of a morning. Plus which, why would he be different from any other slave-holder? The darker thought was that the man of liberty was unable to get himself out of the slaveholding system, much less get the nation he declared and led out of it. This had been a habit of long standing among the freedom loving people of the West.[2]

Still, it shook the habit to know, for *certain,* that Jefferson really had fathered his country in more ways than one. The mental habit of denial was very strong until then. White people could look into the skins of African-American people, see the varieties of color, and ignore the only possible explanation. Yet, in the late years of the twentieth century, the denials were hard to maintain. Not only were there many more "facts" of the DNA kind, but many more people were willing to claim relations long denied.[3] Even in the absence of facts, the oral histories of the relations were enough for more and more people to play the skin and blood game in new and original ways. The differences were palpable.

Some words tell truths people don't want to admit. I don't mean big analytic words like "society," "self," "race," and the like. Words like these tend to tell lies of various kinds. The words I have in mind are both commonplace and simple. Because they are common, they are used regularly in public company. Because they are simple, they resist being twisted around into analytic meanings. Take for particular example words like "we."

As the twenty-first century was beginning, the word "we" suddenly became a troublemaker when used in public. Before the eclipse, one could say "we"—as in, "We the people, in order to establish a more perfect ... [whatever]"—and expect everyone to know exactly who was included in the "we" and who was not. In those days, if anyone thought about it, they seldom said so. After the eclipse, those who used "we" unthinkingly may have had to explain themselves. Someone was likely to jump out of her seat to object to a speaker's assumptions about who was included in his "we." This came to be known as the *Whose We?* problem. It was, and still is, much more than a semantic problem.

All first-person plural pronouns, and their variants, can be trouble under certain conditions. What made the *Whose We?* problem so interesting was that it arose with such suddenness. One day a person who had used "we" all his life would say some local version of "We the people" and one of the people in hearing range would ask *Whose We?* He might have only meant to say something like, "Well, shouldn't *we* have this meeting at breakfast? How 'bout seven tomorrow morning?" And she may have only meant, "Right, and *who's* going to get my kids to school?" Still whenever and wherever *Whose We?* is said, it has come to mean: "Wait one minute. What makes you think I share your experiences, assumptions, beliefs, and feelings?" It is not that those who ask this question don't have their own experiences, assumptions, beliefs, and feelings. They do. That is just their point. They mean to change the way people talk and think about them. They usually begin in the smallest of ways, even when they intend to change something big about their local worlds. One of the better effects of the *Whose We?* problem is that it brought a little sociology into common conversations.

Words are not neutral. They convey much more than their agreed upon semantic value. They are, like it or not, almost always sociological when they are used for public consumption. When words are used in public (as opposed to, say, in the bedroom), they have a fungible market value. Their meanings are being offered for sale or barter if the cost can be borne. When the consumers of public rhetoric, or even of plain ordinary talk in public, are uncertain of themselves (or made to feel that way) they may buy a word's meaning without complaint. When, under other social circumstances, they feel they can complain about the cost, they may not buy at all. Hence, "Whose We?"

Whenever a speaker uses the word "we" out-of-doors, he may be taking the risk of including those who do not want to be included, not to mention those who might want to be included but realize perfectly well that they are not wanted. Speakers should know better. But, until recently, many didn't. The consumers of their talk did, of course, because they were the ones who paid for it. There is, I think, no better illustration of the uneven distribution of sociological competence. Those who pay usually are the better sociologists of whatever value is being sold.

In point of fact, everyone ought to be, or potentially can be, competent to judge when they ought, or ought not, to use a word like "we." This is so because anyone who really pays attention to the prevailing social arrangements on their street will see for himself who belongs and who does not. Except for a few of the more notable secret societies like Sigma Chi or the KKK or the CIA, belonging is the most basic of practical sociological works. Belonging, and the right to belong, is where all "society," whether intimate or not, begins. Whenever and wherever there might be a social contract, its terms have to do with belonging, and not much else. Social contracts ought to be more social than they normally are.

Still, most people have a good bit of commonsense competence about belonging. Nearly everyone knows, almost by instinct, if he or she belongs at a party that may be forming in the neighborhood. You may decide to crash it, but at a risk. The reason there is always a risk in crashing social parties is that those throwing the party are almost always of one of two states of mind, neither of which disposes them kindly toward party crashers. Either, they are throwing the party precisely because they only want to associate with their kind. Or, they throw parties all the time and never stop to think about the invitation list. Of course, it is often the case that people with the second attitude are no more than naive instances of the first. But they who think in the first way are anything but naive. Still, they, in turn, fall into two subcategories. Either, they want to exclude people who, they fear, might want to crash their party. Or, they are sick and tired of not being invited and want to have parties of their own.

It might be said that one of the more devastatingly subtle effects of the eclipse just passed is that of breaking up many of the traditional parties. Ever since people started showing up at parties to which they were not invited it became much more difficult for everyone to figure out who were the included and who the excluded. *Whose We?* is the problem of not being certain which party to go to. Those who were, until then, accustomed to sending out the same old invitation list (and suffering, I might add, the same old characters showing up) are more likely to brood over the dark thought that their membership credentials are not in self-evident order. This is not a new brooding,

The only thing new about it today is that it is now done in public. This is because *Whose We?* is, by its very nature, always a public question. Just the same, even before people started asking it, the dark thought was there, lurking in some corner of the social mind.

Take, for example, the most famous sentence of the most famous American Creole[4] of the early European Diaspora, Thomas Jefferson, who wrote in June of

1776: "We hold these truths to be self-evident: that all men are created equal; that they are endowed by their creator with inherent and inalienable rights; that among these are life, liberty, & the pursuit of happiness: that to secure these rights, governments are instituted among men, deriving their just powers from the consent of the governed." Hardly anyone, anywhere, has not read or heard these words. They are among the most quoted, copied, and beloved words in modern culture. Yet, the careful reader of them, as they appear above, might notice an error. In the second line where one expects to find "certain inalienable rights" there appears, "inherent and inalienable rights." Actually, there is no error. These are the words as Jefferson wrote them. His revolutionary colleagues revised them, in less revolutionary ways. Jefferson himself felt so strongly about his words that he included them along with his autobiography written many years later.[5] In this case, his fellow revolutionaries weren't willing to go so far as to say that the inalienable rights of the people are also "inherent." Even for them, Jefferson's was too strong a We-statement. They preferred the indefinite form—"certain inalienable rights."

Whichever form they may take, since the eclipse, declarations of rights to belongings of various kinds are ever so much more carefully scrutinized than before. This is because they have become ever more complicated. For starters, when you live in a society, or social world, where *Whose We?* might be asked, you have to have an answer at the ready. Curiously, such an answer is no longer simple. Not that it ever was. The difference is that, most places, in the new millennium the answer necessarily involves a claim about one's "self" (as it is said) as well as about one's group affiliation. There is a reason for this. Claims about group membership today require some certification of one's personal right to make the claim.

When the group into which one claims membership is no longer assumed to be the nation immediately at hand—or some other such universally recognizable group (such as whichever social class prevails in the neighborhood)—those who claim the membership have to have their immigration papers in order. These papers are always very personal. When, for example, a member of a persecuted group flees his native "nation" for safety in, say, the United States, he may properly claim the right to stay in the host country if and only if he can certify that his group back home is in fact persecuted. As it turns out, one does not prove this sort of thing merely by documenting the group's political situation. One must also demonstrate that he actually belongs to that group and this proof *always* entails excruciating details of his personal life. That is to say, the right to enter a new group from a previous one is necessarily a test of having a proper *self*. Selves are always and only documented by facts of a very personal and painful nature. In the example, it may take years of waiting (perhaps in refugee camps) before it is determined whether one's self is in order. If it is, the person is allowed to remain in the United States, usually as a member of the official group known as "aliens." "Alien" is a more generous analytic tag than you might suppose. When affixed, it serves to identify, thus to hold, immigrant peoples safe from harm elsewhere as it holds others for work in the host country. Though, as a rule, neither status pays well, both are sought after, hence desirable.

What is true of political refugees and immigrant workers is usually true of any-one who claims a right to belong not previously taken for granted. One of the more interesting of these claims is one made by those who have every reason to assume they are proper members of a group, often a national group, but who, after years of bitter experience, know very well that rights self-evident to them are not self-evident to oth-ers. This, very probably, is why Thomas Jefferson's revolutionary colleagues got rid of the word "inherent." It is one thing to say that rights to belong are "self-evident" and "inalienable"; quite another to concede rights to those for whom they were "inherent" to begin with. To admit the clerical error of exclusion of those whose rights, it turns out, were also "self-evident" is to hold oneself up for trials of all kinds. In Jefferson's day, those who shared in his declaration of independence were, by and large, members of a relatively small, powerful class of men, all of them white. They were among the minority whose education and social standing would have been sufficient for them to use the expression "self-evident." You can see that the expression involves a prefix that would eventually become an important analytic category.

"Self" is one of those words that stands between little, but tricky, words like "we" and robust, but analytic, ones like Society. Still today, self is used as a common prefix or suffix, as when one says without regard to grammar, "I myself did it." This is said to be a reflexive expression pointing back to the one speaking. Eventually, about the time other big analytic terms were coming into their own, the reflexive self was broken off from common language and turned into the very large categorical thing. By the end of the nineteenth century, analytic social scientists were already talking about The Self, as in "Self and Society." In Jefferson's day, this practice was less common. The reason it was is that almost no one ever asked Whose We?

So when men said, "We hold these truths to be self-evident," they were, to be sure, speaking for "themselves." They were also speaking as a class of powerful men who already had the right to use words like "self-evident." Any We that uses such an expression without qualification, no matter how well intended, is arrogating to itself a certain degree of secret knowledge—declaring, thereby, truths the evidence of which is known, if not only, at least obviously, to themselves. Whenever anyone asserts the self-evidence of his or her truth, it is time to hold on to your pocketbook. There is fine print somewhere.

This may be why these men got rid of Jefferson's word "inherent," which then, as today, meant something like "natural or essential." It is one thing to say, "We assert our own self-evident rights to life, liberty, and the pursuit of happiness, and we won't let anyone take them away." It is another to concede that such rights are "inherent" in the sense of being an essential human right. People who are already claiming a relatively Gnostic principle of evidence may have very good reason to put a limit on the extent to which the rights they profess might be thought of as universal. They may like the idea, in principle, but have completely sound social reasons for holding back. Why else would they not want to give the evidence for the rights they were willing to declare? It is well known today that they did have a good reason to hedge their bets.

From the first, Americans overplayed their strong hand. Few national cul-tures make louder, more moralistic, Strong-We claims equating their local rights with those of all human society. American righteousness was trouble from the very beginning—as in the deletion of Jefferson's "inherent." But that was not the only revealing slip of the eraser. Jefferson's co-conspirators also deleted another telling passage he had left with them, one that might seem to have been as agreeable a complaint against the British throne as colonial rebels could make: "He has waged cruel war against human nature itself, violating its most sacred rights of life and liberty in the persons of a distant people who never offended him, captivating and carrying them into slavery in another hemisphere, or to incur miserable death in their transportation hither."[6] This passage was immediately deleted. But why? The line is delicately phrased as denunciations go. Is not Jefferson making reference to the enslavement of the colonial people? No, of course not. Had he been, then it would not have been necessary to drop the line to appease Georgia and South Carolina. Jefferson was being coy with his colleagues and his own situation. He had to have meant "slavery," not metaphorically, but in the definite sense. Yet, he phrases the passage as if to join the denunciation with the same inherent human rights he wanted in the first lines. Everyone knew exactly what he had in mind. How could they not have? The slave system was the most distinctive feature of the colonial economy, and the one that flew in the face of revolutionary righteousness.

This second deletion, like the first, was about much more than politics pure and simple. It concerned what Alexis de Tocqueville would later call "America's most formidable evil threatening its future." But the revolutionary generation did not need instruction from an alien. They knew. Later, Jefferson admitted that the slavery system was as much the responsibility of the colonists as of the British and that he was attempting to slip the abolitionist line past his Southern colleagues.[7] The American revolutionaries knew the limits of their righteous claims. They, like Jefferson, had interests and other inconveniences that kept their values in check. The Americans were, in this, no different from others of strong cultural position who seek to extend their rights to the whole of humanity. Since the giving of rights always carries with it membership costs, and benefits, rights are seldom given away incautiously. Hence, Jefferson's duplicity was America's, and that, *mutatis mutandis,* of all rights givers.

The extent of the dilemma of rights givers everywhere can be seen by comparing the American declaration with, for prime example, the grand charter of English rights. The Magna Carta of the early thirteenth century began, as you might expect, with a very long list of names. John, the king declaiming the rights, had very good reason to implicate all the others in church and court who were signing on to this charter of independence. So it begins, "John, by the grace of God, king of England, lord of Ireland, duke of Normandy and Aquitaine, and count of Anjou." Like today's refugees from El Salvador, John felt he too was required to give a personal history, hence to show that he was a *self* proper to the edict he was announcing. It turns out that in 1215, when the great charter was first given, King John was in fact at some risk of being, if not a refugee, at least a king without a land. He was not, himself, completely happy to be giving away these liberties (which, later, he renounced).

This is one reason (the other being the protocol of the day) that John's declaration of rights begins with a long list of those whom he consulted: clergy, experts, nobles, and the like. This list has the effect of saying what the Americans felt they did not have to say. John did not believe that the liberties were "self-evident." As a result, by the time the Magna Carta gets to "We have also granted to all freemen of our kingdom, for us and our heirs forever, all the underwritten liberties," everyone knows whose liberties are being granted. They were not bad liberties at all; anything but. Still, you see what is going on. This ancient declaration of rights, handed down by one who was only exceptionally exposed to the *Whose We?* problem, nonetheless gives more detail than needed about *Whose We* will have the rights.

It is a very long step in time to the French Declaration of the Rights of Man in 1789. The French had benefited not only from the English but even more so from the American declaration. As a result the French were willing to declare the rights of the French citizen "human rights." Even if, at the time, they were not self-evidently more freedom-loving than the Americans, the French declaration was much more clear on the crucial point. In Article VI, borrowing from Jean-Jacques Rousseau, for example, they said, "The law is an expression of the will of the community." This would seem to be a hedge against the universality of the rights to belong. But these were professed earlier, in Article IV, which said: "The exercise of the natural rights of every man has no *other* limits than those which are necessary to secure to every other man the free exercise of the same rights." This still does not go as far as the "inherent," or essential, rights Jefferson wanted to include. In any case, he was not in Philadelphia when his colleagues excised this and other of his words. He had already gone home to his Virginia plantation in the company of his personal slaves who were constantly at his side.[8] He was so disgusted by the deletions that he called attention to them in the years to come.

Any declaration of rights of belonging, and its benefits, is a tricky business. Those who declaim in the name of a We must be careful either to explain which We precisely (as did King John in 1215 at Runnymede) or, if they mean it, to say "everybody" as the French nearly did in 1789. The very worst thing is to be ambiguous, as the Americans were in 1776 after Jefferson left town. Self-evidence is never evident unless the selves declaiming it mean to include all those who are inherently "human" (which they did not). Alternatively, they may mean to follow King John's example and give the full and explicit list of those selves to whom the rights extended are being precisely restricted. Anything in between creates problems. The Americans, in particular, took a long time to solve them. It was not until the election of Andrew Jackson in 1828 that democrats definitively limited the rights that previously had been narrowly extended in republican fashion to America's ersatz patrician class. It took until 1863 for black slaves to be declared free, and another good century for those rights to become effective. It was not until 1920 that women, whatever their color, could vote. And, oddly, as the century ended there were people in California and Texas and other places who wanted to remove whole groups of immigrant workers from the membership roles that made them eligible for health and education benefits. This was the kind of problem that the French, among others, avoided in the first place by not meaning what they said. They never permitted more than a relatively few of their colonial subjects to become full members. The rest may be evicted at any time. This, I suppose, is much like Thanksgiving or New Year's suppers at various plantations or households. The help are invited for a meal, allowed to clean up, then sent on their way at dusk.

Still, what is most striking about people in comparable positions in present times is that they are so excessively disturbed when asked, *Whose We?* There are two reasons for this. First, the question identifies them as the problem at hand. Second, the problem others have with them is personal as well as political. *Whose We?* is two questions at once: Who the hell do you think you are? Who elected you to decide who belongs?

It might be said, therefore, that those who, as a class, bear the brunt of this rudeness are members of a loose analytic group that might be called the Strong-We. Their situation is, thus, homologous (but not analogous) to the situation of those who ask Whose We? The question that shocks the Strong-We arises in the same or similar circumstances from which it is asked by a Weaker-We. Same origins; different effects. The effect on the Strong-We is to threaten, without necessarily weakening, their social position. They shake because they know their position is no longer taken for granted—because, put otherwise, their Self-understanding is being called into question. Generally, but not always, the Strong-We, being strong, recoup their losses and hold the line. Like I say, none of this is ever simply a matter of semantics; nor, most pointedly, is it in the effects of the query on those who pose it.

Hence, the other side of the story. Those who demand *Whose We?* might be called—though deceptively so—the Weak-We. They are the ones whose strength lies in the anything-but-semantic weakness of their social circumstances. They may not always be actually weak at the time of asking the question, but they know weakness in the social, economic, and political senses. This is why they create trouble. Hence, again, the homology.

So far as anyone I know knows, the various social worlds on the planet have always been divided between those who were stronger and those weaker, socially speaking (where, for simplicity's sake, "socially" is meant to embrace all aspects of social life, including the political and the economic). How those divisions are imposed and enforced is subject to many variations. They are not always permanent. Give a "certain" unequal distribution of human rights and benefits four or five hundred years, and the arrangement is likely to change. Sometimes it may even turn topsy-turvy—though topsy-turvy reversals, like the one in 1848 in Europe, seldom last more than a few months. More often, the changes are readjustments in the inequalities at hand. Some, but not all, who were weak under the previous regime become stronger; and vice versa.

One of the remarkable things about the present situation, however, is that, though things are changing quite a lot, and some of the formerly weak are stronger than they had been, on the whole the weak are getting weaker; and the strong, while a bit shaken (and fewer in relative number), are getting stronger. With one exception: The weak are better organized than once they were; and they speak out.

Hence the Weak-We are those who today are more acutely aware of them*selves* in relation to the Strong-We. Their strength is in their history of social weakness, which allows them to demand Whose We? Which, in turn, has the effect of shaking the Strong-We.[9] This makes the latter more defiant, which may explain why the Weak-We, and those spoken for in Weak-We utterances, generally find themselves in a less equal social position. Like bears in the woods, the Strong-We are more dangerous when attacked. This is when they are most likely to piss on you, or worse.

There are numbers of many kinds that illustrate this peculiar arrangement of worldly things. One set of data has been circulating for years among the Weak-We. Believe it or not, just a minute ago I received a copy of these data from, not coincidentally, a Brazilian sociologist who currently lives in the United States without having given up his concern for the poor in his native country:[10]

> If the Earth's population were a village of 100 people, with all the current ratios as they are today, then that village would look like this:
>
> Asians: 57
> Europeans: 21
> Western Hemisphere: 14
> Africans: 8
>
> Women: 52
> Men: 48
>
> Nonwhite: 70
> White: 30
>
> Heterosexual: 89
> Homosexual: 11
>
> Number possessing 59% of the wealth: 6
> Those living in substandard housing: 80
> Those unable to read: 70
> Number starving: 50
> Number with college education: 1

Some Strong-We types may well dispute these numbers. But even if they are off in minor details, the picture is clear. Most people, by a long shot, are poor, illiterate, and starving. Most are not white. By contrast those able to read this page are, by a large number, likely to be white, wealthy, and members of the European Diaspora. Those not able to read this page are likely to be directly or indirectly related to people who are, or once were, poor, illiterate, nonwhite, starving, and born in the former (or current) colonies of the European Diaspora. This is the world of the Weak-We, or the world they represent, when they say, "Whose We?"

Numbers, like words, can lie. But these numbers are too big to lie too much. Plus which, whoever looks out on the world as it is is unlikely to be all that surprised by them. The numbers are shocking only because they are pretty much what one feared they might be. By the same token, this is why, also, Strong-We people are no longer very surprised when confronted by the Weak-We. This is why the Strong-We very often live in gated communities.

Though, as a rule, the Strong-We are not self-consciously cruel, it does turn out that they, or their agents, are known to have thrown up barriers of various kinds—fences around refugee camps, gated walls around clusters of fancy homes, and reinforced perimeters on borders with regions where there is an unusual number of Weak-We people.

As a result, the Weak-We very well understand borders, fences, gates, border guards, tunnels, guard dogs, surveillance towers, metal detectors, passports, lock-downs, unemployment lines, work-fare offices, green cards, detention slips—and all the other paraphernalia used in border maintenance. As often as not, the lives of today's Weak-We, like the lives of their ancestors, are organized around lines drawn in the sand between them and Strong-We people, who tend to have the bigger homes and the better lands.

Again, these are not semantic lines. But they do determine how people talk.

One of the themes repeated by the Weak-We is of the reversal of fortunes between them and the border guarding Strong-We. For example, a contemporary of Thomas Jefferson, the Seneca chief, Sagaoyeatha, in 1805, addressed some Christian missionaries: "Brother, our seats were once large and yours small. You have now become a great people, and we have scarcely a place left to spread our blankets."[11] Again and again, the Weak-We speak of reversals, including more complicated ones like that made famous by Sojourner Truth in 1851:

> I can't read, but I can hear. I have heard the Bible and have learned that Eve caused man to sin. Well, if woman upset the world, do give her a chance to set it right side up again.... Man, where is your part? But the women are coming up blessed be God and a few of the men are coming up with them. But man is in a tight place, the poor slave is on him, woman is coming on him, he is surely between a hawk and a buzzard.[12]

The Weak-We, in all times and places, are very often people descended from ancestors from whom rights were taken. They know the stories of the original conditions from which what was theirs was stolen. This is part of their power, when they can and do speak up.

When, today, the Weak-We ask their upsetting question, they do from their side of borders fixed in place, over many years, by the Strong-We:

> The world is not a safe place to live in. We shiver in separate cells in enclosed cities, shoulders hunched, barely keeping the panic below the surface of the skin, daily drinking shock along with our morning coffee, fearing the torches being set

to our buildings, the attacks in the streets. Shutting down. Woman does not feel
safe when her own culture and white culture are critical to her; when the males of
all races hunt her as prey.

Alienated from her mother culture, "alien" in the dominant culture, the
woman of color does not feel safe within the inner life of her Self. Petrified, she
can't respond, her face caught between *los intersticios,* the spaces between the different worlds she inhabits.[13]

This, many will recognize, is Gloria Anzaldúa. She speaks of herself as Chicana,
tejana, lesbian, and native to the dangerous economic and territorial borderland
between Mexico and the American Southwest.

One of the ways the Weak-We surprise the Strong-We is that they know who
they are and they recognize each other. When they are asked who they think they
are, the Weak-We have an answer. They very often are those who, as Anzaldúa says,
do "not feel safe within the inner life of her Self." They live, in a fashion, outside
themselves because, among other reasons, they know the stories of the border guards.
They, therefore, recognize others who are similarly on guard, and recognize them
even when they do not speak the same language.

Chicanos of the American Southwest have lived in the United States since they
were trapped by the diplomatic theft of the homelands of 100,000 of their Mexican
ancestors in the 1848 Treaty of Guadalupe Hidalgo.[14] Yet, they understand, needless
to say, the experience of Mexican and other Latino workers in the United States today
because they understand borders and their dangers. And, in turn, they understand
early immigrant workers—contemporaries of their great-great-grandparents—who
were the first waves of many Asian peoples to come to the United States to build the
land, the water system, the railroads. The early generations of Asian workers were
subjected to a growing body of race-based immigration law, which had the effect
of restricting rights in order to control and segregate these workers. Thus, though
strangers to each other, the Weak-We of many different histories recognize each other
in the marks of the legal and physical barriers imposed by the Strong-We.

Lisa Lowe gives one account of this odd fact of life that forms the kinship
between Asian workers in the nineteenth century and Latino workers in the early
twenty-first:

The state, and the law as its repressive apparatus, takes up the role of "resolving"
the contradictions of capitalism with political democracy. The historical racial
formation of Asian immigrants before [the 1965 change in immigration laws] has
mediated the attempt to resolve the imperatives of capital and the state around the
policing of the Asian. In the period since 1965, legal regulations on immigration
include Asians among a broad segment of racialized immigrants, while the policy
has refocused particularly on "alien" and "illegal" Mexican and Latino workers.
Asian Americans, with the history of being constituted as "aliens," have the collective memory to be critical of the notion of citizenship and the liberal democracy
it upholds; Asian American culture is the site of "remembering," in which the

recognition of Asian immigrant history in the present predicament of Mexican and Latino immigrants is possible.[15]

Anzaldua is a poet. Lowe is not. Anzaldua writes more directly out of her life in a Weak-We world. Lowe knows that world very well, but writes in and for the language of analytic peoples. Still, they know each other in more ways than one.

To speak of large membership groups as the Strong-We and the Weak-We is a loose analytic way of getting around the deadly effects of putting people in cells or otherwise on the other side of borders of various kinds. Analytic terms are not, as I say, evil in themselves. They are used, in the name of science, for good purposes. Sometimes they achieve a considerable good. The question is, do they do enough good to cover the damages?

Take this analytic term "Self" which, as I say, has a foot in both camps. As a mere reflexive, *self* allows people to speak emphatically for themselves, to make clear who is saying what, even to insist on the right to say or do whatever is at hand. But, as an analytic notion, *Self* does quite a lot of violence of another kind. The violence done by the *Whose We?* defiance is of another order from the violence done by cutting things up and off. Still, in the case of middling words like "self," the potential for damage in both can be found.

Even in its small reflexive sense, "self has always, from its beginnings in Gothic and Scandinavian, not to mention Old English, borne a potential for a very big idea," identity—as in the 1175 *Pater Noster: "He fondede god solf mid his wrenche."* When a god enjoys intimate society of any kind, he remains a god. It is in the nature of a god to be capable of being identical to himself, without respect for any analytic cut, including gender. Such a meaning was always in the background even, years later, in a later English translation (ca. 1400) of *The Rule of St. Benedict* (original Latin version, ca.[16] 525 CE). Here the subject was not so much a god, as a god's effects on his subject. Still, the identarian principle is at work: *"Oure awn self we sal deny, And folow oure lord god almyghty."* Still, even here, it is plain that self is midway between the common reflexive (formerly used by the gods) and the analytic thing it was soon to become.

Even, however, in the seventeenth century, when the modern analytic form first peeked out from behind the cover of common human ideas of identity, "Self" retained its ties to the past. In his *Treatise on Human Understanding* (1690), John Locke said, for very notable example: "Since consciousness always accompanies thinking, and 'tis that, that makes every one be, what he calls self." Self is that which makes us ourselves. You see the effects of René Descartes who is thought, by many, to be the very first to lay the groundwork for the modern idea of Self. It is said, also, that Jefferson's most important philosophical principles came from Locke's psychology.[17]

In 1690, near the end of the century in which Descartes got the analytic ball rolling, Locke used the term "self" consistently. He meant, clearly, to speak of *self* as a way of speaking about the "consciousness" that had been groping its way toward becoming *the* "inherent" and essential feature of the human. Any being capable of entering a social contract was, necessarily, a very delicate invention. He had to have been like a god (hence, possessed of a conscious self by which he knew himself to be himself). But, also, this human had to have been a being whose self-consciousness—his awareness of himself—transcended the stupidity of animals and other natural creatures who were (and are) considered incapable of identarian thought (which is to say, incapable of using the reflexive competently).

Hence, the foundational anxiety over the beastly savage in human "nature." There could be no finer proof of the tardiness of nineteenth century claims that the culture of the European Diaspora was a rebirth of ancient Greek culture. The English *self* that arose on the back of the Latinate *ipse* was, in a sense, homage to the original dread of a return of Roman impotence before the savages. Had Descartes and Locke and Kant, not to mention Jefferson, been working directly from the Greek, they might have come to a different conclusion about a whole variety of subjects—from self-evidence, to individual rights, to the human consciousness of self, to the moral space between the gods and the animals, to even the *ego* that was behind Descartes' *Cogito, ergo sum.*

Instead, the early modern philosophy of human thought, which came into its own in the seventeenth century out of a virtual Roman culture, served to define the terrain of the modernist utopia. By the nineteenth century that fictional social space came to be known as "history." But in the seventeenth century it was the far more psychological principle of self-consciousness. Without the self-conscious mind, able to think itself first and foremost, there could have been no principle of human action so elegant as Kant's categorical imperative. "Act only on a maxim by which you can will that it, at the same time, should become a general law."[18] This was, not surprisingly, 1785—just shy of a decade after the Americans invented practical history, just a few years before the French Revolution interrupted Kant's walk about town. Kant, famous for his regularity, was stopped in his tracks only one other time—after reading Rousseau's *Émile.* Hence, differences and disputes notwithstanding, the common will among the greatest thinkers of the English, American, French, and German Enlightenments. The Human was nothing less, and not much more, than the possibility of self-conscious action predicated upon self-consciousness itself. One can hardly act so as to anticipate the general will without first being capable of consciousness of self which must be the predicate in any reasonable maxim. If it is true that Jefferson preferred Locke's psychology to his politics this is further evidence of his shrewdness. In the beginning, everything was psychology. History requires moral action; which requires consciousness of the common will; which requires thinking; which requires consciousness of self. This is how such a middling word as "self" came to be, by the end of the nineteenth century, such a big analytic one.

Still, one might wonder what the modern world would have been had it been Greek, rather than Latin, that was read through the dark ages? The Greeks very probably would have solved this little problem differently. Instead of self they would have stumbled upon "psyche," the term that has been carried over into late modern culture by psychoanalysis (much as the Moors protected Aristotle during the dark ages). Among the Greeks, as among the Hebrews, "psyche" (as it came into the modern languages) referred to the life-giving "breath"; hence, "soul." Think how much less analytic moderns would have been had they taken their lead from the Greeks. It is one thing to transpose self-identity into the analytic Self. But quite another to cut up the very breath of human existence, the Soul.

As everyone knows, "soul" is susceptible to all manner of degradations when it is taken over by analytic preachers of all kinds. Still, we have the contradiction that the analytic science known as Psychology became, not the science of the Soul, but of the Self and its cognates. It is true that were psychologists to stop and think about what they are doing (which can be a tricky business for analytic peoples), they would say that theirs is a science of "mind," or "mental life," but they would rarely be caught dead making the transposition of "mind" into "soul" or "spirit."

In a rare instance of parsimony the OED does just that. *Psyche. The soul, or spirit, as distinguished from body; the mind.*[19] It is plain that so parsimonious a definition has been able to maintain its integrity over many years because the *psyche* refers to the breath of life itself. The word is fungible only outside the marketplace of identities. It is metaphoric without being indefinitely substitutable. It is, pardon the expression, a *surd*—a necessary but irrational root that allows no final explanation beyond itself. It is, in short, that which reminds humans of the finitude they see and encounter every day in their differences with others who, against reason, are not exactly identical to themselves. This of course would not do when what one has in mind is modernity.

To speak of the human soul, or psyche, is therefore to resist, if not to block, the identarian impulse. The urge to replace the power of the gods with the power of the Self is a mighty one. Still, it would be a wonderful exercise in virtual history, to imagine what might have been had the late modern West imagined itself as that which was driven by a Soul, not a Self. Except when taken over for the purposes of fund-raising under the fear of condemnation to hell, the principle of Soul has to do more with that which simply is—and is without need of being identical to itself. To speak of a "soul mate," or a "soul brother or sister," is not to speak of one exactly the same as oneself. It is to speak of one who breathes the same air.

A soul, thus, is always something Other. It is that which is basic to life itself precisely because it comes from an Other not the same as oneself. This is why, it turns out, the old skin and blood game turns on an essential ignorance of the principle of Soul. In the strict sense, blood is that which carries the oxygenated breath of life to the various organs (including the skin) by which life, and action, are carried forth. To ignore this fact of life is to head down the path of modern analytic thinking.

To define history as the action of human selves self-consciously pursuing themselves is to set oneself up for analytic trouble. By contrast, had the moderns the courage to steal soul from the preachers of analytic doom, a lot of suffering might have been prevented. To have thus defined "history" as the course of life among breathing beings grateful for the spirit they cannot explain might have led to a little less cutting up. In principle at least, it would have settled the human down into more cooperative relations with all other living beings who, by a variety of means, are grateful for the clean air and light they exchange for energy. This, we now understand, was a virtual impossibility because, already by the seventeenth century (and decidedly by the nineteenth century), the analytic course of human thinking in the West turned on the dark thought of savages. Modernity, it might be said, is the fear of returning too innocently to life among the savage beasts. Hence, the self-preoccupation of so-called modern thought.

Descartes was thus the first to give eloquent expression to the moral principle that it is better for like kind to keep to themselves, even if it means throwing a line or two around the camp. *Cogito, ergo sum* was, in effect, the first analytic line of this kind. The Self is that which thinks itself in order to ward off the dark return of the savage Goths. This is why there is so little soul in so much of modern thought. It could not help itself. It was not possible, given the foundational dark thoughts, to think too precisely about the breath that enlivens the blood which courses alike among many beings.

The psyche, thus, is that sort of *mind* that is always, to some degree, other than itself. The psyche is the soul of differences. This is why it is possible to describe Freud and psychoanalysis as the Moors of modern thought. Until the eclipse darkened the Enlightenment sky, it was psychoanalysis, more than any literature other than literature itself, that preserved the dark thought as a necessary feature of human thinking. Though any number of poets and fiction makers did this in their way, Freud was the only one of the great end-of-the-nineteenth-century social thinkers to counter the analytic urge by an insistence on the impossibility of Self. Thus, for him, even in the earliest, most mechanical and structural of his phases, instead of the Self there stood, simply, the "I" or "ego." This Freudian "I" was, curiously, never an analytic thing, but always a breathing part of the soul by which the mind engaged in its never-ending struggle with the all-too-rational demands of the superego and the all-too-savage drives of the id. It is true of course that Freud himself, and most of his followers, failed to complete the Copernican revolution of removing the Self from the center of human life.[20] Freud himself had more than a few analytic moments between the early hydraulic theory of the psyche and the psyche's eventual resolution into drive theory. Still, from the first great work issued just weeks before the end of the last century, Freud allowed for the possibility of mental life as the work of a soul, not of a self.

In *The Interpretation of Dreams* (1899), Freud, a devoted reader of Sophocles and the Greeks, mapped the terrain of the Unconscious in mental life. Dreams are the ubiquitous language of this *terra incognita*. They are also, in the book's memorable opening line, "a psychical structure which has a meaning and which can be inserted at an assignable point in the mental activities of waking life." Dreams are always with us. They are the representations of that Other-within, which is always other-than-self (so to speak), yet assignably necessary to it. There is no consciousness without the Unconscious. In the central structure of mental life there are no identities. The self is not itself. In the place of the organizing Self of modern thought, psychoanalysis put the psyche—the *soul* that is always up against its necessary limits. This does not mean that psychoanalysis has been immune to the analytic impulse, some of it quite dreadful—as in Freud's own early cutting up of the sexualities based on what today we understand to have been a hasty reading of Sophocles. Still, like many of the social thinkers at the end of the last century, Freud and the movement he started resisted the analytic urge even as they were giving in to it. In Freud's case the resistance was never resolved. He thus was the Moor of modern thought who saved the Greek soul in the displacements of the psyche.

About the same time, another founder of twentieth-century psychology worked the same terrain as Freud's. William James, however, worked it from the opposite border. His *Principles* of *Psychology* (1890) was one of academic psychology's early and enduring analytic textbooks. "Psychology is the Science of Mental Life."[21] This is James's first line, different in every important respect from Freud's opening words, just a decade later. James was on an analytic course. This required that he deal with the Soul. He wasted no time. In the same, first paragraph of the book, James dismisses the spiritualist idea of the personal *Soul* as the original source of the phenomena of psychology. Still, James did not go so far as to say there is no soul; only that it cannot be the foundation of psychological knowledge. When, later, James writes of cognition, he says that "the relation of knowing is the most mysterious thing in the world."[22] His fascination with religion in *Varieties* of *Religious Experience* reveals the full extent of his awareness of the limits of knowledge. For Freud, the Other was the Unconscious; for James, it was religion.

Yet, at the heart of his science of mind lay the Self wherein James reveals his own unwitting alliance with the Strong-We:

> The Empirical Self of each of us is all that he is tempted to call by the name of me.... We feel and act about certain things that are ours very much as we feel and act about ourselves. Our fame, our children, the work of our hands, may be as dear to us as our bodies are, arouse the same feelings and the same acts of reprisal if attacked. And our bodies themselves, are they simply ours, or are they us?[23]

There could hardly be a more gracious illustration of the struggles the better Strong-We put themselves through. James is speaking here of the old, old mind-body dilemma. Consciousness of Self is basic to mind. When that which is ours is called into question is it merely because we possess it, or because it is our Self itself? Is it that we are what is ours? Or that what is ours is us? You see the difficulty inherent to the idea of Self. In the same paragraph, James makes more trouble for himself: *"In its widest possible sense, however, a man's Self is the sum of all that he CAN call his,* not only his body and his psychic powers, but his clothes and his house, his wife and children, his ancestors and friends, his reputation and works, his lands and horse, and yacht and bank-account." You can hear the chorus, *Whose We?*

Thus began what is commonly known in the analytic world as Self-theory. And thus it began on the Strong-We assumption. Here, full-blown, is the universal self—the very Self who owns and works and thrives. He rides horses as did Jefferson till the last months of his life. But then there is the word James himself emphasized: "A man's self is all that he CAN call his own." No respecter of mysteries could possibly deny that ownership is always trouble, especially when what is owned is land and yachts and the like.

It is all too easy to sneer. James tried to think otherwise. In the section immediately following this very gentlemanly definition of the universal self, James attempted to enumerate the constituents of Self itself. Among the more interesting of these are the still provocative pair—the social self and what James called the spiritual Self. The former gave rise to the unforgettable expression, "A man has as many social selves as there are individuals who recognize him." These others are the others within. But they were ultimately, if uncertainly, reconciled. Against the social stood what he called the "Self of selves," which he labeled the spiritual Self. Then, quite outside his analytic cutting apart of the Self, James writes of "the sense of personal identity." Hence the other of the memorable lines from this section. "Am I the same self today as I was yesterday?"[24] This is the existential question of anyone who dares reflect on herself amid the societies to which she belongs, or from which he is excluded. It is, obviously, a very difficult question when asked analytically—when asked, that is, from within the terms of a Strong-We Self.

The reason not to be overly harsh with many of the early Strong-We social theorists is that they very often knew, as did James, that something is wrong in the analytic scheme. He could not put his finger on what was wrong. But he could, and did, acknowledge the difficulty. In *Varieties of Religious Experience,* he returned to the uncertainty at the heart of self theory in a chapter on the "Divided Self" where he described a man's interior life "as a battle-ground for what he feels to be two deadly hostile selves, one actual, the other ideal."[25] James's idea of the divided self was surely a, if not the, major source of W. E. B. Du Bois's double consciousness of the American Negro. Du Bois—one of the most distinguished of Weak-We social theorists—was James's student at Harvard, and long-time friend afterward. Just as James, on his side, suffered the division between analytic certainty and reality, so Du Bois, who knew Weak-We realities very well, for a long while felt that the solutions lay in the Strong-We culture of the European Diaspora. The divide between the Strong and the Weak-We can be harsh, and usually is; but not always.

Still, it was with James, as much as anyone else, that "Self" crossed over from its past as a reflexive to take up its place in the analytic narrative. How is it possible for the human Self, with all its competing social pressures, to be the same today as it was yesterday? All along the way of this distinguished tradition, thinkers attempted to account for what James called the problem of personal identity in complex societies. None was able to outrun the analytical force of the concept itself.

Even so supple a formulation as George Herbert Mead's suffers the limitations of the analytic urge. "The self has the characteristic that it is an object to itself and that characteristic distinguishes it from other objects and from the body."[26] This may be Mead's most parsimonious summary of his idea of the Self. Yet, for all its freshness, it groans under the weight of the ages. Consciousness of self is, necessarily, the inherent human quality. It is that which locates the analytic Self between the world of inert objects and the body's animal passions. Mead's advance over the seventeenth-century psychologists, though considerable in the particulars, is superficial in the basics. The Self remains the organizing center of human variety, the presupposition of moral agency, the axis of cognition, the drive of history. For the several centuries of its coming out, the analytic Self was, always, the de facto Self of the Strong-We. It was the foundational principle of Universal Humanity. As such, it was always vulnerable to the reality of social differences. Its vulnerability lay in its ambition—in its self-claim to be the successor to the human Soul, in its willingness to serve as the zero signifier of all humanity. All that it took was for some wise guy to say *Whose We?* The self-evidence of the Self began to shake.

All Strong-We claims are ultimately moral; hence, political. Strong claims of this sort are, in fact, usually made quietly, as though the truth of them was perfectly self-evident. They are, even, made in silence. Thus, when someone breaks the code of silence, as Erving Goffman did in 1963, the reaction may be no more than a nervous twitter:

> Even where widely attained norms are involved, their multiplicity has the effect of disqualifying many persons. For example, in an important sense there is only one completely unblushing male in America: a young, married, white, urban, northern, heterosexual Protestant father of college education, fully employed, of good complexion, weight and height, and recent record in sports. Every American male tends to look out on the world from this perspective, constituting one sense in which one can speak of a common value system in America.[27]

The silence here broken is that covering the ludicrously over-strong idea that any complex society like the American one, even when it focuses its power on some global purpose, could possibly enjoy anything like a "common value system." It is one thing to believe, even to know, that people in a Society share basic orientations to the grind of daily life. This is not hard to swallow. It would be hard to account for the grind otherwise. But, it is quite another thing to believe—as numerous politicians, preachers, social scientists, and other analytic types have from time to time—that it is possible for a society to enjoy a "common value system" in the sense of that which holds the Whole together. The difference is in the strength of the assertion. The stronger it is, the more moralizing is required to protect it. One might even say that faith in the Universal Self is the last analytic resort before the truth is out.

Still, the idea was defended in the years that followed. Some of the defenses are empty and foolish. One in particular is compelling. In *Sources of the Self* (1989), Charles Taylor composes the history of the Self. He plainly diagnoses the vulnerability of the disengaged subject that stood behind both Descartes' and Locke's self-psychologies. He means to demonstrate the limits of the overly elegant punctual self by exposing its ludicrous doctrine that "we become constructors of our own character."[28] Taylor, in effect, understands the extent to which the Strong-We rely entirely on the myth of the pure subject, disengaged from moral space. His goal is to reconstruct a strong concept of Self on a sociological foundation. He begins:

> I want to defend the strong thesis that doing without frameworks is utterly impossible for us; otherwise put, that the horizons within which we live our lives and which make sense of them have to include these strong qualitative discriminations.

Moreover, this is not meant just as a contingently true psychological fact about human beings which could perhaps turn out one day not to hold for some exceptional individual or new type, some superman of disengaged objectification. Rather, the claim is that living within such strongly qualified horizons is constitutive of human agency, that stepping outside these limits would be tantamount to stepping outside what we would recognize as integral, that is, undamaged human personhood.[29]

Here is a Strong-We statement with a difference. Taylor's "undamaged human personhood" is not lodged in universal properties of cognition, being, or practice. Rather, the Self is defined in relation to moral orientations that, in turn, are unavoidably social:

My self-definition is understood as an answer to the question Who I am. And this question finds its original sense in the interchange of speakers. I define who I am by defining where I speak from, in the family tree, in social space, in the geography of social statuses and functions, in my intimate relations to the ones I love, and also crucially in the space of moral and spiritual orientation within which my most important defining relations are lived out.[30]

Self-definition, thus, is the narrative product of a pilgrimage within moral frameworks for the sense of the good in relations with others. Taylor uses the engaged but still Strong We. "Because we cannot but orient ourselves to the good, and thus determine our place relative to it and hence determine the direction of our lives, we must inescapably understand our lives in narrative form, as a 'quest.'"[31]

The moral quest with others revives the Self as narrative. This is the bold leap beyond the disengaged Universal Self. Even so, Taylor cannot escape its gravity. What he must do to complete the idea is to speak of the concrete human differences against which any such quest must move. Taylor's position remains a Strong-We one because he assumes a social space and a geography of statuses that are wholly friendly to the questing Self. These are the social conditions, and the only social conditions, in which one could expect to find the "undamaged human personhood" for which the Self strives. Taylor moves well beyond even James. His social self is not a receptor of recognitions so much as a social force joined necessarily in framework with others.

Taylor requires a world relatively immune to the damaging force of social differences, which are not, in the end, polite questions of identity differences. Social differences, in the current situation, are about inequalities of such potency as to have the reality of death. Even Craig Calhoun, one of Taylor's most robust advocates, withdraws on this point. "The relationship of social change to change in persons and moral frameworks remains largely an enigma."[32] Calhoun then lists the changes in world order Taylor fails to address: "The introduction of democratic politics, the rise of state bureaucracies, the shrinking size of the family, the transformation in numbers of people working away from their homes and/or among relative strangers, the growth of cities, the increased ease of travel, the conquest and loss of empires, and globalization of the economy, the change in living standards, the increase in capacity to kill in war, and so on."[33] Calhoun is right. Had Taylor not intended to lodge the modern, moral Self in concrete social life, he would not have had to account for the concreteness. He did. So he must. But he does not.

The bind Taylor put himself in is nothing more than the bind of the best Strong-We thinking. It is not enough to uncover the social nature of the Self; nor to embed it in a narrative quest with others. It turns out that these others with whom we are expected to quest can be extremely difficult—even when they are on our side (and most of them are not). This is the understanding that is second nature to the Weak-We.

When even so critical a modern liberal as Taylor fails to recompose the soul of the Western Self, it is clear that there is little good that can be done from within. The Strong-We cannot be other than it has been becoming through the centuries since at least Descartes, perhaps even Martin Luther, possibly Augustine. Strong-We is as Strong-We is. Its power always comes up against that which it cannot get around. The ideal of the strong Self as a universal property of human Being is simply not able to entertain the possibility of differences.

If there is any fact of world life it is that there are gross differences among the various membership groups of humans. These are differences too obvious to list. They arise from social arbitraries to be sure. The play among them is always uncertain. Is race really class? Is gender really sexuality? Or, again, class? Is class global or local?—and how does it play upon sex, skin, and gender? And so on. It is one thing to discover that many of these are social constructs—that there is nothing natural about the differences assigned to skin or blood; that the desire of others, like the desire for lucre, is plastic as much as it is given; that we are driven as much to destroy as to build; and so on. Social constructions are real. But in what sense? From whence do they come? Are they mankind's original nature?—or its original sin? After all these years, no one can even begin to answer.

When one day someone does, she will have to begin outside the culture of the Strong-We. For, if it is assumed from the start that social differences are either the accidents of failed progress or the necessities of nature, it is impossible to give those differences their due. Neither the left-liberal nor the right-conservative—the one affirming a vague progress, the other defending a just as vague naturalism—will ever convince the other. This is why both suffer the contempt of the Weak-We in roughly equal measure.

In the end, the question the varieties of liberal modernism—those of the right and the left—can never answer is the question they, together, pose. How is it possible to dream of the future while remaining true to the real present? Without the dream, the present is unbearable. Without present realities, the dream is a fantasy. The future of the present is—and always has been—the riddle of modern culture. This is where its left hand, bent back where it cannot see, touches ever so gently its right hand. This is where Marx meets the political economists he could never shake off.

Among the Weak-We this riddle is familiar. More than familiar, it is the most apparent necessity of their self-understanding. It is the social space of their souls. The

Weak-We understand what, very probably, can never be truly understood by those who assume the upper hand. They understand, as Patricia Hill Collins puts it, "the necessity of linking caring, theoretical vision with informed, practical struggle."[34] Put this way, one sees the wisdom, but still may ask, Is not this no more than the familiar analytic question of the dialectic between theory and practice? In a sense it is. But the sense in which it is not lies in where the answer is sought. It is sought not in the analytic remove of technical elaborations that refine and comprise the theoretical vision to the empirical necessities of the practice. The analytic remove always, and necessarily, destroys the dialectic. This is its first cut—that by which Strong-We thinking is all too ready to squeeze the blood to fit the skin.

If the Strong-We were willing to look closely, they would see that just before the squeeze, the Weak-We stop, to make another move. They do it often, regularly. This move is always disturbing, upsetting, annoying, insistent. It is rude in its fashion. It is the move of story telling, as in Collins's prelude to her discussion of visionary pragmatism:

> As a child growing up in an African-American, working-class Philadelphia neighborhood, I wondered how my mother and all the other women on our block kept going. Early each workday they rode long distances on public transportation to jobs that left them unfulfilled, overworked, and underpaid. Periodically they complained, but more often they counseled practicality and patience. Stressing the importance of a good education as the route to a better life, they recognized that even if Black girls married, big houses, maids, and blended family bliss as idealized on the popular television show *The Brady Bunch* were not guaranteed for us. Their solution: we, their daughters, were to become self-reliant and independent.[35]

Then, she says, "The Black women on my block possessed a 'visionary pragmatism' that emphasized the necessity of linking caring, theoretical vision with informed, practical struggle." Collins then cites other black feminist women. But the citations, if one looks closely, are not the analytic move one might suppose; everything Collins writes, even when she is writing to address the analytic terms of her disciplines, is always written in relation of the Weak-We others who know what she means.[36] At times, it is true, Weak-We academics like Patricia Hill Collins and Lisa Lowe, even Judith Butler, among others, write as though they were content with the analytic words of their professional fields. But, even when they are making careful, patient, practical moves against those fields, they begin with stories meant to affirm their ties—their Weak-We ties—to mothers, and to the other mothers, and others still. As I say, stories of this kind are disturbing to the analytically strong. They violate the methodological rules. They are so very local, particular, variable—hence, unscientific.

The Weak-We are annoying, insistent, unrelenting because they are the better sociologists of the particulars. They begin with the experience of damaged personhood—if not their own, at least, that of those they know, or love, or heard tell of. They know very well that, whatever is common among human beings, there is a certain power to be had in recognizing the plain facts of life. Their weakness, so to speak, is weak against the claims of those who insist on a universal Self, of whichever kind. The Weak-We assert their differences not to psychologize but to define moral and political frameworks just as Taylor would like. Their strength lies in the stronger grasp of societal relations—of the important bonds to which one must cling in a dangerous world. They, thus, remind the Strong-We of their limits, of the trouble at the heart of the analytic world, of the insufficiency of gentle sociologies of the moral quest. Their *Whose We?* is the darkest possible thought the Strong-We could imagine.

NOTES

1. Joseph Ellis, "A Note on the Sally Hemings Scandal," *American Sphinx: The Character of Thomas Jefferson* (New York: Knopf, 1997), 303–307. The facts about and interpretations of Jefferson in this section are based on Ellis, *American Sphinx*. It should be said, however, that Ellis, probably the most astute interpreter of the American founding fathers, takes a dark view of Jefferson, darker than of the others, like Adams, Madison, and Monroe, even of Hamilton. See, more recently, Ellis, *The Founding Brothers: The Revolutionary Generation* (New York: Knopf, 2000).

2. One of the most striking events in the first months of the new century is that so shortly after Jefferson's blood was found under the skin of other than white children, there began a major revision in the pantheon of founding fathers. Both Ellis's *Founding Brothers* and David McCullough's *John Adams* (New York: Simon and Schuster, 2001) were atop the best-seller lists through 2001.

3. Among the many stories of people coming upon racial surprises and crossings over, see Shirlee Taylor Haizlip, *The Sweeter the Juice: A Family Memoir in Black and White* (New York: Simon and Schuster, 1994) and James McBride, *The Color of Water* (New York: Riverhead, 1996). For an account of one white man's attempt to travel on the other side of the color line, see Walt Harrington, *Crossings: A White Man's Journey into Black America* (New York: HarperCollins, 1992). On the biracial life, see Use Funderburg, *Black, White, Other* (New York: William Morrow, 1994). And for a brilliant discussion of the whiteness of famous blacks (Frederick Douglass, Ralph Ellison, Bob Marley), see Gregory Stephens, *On Racial Frontiers* (New York: Cambridge University Press, 1999).

4. Though originally "Creole" referred to blacks born in the New World, it soon took on the meaning of all those, whether of African or European descent, born in a New World or other colony. As in many other things, the best discussion is Benedict Anderson's "Creole Pioneers," *Imagined Communities* (London: Verso, 1983).

5. *Jefferson/Autobiography/Notes on the State of Virginia/Public and Private Papers, Addresses/Letters* (New York: Library of America, 1984), 1–102. The autobiography was written in 1790.

6. Ibid., 22.

7. Gary Wills, *Inventing America Jefferson's Declaration of Independence* (New York: Doubleday, 1978), 66–68.

8. Ellis, *American Sphinx*, chap. 1.

9. Among other important sources, see Alberto Melucci, *Challenging Codes* (New York: Cambridge University Press, 1996), on the importance of the marginal in the new social movements.

10. H. B. Cavalcanti of the University of Richmond in Virginia transmitted the data following on November 18, 1999. His version is attributed to Phillip M. Harter of Stanford University. I have previously seen copies of the same numbers distributed by the Commission on Racial Justice of the United Church of Christ (U.S.).

11. Chief Red Jacket, "We Also Have Religion," in *Our Nation's Archive*, ed. Erik Bruun and Jay Crosby (New York: Black Dog/Leventhal, 1999), 208. One of the more remarkable reversals found among the Weak-We is their sense of the reversals of space and loss brought on by the Strong-We

colonizers. Another notable example is the telling line in a speech given by a Stockbridge Indian before a congress of whites in 1775: "I was great and you were little" (ibid., 123).

12. *Narrative of Sojourner Truth,* ed. Margaret Washington (New York: Random House, 1993), 118. These are the concluding words of Sojourner Truth's famous 1851 "Ain't I a Woman?" speech, which is the subject of considerable controversy. For the history of the conditions and distortions of this famous speech, see Nell Irwin Painter, *Sojourner Truth: A Life, a Symbol* (New York: Norton, 1996). And for an insightful discussion, see Donna Haraway, "Ecce Homo, Ain't (Ar'n't) I a Woman, and Inappropriate/d Others: The Human in a Post-humanist Landscape," in *Feminists Theorize the Political,* ed. Judith Butler and Joan W. Scott (New York: Routledge, 1992), 86–100.

13. Gloria Anzaldúa, *Borderlands/La Frontera: The New Mestiza* (San Francisco: Spinsters/Aunt Lute Press, 1987), 20.

14. See Gloria Anzaldúa, "The Homeland, Aztlan" in *Borderlands,* chap. 1, for her history of the borderland.

15. Lisa Lowe, *Immigrant Acts: On Asian American Cultural Politics* (Durham, NC: Duke University Press, 1998), 21.

16. A sociological bonus of Benedict's *Rule* is that, though his birth and death dates are established, the exact authorship of the *Rule* can only be estimated. The principal biographical source on Benedict is Gregory I the Great (540–604), who as pope the last fourteen years of his life can be credited with recognition of the revolutionary sociology of Benedict, who was admired by Gregory more for the monastic movement that followed the *Rule* than for the text itself.

17. Also, according to Ellis, *American Sphinx,* 56–59, Jefferson seems to have read Locke's psychology more closely than his politics.

18. Immanuel Kant, *Metaphysical Foundations of Morals,* from *The Philosophy of Kant* (New York: Modern Library/Random House, 1993), 187.

19. For whatever it may be worth, the OED entry for "psyche" prints out to a mere four pages, while that for "self" is twenty-four.

20. Jean Laplanche, "The Unfinished Copernican Revolution," *Essays on Otherness* (New York: Routledge, 1999), chap. 1.

21. William James, *Principles of Psychology* (1890; reprinted, Cambridge, MA: Harvard University Press, 1981), 15.

22. Ibid., 212.

23. Ibid., 279. All quotes immediately following, ibid., 279–288.

24. Ibid., 316.

25. William James, *Varieties of Religious Experience* (1902; reprinted, New York: Fontana Library, 1960), 176.

26. George Herbert Mead, *Mind, Self, and Society* (1934; reprinted, Chicago, IL: University of Chicago Press, 1962), 136.

27. Erving Goffman, *Stigma: Notes on the Management of a Spoiled Identity* (New York: Simon and Schuster, 1963), 128.

28. Ibid., 123.

29. Charles Taylor, *Sources of the Self: The Making of Modern Identity* (Cambridge, MA: Harvard University Press, 1989), 197; see chaps. 10 and 11 especially on Descartes and Locke.

30. Ibid., 27.

31. Ibid., 35.

32. Ibid., 51–52.

33. Craig Calhoun, "Morality, Identity, and Historical Explanation: Charles Taylor on the Sources of the Self," *Sociological Theory* 10, no. 2 (1991): 260. Quote below same page.

34. Patricia Hill Collins, *Fighting Words: Black Women and the Search for Justice* (Minneapolis: University of Minnesota Press, 1998), 188.

35. Ibid., 187.

36. For an exposé of the way in which analytic social scientists use citations and other formalities to keep the secrets of their guild, see Ben Agger, *Public Sociology* (Lanham, MD: Rowman and Littlefield, 2000).

11
Can Worlds Be Changed?
ETHICS AND THE MULTICULTURAL DREAM

The philosophers have only interpreted the world, in various ways; the point, however, is to change it.

—Karl Marx (1845)

One can hardly avoid the talk of ethics today—the ethical turn in social theory, the new morality of foreign policy, the ethics of a global environment, biomedical ethics, the clash of civilizational values, etc.[1] Yet the early years of the new millennium are a very strange moment for such talk. Strange, that is, because, if anything is true of the end of the world, as we knew it (Wallerstein, 1999),[2] it is that the social conditions on which ethics are usually based have all but disappeared. At the least, global social arrangements are reconfigured in ways that call into question the empirical grounds upon which ethics have traditionally been founded. In brief, if, as it is often said, ethics is the art of thinking through which *ought* applies to a given *is,* then ethics is always, implicitly or explicitly, *social* ethics—a variant, thus, of social theory.

An ethic must, thereby, arise from a social setting wherein the empirical *is* requires a normative *ought.* For the most part, even the more universalizing of ethical doctrines (natural law theories, for example) arose from a social circumstance in which there was reason (not necessarily a good one) to assume that there could be social consensus as to the universal (or even merely general) norm. All this goes by the boards when the multicultural is taken as a proper descriptor for the empirical *is* of global realities. The multicultural, by whatever name, necessarily undercuts the very possibility of a social consensus as to the values meant to guide practical judgments about the best (if not good or right) actions required for social order (if not social progress or social propriety).

To make matters worse, if ethics is a variant of empirical social theory, then social ethics are in principle, if not in practice, political. Hence: if, as Marx said, the idea is to change the world, the dream of the multicultural presents even more problems than may meet the abstract eye. First, to speak of the multicultural as the "is" of an actually existing global reality is to speak of *worlds,* not world—to speak, that is, in an empirical plural where the variance outruns the modal means. Second, to speak of changing these worlds, as Marx did in reference to a purportedly single world, is to speak in the language of social ethics—to speak, that is, of the *ought* or *oughts* that may apply to the worlds for which changes are prescribed. Third, even to allow for the possibility that the classical *ought* of social ethics might be *oughts* is to raise the question entailed by the numerical ambiguity of the word itself: is the term *ethics* actually plural, thus necessarily meant to convey *oughts* appertaining to a plural *is* (or *are*) in worlds where the directions of change may be incommensurable (as opposed to simply different)?

To consider the multicultural, whether to support or oppose, is to consider changes in the deep structure of the One World ideal, such that the dream of a universal value must itself be set aside in favor of ethics as, at least in principle, incommensurably plural. The world, if we are to do more than think it (or them), cannot be changed without a plan, which is to say a principle, which in turn is to say an ethic or ethics. The ethical principle need not be transcendental (since Kant, few have been), nor must it even be quasi-transcendental (the impossibility of which Habermas has proven by a lifetime of futile labor devoted to putting the transcendental genie back in its one world bottle). Nor, at the other extreme, may the ethic be merely contextual (which is demonstrated by the foolishness of neo-utilitarian, quasi-structural bets on third-way political strategies). None of the usual and traditional ethical positions pass muster when considered against the prospect of a multicultural *is,* wherein the question is quite at odds with any and all theories as to what ethics are: can you change the world in directions that are at once both multiple and different?

WHAT IF THE MULTICULTURAL "*IS*" IS REALLY AN "*ARE*"?

The multicultural, whatever else it may mean to its scores of fans and opponents, surely stands for and is brought about by the breakdown of a long prevailing social consensus—one of purportedly global relevance—as to the core values applicable to human behavior in social settings of important magnitude. Since the first among social magnitudes that can no longer be avoided is the far reach of global social realities, the very idea of an ethical consensus is rendered virtually nonsensical. Strictly speaking, an *ethics* has been the well-considered theory of the values pertaining to an *ethos*—that is, to a prevailing social consensus. Hence, the strict meaning of morals is the customary norms governing social practices, or mores—that is, a prevailing condition of normal practices in a social group of whatever scale. Notwithstanding their different origins in the ancient Greek and classical Roman languages, the terms *ethics* and *morals* refer necessarily to some agreeably coherent degree of social coherence. That modern usage more or less assigns the theoretical work to the term *ethics* and the practical accomplishment of the theory to morals does not alter the strict sociological foundations for the use of either or both terms.

This is why one must ask whether ethics are possible in a multicultural world. Even the asking of the question demands reflection on the language and the realities themselves. It hardly makes sense, in the first instance, to use the term *multicultural* in reference to the existing, purportedly real world without transposing the naïve classic ideal of a singular world (as in One World, an essentially theological and metaphysical concept) into the necessary plural, *worlds*. If the world is multicultural, in any plausibly real sense, then the world is many *worlds*. Otherwise, the term *cultural* is being used figuratively and not with complete empirical seriousness. The trouble with so many discussions of the multicultural is that they seldom abandon theoretical privileges for the sake of serious sociologies of the worlds purportedly made real by the cultural forces (including the real values and norms behind morals as opposed to ethics).

If indeed the worlds are experiencing an ethical turn, it is a turn that demands clear thinking about the nature of ethics amid global social realities wherein cultural differences are seldom settled well, save by the deployment of economic or military power, and then of course they are settled artificially, at best. Or, to put it to the multicultural point: the reason social differences are seldom, perhaps never, well settled is because, when the fact of social differences is held stubbornly enough, differences between cultures cannot be viewed as mere semantics or short-run disagreement (as the all-too-polite liberal-left puts it) or as the failure of the "different" ones to do or be well enough (as the impolite right puts it).

Right wing hostility to the multicultural, while grossly ignorant of the facts pertaining to the idea, is at least the more robust ideological position. Those who hate the idea that social differences may be real are surely right to object to multicultural theories. And when they do, they object vociferously to the multicultural dream precisely because the very thought of such a state of public affairs makes their consensus as to the ethical rules untenable. They at least know on which side their ideological toast is buttered. Those on the other ideological hand, the weak-kneed left, usually hold the less tenable ground, if only because they are so ready to compromise. The liberal devotion to civil discourse (as if any of the other players cared a damn about this) forces them to treat multiculturalism as, in fact, not much more than a warmed over version of what in the USA was once the melting pot doctrine. The only difference between the old and new versions of the idea is that the liberal-left cannot afford to do more than warm over their tried and untrue doctrines of pluralism because they, in fact, do not believe in social differences as either an empirical reality or a state of nature. As a result, the left gives away its one solid political weapon—the facts of the matter. If we are to use the term *multicultural*, we can only use it with reference to the facts of global realities. As a dream or an idea, it is just as bad a soup as that made in the melting pot—the meat is tough because it resists tenderizing by holding fast to its fibroid integrity.

Social differences, in other words, are butchered by the most pervasive ethic of the European Diaspora, an ethic that stands behind political and ideological positions all along the continuum. That is the ethic of Universal Humanity, which was a general, if not universal, value of reasonable plausibility only under such conditions as may have obtained when the structures of the capitalist world system held the upper hand. That system, which Wallerstein and his co-workers have defined, described and criticized, was founded in the long 16th century on the economic exploitation of colonial subjects, of which the remains of the pre-feudal slave mode of production in Africa, the West Indies, the Amazon basin, and the American South were the principal structural means. Although with the suppression of the Atlantic slave trade early in the 19th century (a suppression that did not become effective until much later; DuBois, 1896) the feudal elements of the system were ultimately doomed, their continuing effects—what Adam Hochschild calls, referring to the Congo, their ghosts (Hochschild, 1998)—remained well into the late 20th century. To speak, in this connection, of an ethic of Universal Humanity and its self-moralizing correlate, One World, is, of course, at best to speak of hauntings of the vaunted reasonableness of the European entrepreneur—or in the pseudo-history of modernity: the Age of Man.

The covering principle of modernity might best be described as the Age of [the] Man who can only live in One World. The pseudo-history entails perforce a pseudo-geography. The One World dream was nothing more than a projection in social space of a distorting moral geography of the One Man, which of course made sense only to those immediately possessed of the superficial attributes of the European gentleman. All others—that is, those not thus possessed—held to the value only out of fear of the consequences or at the deeper and interior level of the colonized mind. Colonial subjects become subjects only to the degree that they submit to the years of patient instruction by the white world as to the moral necessity of the One Man ideal. As early in the decolonizing movement as 1952, Frantz Fanon's *Peau noire, masques blancs* told this nasty truth in terms that made an impression among the liberal-left of the colonizing Europeans. Fanon's idea, formed by his own experience as a colonial subject of France in Martinique and Algeria, was that the colonized took the white colonizer's manners into their inner-selves, a perversion of the rational principle of socialization, which had the effect of blotting out their Negritude (Fanon, 1967).[3]

Hence, were one to generalize from Fanon's commentary on the colonized of the mid-20th century to the post-colonial rebellions of the early 21st century, the long-run effects of the European Diaspora's colonial world-system is the necessity of violence as a normal stage in the overturning of the colonial system. The smart bombs of the Europeans and their successors in North America may not calm the post-colonials in Central Asia, the Middle East, the Koreas or Cuba, who smart under the centuries of exploitation in the name of the One World, Age of Man, ethical doctrine, which served as the Euro-American Enlightenment's philosophical opiate to the Capitalist World System's Enwhitenment policies.

One of the most astonishing effects of the controversy over the multicultural premise that the world may in fact be many is the hysteria over the prospect that relativism is the one solid truth of an ultimately (that is, empirically) soft world. Why exactly this panic is hard to say. Relativism is as old as the Greeks, if not as the hills. It pervades the practical experience of hard-to-resolve encounters with others like the bourgeois obsessive, once my neighbor, who insisted I remove several inches of driveway gravel from his side of the property line. We lived side by side, but we lived in worlds so different that it made no sense even to think of discussing the matter with him. When it comes to property rights the bourgeoisie will unrelentingly defend their absolutes. And there, perhaps, is the answer. The One World ethic is founded on absolute property rights. Thus, the Age of Man began in earnest when, late in the 18th century, enlightened Europeans set out to measure their lands, which in turn was necessary to complete the earlier efforts to establish universal weights and measures from which, by algebraic transposition, were derived the equivalency measures necessary for international trade in slaves (among other commodities) upon which, in turn, the Capitalist World System was able to flourish (Scott, 1998).[4] Giving up the universal entails giving up on the world itself, which is exactly what is at stake. The enwhitened European Diaspora is the principal stakeholder in the One World Order—hence, its panic that the truth of the world may be several or many.

One of the more bizarre *sequelae* of the multicultural hysteria is how the polite liberal-left sings the same note when faced with the multiple realities of the worlds as they are. The impolite right, by contrast, knows what is at stake and is prepared to fight to the death—an especially easy commitment to make when, as in Iraq and Afghanistan early in the 21st century, the number of their own children killed by the smart bombs is so improbably small. No more Vietnams, to be sure. But the left-liberals, with all their smarmy talk of third-way compromises, and other gestures of political *politesse,* are the true hysterics. For them, to give up on a One World ethic is to give up, in a word, hope. I have heard this note sung monotonously in the corners of the European Diaspora. From Bristol to New Orleans you will hear the chant of the virtuous left, in almost the same words: *Multiculturalism means there is no hope.* What they mean, of course, is that the liberal-left is founded on its own one world theory of the Necessary Revolution—that is, of the hope that one day the oppressed will have their 1789. Has the left ever stopped dreaming of the revolutionary moment when the oppressed would rise up, as the universal class, to cut off the heads of the tyrannous regime? Never mind that 1789 led to the Terror and to restoration, then to such tame projects as the Third Republic. World change doesn't work that way. Revolutions are few and far between, and none has ever approached the ideal left revisionists would transport back, over the record, into the dream of a global Bastille Day.

Thus Marx, right in so many things, was wrong on the crucial point of real politics. Yes, the idea is to change the world, which is indeed filled with contradictions, but you cannot change the Master's world with the Master's One World ethical tool. In this, Weber had the better grasp of the political calling as "the slow boring of hard boards" (Weber, 1946: 128). The boards come off the mill one at a time, filled with knots that slow the work already burdened by the market demand that each be cut to size. Without hope, to be sure, there would likely be little motivation for collective politics. The irony of the political vocation is that, as Weber also said, in the same place, "it takes both passion and perspective." Hope may fuel the passion, but the boards must be cut against the measured grain of market demands.

The multicultural, if it is to make empirical sense, is about social differences only occasionally susceptible to the hope of reconciliation. To speak, thus, of a multicultural world is *not* to speak of an all-too-hopeful world in which short-run compromises are assumed to be the harbingers of a long-run universal pragmatic. If the ideal of the multicultural is worth anything at all, it must take with hard-boring seriousness the perspective that the differences are real, worthy of respect, and unlikely to disappear.

For once, the language used tells the whole story. To speak of the multicultural in reference to the social realities of the human situation demands that the word *world* be retired to its proper semiotic home as a metaphor, at best. The multicultural, in effect, exhausts the original meanings of world, which come down by obsequious passage from the Latin *mundi* (from which the French, *monde*) by way of the German *welt*—which in nearly all instances designates the entirely moral (as opposed to empirically geographic) sphere of human space or time, as in, no less, this world or *the Age of Man.*

If the word *multicultural* is meant to designate some empirical reality of the worlds as we are coming to know them, then it must be taken back from the word hacks who use it, for good or bad reasons, as a mere slogan. In many ways, the very idea of the multicultural is itself a defensive notion, construed in alarm against the mounting evidence for the decline of the One World doctrine (Boyd, 2003).

CAN OUGHTS BE PLURAL?

On the surface, the question would seem to be absurd. *Can oughts be plural?* Hardly anyone even half-alert to the worlds about could well deny that values differ. In fact, it is easier to trust the fact that oughts are manifold than to believe the worlds are plural. This incongruity of naïve practical faith is precisely the issue at hand after the world, as we know it, came to be understood as worlds. The instinct that inclines members of a human group, if not of the species *tant mieux,* to desire that the world be One is itself a kind of primary process ethic—a value of a juicy, emotional kind that no doubt rises to the breast for which the infant longs against the harsh realities of the postuterine world. Whatever its source (very likely impossible to say for certain), the wish that the world be One is a very basic human instinct. This may well be why the colonial subject of Fanon's experience so readily allows itself to be taken into the white world of Universal Humanity. To wish to be at one with all others is so powerful because those so manifestly other to the grand and modal One of the Age of Man wish they were not who and what they are.

Who has never had the experience of denying a secreted truth of one's difference in order to be like the rest? This quite natural instinct has come to be called, in certain circles, "self hatred." It happens, of course, but deeper still: is the desire to be one with all others really anything more than a radical trimming of the sails of selfhood against the winds that can leave one so out in the cold? True, when heading up against the wind, if the helmsman trims too ferociously, holds the mainsail too fast, in order to seek every ounce of energy the wind can offer, the boat itself can capsize—from which the only rescue is to let go of the main sail, which, as they say, will put you in irons and out of the race. Then, again, those who are said to hate themselves are often made to feel that their self-disgust is well merited—as when upon failing standardized school-entry examinations their ignorance of yachting leaves them confused before the extended metaphor of sail trimming—even when it is put forth, across the lexical differences, in the intention to feel the pain of those who, far from owning a pleasure boat, cannot even find the words to describe a life-time spent bailing water against the bilge of economic injustice.

Hence the paradox, perhaps even a theorem: *A One World ethic will trump all more regional ethical principles precisely because this ought applies so poorly to the worlds members wish without hope could be better gathered together.* Who would not choose a world that is One over the worlds as they are with all their intractable differences? When the worlds are many, those who send their noble troops to save a people from evil only find themselves in a fast rising tide of differences not taught at Sandhurst and Quantico. Innocent boys and girls die for what? When the worlds are many, the cashiers change the rules without notice, only in the end to close down the dispensaries to ghetto despair. Innocent babies die for what? And on it goes.

In point of real politics the theorem of modernity's paradox operates against the facts of life—and never more assuredly than in the secret councils where foreign relations policies gestate, where it is impossible that this or that minister of defense or of state could come to office were she to suppose that the world as we knew it has ended. The foreign policies of the core state and its allies (what few may remain) rest assuredly on the premise that the worlds of which they are the Core itself will bow ultimately to the One World principle. These are the managers of the core/periphery arrangement, such as it once was and still may be. Without the One World doctrine, they would have little or nothing to manage.

This is why, among other sure signs of the post-1990 vulnerability of the capitalist world system, the inner circles of foreign policy analysts so often take their lead from a debate joined by two books—one of them certifiably silly in its claims; the other, not silly, but unremarkable as to its multicultural idea. The former is Francis Fukuyama's *End of History* (1992), the University of Chicago circle's ode to the new world order after the fall of Ronald Reagan's Evil Empire. The book's half-baked Hegelian notion that with the decline of the world communist antithesis, the capitalist thesis, lacking a viable Other, had brought history to its End by establishing the One World ethic. Such fluff leaves its left flank open to ridicule and attack, of which the most restrained and well-documented is Samuel Huntington's *The Clash of Civilizations* (1996), which argues that the Eurocentric civilizational core, its economic and military power notwithstanding, is now a lesser and declining civilization against the other major world civilizations. Huntington's book is in effect a brilliantly composed map of the worlds of social differences, but like most original maps once they are drawn and committed to public view, they seem all too obvious.

In between these two positions—Fukuyama's one-worldism and Huntington's map of global differences—the excluded middle languishes.[5] What strikes the skeptical reader is that the debate over the policy implications of the New World Order is not so much the premise of an emergent world, or even of a declining one, but the unwillingness to consider the world as new in some disjunctive degree—even if its newness is the coming out of the dark of a half-millennium's oppressions of the always other within the world system.[6]

Hence, again, the paradox: *Can oughts be plural?* Yes, of course, they can, and are—save for the organizing Ought of Modernity, which requires an ethical doctrine that denies the realities of social differences. The One World Ought is, in effect, an *ought* with no possible *is*. It cannot face the empirical realities that would fracture its delicate structure. This, one supposes, is why, as the modern world lurches awkwardly toward its end, the culture of modernity grows more and more unreal—more and more, that is, drawn into the virtual space of reality television and the like where even Jean Baudrillard's Disneyworld simulacrum is stark reality by comparison (Baudrillard, 1988: 166–84). The final irony of Euro-modernity's overwrought obsession with ethics is that its organizing ideal is one that makes ethical judgment implausible if not impossible. All *oughts* require an *is*. The One World Ought can only be transcendental to the global differences that were, in fact, first discovered in the long-ago 16th century when Europe colonized the global spaces by squeezing their many and variously incongruent parts into the World it was then just inventing.

The multicultural is, thus, little more than the whimper of that world—a generously liberal whimper, to be sure; but still a sad moan in the face of the noise of global differences. Again: *Can oughts be plural?* Yes, of course—all, perhaps, but one.

MIGHT GLOBAL CHANGES BE INCOMMENSURABLE?

If the worlds are different, then it must be that whatever changes they may undergo would, at least in principle, be incommensurable. The difference between differences and incommensurabilities is, of course, that the former kind of differences could possibly be resolved while the latter could not reasonably be expected to be resolved. The difference made by social differences turns entirely on that distinction—on the question of whether the worlds will come together, or not. The multicultural, if it is to be empirically sensible, must at the least consider the prospect that the worlds of social differences are just that: different in an incommensurable way. Whatever ethics, whatever social policies, whatever politics are associated with the idea of a multicultural world depend on a rigorous examination of this possibility.

Few others, to my knowledge, have made better sense of this limiting condition than Avery Gordon and Chris Newfield, who were among the first to describe the multicultural dilemmas:

Is multiculturalism antiracist or oblivious to racism?
Is multiculturalism cultural autonomy or common culture revisited?
Is multiculturalism grounded in grassroots alliances or diversity management?
Does multiculturalism link politics and culture or separate them? (Gordon and
    Newfield, 1996: 3–6)

The dilemmas could hardly be better put. In the modern world, every consideration of social change or social differences ought to begin with race (though they seldom do), if only because race is at the foundation of modernity's analytic cuts at the heart of human Being (Lemert, 2002). If arbitrary social divisions assigned to race are taken seriously as real social differences (as opposed to natural ones), then it is possible to consider that the social history of the modern world system is a history of those cuts—that the differences created are real, not by the natural failings of the ones cut out, but by the nature of the social system itself. If this, then the remaining three must follow as propositionally interesting.

If social differences, beginning with race, are real in themselves, then the multicultural must entail an authentic principle of cultural and social autonomy— hence, incommensurability. If this, then the multicultural entails, by necessity, a grassroots social movement, not a new strategy for co-opting, managing, or appropriating the differences. If this, then we are back to Marx's eleventh thesis: If we are not merely to think the world, then the cultures in, and by, which we think must be political, that is: devoted inextricably to changing *them*—the plural worlds. Nothing short of a correct (and I mean to use the word, against all odds) sense of the multicultural can possibly make good sense of the word, or the empirical possibilities, or finally of the possible ethical judgments that may be thus, and variously, required. Indeed, the idea is not to interpret the worlds but to change them. But will they change in ways that can be expected, in the end, to come together into a world, as once we knew it? Not likely; or, if possible, then it cannot be taken for granted.

In the social sciences all of the standard variants of social change theory have assumed, by one or another means, that the changing worlds are commensurable. The classic version, rooted in antiquity, but prevalent in modern times through the writings of Oswald Spengler, Arnold Toynbee and Nikolai Dimitriyevitch Kontratyev (Kondratieff),[7] among others, is the cyclical or wave theory of change. It assumes that history moves, if not round and round, at least back and forth between peaks and valleys—but always in a coherent pattern, always seeking, if not a resolution, at least a steady state of change whereby a location in one phase of the cycle permits one to anticipate the direction of change toward another phase. Similarly, according to a different figure of social time, the modernist theory of social change, codified in economic policy by W. W. Rostow but omnipresent in economic theory, even in radical forms (Amartya Sen), is that social history moves progressively forward, at locally irregular rates, such that the regions and nations of the world (sic) can be classified according to their level of development (Rostow, 1971).

Some places are developed, others less so—but all have their locations along the linear incline of the scheme, which assumes (if somewhat disingenuously) that all short-run differences might be commensurable. The radical modern version of the modernist scheme, the one that owes to Marx in particular, makes much the same assumption save for its adherence to the principle of contradictions interior to the mode of production from which the possible resolution might issue. Finally, one might suggest that any and all forms of anarchism are to cyclical theories as Marx is to Rostow in that they assume that the ought of short-run anarchy is the possibility of renewal after the present forms have collapsed (differing thereby from radical modern theories of social change by the refusal to prescribe the terms and conditions of the social forms that might arise from the ashes of collapse).

The remarkable (or, depending on your point of view, unremarkable) thing about most, if not all, meta-theories of social change is that they trust so unflinchingly in the commensurability of social differences provoked (or brought into the open) by changing times. Not only that, but also most (with the possible exception of wave or cyclical theories) look to the future as likely to be brighter in some ways than the present, certainly than the past. You can search a long while for any hint of possibility that social changes take the form of reversals, much less that they serve to separate the social parts in definite and incongruent, perhaps even irreparable, ways. The force of the One World ethic is so great that it does not permit, even in the wisdom of the ages, consideration of the possibility that were the world worlds, then the worlds are not necessarily headed from or to the same social time or space at all. And here is the point at which theories of social change ought to converge with theories of social differences. For the most part (with the exception of thinkers in the Matrix layer of post-Lacanian social theory),[8] they do not. Theories of social change that disallow the possibility of incommensurable changes are, in effect, not so much theories as beliefs—or social ethics of the One World.

Still, the ever more remarkable quality of the governing theories of social differences and change is that, bad ethical theory aside, they run so counter to everyday experience in politics, even of moral practices. Truth be told, and a few triumphal moments notwithstanding, Weber was being optimistic when he described politics as a slow bore on hard boards. Politics are impossible, and never more so than at the local level. You can get people to come together for a while on the lesser matters—organizing the town picnic, keeping the undesirables out of town, passing referenda on the schools, voting creeps out of office, and the like. But even these seldom hold for long. Sooner or later the picnics wither, *those people* break the housing code, people vote against the kids, some other creep sneaks into office. And these are references to the lesser political issues. When it comes to truly serious and urgent ones—like war, global markets, AIDS, environmental policies—the boards bore roughly at best, and slowly to the point of entropy. Still, again, what is true of real politics, lesser or grand, is already more optimistic than the honest truth of moral behavior.

One need not take Erving Goffman's strong point that, quite apart from misrepresenting ourselves to the worlds about, we are all miserable and necessary liars or worse (Goffman, 1963). In point of ethic reality, not only do we, on average, seldom do the good that we would, but it is very hard to be moral in any coherent sense when the imperative is to put every *ought* to which we may hold to the test of its immediate *is*. Moral practice is more about slippage and backsliding than the myth of the ideal and coherent Self. On the ground of common social things, differences generally prevail. There is no workable *we,* for very long—not with the neighbors, not with ourselves for that matter.

There is actually a body of work on the question of the incommensurable differences in political life. George Lakoff, referring to national politics in the liberal states, argues that even when the right and left think they are in agreement, their accord is based flimsily on ignorance of the real differences. Political animals on the right, for example, may agree for a moment that governments ought to do something for, say, the poor. They may even share the paternalistic views they attribute to their opponents. But on the right, the State is seen as the strict Father who must teach his children fiscal responsibility, while on the left the Father-State is the one who must care for children in his charge (Lakoff, 2002). I grew up with the former kind of father, who on occasion may have seemed to have been the care-taker kind, when in reality he was a bottom liner (and not, I should add, a very good one; he, like American political conservatives, demanded fiscal responsibility more for the kids than for himself). There is a difference, even if neither is by itself a particularly apt model for parenting, much less governing—though the gods know this does not keep the World Bank and the IMF from enforcing their loan agreements with a paternal expectation of fiscal responsibility, defined of course in stringently One-World ethical terms. What Lakoff means to say is that the two governing figures of state benevolence have little or nothing in common. The right and left, like my driveway-obsessed neighbor and I, simply live in different worlds—so different that we cannot even see the property lines that divide us.

If so—if only possibly so—then the dilemmas of the multicultural as Gordon and Newfield define them are all the more telling. Cultural and social differences are about real and not necessarily manageable differences. All the more so when the sphere of social differences is measured in global proportions. The crucial difference between worlds and the globe is that the former term is moral, the latter geographic. Global space begins and, in a definite sense, ends in real physical places. On the face of the globe the worlds are not simply visible, they are physically located in their various and well-engineered places—some much better than others. The difference between, say, New Jersey and Somalia cannot accurately be measured according to scale. It is not a question of infant mortality rates, number of persons with AIDS, racial percentages, number of television sets or internet connections, or anything of the like. Nor are they differences measurable by the hope that Mogadishu, being underdeveloped, will eventually one day have a good mall like the one off the turnpike at Paramus, NJ. Nor are they differences resolvable by contradictions, or take-offs to growth, or Kondratieff long waves, or anarchic dissolutions. It is not that the development metaphor is worthless. In fact it is noble. Nor is it that there is no hope for New Jersey. What it is, though, is that the *is* of Somalia is something unto itself, whatever it might or might not become one day.

Might global changes be incommensurable? Of course they might be; very likely they are—or perhaps not. Whichever way the worlds turn, no sense can ever be made of the multicultural and the social differences such an idea entails without sober thought on the true nature of worlds as they are and the autonomy of the values they inspire (or not), if they are as they seem: worlds—many of them, all crying out, in their different ways, for someone at long last to take Marx seriously.

NOTES

1. Among the countless examples, beginning with the *locus classicus* of the so-called ethical turn: Michel Foucault (1996), Garber et al. (2000), Harpham (1999), Campbell and Shapiro (1999), Huntington (1996), Gelb and Rosenthal (2003), Greider (1997), Reamer (1991) and Žižek (2001). To which list one might add the nauseating soup in the debates over family values and the culture wars, not to forget multiculturalism itself and the subtext of virtually every book written on globalization.

2. On Thursday, March 11, 2004, it took Google 0.49 seconds to generate 551 uses of the phrase "End of the World As We Know It," which may not be interesting since on the same date it took Google only 0.16 seconds to generate 4080 references to "Immanuel Wallerstein." The difference between Wallerstein and Google, not to mention countless others, is that Wallerstein provides a coherent argument based on historical evidence from his multivolume history of the modern world-system and other works, of which *Geopolitics and Geoculture* is one striking and early example.

3. See especially chaps. 5 and 6. In this formulation Fanon anticipated by a good twenty years Foucault's play on the modern notion of subjecthood as a consequence of subjugation to the governing regime of power/knowledge.

4. Scott (1998), Alder (2002, 11–52), Linklater (2002); compare Berlin (1998).

5. On the centrality of the Fukuyama-Huntington debate, see in particular Hoffman (2002). As regards Fukuyama, see his *The End of History and the Last Man* (1992). (A sign of Fukuyama's self-assurance is that in the few years it took to make a book out of an essay, the crucial question mark disappeared; see Fukuyama, 1989) On the tensions within the triumphant core policies, see Mead (2001).

6. I have personally been present at an afternoon's seminar of senior U.S. foreign policy analysts, for which the price of admission was keeping the seal of confidentiality. Yet, otherwise, I do not violate the oath by observing that, as in public discussions, the Fukuyama-Huntington debate was much discussed. When several outsiders (myself included) proposed Wallerstein as a third position on the state of global change, it is apparent those gathered knew the world-systems theory, though none would consider it applicable.

7. Spengler (1926); Toynbee (1957); Kondratieff (1984). One of the surprises is that Kondratieff's long wave theory is widely used among members of the world-systems analysis group with reference to the economic cycles of the capitalist world-system, even though a cyclical theory of change could not have predicted (as Wallerstein in fact did) the end of the capitalist system (which he analyzes in terms much more consistent with contradiction theories of social change).

8. The reference is to *The Matrix* hyperreality films. See Gopnick (2003), where the connection between Slavoj Žižek and other theories of the social discontinuous and cinema is drawn. The most serious, if mostly impenetrable, book on the subject of social discontinuities is Gilles Deleuze and Félix Guattari (1987).

REFERENCES

Alder, K. (2002) *The Measure of All Things.* New York: Free Press.

Baudrillard, J. (1988) "Simulacra and Simulations," in M. Poster (ed) *Jean Baudrillard: Selected Writings.* Stanford, CA: Stanford University Press.

Berlin, I. (1998) *Many Thousands Gone.* Cambridge, MA: Harvard University Press.

Boyd, T. (2003) *The New H.N.I.C., the Death of Civil Rights and the Reign of Hip Hop.* New York: New York University Press.

Campbell, D. and Shapiro, M. J. (eds) (1999) *Moral Spaces: Rethinking Ethics and World Politics.* Minneapolis: Minnesota University Press.

Deleuze, G. and Guattari, F. (1987) *A Thousand Plateaus.* Minneapolis: University of Minnesota Press.

DuBois, W. E. B. (1896) *The Suppression of the African Slave-Trade to the United States of America.* New York: Longmans, Green.

Fanon, F. (1967) *Black Skin, White Masks.* New York: Grove Press.

Foucault, M. (1996) *The Care of the Self: The History of Sexuality.* Vol. 3. New York: Random House.

Fukuyama, F. (1989) "The End of History?" *National Interest* 16: 3–18.

Fukuyama, F. (1992) *The End of History and the Last Man.* New York: Free Press.

Garber, M., Hanseen, B. and Walkowitz, R. L. (eds) (2000) *The Turn to Ethics.* New York: Routledge.

Gelb, L. H. and Rosenthal, J. A. (2003) "The Rise of Ethics in Foreign Policy," *Foreign Affairs* 82: 2–7.

Goffman, E. (1963) *Stigma.* New York: Simon & Schuster.

Gopnick, A. (2003) "The Unreal Thing," *The New Yorker* (12 May): 65–73.

Gordon, A. and Newfield, C. (eds) (1996) *Mapping Multiculturalism.* Minneapolis: University of Minnesota Press.

Greider, W. (1997) *The Manic Logic of Global Capitalism.* New York: Simon & Schuster.

Harpham, G. G. (1999) *Shadows of Ethics.* Durham, NC: Duke University Press.

Hochschild, A. (1998) *King Leopold's Ghost.* Boston, MA: Houghton Mifflin.

Hoffman, S. (2002) "Clash of Globalizations," *Foreign Affairs* 81: 104–15.

Huntington, S. P. (1996) *The Clash of Civilizations and the Remaking of World Order.* New York: Simon & Schuster.

Kondratieff, N. D. (1984) *The Long Wave Cycle.* New York: Richardson & Snyder.

Kueng, H. (1998) *A Global Ethic for Global Politics and Economics.* New York: Oxford University Press.

Lakoff, G. (2002) *Moral Politics: How Liberals and Conservatives Think.* Chicago, IL: University of Chicago Press.

Lemert, C. (2002) *Dark Thoughts: Race and the Eclipse of Society.* New York: Routledge.

Linklater, A. (2002) *Measuring America.* New York: Walker & Co.

Mead, W. R. (2001) *Special Providence: American Foreign Policy and How it Changed the World.* New York: Knopf.

Reamer, Frederic G. (ed) (1991) *AIDS & Ethics.* New York: Columbia University Press.

Rostow, W. W. (1971) *The Stages of Economic Growth.* Cambridge: Cambridge University Press.

Scott, J. (1998) *Seeing Like a State.* New Haven, CT: Yale University Press.

Sen, A. (1999) *Development as Freedom.* New York: Random House.

Spengler, O. (1926) *The Decline of the West.* New York: Oxford University Press.

Toynbee, A. (1957) *A Study of History.* New York: Oxford University Press.

Wallerstein, I. (1991) *Geopolitics and Geoculture.* Cambridge: Cambridge University Press.

Wallerstein, I. (1999) *The End of the World As We Know It: Social Science for the Twenty-first Century.* Minneapolis: University of Minnesota Press.
Weber, M. (1946) "Politics as a Vocation," in H. G. Mills and C. W. Mills (eds) *From Max Weber: Essays in Sociology.* New York: Oxford University Press.
Žižek, S. (2001) *On Belief.* London: Routledge.

VI
Globalized Worlds

12

If There Is a Global WE, Might We All Be Dispossessed?

Is there a WE in this global world? The question is one that must be asked, if not in so many words. Who are WE? Are WE a WE? This is the question of practical life in a global world. Few are privileged enough to avoid the everyday situations—many real, some virtual—wherein the uncertainty of global things confronts and disturbs. Even the privileged cannot avoid the question altogether. Most of the people on this globe today are continuously aware of the unsettling fact that "our" people (whoever we are) are in a different global circumstance than once they were. We encounter the differences many times a day, even when we fail to notice.

What does it mean to use the pronoun "we" in such a world? In the West, "we" is as much an assumption as it is a word. We in the West have been taught a philosophy that holds that "all men are equal," that there is such a social thing as the "human community." We know that the idea of universal humanity is not practically real, but our culture believes it just the same. Chinese and Korean cultures of course retain traditional elements of belief in the idea that all Koreans and all Chinese have important things in common, even when it is obvious they do not. Yet, people from East Asia understand our Western philosophy, as we do not theirs. Like millions of others around the world, East Asian people have experienced economic or political colonization by Western powers. They are keenly aware that the Western idea of "common humanity" is, if not an illusion, at least a remote ideal. They know firsthand the effects of the arrogance of Western culture. As a result, whatever they think philosophically about "community humanity," they think it in relation to real experiences of human social differences—differences that sometimes kill, almost always injure.

In a world where it is very difficult, perhaps impossible, to avoid the conflict of social differences, there may be only one universal WE—only one way to refer with some accuracy to the experiences of all people on the globe who are old enough to wonder who they are and what they do or do not have in common with the others they encounter in their daily lives.

If there is a global WE, might we call ourselves the dispossessed? Who are the dispossessed? First, they are the millions of human beings worldwide who leave home for a better life in the city or abroad. As many as 178 million people are dispossessed in the sense that they are living outside their countries of birth, roughly 3 percent of the world's population.[1] The number would likely be higher were it possible to observe the movement of illegal migrants and political refugees who, by the clandestine nature of their dispossession, are hard to count. Some 10 million leave their homelands each year. Some estimates are of many millions more than that. Though a great many move not out of desperation but to improve already secure lives, many are fleeing genocide, hunger, poverty, disease.

On top of this add the global migration of people from the countryside to the city. In the last two decades, China alone has undergone the largest resettlement of human beings in history. In 2003 approximately 40 percent of Chinese people lived in cities; but in the next generation that number will become 60 percent. The percentage is relatively small compared to neighboring countries like Korea where 80 percent live in cities, but given China's population the human movement is both rapid and massive beyond comparison. Worldwide, the movement of people from underdeveloped regions to North America and Europe is only marginally less dramatic.[2] In other words by the time young mothers today in the poorest regions of the world give birth to their babies most of their children will be unfamiliar with the traditional village life of their parents. The change is comparable in kind to what occurred in North America in the twentieth century but the numbers are staggering by contrast.

Of course, the simple fact of moving from home does not necessarily mean the loss of a home place. A good many people of all social classes resettle comfortably into their new cultures. But not all; many remain in their homelands and towns, but suffer impossible conditions because they are too weak or too poor to flee. Others get by in economic terms; but whether in a new or old homeland, they are deprived of the most basic human rights. Still others live well enough but are jolted by the changing world, uncertain of their ability to hold on to what lives they have. Then there is a special class of people who have done very well in life but are surprised by the defiance of ordinary people to the authority once accorded people of their status.

Between the starving refugee and the anxious elite, there is a world of difference. The word "dispossessed" does not fit them all in the same way. Yet, in another sense it does. Without trivializing the unthinkable suffering of the global poor, it is fair to say that globalization takes away from nearly everyone the assurance of a settled home place. True, the very rich may complain as usual, "You cannot find good help anymore." But in the globalizing worlds those who depend on the poor to pick their crops, build their computers, mind their children, mow their lawns, haul their trash are much more likely to be aware of migrating workers who may not speak their language, understand their culture, or worship their gods. It is not a question of the plight of the well-off, so much as the extent to which—economic differences aside—the most well-off are more aware of being in the same boat with the very poor. Personally, one might say to them, "Welcome to the real world." But sociologically, one must note the contradiction. In a day when the economic distance between the rich and poor is greater than ever, the social distance is strangely closer.

When people of sharply different experiences come into contact—either in person or at a televisual remove—the contact has an unsettling effect. Those in the disadvantaged position see firsthand what they lack. Still, even the privileged are aware, however vaguely, that there are others who would take it all away if only they could. This is so in all times and places, but more so in a globalizing world—both in the kind and degree of the risks. In the past the poor were certainly not better off not knowing just how unfair their lives were, but in a world where they see images of affluence everywhere from dawn to dusk and through the night, the difference grinds harshly. The rich may have been better off (if that is the word) when they hired their servants from the nearby villages, but in a global place they surely must begin to sense that their privilege is not so much a natural right as an extravagance arbitrarily gained. For both and all in the between their homes in the world are put at risk.

Home is not a house. The unhoused may find a home in a street shanty. The overhoused may never be at home in their several houses. Home is a place, yes; but above all it is a social place. Home is where, as the expression goes, we are *from*. It makes little difference whether or not one currently lives in the place she is from, so long as the *from-place* remains a fixed star on the horizon of consciousness. I would never, even remotely, consider returning to live in any of the neighborhoods where I grew up. Yet, I am well aware, when forced to think on it, that these places have something to do with who I am—if only because I have managed to escape them. I'm not a home-boy; still I have these places in my heart-of-hearts. Others, of course, long for down-home or the old country. But, either way, the home is the social place where, in another phrase, one has her roots. So long as somewhere in the world one has, or believes she has, a home, then she possesses a homeland which, again, is more a figurative than a literal place.

The modern world was (or is, as the case may be) a world in which, in principle at least, everyone had a right to a home, if not a house. Modernity was the culture of social space—the space of the territorially defined nation-state, the space of exploration and colonization, the space of new frontiers and new conquests, the space of future time toward which one moved in the search for the good life. If there is a postmodern world aborning, postmodernity is the space of time—of a time so fast that when one moves house it is very difficult, even a bit bizarre, to backtrack. Some still go home to die; but most do not, if only because the hospitals back there, if any, are lousy with lice. Some still visit kin during the holidays, but rarely if home is oceans away. And the millions displaced by civil strife or poverty would not think of going back, even if their current home is a shanty town on the filthy outskirts of an urban sprawl.

Globalization, whether it turns out to be postmodern or not, is a social process in which the grotesque failures and social evils of the modern world cannot be easily painted over. One sees the homeland for what it is, filled as much (or mostly) with misery as with what pleasures one may have. It is not merely a matter of virtual experiences of distant realities—by television or other information technologies—but of the fact that even the beggars may beg outside the all-night convenience store with its tiny black-and-white television blaring away the news of distant realities. In a world—if this one is what once was meant by the word—where it is next to impossible to avoid the realities as they are, the fable imagined community is seen for *what* it is and for what it requires of us, however different we, if any, are.

The dispossessed is no longer a science fiction.[3] To speak of the dispossessed is increasingly a way of naming normal life amid the pressures and possibilities of globalization. In particular, *dispossessed* may be what we—if one is to dare speak of humans as a WE—might have to call ourselves in a globalizing world. To *dispossess* is to oust or dislodge someone from what he possesses. Curiously, the history of the word in the English language seems to be limited entirely to the modern era and to refer almost exclusively to an action directed at persons—literally "to put (anyone) out of possession; to strip of possession."[4]

Of all the possessions, the loss of which would be most widely felt, the first would be home—and nowhere more so than in the modern world. If home is where a person is *from,* then *not to be from anywhere* in particular is to suffer a terrible fate in a culture that values the conquest of social space as much as modernity has. The colonizing ambitions of the masters of the modern world are not limited to the taking of lands and lives for economic gain. As Jürgen Habermas has repeatedly said, the personal world in which we live, our lifeworld, is continuously at risk of being colonized.[5] More specifically, in the modern lifeworld, the social space in which one lives is a way of saying who she is. In bourgeois circles of the modern rat-race, when strangers meet, after names are exchanged, one of the two questions they will ask the other is "Where are you *from?*" The other is often, "What do you *do?*" What a member of the privileged classes *does* (her profession or job) is a function of where she is *from.* In more traditional times, the tie of one's place in the social world to the place of her home was direct and intimate. People worked, if not *at* home, in nearby fields or enterprises. Roads were few and made of mud and dirt. In modernizing times, the tie is indirect and conflicted. People must leave home to find work; if they find it, then they are often able to pay the price of putting down new roots, but seldom a home from which they derive their sense of who they are. They may pretend of course, as *les nouveaux* must, that they are at home in the new playpen, but eventually a slip of tongue betrays them as strangers. Modernity's roads and sidewalks are many and made for speed. But in a globalizing world, people more and more work at home; but when they do their work is on the electronic highway. Those still in traditionally modern employment understand very well that it is their jobs that are on the fast track to somewhere else. Global roads to income are made for speeds early moderns could not imagine, speeds so great as to collapse the social value of being from anywhere and, at the extreme, of being anyone in particular; or at the worst, of being consigned to the lot of the economically and socially doomed. Consider the factory worker: globalization's blacksmith, if not exactly a court jester.

Home is a place—as much social and virtual as geographic and durable; hence, also, a social location inseparable from social meanings—from identities, statuses, classes and natures; from freedoms, bondages, gains and losses; and everything else in the conceptual schemes of the sociologies of real live collective things. In modern sociologies, a status is tied to a class, which in turn hints at identities, which in their turns are as much the right to social inclusions as to interior understandings of self, which in another turn of the screw defines whether, if high in the scheme of social things, they can claim to be normal or, if low, they are considered below human nature itself. Likewise, freedoms are mostly escapes from bondages, which in turn are always more available to those whose luck gains them income enough to escape the losses that can land one at the bottom of the stratification scale allocated to the untouchables that, truth be told, are not really in the human race. The road to social death is no longer paved with good intentions. In the global worlds the needle executes by the terrible swift sword of exclusion from the race. And on it goes. Concepts of social differences arise, when they do, in local practices of social differences where feet-to-the-ground people come up against each other. Most of the time, they pass by the other without admitting, even to themselves, that they notice the difference. From time to time, more often these days it seems, they brush against the others; sometimes rudely enough to strike out, often with hand or foot where word or grimace would have been sufficient.

Who are these fractured global groups who, by their rude differences, cast doubt on the cherished idea of a modern human WE? Without admitting, even in the fine details of language, that they are a *they,* they are the several competing local civilizations that clash violently enough to disabuse themselves of the former pretense of a common humanity. Samuel Huntington is famous, if that is the word, for claiming that the globalizing world can be understood as a clash of civilizations.[6] Against which, among others, Edward Said insists that this way of putting it is a clash of ignorance.[7] To speak of global realities as organized neatly according to large, unifying cultural systems that serve to mark off the different ways human beings define what is civil to them seems, at first, a progressive move beyond the silly universals of the modern age. But the ignorance behind even this superficially wise division of social things is that it carries forward the organizing principle of human community in the modern world—that human communities, whether global or regional, are gatherings of people of a collective like-mind. Hence, Huntington stipulates Islamic, Chinese, Latin American, Hindu, Buddhist, Japanese, African, Orthodox, and, to be sure, the West—as if any one of these is a proper name for a civilizational order without significant interior clashes. What looks like a serious liberal qualification of humanistic essentialism turns out to be nothing more than the same thing writ smaller. In fact, the sensation stirred by the essay and the book that followed owes to its catchphrase: the West and the Rest that threaten the modern West. The Rest, it happens, usually know better, at least when they are willing and able to reflect on the nature of local conflicts. Edward Said, in an essay critical of Huntington, writes of the ignorance of civilizational thinking. He knew better because, his wealthy upbringing in Egypt, Lebanon, and the U.S. notwithstanding, Said lived also in Palestine and as that local conflict grew nightmarish, particularly after the 1967 war, he tried to remake a cultural home out of his privileged past as a Palestinian who became an exiled.[8]

If, as Claus Offe has suggested,[9] Prague is the ideal city of modernizing civil society wherein a vital public sphere grew out of political oppression and chaos, then perhaps the West Bank would be the metaphoric noncity of globalization wherein differences like those between Palestinians and Jews in the West Bank and Gaza are so unbridgeable as to be beyond reasonable hope of resolution. Anyone who struggles to any important degree with real and complicated social conflicts realizes that real conflict is always local, always tied to local interests, always remembered because the opponents cannot ever move far enough away from the other—in real as well as symbolic terms—to forget, much less to forgive.

It would be better, when speaking of differences among global things, to speak of ways groups have been dispossessed of their home places. The number of social theorists attempting to think through the misery of the world is small,[10] but it is growing in some more or less direct proportion to the unyielding strain of global differences. In the wake of global violence and suffering, social theory is just beginning to consider the dispossessed according to their several different kinds of losses of home, thus of a social place, thus of a *from where* wherefrom they might make a single, uncomplicated identity in the worlds. There are at least the following types, somewhat schematically drawn up, none fully understood, each requiring explanation:

- The Political Nostalgics who have means and method but are unwilling to settle in.
- The Truly Dispossessed who are without means or method to find a home.
- The Economically Uprooted who have the method but not the means to root themselves.
- The Socially Unsettled who have the means but not the method to make a home.
- The Cultural Exiles who, possessing means and methods, work to unsettle the worlds.

What defines the dispossessed in a sociology of global misery is the extent to which people are defined according to the economic means they possess or lack and the social methods by which they succeed or fail to come to grips with globalization. The differences among them are uneven as to justice, leaky as to analytic precision, uncertain as to the meaning of their global situation. The differences within and between the five groups—better put, social movements—provoke conflict within each and with each at the others. In a global world the fundamental structural conflict is neither class nor race nor gender, but global position—a more complicated structure even than all the hitherto existing categories: first/third world, core/periphery, North/South, developed/underdeveloped, colonizer/colonized—which turn out to be vulnerable to critical traditions of thought like queer theory and subalterity, among others. To speak of the dispossessed in this way comes down to the risk of using analytically loose, politically temporary, and culturally partial methods as a means to think the global unthinkable.

One of the more appealing, if not yet worked through concepts for locating the differences among the dispossessed may be Patricia Hill Collins's matrix of domination, which has the potential for application to the struggle among people at odds with each other in the terror of local conflict as in the articulation of a global matrix of domination.[11] Collins's matrix is used to illuminate the moral power of the Black woman in America—a power that is ironically due to her being the subject of so many vectors of domination. Though in *Black Feminist Thought* (1990) Collins does not consider the matrix of domination in relation to global process, it is obvious that in the background is the contention that, worldwide, women of color suffer from their social locations—as Black in a white world, as postcolonial and subaltern in a modernizing world, as women, as poor, as members of the lowest classes and castes in their societies. And yet it is very well known that, as in America, the woman of color is very often the pillar of strength of her village and community and, even, her national society. To say that domination is a many-sided and multidimensional system in which, so to speak, power moves in all directions is to describe a system that seems, more and more, to apply to the globalized world.

Globalization uncovers the rough-edged universal facts of the matrix—that even the privileged are afflicted, at least relatively, by elements of their social privilege—the afflictions of exaggerated responsibility for the world order, of defensiveness against attacks on all quarters, of guilt for the evil they inflict and so forth. One need not pity the powerful to understand that they use their power as they do with the trembling hand of uncertainty. Think of George W. Bush, panic-stricken before the children, when first he heard of the 9/11 attacks. Wherever one is in social space—a space that while virtual is usually neatly superimposed on the global economic geography of first and third worlds and the like—one is in a local place where the sewers overflow, the relief foods are distributed (or not), the fields are parched, the diseases are communicated, and all the rest that goes with suffering and its absence in real social time. One notices the effects of misery from whatever home she has, whether well furnished or barren.

To allow for a matrix of domination is to allow for a social condition that becomes epidemic under globalization in which any given local place is as likely to be uprooted or looted as any other. The realities are that the poorer, more dominated places are in fact unsettled and looted more often and more severely, but the threat seems to be ubiquitous. In form and, to a remarkable degree, in style, the gated community in Los Angeles and the political prisons in places like Guantánamo are much the same in principle. The guards may be differently armed—with electronic alarms or digitalized weapons of personal destruction—but the social function is much the same: Keep close guard at the walls in order to keep the undesirables in or out as the case may be. The common result is that, whether one locks himself in or is locked up, all are to some degree dispossessed of their freedom, prisoners in an open world. It may sound flippant to equate wealthy scum in their gilded mansions with the political prisoner of uninspected guilt, but sociologically the equation is just even if the human injustice is out of any known proportion. Hence, the irony of global things—they turn modern social assumptions on their heels, if not their heads.

THE POLITICAL NOSTALGICS

The still dominant political culture in the West is rooted in liberal individualisms of the seventeenth and eighteenth centuries in Europe. Though the most visible structure of modernity is the capitalist system of economic exploitation, the deepest cultural aspect of modernity is the liberal dream of rational progress toward a good society. If it is even remotely possible that the most salient historical fact of modernity is the contradiction between its political promises and its economic realities, then no wonder that nostalgia is a leading form of dispossession for moderns with a stake in the world that was.

Nostalgics are unsettled by global change precisely because globalization, like modernization, promises what it cannot afford to give. Unlike modernization, globalization spreads wealth thickly on the global upper crust, all too thinly to the rest of the pie. In the United States (and there is no country more boastful of its human values), early in the 2000s, the miniscule top one-tenth of 1 percent (0.01 percent) most rich gained 8 percent of the nation's personal income, while the top 20 percent received 62 percent of the income, compared to the bottom 20 percent's 2.5 percent. In other terms, the wealthiest 0.1 percent (about 145 thousand taxpayers) earn (if that is the word) roughly the same income as the bottom 40 percent (60 million taxpayers). Or, still worse, in the United States (the least egalitarian of modernized nations) the ratio of very rich to poor is better by far than the same ratio in the world as a whole. Globally, as noted, the 400 richest are wealthier than half the world's current population. In the modernized West, the 400 richest taxpayers have average annual incomes of $87 million or more, while the 28 million poorest live (if chat is the word) on average incomes of $13.5 thousand or less each year.[12]

In between the most poor 20 percent and obscenely rich tenth-of-a-percent in America one finds the nostalgics—aware that the very rich live in another reality altogether, while they have mortgages and tuition checks to write, if they are lucky. What the nostalgics realize, whether they admit it or not, is that, when a great nation in which they have placed their trust fails to come even close to its professed commitment to human life and fair play, something is wrong with the system. Hence, the acute nostalgia for a better time in a simpler past or a (remotely) possible future—a dilemma that is fundamentally political because in allegedly free and democratic societies, granting the differences in governmental and social forms, politics ought ultimately to be the art of distributing the goods by some reasonable scheme that, at the very least, preserves and protects individual rights even when it falls way short of economic justice. If the modern West cannot do better for its own (granting the burgeoning number of immigrants who get, sneak, or want in), then how can the modern world be moving globally toward anything like the ideal of a good society?

The genius of the modern world system was that it colonized at a distance in foreign lands (or segregated states) from whence the bad news seldom travels far. The stark honesty of a globalizing world is that it is possible for almost anyone to dig up the bad news and with very little digging at that.

The politically nostalgic are many in number, irregular in kind, and more sympathetic than previously thought.[13] They are the moral and demographic core at the core of the global system—those with hard-won investments in the world as it once was. Nostalgics, while wealthy beyond the hope of the poor, are seldom among the obscenely rich. Many do quite well, but most are of comfortably modest means, and some have fallen to the economic margins.[14] They are, almost always, privileged in the local sense of being near to the upper reaches of the social scheme. They may be of modest, even threatened, social statuses like that of the working poor but they cling to the hope that social things will get better. Their hope is rooted in the modern idea that progress is a necessary history that suffers occasional setbacks, but never a reversal of fortunes. Their hope is troubled by globalization, if not completely dashed, because, seeing (often against their will) the terrible misery of the truly dispossessed, they are made to see that their advantages, however modest, are real because the number of those, worldwide, who are homeless, hungry, sick without care, and poor without prospect is growing, not declining; and that the truly dispossessed are more the global norm than they were a good century ago (even perhaps a millennium ago). The effect of the realization is created by the visible evidence that progress, being far from inevitable, may have been, if not a joke, at least a moral trick their forbears turned on those they colonized and raped.

In a world where the combined wealth of the 400 richest individuals is greater than that of half the global population, the emperor is more than naked. He's a prick. The inequality is so far beyond obscene as to be salacious—the asymptote where violence and pornography meet on the curve of their true and identical natures. Modernity's culture always claimed to be, first, the most human—hence, by implication, the culture most free of inhuman violence; and, second, to be the most progressive because it was morally the most pure—hence, by implication, the one puritan culture that transposed raw sexual energy into wealth. Neither is true to its claim. The price of the formula was that the wealthy few relieved their pent-up libidos by screwing the miserable many. There is a saying among philanderers, borne out in divorce courts: "The screwing you get isn't worth the screwing you get." Yet, the one sphere of marital life that rewards the capitalist pricks is their devotion to economic gain. They fuck the rest to save the West.

Harsh though it necessarily is, there is moral room left over for a degree of sympathy for the nostalgic who is only occasionally able to laugh at his global situation. His lack of perspective (and one uses gendered generic because his or her roots are in the classically homocentric nineteenth century) is not due to failure in deeds. The modern era, from 1500 to 1990 or so, sparkled with brilliant achievements one might fully enjoy were it not known that the brass and silver were polished by the indentured poor. Given that no other previous age, nor the one that may be succeeding the modern, has shown any great capacity to do better at doing good honestly, it is wrong to be too harsh on the moderns. To paraphrase whoever it was, the trouble with modernity is that it is the worst possible system, except for all the rest. Modernity's evil is not so much in the evil it does, but in the lies it tells to pretend it is better than it really is. To be a civilizational culture better than, say, the slave or feudal modes of social production is not exactly an assurance of human progress.

Hence, the sad nostalgia of the late modern era. Those with a stake in modernity rightfully appreciate the cultural, scientific, and even political accomplishments of their forbears from whom they inherited their advantages. But as the global truth dawns, they find it more difficult than did their predecessors to believe the deceptions upon which their claims to superiority rely.

In the modern West, the romantic promises were always projections across the myth of history of the allegedly elementary forms of political necessity. To be sure, some nostalgics are real bastards, but not as a rule. For safety's sake one might do better choosing them over the romantics who tend to turn the bully when the romance is over. Still, either way, the political nostalgics stalk the lost object of their desire for a good that, however plausible as a value, is at best the bitter pill of a notably superficial and time-bound culture.

THE TRULY DISPOSSESSED

When, in 1987, William Julius Wilson published *The Truly Disadvantaged,* he was deliberating on the most poor in American urban society, who were most visibly Black. Over time this book established a midpoint in the trajectory of controversy surrounding the relations between race and class in the determination of urban poverty. By 1996, in *When Work Disappears,* Wilson was more pessimistic than he had been a decade earlier. In the decade between, globalizing had begun to have its discouraging way with the most poor even in the fine cities of the modernized world. In the modern world, "disadvantage" is a fungible term in the vocabulary of social hope and economic progress. What Wilson saw in 1996 in the fieldwork in Chicago's worst corners was the terrible degree to which globalizing labor markets were taking all the jobs away from the most poor. To say that income gained from meaningful employment was no longer a reasonable dream was to state the increasingly obvious fact of globalization.

Not only does globalization threaten modern politics, but modernity itself is uprooted when the economic promise that hard work at a job will lead to socially good outcomes and personally satisfying lives is broken. As globalization produces more absolute wealth than ever before, it does so at the expense of the foundation of modern work—the job, as the method for distributing income and the means to assuring human decency, was disappearing. *The Truly Disadvantaged* are the millions worldwide who have scant prospect of finding the method or the means to income sufficient to make a home.

The most devastating fact of life for the truly disadvantaged is that those to whom they might turn for help turn elsewhere—to the Middle East, instead of

Rwanda and Sudan; to debates over fine points of religious doctrine, instead of relief for the poor; to frivolous platitudes reinforcing tried and untrue policies, instead of a deep rethinking of social programs; to a series of doctrinal nullities like third-way, neo-liberal, neo-conservative, instead of honest consideration of the modern state's failure to deliver modernity's promises. The distractedness of the normally well-intended and morally well-dressed at the core of the modern world means that, apart from the numbers that tell the stories of global dispossession impersonally, one only rarely hears tell of the true misery. But occasionally someone, like Nicholas Kristof, digs out the story that is hard to ignore, such as that of Magboula.[15] She had once lived in the countryside in the war-torn Darfur region of Sudan. She had a home until, that is, the janjaweed came to town. She and her family escaped for another town that they soon fled when Sudanese Army units arrived. Then began two months of running from the terror. Eventually the janjaweed overran them. In Kristof's report of Magboula's own words:

> The Raiders shot her husband dead, she said, her voice choking, and then they whipped her, taunted her with racial insults against black people and mocked her by asking why her husband was not there to help her. Then eight of them gang-raped her.... After the attack, Magboula was determined to save her children. So they traipsed together on a journey across the desert to the Kalma Camp, where a small number of foreign aid workers are struggling heroically to assist 110,000 victims of the upheaval. Magboula carried her 6-month-old baby, Abdul Hani, in her arms, and the others, ranging from 2 to 9, stumbled beside her.

Magboula survives. Her baby dies. She and the remaining children beg from others in the refugee camp—others as homeless and hungry as they are. This while those with the power and the money to help do nothing. The misery of this sort of dispossession is enough in itself. But when the dispossessed tell their story to a New York reporter they know that the rest of the West will know, if only they would. They have neither means nor method to do more than survive. They have escaped the genocide to wait, in the dirt, for death.

THE SOCIALLY UNSETTLED

While the truly dispossessed are without means or method even to hope for more than the worst, the socially unsettled very often manage to find the means to settle in safety but, usually through no fault of their own, they are denied the method to make a home. Many of them live in the next neighborhood to the well settled.

The socially unsettled have enough method to make the means to find a home after dispossession of their home "back home." But they are limited by the social conditions in the host country or city. To put it crudely, American whites have never known what to do with American Blacks. Still today they hardly understand the differences among people of the global Black Diaspora. For that matter, whites in

Africa, being settlers themselves, are just beginning to come to terms with the reality of a Black majority. Americans are far enough behind that they actually believe that because their foreign ministers are Black then America is making racial progress—an attitude but slightly different from calling a continent Africa without recognizing even the most apparent of internal ethnic and cultural differences.

The socially unsettled have means, as I say, but not a method sufficient to make a life in the new place. But they seldom are permitted to settle in fully. Modern societies, their rhetoric notwithstanding, are not very welcoming. European societies never in fact tried as America has and now they face a similar crisis of being able to afford the immigrant laborers who make their welfare states possible. Australia still is struggling with its indigenous populations, not to mention the dispossessed who come seeking a new life. The South African whites gave up their status only when forced to do so. Only Canada, it would seem, has done better than average in welcoming the dispossessed. But then, their scarcest resource is people. Modern societies are, in a word, begrudging, even when they smile and slap your behind as they pass by on the street.

THE ECONOMICALLY UPROOTED

If the socially unsettled have the means but not the social method, then the economically unsettled have a method that fails to generate the means to set down roots. In a globalizing world dispossession works more often through economic means than social or political ones. Were it the case that the world was supplied with an overabundance of goods, enough to make life free for the asking or picking, then many of its social and political problems would likely disappear. One says likely because there is little evidence in the history of modern peoples that they are especially keen on peace, not to mention justice. But then again, though their ancestors taught that prosperity would come in time, since it never came, moderns have never known more than occasionally passing illusions of prosperity sufficient to eliminate scarcity. Hence, the contradiction in the modern scheme of social ideals: It promises that which may be impossible to provide under any circumstance. It underestimates the Malthusian prediction that sooner or later scarcity will catch up to the promises.

In a superficially generous but profoundly begrudging society, some people will remain, on the margins, constantly at risk. Why do some obey the norms and find a way to health and home through work? And some not? In a culture that so values individualism you would think that it would occur to people that the economically uprooted are themselves modern people in the human sense of living in a modern world. Why should they be deprived of the right to choose what methods they have so long as they are little more than a political burden on the comfortable? Yes, support costs the public money. But not a fraction of what the public pays in taxes to subsidize the hyper-rich (who pay proportionately fewer taxes than the poor); nor even of the benefits the well housed have of deducting a portion of the cost of their mortgages from their tax debt. One supposes, though I have not done the calculations, that if in all the modern nations everyone paid a fair share of the global costs of human survival (survival, that is; not even comfort) the world would be a better place—and certainly one more in line with the ethical pretenses of modern culture. This, in effect, is the idea behind Jeffrey Sachs's proposal to end world poverty. If the well-off in the West would sacrifice but a fraction of their wealth, there would be resources sufficient to save the rest.

Economic uprooting is, of course, a short-run effect of a rapidly changing global economy. It would be stupid to deny the complexities. But how less stupid is it to deny the human realities that over the long run of modernity have grown worse, not better? Economic uprooting requires an economic answer but the answers will not be considered until modern nostalgics give up even a portion of their modern moralities. Moderns talk about values. They seldom reach beyond their nice local circles of comfort to rethink the values that would serve the more needy. That fact is a moral issue.

THE CULTURAL ELITES

More than anyone else, I think, Edward Said has transformed the experience of dispossession into a prerequisite of the culturally elite. He would have meant "elite" in another sense than customary. He would have meant not the capitalist pricks but the socially and politically alert intellectuals who use their cultural capital to stir the social pot. Pierre Bourdieu, who invented the expression "cultural capital," once described the role of the sociologist as being a cultural terrorist. For reason of his attachments to Palestinian politics, Said would have put himself at risk were he to have used such an expression. Even if, as was the case for Bourdieu, one is born to modest circumstances, once one has a cultural home in Paris, there are freedoms denied others. Said was born to wealth, but to Egyptian-American parents. He was "delivered" in Jerusalem because there alone were the best hospitals, even for Palestinians. His father's wealth sent him to the elite schools in Cairo and Beirut, eventually to Princeton and Harvard, then to a literary life based at Columbia. He was a Palestinian who possessed both the means and the method to attain a good life, which he had and enjoyed.

But Said refused absolutely to squander his elite status by dismissing his Palestinian past. Many worldwide accused Said of pretending to be a real Palestinian. Yet, Said refused to let this deter him. In one of his smaller but most important books, Said describes the role of the intellectual as being rootless, unsettled. The model for his intellectual and political work was the exile he was, in spite of the family's wealth. In the memoir of his life as an exile, *Out of Place,* Said describes the personal effects of his willingness to embrace his status as one of the dispossessed:

> Sleeplessness is for me a cherished state to be desired at almost any cost; there is nothing for me as invigorating as immediately shedding the shadowy half-consciousness of a night's loss, than the early morning, reacquainting myself with or resuming what

I might have lost completely a few hours earlier. I sometimes experience myself as a cluster of flowing currents. I prefer this to the idea of a solid self.... These currents, like the themes of one's life, flow along during the waking hours and, at their best, they require no reconciling, no harmonizing. They are "off" and may be out of place, but at least they are always in motion, in time, in place, in the form of all kinds of strange combinations moving about, not necessarily forward, sometimes against each other, contrapuntally yet without one central theme.[16]

Could there be a better description of, first, an attitude that may be necessary for getting by in a globalizing world where everything sooner or later comes up against everything and everyone else? For Said, the figure of the exile was the model for what others would call the social theorist. In *Representations of the Intellectual,*[17] Said describes the culturally elite intellectual as an exile by identifying a fact that is seldom considered. Said mentions, in particular, Theodor Adorno, the founder of German critical theory and, if ever there was one, an elite intellectual. But Said also reminds us that Adorno and Max Horkheimer, and all the others associated with that form of critical theory, were exiles, dispossessed by Hitler. In fact, one could hardly imagine the history of social theory without the exilic factor: Marx and Durkheim left their homes; Du Bois and Weber stayed home, more or less, but put themselves in exile to the prevailing ideas of their times. There would be no feminist theory had not women left home; nor queer theory; nor postcolonial theory. Frantz Fanon and Aimé Césaire were exiles from Martinique, as Foucault and Derrida were from native homes in a rural city and Algeria. Though the types of dispossession differ in degree and kind, Said is surely right. Like it or not, to do the critical work of using one's elite cultural capital to unsettle the world is to become an exile—even a traitor to the class, even a terror to the prevailing culture. One cannot do social theory without being an exile. The modern world, so pleased with itself that it welcomes immigrant labor, has never taken well to free-floating intellectual social critics, many of whom find their way to prisons of one or another kind.

One supposes that modernity would have been better off not promising what none before, or since, have been able to provide. The good life may from time to time extend beyond the tiny higher circles of the fabulously or near-fabulously rich, but never has it embraced all of humankind. This was the genius of Robert K. Merton's famous essay on values and jobs. In 1938, well before the current situation, he recognized that the worldwide Depression of the 1930s was not an aberration except in degree. In the best of times, he taught, only a relative plurality, seldom a majority, of people living in the most modern of nations would be able to conform to the norm of hard work at jobs of dignity providing income. The fault is not with the promise or the ideals but with the underlying cynicism of those, unlike Merton, who know better and do little or nothing.

The terrorism of economic dispossession lies in the reality that there is indeed enough wealth and technically clever-enough method to provide the means to, at least, a decent human life in a home of some kind. Consider: Everyone should have one home before anyone gets two. Rob Rosenthal, among others, has calculated that were all the homeowners in the United States alone to sacrifice but a fraction of the tax relief they receive from the mortgage interest tax exemption, there would be sufficient revenue left over to provide a home of some kind for everyone living in the United States, legally or not.[18] Plus, one of the world's most accomplished practitioners of the art of economic transformations, Jeffrey Sachs, has argued, in *The End of Poverty* (2005), that it is possible by relatively simple measures virtually to eliminate global poverty.[19] After the disappointments of the previous half-millennium, one must be cautious before any new promise of a way out of the uprooting effects of economic injustice.

Yet, what encourages a renewal of hope is that there are those, like Sachs and Rosenthal, and many others, who are willing to press the hard numbers to calculate the means to supply a social method to the many. They differ, I think, from the nostalgics and romantics because, in principle at least, they reject much of the logic of the past in order to think the future afresh. Third-way policies are illusory. Debt-forgiveness and other strong economic redistribution policies are at least possible because they are thought outside the confining box of liberal ideology. If people would think as some do then it might be possible to save the globalizing world from itself—not by reestablishing the older modern synthesis, but by using what one can of it and leaving the rest.

For many dispossession is a terrible fate. Who will help their worlds if none accept the seemingly necessary vocation for thinking and acting clearly in a globalizing world? How else is one to act or think clearly in such a world as this? How else is one to take in the unthinkable misery of the truly dispossessed? Perhaps, like Edward Said, the key is to embrace sleeplessness as the proper and necessary gift for life as the exile in a world where all are dispossessed.

NOTES

1. In 2004, 175 million people were living outside their country of birth. At the ten-year average annual migration rate of 2 percent, the number could be as high as 177–178 million in 2005. Source: *World Economic and Social Survey 2004/International Migration* (New York: United Nations, 2004), 24.

2. The estimate is between 2003 and 2030 (rate of change 3.1 percent). Source: "Urban and Rural Areas 2003," *United Nations Department of Economic and Social Affairs/Population Division* (New York: United Nations, 2003), 1. Estimates following are from the same source.

3. Ursula Le Guin's *The Dispossessed* (1974) is a science fiction novel.

4. *Oxford English Dictionary,* 2nd edition (1989).

5. Jürgen Habermas, *The Theory of Communicative Action,* vol. 2, *Lifeworld and System* (Boston: Beacon, 1984).

6. Samuel P. Huntington, "The Clash of Civilizations?" *Foreign Affairs* (Summer 1993).

7. Edward Said, "The Clash of Ignorance," *Nation* (October 21, 2001). See also Stanley Hoffman, "The Clash of Globalizations," *Foreign Affairs* (August 2002).

8. Edward W. Said, *Out of Place* (New York: Random House, 1999).

9. Remarks were made in a seminar discussion based on Claus Offe, "Civil Society and Social Order," paper presented at Seoul National University seminar, Rethinking the "Modern" in the Globalizing World, May 26, 2005.

10. The phrase is Pierre Bourdieu's, but the task is perhaps better defined by Said, for one, and Jacques Derrida for another, in the writings at the end of his life on globalization and forgiveness. Derrida, *On Cosmopolitanism and Forgiveness* (London: Routledge, 2001). The tradition has its roots, theoretically, in Gilles Deleuze and Félix Guattari, *A Thousand Plateaus: Capitalism and Schizophrenia* (Minneapolis: University of Minnesota Press, 1987) and the emergence of subaltern studies at about the same time; for example, Gayatri Chakrovorty Spivak, "Can the Subaltern Speak?" in *Marxism and the Interpretation of Culture,* ed. Gary Nelson and Lawrence Grossberg (Urbana: University of Illinois Press, 1988).

11. Matrix of domination owes to Patricia Hill Collins, *Black Feminist Thought* (New York: Routledge, 1990), who uses the concept (borrowed from bell hooks, among others) to account for the political and cultural standpoint of the Black feminist. The idea of the matrix of domination is, in part, Collins's attempt to rethink domination, somewhat in the manner of Michel Foucault's theory of power as knowledge, as diffused up and down and across social and global spaces. The Black woman in America (and by implication everywhere) may be in some social sense among the "most" dominated figures (which as many have argued may also be a source of her moral power), but if power dominates ubiquitously then all suffer its effects according to their social position. What Collins leaves out, I think, is a reckoning of the Black woman's global position. To begin, any social position in a region like the core of the American hegemony who owes her home place to the slave trade is, one would suppose, necessarily in a global position—one more enduring and definitive than any other. The *locus classicus* of the Black woman's moral power as a function of her domination is Anna Julia Cooper's 1892 classic *A Voice from the South*—in respect to which, one notes in passing, that the argument turns on the tide's phrase "from the South"—the Black woman in Jim Crow America in the 1890s was from the South, even if in the North, in the sense that her moral home is the feudal South of slavery and its subsequent entailments.

12. The comparisons here are loose in places where I compare wealth to incomes, a move justified only partly by the fact that the point made is about differences so extreme as to be unthinkable. Thus, as rough measures the income of the wealthiest is a good enough estimate of the degree of wealth relative to the income of the most poor who, in fact, have virtually no accumulated wealth in the sense of investments, real estate, and personal property. The estimates and precise numbers are reported in the *New York Times* (June 5, 2005), A27. See for sources http://www.nytimes.com/class/sources; in particular for income estimates, Edward Wolff, "Changes in Household Wealth in the 1980s and 1990s in the U.S.," *Working Paper* 409, The Levy Economics Institute of Bard College (May 2004), which actually attends to wealth while the *New York Times* report is for the most part on income.

13. The reference is, in part, to the first edition of this book, where I took a wholly unsympathetic attitude toward certain of the more prominent nostalgics. Now in the passage of time I think of some of them as merely pathetic; others as struggling in, to me, a strange way to come to terms with their loss. I am sure that the ability to accept loss has grown from the loss of my son Matthew in 2000.

14. The allusion to core and margin is a serious play on Immanuel Wallerstein's terms.

15. The following is based closely on Nicholas D. Kristof, "Day 141 of Bush's Silence," *New York Times* (May 31, 2005), A17.

16. Said, *Out of Place,* 295.

17. Said, *Representations of the Intellectual* (New York: Pantheon, 1993).

18. Personal communications over several years of discussion with Rob Rosenthal; see also Rosenthal, *Homeless in Paradise* (Philadelphia, PA: Temple University Press, 1993).

19. Jeffrey D. Sachs, *The End of Poverty: Economic Possibilities in Our Time* (New York: Penguin, 2005).

13
Surviving the New Individualism
With Anthony Elliott

Individualism has become so prevalent in talk among modern people that many will be surprised to learn that the word is of relatively recent vintage—not much earlier than the 1830s, when the great French social thinker and observer of American life gave the word a still-cogent meaning: "Individualism is a novel expression, to which a novel idea has given birth. Individualism is a mature and calm feeling, which disposes each member of the community to sever himself from the mass of his fellow-creatures, and to draw apart with his family and friends" (Alexis de Tocqueville, *Democracy in America,* 1835). What was novel about the idea and the word in the 1830s was that Tocqueville, himself quite a serious individual thinker, was commenting on the social consequences of a moral and political principle that gave rise to the modern world. The idea was that the proper and primary condition of the human individual in society is a state of composure within and without comfort among those few to whom one is most closely bound. To achieve this idyllic state the individual must "sever himself from the mass of his fellow-creatures and draw apart."

Tocqueville's definition begins to suggest the degree to which, prior to the modern world, individualism was far from a normal first consideration when people thought about the purpose of their lives. Individualism, as a commonplace moral ideal, was not just unique to the modern world, but in many ways its prevalence has been one of modernity's identifying social facts. This is why, years later, we recall Tocqueville's nineteenth-century observations with interest, and why the fate of the moral individual and his freedoms (or lack thereof) have long been a worry of social critics in the twentieth century. Yet the story of the concept's origins, like that of all important social facts, is not entirely clear cut.

Before the revolutionary eighteenth century, people thought of themselves as mere particles of a mass of social order. Certainly, those of the noble classes gave evidence of an extreme confidence in their subjective worth; and long before that, men and women like Aristotle, Augustine of Hippo, the biblical Ruths and Marys, and many others, knew how to think for themselves. And we have seen how the concept was put into practice before the word had been coined—in the thinking of eighteenth-century revolutionaries like Jean-Jacques Rousseau and Benjamin Franklin, among many others.

What distinguishes Alexis de Tocqueville's definition of *individualism* in the complicated path of the word's prehistory as a political and moral ideal is one important, little-noted aspect of the work that led to *Democracy in America*. Tocqueville was not engaged in philosophical work so much as an early form of sociological observation. In the 1830s the line between was fine indeed; still, there is something to be said for an idea that begins not in logic but in systematic observation. The individualism Tocqueville defined was a social phenomenon as much as an idea—and one that was already widespread in North America in the early generations that grew up after the French and American revolutions. And, in the nineteenth century, nowhere else was *individualism* more in evidence than in early modern America, where, long since, it still finds its most acute expression.

This being said, it could well be asked as we come to the conclusion: *So, what then is all that's new about the new individualism?* In one sense, the honest answer would appear to be: not all that much. The theories of the new individualism we have presented throughout the book still exhibit traces of a search for a "calm and mature" state of individual life apart from the unsettling complexities of society. The differences over time are in the changing social realities faced by individuals.

When the word came into use—in the 1830s in North America especially, but also in Europe—the modern societies were, by contrast to today, anything but complex; nor were they utterly simple for all social classes, as we know from the fictions of Charles Dickens. Life was hard for many in mid-nineteenth-century Europe and America, where the early factory system brought misery upon misery for those forced to leave the worlds they knew in search of what livings they could earn from long days pressed against the machinery. Still, this was a world in which individuals (so-called after the fact) could imagine themselves enjoying a private life cut off from the public sphere. It is true, we must say immediately, that the individuals who in fact enjoyed the freedom of a mature and calm individualism in a settled life among friends and family were, with rare exception, white men; and men in particular of the middle and upper classes. The people in Jane Austen's novels who enjoyed their luxuries in estates in Bath were people of privilege. Yet, as we also know from the great nineteenth-century novels of English literature, if any among the landed classes were deprived of a sense of individual self-composure it was women like the Jane Eyre of Charlotte Brontë's imagination. No blacks needed apply for the status, save for the now famous madwoman in the attic in *Jane Eyre* and other accidents of the colonial system. Nor too did it happen that the poor—those today we call the working poor—had much assurance of the benefits of individualism as a way of life. Yet we know very well that they understood the principle and aspired to it.

This we know from the ease with which former slaves and subjects of the world colonial system were able readily to adjust to the trappings of the bourgeois life once they gained their freedom. Late in the nineteenth century, men like Frederick

Douglass and women like Anna Julia Cooper, both born into slavery, lived their adult lives according to the principles, if not the exact social realities, of the bourgeois individualism that then prevailed in the dominant white middle and upper classes.

What, then, and again, is new in the new individualism? Well, first and foremost it helps to realize that individualisms of all kinds, new or old, are moral and social codes before they are concepts. This is the conclusion we draw from the origin of the word at a certain time in the early evolution of a new form of bourgeois civilization in the modern European diaspora. Social ideals (even after they become concepts of various kinds) are always linked to what the great German social thinker Georg Simmel called "social forms." The ideas men and women live by necessarily must fit to an efficient degree the society in which they intend to live. Otherwise, as monks of all kinds will tell you, they must quit the social order to find another that will tolerate their peculiar ways.

This is an important point to keep in mind as we consider the question of how one survives the new individualism. And one of the best ways to keep it in mind is to note, and remember, that the three expressions of the theory of new individualism we have described each arose in a specific social setting. While there were variations on the theme of Tocqueville's definition in the century or so between his definition in the 1830s and 1930s when in Germany critical thinkers revised the term's meaning to suit the times, the old individualism remained, for the most part, a near, if not perfect, constant. The century from the 1830s on was the period when in the West (and in selected quarters of its vast colonial system) the bourgeois class rose to the prominence previously reserved for a nobility. In business, the arts and literature, as in the values in which they were formed, the new bourgeois class lived in families amongst their kind. Even Marx in London, poor though he was, and the most radical of critics of the bourgeoisie, aspired to live a bourgeois life. He withdrew from the public order for great periods of time to write and think in the British Museum—and was afforded this luxury by the generosity of his wealthy comrade, Friedrich Engels. Marx's detested bourgeoisie, like Jane Austen's more benign class of a certain cultural refinement, was a new and original social class—one as different in kind from the nobility of old as it is from the so-called middle classes of today.

THE DEADLY COSTS OF GLOBAL VIOLENCE

The question we would ask of today's world is whether individuals, new or old, living in the 2000s can reasonably expect war and violence to disappear from the global scene. A century before, the First World War was fought, according to the optimistic, as a war to end all wars. The record of the intervening century, however, is one of near-continuous war. And, to make matters worse, even when the wars are more regional than global, one can hardly look forward to a moment when peace might reign. The globalized worlds seem to be ones in which social and economic violence is more, not less, in evidence. It may be, some would say, that with our brilliant new information technologies it is not the violence that is greater but our capacity to know about it instantaneously and thoroughly, in more televisual detail than anyone with a life could want. This of course is possible, a possibility only time will tell. But it is also possible, and just as likely, that the pattern of war and violence that grew across the twentieth century has now become commonplace.

It is certainly true, though its enthusiasts deny it, that globalization has led to deeper and deeper cleavages between the world's haves and have-nots. While parts of South and East Asia have joined the lands of the haves, Central and North Asia, not to mention southern Africa, much of the West Indies and the central and southern Americas, the far north of first-peoples in Canada and economic refugees in Russia have become the land of the have-nots. And the gap between the two has widened in near exact proportion to the appalling wealth in the lands of the haves. It is a topic of much discussion among policy-makers whether poverty incites violence. What is hard to deny is that when the poor see the wealth from which they are excluded they have confirmed reason to feel anger and much else. In Dickens's day the poor in East London, lacking television or radio, even telephones, had little direct knowledge of the rich in Kensington. Today those fleeing Taliban warlords know that some in Kabul had a better life, as even those in border camps in Darfur or makeshift shelters in post-tsunami Indonesia have contact, perhaps even televisual, with the affluence of others which were, until disaster struck them, comforts they themselves had tasted.

Whether it is actual warfare, or civil strife, or the spread of AIDS, or the selling of children into the sex trade, or grinding poverty, or sewage flowing before the opening of a shanty, violence is present whenever those with the means use their means to protect their privileges against those who want a share of them. And, to come to the unique feature of globalization, when money and time move as rapidly as they do today on the wings of a digital bird any one person knows that he or she is at some risk—even those most securely ensconced in their gated villas.

The global worlds are risky in ways that go far beyond the historically normal risks of famine, drought and warfare. Risks now are ones from which no one can be assured a free pass and into which the millions upon millions tumble day by day. The very idea of a mass society as an imposition on the individual is eclipsed in such times as these by the mass of human misery. It is true of course that those who wake to the smell of sewage are very much more at risk than those no longer able to find good help to clean the apartment. Yet, what ties shit on the streets to the inconvenience of dirt balls under the sofa is that the shit is likely to have been left, in shame and mortification, by the woman no longer able to travel north far enough to find meager work cleaning the master's shit from the master's toilet. In a global environment everything is linked to everything else. A principle that was for centuries a matter of Buddhist belief has become a hard social and economic reality. No one sees the butterfly that sends an economic or social tsunami our way. No one believes that wave of global flooding can rise up to the penthouse. But it can and it has—today with ever so much more regularity. And whether you fall asleep plotting a way to slip across the border to San Diego or feel the backache from doing your own cleaning for a change, the one inevitable fact of life in the 2000s is that everyone must think—and think about themselves, deeply and seriously. Some will adjust and make a new individualism. Others will not because the risks are too real and their resources too few.

Deadly worlds are violent worlds. They may not lead immediately to the death of the body, but when violence is pervasive, either in the neighborhood or across the world, that violence is experienced and has its effect. One no doubt feels at risk, and especially so if one is a child, little aware of the whys and wherefores of the gun shots down the street. There is a risk to be sure, but the ubiquity of violence in the world is something more.

Individualisms, whether old or new, are, first and foremost, practical moral principles by which men and women measure their personal worth. They may come to be accepted by, or embodied in, literary or social theories, but before they rise to the level of intellectual curiosities they are the mundane theories of men—and men living, not always well, in the quotidian. Thus began the old *individualism* in the decades and centuries before Alexis de Tocqueville put it into words. What he saw on his visit to the United States was a then just-emerging bourgeois class, a class to which those who, a century later, would be called "lower" or "middle class" aspired. It was a social type he had seen fully formed in Europe where the bourgeoisie had emerged somewhat more by descent from the declining nobility. By contrast, in the US the bourgeoisie had arisen, rather more, from a yeomanry whose ties were not to the court but to the independent farmers that Thomas Jefferson thought were the promise of American democracy. Jefferson himself, while a landed slave-holder and a man of noble culture, lived most of his days as a reluctant patriot and revolutionary— services that caused him to exhaust his wealth and to die a man of limited means in the moral debt of those who had covered his financial obligations. Benjamin Franklin, likewise, began life as a shopkeeper and tradesman—a printer first, then a newspaper man, and only then a statesman and scientist. These two extremes were the typically American old individualists—men engaged in society, yes, but engaged on the basis of duty not privilege, and men who made their mark by bringing to their callings and avocations unique and individualist talents. By the time of Tocqueville's observations in the 1830s both were gone from the scene. Still, as Max Weber would put it, they were ideal types, historical individuals who represented in practical terms the old individualism Tocqueville saw a generation later spread across the land—the old individualism that cherished the independence of spirit of being cut-off from the masses. Thus, the old individualism, while aspiring to the unique calm of the private self, was just as much a product of its social conditions as were the later new individualisms of the twentieth and early twenty-first centuries.

Individualisms, old or new, practical or theoretical, are more social things than psychological ones. If they are to be studied, they must be studied by the rules of a sociology—that is, as facts of a social kind that cannot be explained away as having been caused by the impulses of the mind or psyche. This is why not only Tocqueville but all the subsequent theorists of modern individualisms were and are either professional sociologists outright or, in Tocqueville's case, proto-sociologists. From Adorno to Marcuse and Habermas, from Riesman to Sennett and Bellah, from Giddens to Beck and Bauman—all the major theorists have thought as sociologists. This is not a fact of convenience but one of moment. It calls attention to a theme that has always been in the background of thinking about moral principles in social history, and certainly about books (including this one) and essays of the old and new individualisms.

In a sentence: moral principles of individualism, while they are clearly of keen interest to actual individuals, are also of broader interest for the ways they represent practical theories of how individuals facing dangers greater than mere risk must think themselves in order to deal with real social conditions.

Hence the merciless elegance of the liquid world: the comforts come with the violence; the violence accentuates the longing for comfort; and, in times like these, neither is likely to win the day. These may be days that cannot be won. But they must be lived in because they are the only days we have. This may be why the British theories of reflexive individualism are in their way both cautious and sober, while at the same time being less bitter than the earlier German criticisms and not at all nostalgic like the American ones.

SURVIVING THE NEW INDIVIDUALISM

Thus we come to our final question. How does one survive the emotional costs of the new individualism? And how especially can men and women come to terms with worlds so liquid, the very liquidity of which is the source of their risks and dangers, the dangers of which are the source of its deadly violence? As we have throughout, we answer these questions with the stories of two individuals—both well-enough known to us as they are to many who learned to live and think by their teachings. Had they lived they would both have been in their eighties early in the 2000s. Ironically, they knew each other for a time in the 1940s, which makes their different paths to individualism so striking. It is not incidental that one was a man, the other a woman.

The man was C. Wright Mills (1916–62), one of the most influential social thinkers in the United States in the 1950s. Mills, in many ways, stood at odds with some of the social critics of that day. While he certainly shared, say, Riesman's concern over the rise of other-directedness, he was unusual for an American intellectual of the day in that he attempted to bring more European ideas into his writing—and especially the ideas of Max Weber and Karl Marx. As a result Mills's criticism of modern society had many of the features of the Europeans. He saw the problems not simply as a failure of the individual to keep a sense of discipline and hard work in the face of consumer culture, but as, even more, the result of systematic exploitation on the part of an elite. One of his well-known books was *The Power Elite* (1956) in which he systematically, and for the first time in a popular book, described the actual existing relations among business, military and government elites. The very expression "power elite" then entered the American language, as did the idea that an elite that included people who were elected by no one in particular exercise unusual power over the policies that affected American life. By 1960, Mills's idea was so well known that it is hard to miss its influence on the then president of the United States, Dwight D. Eisenhower, who in his farewell speech upon leaving office warned the American people of the dangers of "the military-industrial complex."

Even more famous, and important for our purposes, was an earlier book, *White Collar,* which appeared a scant year after Riesman's *The Lonely Crowd.* This earlier book was less a lament on the passing of the old individualism than a critical analysis of the new middle classes of white-collar workers then defining a new social location between the working class and the older bourgeoisie—those who were more inclined to work in lesser administrative or managerial office jobs than in factories; and, in contrast to the older bourgeoisie, they were unlikely to be the owners of their workplace. They worked increasingly in larger and larger corporate firms that in the 1950s (and since) demanded the very other-directed conformism that bothered social critics like David Riesman. Yet, Mills's purposes in his work were not merely to analyze the sociology of modern life but also to provide the people affected by it the tools whereby they could engage themselves in political action that would take power from the elites, power they would then use to participate in the social world both to make it more human and to improve their personal circumstances.

This led in time to what Mills called, in the title of a later book, *The Sociological Imagination.* He was nothing if not a believer in sociology. His idea of the sociological imagination was not, however, so much concerned with social science as with the political importance of a practical sociology for ordinary men (he spoke that way) who lived personal lives as individuals, but their personal lives were determined by the history of the larger social structures. Individuals, he argued, tend to see no far- ther than their own noses. As a result, when something goes wrong in life they tend to blame themselves for their "personal troubles." It was here that C. Wright Mills shared a concern of the other social critics of the 1950s. But, putting the concern to practical and political purpose, Mills said (to the astonishment of some) that what these "men" needed to do was to become sociologists. His sociological imagination was the art of seeing beyond one's personal troubles to the larger social structures that, as often as not, aggravate (or created in the first place) the troubles. The wives and mothers of Levittown come home from a long day at the King of Prussia Mall. In their fatigue they look at their haul—with remorse. They spent too much. They consider themselves moral failures. Being isolated in one-dimensional suburbs they have few resources with which to imagine sociologically—to examine their moral failure as individual in the light of the social issues in the wider culture. They lack not intelligence but the intellectual wherewithal to consider that their shopping is prompted by the structures of post-war life—affluence, media, advertising, fads, proximity to others, the malls themselves, not to mention the elites with an interest in manufacturing a consumer mentality. It is evident, therein, that C. Wright Mills straddled the critical fences—while acknowledging the plight of the individual (as did the Americans), like the Germans he put the blame on the culture itself. Mills was not alone in his thinking in his day or since. Among his influences were those on the radical political movements of the 1960s, especially the student and anti-war movements. Though he died in 1962, his influence grew in the years after and remains important today.

Just the same, we introduce him here not so much for his ideas as for his own way of living, which, in many ways, illustrates both the promise and the tragedy of the new individualism—especially so for men who came into adult life in the 1930s and devoted their mature years to living in the face of the changes in the United States in the 1950s.

C. Wright Mills was anything but an old individualist. He loathed bourgeois refinements. At the same time, he was driven from youth to become an American original. Everything about his approach to education, and later to shaping a career as what today we call a public intellectual, cut at odds with the prevailing norms—anything but cut off from the mass of society so much as determined to be the critical individual of social ways. The man was, in his way, the epitome of the inner-directed individual and the antithesis of the other-directed conformist. Mills was born in Texas, from which he took the rough-and-tumble independent ways. Already as a green first-year student at Texas A & M, the most unlikely of places for such a character, he wrote a most literate indictment of the school as feudal, and worse. He quit the place for the rather more urbane University of Texas, where he studied philosophy before graduate studies at the University of Wisconsin. He was never satisfied with work in one field to the exclusion of others, yet at Wisconsin both sociology and the school's progressive culture encouraged his individualism. Even in this Mills worked at odds with prevailing disciplinary norms by writing a doctoral thesis on American pragmatism while beginning his work with Hans Gerth on Weber and European social theory—in the United States at the time a rare combination of interests. By the 1940s he was teaching at the University of Maryland; then in 1945 he moved to New York, eventually to teach sociology in the college at Columbia University.

Through it all Mills refused to adjust—either to the dreary norms of academic sociology or to accommodate its, to him, creepy narrowness and mind-numbing abstractions. He was never accepted as a full member of Columbia's graduate department of sociology, then the leading program in the field. He refused to write as they wrote or think as they thought. His first major book, *White Collar* in 1951, brought him public acclaim, as did all that followed. In short order, Mills was, in the public eye, one of sociology's most famous writers, while many of his academic colleagues shunned him. He lived his intellectual life as he did his personal life. He dropped his kids off at school on the motorcycle that became his public signature. He loved guns, it is said, but even if this was a rumor from his Texas origins, Mills thought and wrote and dealt with the world in the style of a gun-toting, quick-draw artist on the frontier of modern life. He built homes and ploughed gardens by hand, traveled the world, while reading and writing prolifically.

His travels led him to Cuba and meetings with Fidel Castro and Che Guevara just after Cuba's 1959 revolution. After, Mills wrote *Listen Yankee* (1960) which praised and defended Castro's revolution. The liberal foreign policy establishment rose up against him, as had the Columbia establishment earlier. Behind all the bravado of his public face, Mills no doubt felt the sting of rebuke. He suffered a massive heart attack days before he was to defend *Listen Yankee* in a nationally televised debate. Fifteen months later, after trying to recover his health, he died of a second heart attack. His tombstone in Nyack, New York, reads: "I have tried to be objective. I do not claim to be detached." Mills had lived his 45 years with speed and audacity, even defiance. All of his important intellectual work was written and published in the nine years between 1951 and 1960. In the same decade he built three houses and one BMW motorcycle. Liquid he was not, but his living was as a flash of aggressive speed.

Mills lived in his own way, and certainly his brand of individualism was new, if not settled. His was a life lived with courage, to be sure, but also with insolent protest against the one-dimensionality of modern culture that reduced individuals to empty vessels lacking, in his words, the sociological imagination to resist the power elites; and, also against the mindless conformities of the new middle classes of the suburbs, the shallow privatism that bred the isolating detachment of an individualism cut off from the masses—cut off not by choice, as in Tocqueville's day, but by the destructive forces of the modern world. He did not come close to living long enough to witness the globalizing extensions of these forces. Had he, you can be sure that while he would have argued aggressively with the British proponents of the risk society, he would have taken their point—especially the basic concept of the reflexive self. Mills was nothing if not a man (too much a man perhaps) who lived with an objective eye on global realities and a heart engaged in reinventing himself.

Yet, he did not survive either the global realities or his own masculinist style of individualism. Did the very public controversy over his daring attempt to defy the American establishment by praising Castro kill him? It is tempting but facile to think so. It is enough to regret that his heart gave out at a young age—perhaps because of disease, perhaps because of the speed with which he lived, perhaps because of emotional and physical toll inflicted by his way of setting himself against the dangerous worlds. C. Wright Mills was a new individualist who understood, or would have understood, the entire history of modernity's attempts to come to terms with the cuttings apart and comings together of individual *Character and Social Structures* (1953)—the title of one of his books and the key terms of his famous idea: *The Sociological Imagination* (1959).

THE PROMISE OF AGGRESSION

How indeed do individuals survive in worlds made deadly by social structures? Mills understood the question, but not the answer. The answer may be suggested in the life of a woman of our acquaintance and friendship who, for a time in the 1940s, worked with Mills and whose own professional and personal career was devoted to many of the same concerns, though in a much different way and with markedly different life consequences.

Phyllis Whitcomb Meadow was a survivor, if ever there was one, just as she was one of the more unusual individualists anyone could hope to meet. Though but a few years Mills's junior, she not only lived but lived actively well until a particularly virulent form of cancer limited her days. Even then, between visits to hospital for care, while suffering dramatic weight loss, Meadow continued her life's work. One winter day in December 2004, just weeks before her death at age 80, Phyllis took herself from the hospital in New York City, dressed herself grandly, and went directly to share the stage in a long-planned public discussion with the world-famous French psychoanalyst Andre Green. Most in the audience of 500 were unaware of her illness. Those who were marveled at her energy, as they always had. Phyllis Meadow was famous—and to some notorious—for a level of human energy that would have shamed those about her were it not that she used the energy almost always for constructive purposes that gave life to others.

Phyllis met C. Wright Mills early in the 1940s at the University of Maryland. She was drawn to his intelligence, as he must have been to hers. Still, in one class he gave her a C+, apparently to shock his young student. Mills loathed the University of Maryland. If Phyllis had been a loather, she would have too, but her style was to embrace where possible, transform where necessary, whatever institutions were before. Soon she became Mills's research assistant. When he moved to New York in 1945 she followed him, taking a day job in publishing, while serving as his research assistant for, among other projects, *White Collar*. Late in life, Phyllis recalled her few years working with Mills:

> His main impulses were for work. He once told me he wanted to learn more about literature, so I made a list of all the great works and brought the books to his apartment on West 14th Street. The place was lined wall to wall with books. They soon disappeared. He had the ability to read three or four books a weekend ... He died a terrible death at forty-five. He just burned himself out.

She by contrast lived on, four decades longer than Mills, working and living every bit as hard and fast as he had. What accounts for the difference between two people of enormous energy and intelligence, both roughly of the same age and living through the same social times, both conspicuous individualists in several of the new senses of the term? The one survives; the other does not. Again, we ask, how does one survive the new individualism which, as Mills's life shows, can be risky, even dangerous, perhaps even deadly?

It may be too simple to suggest that the difference that led to Mills's early death is genetic. Something was physically wrong with Mills's heart. After the first attack he did everything then known in order to survive, including visits to clinics in Russia. Yet Phyllis Meadow may be right that, whatever the underlying illness, he burned himself out in the sense that his human energy, so great and brilliant, somehow did not serve to keep him going.

One might dismiss Phyllis Meadow's remark as pop-psychology were it not for the fact that, after her few years working with Mills, she went on to become one of

America's most original and important psychoanalysts. In the 1950s she was trained in psychoanalysis at one of New York's many institutes, where she sought out teachers and training analysts who were themselves individualists, people who cut against the grain of establishment psychoanalysis as Mills of resisting the confinements of establishment sociology. After becoming a certified lay analyst (then a rebellion in its own right), Phyllis took a Ph.D. in psychology because she was devoted to learning, but just as much because she was smart and knew that in that field, as in others in that day, a woman without an MD had to be otherwise certified. She was nothing if not ambitious, like Mills; but her ambitions led her in quite another, though just as defiant, direction.

Phyllis began her life's work in the 1950s, in a day when in the United States feminism was unheard of, which meant among other things that an independent woman faced odds that were, if not impossible, certainly more severe than she would today. In point of fact, never in her long life did she, so far as anyone we know knows, think of herself as a feminist. Certainly she refused to talk the talk of any social movement. But she did walk the walk. One might say that like many other courageous women of her day and before, Phyllis was a feminist before the fact (and without the label). She married, had a child, left a husband, built a home, remarried, trained, and went into private clinical practice. The year after her daughter left New York in 1969 for medical school at Wisconsin, Phyllis Meadow joined in the founding of the first of her several psychoanalytic institutes, The Center for Modern Psychoanalysis on West 10th Street in New York, just blocks from where she had worked with Mills. She was, at the time, already well into middle age, an age when others are beginning to think of retirement.

From there she went on to found and lead two other graduate institutes in the field—one in Boston in 1973, another a quarter of a century later in Vermont—both of which are fully certified to offer clinical certification and doctoral-level degrees in psychoanalysis, and both are research-based training centers. As a nod perhaps to her beginnings as a sociologist, one of the advanced degree programs in the Boston Graduate School of Psychoanalysis is the Institute for the Study of Violence, a program she founded, along with the Vermont Center, when she was well into her seventies. Approaching her eightieth birthday she took up the study of Jacques Lacan, the notoriously obscure French analyst, whose thinking she incorporated in her most important book, *The New Psychoanalysis* (2003). Not only that but at the same time she took up the study of neuroscience, which she required as one of the elements in the training of students in the Institute for the Study of Violence. All the while she continued to treat patients in New York City and Boston, to edit an academic journal she also founded, to push all of her centers and their students towards developing their research skills, to lecture and to travel the world.

We will never know what C. Wright Mills would have been like had he lived a long life, but Phyllis Meadow at 80 and mortally ill would have given a much younger Mills a run for his money. Many describe her as a force of nature. The physician who diagnosed her cancer could not believe it when, after he examined her physically, she told him how old she was; nor over the years could her students and patients. Her most urgent clinical work in the last months of her life was to help her patients and students work through their feelings about her pending death. She kept no secrets, and was willing to hear or say anything—including talk of her own death. She was, thus, a woman who faced squarely the dangers of the deadly and violent worlds, reflexively to take them on and in—thus to reinvent the local worlds about her. One of the more puzzling statements she would often make when people tried to tell her she could not do what she set about doing was: "Of course not. Life is impossible. Don't try to change me." Then she'd do the impossible.

How is such an individual possible? As one could say, that biology may have contributed to Mills's early death, so one could say that the luck of the draw of her early life may have stood behind Phyllis's astonishing personal qualities. When she was 7, her parents separated. Her mother moved to Maine. She chose to remain with her father in Massachusetts, largely because she could not bear to leave her grandmother who, though prim and proper in appearance, was a woman who talked about anything, saying whatever needed to be said. There began Phyllis's childhood appreciation of the most important work of psychoanalysis—the skill to support the patient's courage to say everything about his feelings. Then too the separation she suffered from her mother also had its effect. As a child she longed for the absent mother whom she saw mostly in the summers until she moved to Washington, D.C. when Phyllis was ready to join her (which led of course to the meetings with Mills at the University of Maryland). Late in life Phyllis attributed her ability to feel and talk about these longings for both parents, and the anger at the loss of her primal family, as important emotional elements in, again, her interest in psychoanalysis. But, at an age when she could not have spelled the word "psychoanalysis," it would seem a stretch to suggest that her adult life was already determined by childhood experiences; far from it.

There are many children separated from parents at a young age who go nowhere in particular, some even who suffer lifelong disorders that block their energy and frustrate their lives. This happens as often as there are young men who may or may not have congenital heart disease but who find a way to manage disease and live to old age. Neither family circumstances nor biology are destinies. They can help or hurt, to be sure, but the question of survival is one of how one plays the hand dealt at birth.

There is one word that Phyllis Meadow used to describe her own ability to survive full of creative energy to live a long life: aggression! This may seem odd, and especially so in a culture where aggression does not have a good reputation. But if one stops to think about it, aggression may well be the key to survival. It certainly is with the animals that face natural worlds ever more deadly than the ones humanoids have created over time. If Alpha wolves could think, they would surely know that their day of death and defeat will come. Yet they rise, perhaps by instinct as much as by physical prowess, to conquer the males that would kill them for the status of head of the pack with all the sex you could want. Somehow, over the same cultural history of the modern world that has led to more and more social violence, the culture itself has lost the ability to think of aggression as a natural human virtue.

Perhaps we have lost or neglected the instinct for aggression as a key to the survival of the human animal in large part because we have witnessed, on the social scale, the terrible effects of aggression in world affairs.

There is, however, a difference between aggression that leads to violence and the kind that leads to rich and powerful living. Even the Alpha wolf does not kill when he is not threatened. Curiously, behind the timid moralities of modern culture, the only places one can find positive ideas of aggression are in the cases of a just war against an evil enemy like Hitler or in the face of violence against oneself or one's family. The self-defense argument seems, however, to stand alone in the meager debates over aggression, and especially so in a world where it is attributed to the male of the species who is said to be more inclined than the female to be the Alpha-killer and rapist.

Never, however, have we heard of anyone who thought of Phyllis Meadow as having masculine qualities. She was, if any one personal thing, mostly sexual and seductive (and this until her last days of life). People did call her, as she would have agreed, a killer, meant mostly but not entirely metaphorically. She was a woman filled with available sexual energy, who focused her career always on building groups and motivating individuals. But her way with people was not unrelated to her status as a killer—that is, as a woman who would not tolerate anyone trying to change her or to stand in her way. More than a few times people would storm away from her or her institutes outraged at her aggression. I personally know of at least four senior leaders of her institutes (me included) who quit in disgust because she was willing to run over them to get her way. Some never came back; some did (again, me included). She was more than glad to embrace the prodigals. But she refused to be swayed by their resistance, even when she may or may not have been right in the actions to which they objected.

This we should say right off is a very unusual kind of aggression—a killer instinct that arises not so much from self-knowledge or, even, self-confidence (though surely that is part of it). Phyllis's aggression was rooted in her willingness to know the worlds for what they so messily are—impossible and aggressive and violent. It is one thing to be ambitious or brilliant as Mills was. It is another to have these traits of character and to pursue them against those who wish to kill to protect the comforts of their (usually) bourgeois positions. Mills refused to let the academic establishment rein him in. Nor did he allow the prevailing norms of political liberalism to dissuade him from making noise in favor of Castro's Cuba. Yet we know that he suffered under the exclusion and criticisms to which he was exposed in his intellectual worlds, as he seems to have been affected by the challenges to his radicalism in *Listen Yankee!* The title is bold and aggressive, but his first heart attack came just when he risked embarrassment and exposure before the nation.

Risks are everywhere, more so today than ever. Ulrich Beck and the British thinkers are right on this score, even if they come a bit short of describing the violent nature of a globalized world. In this sense they are closer in their understanding of human nature to Mills than to Phyllis Meadow. Mills's famous slogan of the sociological imagination put all the hope for power in knowledge—the ability of the individual to study the sociology of social structures. There can be no doubt that he, like many intellectuals, put a good deal of his personal faith in knowledge. "I tried to be objective...." If objectivity is the standard for truth, then however much one tries to overcome detachment there is a point beyond which facts will not carry you. In a somewhat similar way, thinkers like Anthony Giddens and Beck, and certainly ones like Richard Sennett in the tradition of lament over the isolated individual, are closer in spirit to Mills. They may not suppose that sociological knowledge is the answer to the risk society. But they do seem to write about the reflexive self as if the reflexive coming to terms with global risk were a naturally available, if traditionally ignored, human quality.

To face risks, when the risks are real, is to face the possibility of real dangers, even violence. We will never come to terms as individuals with the new global realities if we begin with any sort of innocence about just how deadly these new worlds are. We certainly respect the now long history of men and women who have attempted to salvage their inner sense of integrity as individuals while living against and in an inhospitable world. We respect also every bit as much the social critics from Adorno to Giddens who have sought to account for the transformations, even fundamental ones, in the social structures affecting and very often limiting the individual's capacity to survive and flourish. We even (and obviously) agree with them that there is a new kind of individualism abroad on the planet—a necessary one, and one that can be thought to hold a promise of new possibilities for humankind.

Where we hold reservations is on the point of assessing the risks before individuals in the globalizing worlds, in respect to which we propose that a more seriously critical theory of the new individualism is required. If we live in a risk society, then we live with danger. If the dangers are real, they put individuals at risk of violence. If the violence in the social order is real, then how will the new individuals ever be able to survive if they do not develop their own inner capacity for aggression? Aggression on the inside of the individual is not an idea but a feeling—a feeling that some say is due to the residual of the animal within us; and it is not (at least not first and foremost) a theory or a concept. Try to *think* of yourself as aggressive in a culture that teaches the contrary and you will draw a blank. Try, however, to *feel* the aggression within you—those impulses to speak an angry word, those actions that could lead to the breaking of a relationship, those fantasies to murder or otherwise silence an enemy. So far as is known there has not yet been an individual without *feelings* of this kind. The difference between us and the wolves, however, is that, though some do, we humanoids do not, in the normal course of events, need to kill in order to survive. We can use words. But to use the words, or take the actions that allow us to *be* aggressive, we must be willing and able to experience our own personal feelings of aggression. The talk does no good if you do not feel the aggression—and accept the hard truth that in the worlds in which we live there will be aggression, aggression not unrelated to that within us all. Nor, on the other hand, does it serve the individual if he can only act on the feeling without first experiencing it and coming to a conclusion as to whether talk (or silence) or action might be the way to achieve the goal at hand in the situation.

Phyllis Meadow lived by her feelings, but not by feelings alone. She was a genius as a thinker and a therapist and a powerhouse as an organizer. Without question she was a risk taker, and one who could reflect on herself thus to invent her unique and individual self as she went along. But she could not have done any of what she accomplished just by being aggressive. The aggression was always balanced against the love of others and the constructive desire to join them working to build a better world. She had her psychoanalytic theories for the way she lived. Anyone interested in them can consult her books and articles. But we do not tell her story here, as we do not tell any of the stories of others in this book, to set up anyone as a paragon of virtuous accomplishment or of disgracing failure. If the costs of the new individualism are real, thus more than mere risks, then some will fail and some survive, while most will make do with both.

The issue at hand on the globe today is how do individuals survive and thrive amid and against deadly worlds that would take it all away? The question may be more acute on the plains of Darfur or the *bidonvilles* on the margins of economic progress. But it is a universal human question. Phyllis Meadow would not have thought of herself as a universal hero—a model for the new individualism. She was way too occupied with the local and human work to which she devoted her life, not to mention enjoying what pleasure could be on hand along the way. For her the key was joining the aggression with pleasures to lead a whole and honest life.

If her story rings less true as an example available to all, then at the other end of the social and economic scale keep in mind Norman Bishop. He has little education, no money, no particularly acknowledged training or skill—beyond, that is, his acquired capacity to focus his life on living and helping others to survive. Remember him as one who had lost his life to drugs, disease, and the poverty that follows therefrom. But he is also the most self-reflexive individual you could hope to meet, and this because he faced the risks before him. Anyone suffering HIV, not to mention poverty, in his part of the world has a chance that thousands in Africa will not. But Norman's survival is far from an accident of his birth. He survived to thrive in life only because he was able to look at his life *and* his world (call it "reflexivity" if you want, or not).

In his own surprising way, Norman is aggressive. Just as Phyllis Meadow's aggression was always mixed with her drive to form creative relations with others, so Norman Bishop's was displaced into a powerful energy that serves his own desire to shape a better life for the ill and poor. Though not a man who confronts, Norman is one who persists. Though his manner with others is quiet, even saintly, he does not let go of a good idea. Though he respects others, he does not let them go until they've agreed to do something to help. This remarkable brand of positive aggression did not come easily. There was a day when Norman's life could not possibly have been more miserable, and miserable because he was unable to focus his aggressions which, with the aid of drugs, he turned against himself—until that day when he had to turn his life around. Such a day is the one addicts call hitting bottom—the day when they must decide whether to continue the risk-taking life that leads to death or to take the very different risk of giving up the worlds of addiction for a new life impossible at the time to imagine. Addicts cannot take the steps they must to be free of the addictions until and if they take the step away from the old life. When and if they do, then the only way they can live is by, first, giving themselves the experience of living, as it is said, one day at a time. Each day they must remember who they are (a drunk or a junkie who had ruined his previous life). Every day they must several times over decide not to use or drink or whatever it is. They must, in a word, live in continuous reflection on themselves, while always looking at the worlds about. This they must do until they come to believe that the risks of this life are deadly, which in fact they are for them in the most personal and emotional ways.

If the globalized social worlds are risk societies, then the risks must be real enough to be deadly. And if there is a model for surviving the new individualism it could be (though cautiously so) the lives of those who survive a real encounter with the deadly worlds and live to tell the story. The death before them may be their own, or of a marriage, or of war, or of neighborhood violence, or of a child lost to street wars, or of a criminal past, or of any number of things that, being enumerated, we realize are all too commonplace in these worlds today. The new individual may well be a woman of culture and means like Phyllis Meadow. But, more often than not, as Hegel once taught, it may be better to look at the slaves and their heirs; at those who suffer on the margins of the fast worlds—that is, those who have little choice but to feel and experience the suffering of life as they look in their own ways for the new individualism. However one thinks of the new individualism—and it is necessary to think about it—one must think of it as the hard and aggressive work by which what accomplishments are achieved are ever exposed to the aggressions of others who would take it all away.

Yet the remarkable thing is that those who try and fail, or those who come through it awkwardly, and those who seem to have succeeded at it, know very well that there are millions the world over for whom life is not a mere adjustment and culture not so powerful as to reduce them to one narrow dimension. They are men and women, and more children than you would suppose, who see and feel the self within, accept it for what it is, and use its aggressions and drives for attachment to others with whom they remake themselves and what corners of the worlds they can.

REFERENCES

Breines, Wini. *Young, White, and Miserable: Growing Up Female in the Fifties* (Boston: Beacon, 1992).

D'Emilio, John. *Sexual Politics, Sexual Communities: The Making of a Homosexual Minority in the United States, 1940–1970* (Chicago, IL: University of Chicago Press, 1983).

Douglas, Ann. *Terrible Honesty: Mongrel Manhattan in the 1920s* (New York: Farrar, Straus and Giroux, 1995).

Halberstam, David. *The Fifties* (New York: Ballantine, 1994).

Hobsbawm, Eric. *The Age of Extremes: A History of the World, 1914–1991* (New York: Vintage, 1994).

Hodgson, Godfrey. *America in Our Time: From World War II to Nixon: What Happened and Why* (New York: Vintage, 1976).

Lemert, Charles. *Social Theory: The Multicultural and Classical Readings,* 3rd ed. (Boulder, CO: Westview Press, 2004).

Martin, Jay. *The Dialectical Imagination: A History of the Frankfurt School and the Institute of Social Research, 1923–1950* (Boston: Little, Brown, 1973).

May, Elaine Tyler. *Homeward Bounder: American Families in the Cold War Era* (New York: Basic Books, 1988).

Mead, Walter Russell. *Moral Splendor: The American Empire in Transition* (Boston: Houghton Mifflin, 1987).

Meadow, Phyllis. *The New Psychoanalysis* (Lanham, MD: Rowman and Littlefield, 2003).

Mills, C. Wright. *The Power Elite* (New York: Oxford University Press, 1959).

———. *The Sociological Imagination* (New York: Oxford University Press, 1960).

Riesman, David, et al. *The Lonely Crowd* (New Haven, CT: Yale University Press, 1961).

Sennett, Richard. *The Corrosion of Character* (New York: Norton, 1998).

Wallerstein, Immanuel. *After Liberalism* (New York: New Press, 1995).

———. *The Decline of American Power* (New York: New Press, 2003).

Zinn, Howard. A *People's History of the United States: 1492 to the Present* (New York: HarperCollins, 2003).

VII

Intellectual Memoir

14

The Race of Time
and the Lives of the Dead

In *Negotiating with the Dead,* Margaret Atwood says "all writing of the narrative kind, and perhaps all writing, is motivated, deep down, by a fear of and a fascination with mortality—by a desire to make the risky trip to the Underworld, and to bring something or someone back from the dead." If to write is to get down with the dead, then to write a memoir is the most down and dirty of all negotiations of the kind.

To live in the worlds at hand without due regard for their underworlds is a terrible conceit—that life is a stand taken against death. Against which, Emmanuel Levinas has said in *Time and the Other:* "The unknown of death signifies that the very relationship with death cannot take place in the light, that the subject is in relationship with what does not come from itself." The time that flies away or runs out is at once dark and shimmering with the meaning that we are other than we had supposed. To the living and the dead, the race of time is filled by the emptiness of the grievous losses that give human suffering its vitality.

Still, we may ask, what have the living to do with the dead? Atwood again reminds of the many and seemingly ubiquitous cultures that not only allow for visits to an underworld, but insist on them. What, she asks, is sought in the descent? Her list—drawn from Odysseus and Gilgamesh, Hamlet and Borges, Rilke and others—is: riches, knowledges, monsters, and lost loves. What are these riches sought in a descent to the land of the dead if not some knowledge of loved ones with whom we are forever bound by the necessity of life's endings? We negotiate with the dead against monstrous odds, but bargain we must to keep the dead from haunting what remains of life.

Writings of all kinds breach the line that severs the real from the other it becomes when all is said and done. Life with others is lived against the possibility that those who have gone before possess a wisdom that bequeaths the one unqualified value that is beyond all exchanges—the secret of what, if anything, lies beyond. Do they, the Dead, speak to us in the bargain? This is harder to deny than skeptics would admit. At the least (if not the entirety of the matter) the Dead speak to us when we constitute and correct ourselves in the stories we tell of what pasts we think we know.

Life's time is a race to overcome the dark skin of this most vital of ignorances. The race is won, if at all, only when we cast our stories into the void of those who attend to us. They may listen for no better reason than the wish to preserve the delicate social ties that make it possible for them one day to tell theirs to whomever, if not us. There is no telling without the void our strangers kindly offer.

Telling the stories of pasts are negotiations with the Dead we remember, if at all, only in the telling. A past is always, irrevocably, just as dead as a future. We are dealt a passing moment, the present that we check, raise, or fold on the gamble that we can win a pot against the odds of life. A bet is always against an outcome that is never present in the instant we must play what hands we have. The land of the living, like the time to bet, passes in a flash. Writing stills the light into a negative in which the dark stands in for the real that quickly becomes a false positive. Yet, against all this, we tell others what we think we saw before the image passed.

Once upon a time in the low valleys of a river town, a boy was born after a flood. He thinks he was told that the waters had forced his parents to flee for higher ground. The next year they built a new home high in the western hills of the river town. Theirs was the first of many to come that would blot their view of the valley below. Just the same, at the first, their new hill home was high enough to secure the modest aspirations of a young doctor and his beautiful Balkan bride. When the boy was still of nursing age, the parents, newly housed but domestically unsettled, sought help of a sort the better, so to speak, white people of the region customarily sought. As he grew older, the boy came to think, so far as anyone can think such thoughts, that she who came may have offered the breast the mother was told she could not.

Late in the 1930s, the younger woman entered the household of the boy and his unsettled parents when the river town, just north of the South, was still segregated. The year before, Florence had followed her family star to join kin in the near North. She came from Florida where, her parents gone, she had been raised by a white woman. She had been thus raised out of time, an innocent outlaw to the deadly racial exclusions. After settling in a room of her own in the dark but dry basement of the doctor's new house, Florence, her young age and humble status notwithstanding, came quickly to rule the roost. She slept below and ate in the kitchen but she held the family in her hand as had, before and since, so many women of her lineage. Evenings and weekends, the doctor moaned and barked. Weekdays, the mother and wife acted out her stated role as mistress of the domestic scene. Amid the trouble and pretense, Florence made it work in ways that went beyond her prescribed duties. A brother was born to the boy.

In time, war called away the father, Charles. The mother, Helen, was left with more than she was meant to handle. To the amazement of all, she managed well, even after Adele, her mother, being of the old world, insisted that Florence move out. For those years, the boy took to the mother's bed, or so he believes. Florence commuted by bus from a house of her own in the valley from which the doctor had led his family. Adele worked as a nurse across town but commuted on the same bus line, thus replicating the flow of the races. Mornings, whites rode toward the city, Blacks to the suburbs; evenings they took the seats the others had warmed. The boy does not remember where the mother's mother slept, though he is certain as certain can be that it is not in Florence's room.

In time the war came to an end. The father flew home from his far Pacific station. The day he landed at a nearby Air Force base, the late summer air was bright against a cloudless sky. Years later the boy remembers the light, and a strange sort of peanut butter and banana sandwich he devoured while waiting. After lukewarm embraces, the four of them—the doctor, his wife, and two boys—drove home by cornfields freshly cut. On the way, the light disappeared behind some imperceptible horizon. It was already apparent that something had happened to the doctor in the long absence—or, at least, that was the theory. Perhaps whatever it was might have been nothing more than a dimming of the not-yet-latent wishes—or the dawning of the fear the boy would not have the father of whom he had dreamt while sleeping, if he did, close to the mother. Whatever it was, the father thereafter was a missing man.

The doctor returned to his bed by rights and, by necessity, to the private practice of medicine. Legend has it that he was good at what he did outside the house. Mornings, he made house and hospital calls before driving deep into the valley to his downtown office. At noon, he had lunch at the Cricket restaurant just off Vine Street. No matter what, even if in later years the boy had come along, the doctor read the morning papers over a silent lunch. After, he saw patients for three or so hours, then left for home.

On the way home—more often than the boy thought necessary—the father would stop to restock the liquor closet with bourbon and the fridge with meats. At Scheibe's Market, in the stockroom, he would give the butcher regular shots of whatever medicine doctors then thought a diabetic needed. Once home, the doctor had the first of a string of bourbons with water and rocks. By dinnertime he was irritable or distant according to whichever cloud had passed over his head. After, he would nap on the same long sofa that decades later could be found in the home of the boy's brother, himself now a doctor. The father's evening naps would last much of the evening until after the boys had retired to their rooms. The boy, ever keen to his removal from the mother, would listen for the sounds of the father's awakening. After a shower, the doctor dressed for bed to watch late-night television while sipping one or two benedictory bourbons. It seemed, so far as such things reveal themselves, that the long evening nap refreshed the father enough to end the day, house lights down, perimeter checked, and the last drink in hand, by talking things over with Helen. All these years later, the kitchen scene stands out in the grown boy's memory as the one and only fully generous parental habit that brought him to the fore of the attentions. He of course heard only the muffled tones of their talk. In the absence of the real thing, this was what comfort there was in the unrequited possibility that the father loved him.

As the boy grew older he accepted the family routines for what they were. Florence remained a presence. He had the idea that she and Helen had become, if not friends, sisters of a remote kind. But as adolescence gained on him, the one the boy loved most faded to the penumbra of his awareness. To fill the empty time, Florence went to night school for the elementary education she had never had. Many years later she told him (or so he believes) that she worked on her reading and writing in order to keep the bond with him. After the parents died on either side of 1970, she and the boy renewed their primordial intimacies.

The boy, once grown, came to terms with the quirky family story. The indefinite terms he had come to were of those of this story—a story of floods, war, migrations, homecomings, and goings; of inclusions and exclusions; and of wishes disappointed only to be acted out with one who was real in her effect but lost to the well-structured realities of the worlds in and between which they lived.

The story, like all stories, is told from memory. Save for the storyteller and his brother, all of the principals of a local drama that played out long ago are dead. Yet, decades later, the dead ones live on at a time when the teller must renew his negotiations with the land of the Dead. His death, like all deaths, will come at some time sooner or later to the present in which he remembers events that could well have taken place. If they did, then what of the one who remembers them? Is he, *that* boy, alive or dead? If alive, in what sense more real than the stories he tells on the wings of memory's flight? If dead, then who tells the story of a boy who once lived, and may still, but whose encounters with certain events and persons are buried in the dust of structures now abandoned?

In this telling, the boy's story is neither true nor false—neither fact nor fiction. Those who dare tell even the simplest story of some boy or girl they think they might have been are negotiating with their dead. The teller of any one story tells but one iteration of the several truths, realities, or accounts that could be told, each different in important ways from the others.

This is how time races on from the lives of the Dead. It is not so much the speed of its passing as the feeble grasp memory allows on the time in which we negotiate with our dead; hence, the riddle of the past that is always fixed somewhere in a land to which we must return without map or clock to mark the way.

Then too, there is the enigma of tellings. Whether written or sung, by pen or voice, stories must find a way between the voice and the text—between speech that has an aura of immediacy and writing that puts the story into a nether region that is neither here nor there.

One supposes that when it comes to negotiations with the Dead of one's personal past, writing trumps speech if only because the past told is always at a distance from the story. Yet, at the same time—the differences Derrida had with Saussure notwithstanding—the telling must call immediate attention to the dead events in the story as if they were still somehow alive. In the difference—which entails but does not contain the differences between presences and absences—stands the essential riddle of social things. They can only be real to us by our speaking of them, yet even our speech in time forms archives—from the neurological to, now, the digital—that in due course are corrupted as they recede into a cyber-ether. Still, the necessary dependencies and differences between speech and writing remain the primary theoretical vectors of serious understanding of the moral conundrum of social life. The *between* of the individual and her collectivities is a practical negotiation that requires a social contract to and from which no map or clock can guide the way.

On the one hand, for the spoken word to have its effect on those to whom it may be addressed, there must be some reasonably well-inscribed and shared accord by which signifiers, unable to sustain a link to real things, come to convey a world of social consciousness with respect to what things there may be. This would be Durkheim's insistence that social consciousness is the origin of collective representations that, in principle, are the moral and social codes that make meanings necessary, thus possible. This too is the idea that seems to have influenced Saussure's theory of social values as the articulation in the waning present of a sound that evokes not just the shared meanings that come to mind in that present but all the worlds of possible meanings that must be left out in the instant of the utterance. If any speaker tried to say everything that could be said at a given instant then he would emit a babble that could certify him for hospitalization, which is to say for removal from the prevailing social order. With Durkheim and Saussure (but also, and shockingly, Marx), social values are without exception marked for exchange not according to their inherent utilities but by a prevailing (which is to say corrupt and deadly) social form covering the modes of production of the meanings offered for sale.

On the other hand, that of writing—let us call it Freud's (but also to a lesser degree Marx's)—social meanings are riddled with terrible turns of the table. They may arise from some utterly inscrutable voice—like sleepy slips of the Unconscious in Freud (or of Mr. Moneybag's secretive modes of production in Marx)—calls out the repetitions of actual human behavior in which the hidden but absent truth of the past. That voice, of course, is never truly spoken to be heard as such. It is always written in the sense that, as Lacan made clear, in the interior discourse of the Other revealed in dreams, the contents are always metonymic, which is to say pictograms that fuse speech with pictures that condense meanings beyond any possible vocalization. Derrida's famous theory of the priority of writing over the voice was at least homologous to Freud's broken and condensed voice of the Unconscious. Better yet (and this is the point too often missed in attempts to characterize poststructuralism) the truth of presences is cast adrift in the indefiniteness of structuring wholes of all kinds. Being, power, centers, selves, histories, and the like are, Derrida rightly said, the enemies of the free play meanings signified by arbitrary signs.

At the same time, the whole point of stories, whether written or spoken, is that they occupy an inordinately prominent place in both traditions—let us call them again Durkheim's and Saussure's as distinct from Freud's and Derrida's. In the one, Durkheim's (and only slightly less so Saussure's and even Marx's), the primary story is one spoken in the social truth of collective representations (or with Saussure of *la langue* and with Marx the system of exchange values) that give expression to purportedly sensible (but actually obscure) social meanings. In the other, Freud's (and, differences being granted, Deleuze's and Derrida's) meanings, such as they are, arise not from a well-rooted source but in the folds that generate rhizomatic branches that break open the social space of meaning. In the one case, the stories imply that there is a root from which the social truth of the story springs; in the other the idea is that there is no breaching of the past's deadly power over what we know or think we know.

Thus, either way one plays it, what remains is that the written story is much more than a deferral. It is itself an incarnation of the storyteller's negotiations with the dead past. Once there was a boy or a girl … then what? This cannot be said absolutely. It can only be told but never in so many words.

My relations over the years to the ever vanishing little boy of the story account for the race of time across which my writing has sprawled. Some have generously told me that this or that text mattered to them. These remarks are always much appreciated but, with no disrespect for those who have made them, they have also been a surprise.

At first, I thought they were confusing me with my uncle Edwin, now dead, but still one of sociology's finest, most elegant writers, not to mention creative thinkers. In the early days, many did in fact confuse me with him to the point that I had to look up *potlatch* to understand whatever Edwin had said on the subject. Still, when (in Goffman's hilarious locution) in some "vasty Hilton field" I realized they were referring to a hobby horse I had in fact ridden, it became necessary to dismount the pleasure in order to adjust the harness. Usually, not always, I came to realize that, if there is a conceit more grievous than taking compliments too seriously, it is that of dismissing them out of hand. The one conceit is the fable that we who negotiate with our dead have slain the monsters and brought back the rich truths others have lost, or not found; the other is that of failing to understand that those who attend to the stories we have told have their own stake on the table—that of respecting conversation that suspends the social whole in a web mysteriously spun in the cool of the night. We awaken to behold the dew-sodden filaments that trap the food we consume. Eventually, the sun dries the dew; the fine filaments collapse into the dust from which we had sprung and out of which, another day, we compose the stories.

The stories that at first seem to be acutely personal are in fact caught up and suspended in social space. All structures, of whichever kind—from stellar to social to mental to molecular—are suspension bridges over times and spaces. Otherwise, they would not endure and, by definition, would not be structures. The story of the boy, on one level, is localized for a few years in a specific river town through which, along the river and across the ferries and bridges, thousands upon thousands found their ways west toward the reputed freedoms of the plains, while other thousands, on a different kind of freedom journey, made their ways north out of the deep South. Neither, in their short runs of time, found the pure freedoms they may have dreamt of. They found, if anything, relief from bitter pasts. Along their ways they met others with whom they forged ties when not forging weapons. In a sense, this one kid in his place and time does not matter. In another sense—that of the threads of a story that bind him to others and their stories of other places and times—he is like (not the same as, but *like*) all others. Somewhere in the between, social things are structured for a while until they no longer are.

It is not a question of a common denominator of the human condition; nor of a universal truth; nor, even, of one or another of the more potent myths, like that of Oedipus, that recur in many times and places. The boy, in this case the little boy of my recollections, was, indeed, caught up in what, over several generations, had the taint of an oedipal conflict. But, in the race of time, where exactly does such a conflict act itself out? If one were to grant that beyond the particulars of unrequited passions and unexamined struggles over the right to bed down with either of the two women in the family romance, there is another—let us call it, tentatively—still more grand narrative, which is to say: that of the apparent, if not certifiable, universal quest for objects of desire that are displaced by culture beyond what words can tell. Incest may well be the universal taboo, or the next best thing to it. But incestuous desire is certainly well within language—that is the point of the variations on the Oedipus legend, which makes it speakable if not coherent. What else moves a young heart to wish for the unspeakable is beyond words, even if and when it presents itself in the guise of the powerful taboo that only begins to get at the heart of it all.

To be human is to long. All longings sooner or later settle upon a territory one would rule were it not that the ghosts of what and whom we killed within know we coveted a throne much less a prohibited woman. To long for one who cannot be had is, in itself, to slay, however innocently, all who stand in the way of the impossible. In this sense, all well-structured social things—from the domicile to the mosque or fraternal order to the party or the trade union to the state and its cultural apparatuses to the global pathways and networks—these and more are the enduring remnants of the desire to stand up to the ones who would take it all away.

Is there anyone who does not tell some story of her early life? However refracted and opaque one's story may be—however little she is aware that what she is telling is a story that matters; or, for that matter, however deranged the teller might be in making up a story that could not possibly have much to do with reality—personal stories are what remain of whatever pasts there are. All stories are *opaque*—that is their point: they serve to hide as much as they reveal. All stories are *fictions*—that is how they disguise what they reveal; they could hardly be repetitions of original events. All stories are *personal*—that is why none is truly personal for if it were then the story would lack the power to tell what truths it tells of the larger array of enduring structures against which whatever may be personal is hedged.

Herein stands the most formidable obstacle to empirical social studies. To study the worlds comprising, *and* composed by, storytellers leaves the student of the social with but two options, both of which involve the problem of data. All data, before they become data, must be cooked. Data are never, ever evidential if cut fresh from the kill. When it comes to social research the only question is what kind of stew you want and how, if at all, your pot preserves or lends taste to the butchered meat. As many since Kant have known (but few accepted), things in themselves are never directly available to taste as such. By consequence, we who cook the meat of social worlds are caught on the horns of a bullish dilemma. Either to believe, as many do, that their stews have only clarified the sauces of life, leaving the essences to speak for themselves; or (the only alternative) to tolerate the only pure fact of social research: that the pots we stir, we stir by our own hands, leaving the sauces vulnerable to our imperfect ways. Truth be told, when it comes to social things, there are no truths—which is not at all the same thing as believing there is no truth.

How, given this, does it happen that a boy with a story ends up where he ends up? The stories of the stews we make for ourselves are as good an account as we may have, on one unimpeachable condition: that we swallow the whole mess, the bitter with the savory, the bloody with the burnt.

I have, as those who know me best are aware, made quite a few messes. Often against good advice, I have tried to take them all in. I can only suppose that these facts of my life—the messes and the attempts to swallow them whole, have something to do with the domestic soup into which I was born.

No confession of this sort is ever simple. I have also done some things well, and a few very well. In the remainder what counts, or so I suppose, is less the why than the how of cooking my way into and out of the stews of ordinary life. Mine were the stews of hoping for the only thing a little white boy, suspended as I was in a local matrix in the early 1940s, wished for. We whose fathers appeared to us to be missing for reasons beyond their or our control wanted to know: Where is the missing man and what does his absence mean? Some boys, of all the races, never have that man around and thus never know what his absence means. Boys of my generation encountered this preoccupying mystery because of war. This did not make us special. It only brought us down into the norm of global boyhoods. Yet, since we were led to believe it was not meant to be as it was, we may have been more confounded by it. This alone does not exact an important measure of sympathy. Boys whose fathers or mothers were sold off in the slave trade or killed off in the Indian wars no doubt stumbled on this mystery long before we did. I can envision what others have experienced but I can only give tell of what I knew and what the boys of my vague acquaintance in those days seemed to have known.

All mysteries wrought of unrequitable desires are deep precisely because they come into emotional play at precisely the point where all should be clear. This unsettled state of confusion—however widely it may be distributed among the classes and races—puts those therein consigned in an impossible situation. One acts on what one knows without realizing that one knows very little, if anything, about the facts of his life. The actions are attempts to stir the pot in ways that will render the meat edible. Still, one desires the raw meat that, sushi aside, is not to be taken in.

When the boys in question are of the higher classes in regions laden with racial hatred, the mystery of the missing man can be more puzzling. What white people have in mind when they entrust their precious babies to women not welcome at the dinner table is itself a good measure of the peculiar way social things work. Where apartheids are well structured into the social fabric, the political economy of intimacies expands and contracts with the heat of perceived needs. In the case of the little boy, the white parents are said to have realized that they were swimming in the deep end when it came to managing small children. It was the colored woman herself who told me that as Charles, the father, lay dying, he rose out of the morphine long enough to say to her, uncharacteristically: "Thank you for taking such good care of the boys. We couldn't … " All I know about what was said is what was later told me *and*, crucially, the fact that these were the last words my father uttered before the painkillers took him down below the set point where speech and consciousness are possible. All I can say about these sayings is that they seem right to me.

Thus it was that I was formed not just in any old stew but in one spiced by racial tastes of a particularly ancient, thus refracted, sort. Long enduring evil is cut over time by necessity. Those able pay. In their relations to Florence, for reasons quite out of character, my parents paid the true as opposed to market price for domestic labor. They paid well and, already in the 1940s, they voluntarily contributed to her social security account. Noblesse oblige among the nouveau is an obligation of vague but true recognition either of the failures of the one who pays or (in the instance of my white mother) of an awareness that her station in life was but a hair's breadth above the misery she had herself known in her childhood. Boy children (and perhaps the girls as well) of these arrangements *can* suffer the indignity of loving the one whom the prevailing structural order forbids. When this happens it is far from clear to them whom they love. Like all children of the type they are taught to compose affectionate cards and notes to the legitimate parents while keeping silent as to the forbidden one. But who is the parent when the legitimate parent realizes at the end of his days that he was not? When did he realize this? And how did his late-dawning snatch of the arrangements he created affect the children? What, for that matter, does a child understand of these things? If at all, how does he come to understand them?

The mystery deepens when economic fluctuations, wars, and other intrusions upon the civility of the domestic order take away, for however long, the man who, truth be told, may have already been missing in the crucial sense before he went to war or to whatever it was that made him the lead character of a missing man story. War comes down on all wherever they are in the affected regions, tribes, and nations.

Still, the hard penultimate rule of structural effects is that they come down unevenly. Otherwise there would be no differences explicable according to general theories of social justice or, in the case of empirical social studies, of stratifications. Thus, at the extreme, the mysteries of personal life—like the mystery of the missing man—are inextricably bound to the mysteries of structured social things. One supposes that the personal ones are the more poignant. This is true, but it is not the truth. The truth is that there would be no poignancy in personal life were it not for the structured injustices in the uneven distribution of means and ends. Poignancy is as poignancy does, and feelings arising from absences always arise more acutely in individuals. This is not, decidedly not, because any particular class of individuals gathers the only true members of the order of things. Injustices are social things that bear on any and all who are members of the flawed commonwealth. All experience inequality's differing degrees of pain or pleasure. If there is a primary threat to the ones with more material pleasures, it is that their educations and comforts do not often enable them to feel the pathos of the social wholes except when, in rare moments of collective excitement, their feelings are joined with those of others not of their class.

Why structures like those governing the effects of time, race, locale, war, floods, droughts, and the rest fade in and out of reception is not known. What is known is that they do, which is not to say that collectivities are unable to feel. Of course individuals do not feel anything totally or continuously either. What they do—and do it so much better than do structured wholes—is remember. Tribes have their oral traditions, nations have their archives, ethnic groups have their lingering resentments, but none of these encourages immediate access to the raw feelings that are the uncooked inner fiber of longing and desire.

Access to the truth of these impossible truths is, to be sure, opaque—through a glass dimly. "For now we see through a glass, darkly; but then face to face: now I know in part; but then shall I know even as also I am known." Unapologetically biblical (Paul, I Corinthians), this oft-quoted line comes agreeably to the point. The mysteries of the personal life are those of the social life, as Émile Durkheim insisted whilst trying to explain away the mysteries. Where they meet, if they do, and how they might be joined, if at all, is the foundational mystery of social theory and social studies in general.

Whether as professional theorists or practical seekers we would like to know now what we know but dimly and may know, if ever, only in some other time than the one with which we must live, and move, and have what being we have. We are left to cook the stews we make. The great failure of social studies, in my opinion, is the failure to heed the lessons Marx and Freud understood dimly—that in the end, nothing is exactly what it appears to be. The only distinguishing difference that separates Marx and Freud from Weber is that Weber knew that the truths, such as they may be, do not present themselves, if they do, on our terms. As he confessed in "Science as a Vocation," ideas cannot be forced. "No sociologist should think himself too good, even in old age, to make tens of thousands of quite trivial computations in his head and perhaps for months at a time." Even the slightest idea will not be born without labor. Like politics, science is the work of boring hard boards. Marx and Freud, also hard workers, both took the easier way to politics and science—the illusion that the structures would necessarily provoke the definitive contradiction; the faith that an analytic science would uncover the etiological trauma. Weber was the only true Lutheran—work hard, believe, accept.

It is one thing to work hard at science as a calling, quite another to live according to the rule of irresolute mysteries. Mysteries dim the vision in both instances but somehow, in the long run, it seems easier to accept the frustrations of scientific work (even the acceptance takes the form of succumbing to a false confidence in the brilliance of one's methods). But when it comes to life itself, the ubiquitous truth that we cannot know the truths face-to-face is more disturbing. This is why I do not suppose that I am the only one to make messes along the way. We make trouble, often for ourselves, because not knowing is so unbearable that we take flight hoping against hope that the moment or two in midair will land us in a different place. It never does. We are neither birds nor ghosts. Though, if neither, we are closer to the ghosts than any other creature—this because we live, when we live honestly, with the disembodied truths that come and go as they please.

What, if anything, might all this have to do with a life lived in and around social theories of various kinds? The question, like all questions put to apparently "individual" stories, is of slight general interest—unless, that is, there is some good reason to think that there is no such thing as a completely personal story. Another thing that is known, in this respect, is that in the strictest of senses there certainly is no such thing as the pure, perfect individual—neither in the analytic sense of the pure "one" nor in the practical sense of "perfectly distinct." The more science-bound social theorists have clumsily conceded this point. Without knowing exactly how it works, students of the social have long attempted to define the means by which individuals are made, or make themselves, qua individuals while remaining plausibly obedient to the social norms without which, individual or other, they would die.

Social death is the border guard between individuals and social things. Cross over, either way, without a valid passport and you are a goner. In this respect, social death is more final than bio-death. The living remember those who died in the good graces of the social whole but the rule of governing the excommunicated is strict and unforgiving. They are to be forgotten or, at least, not spoken of again—otherwise the excommunication fails to put them forever outside the communicating community.

The prospect that the individual's social death sets the terms within which social studies must think the individual is at the broken heart of the mystery of social theories. Individualism, a shared ethic of the discrete if not supreme value of the individual, is not a complicated problem. As an ethic, it is inherently social. The problem, instead, arises for those who would make a science of the individual's distance from and relation to the social. No single answer to date is satisfactory. The classic American one is *socialization,* which as many have shown is just too optimistic in its assumption that social things always and uniformly get inside the hearts and heads of individuals. Talcott Parsons, some time ago, tried to patch Freud into this scheme by proposing the somewhat more subtle dynamic of *introjection,* which in the long run did little except perhaps call attention to the Durkheimian elements in his theory by which, once the individual was reset within Parsons's general theory of social action, the action elements became so ubiquitously engaged with each other that the fabled individual was effectively swallowed up in the dynamic.

In due course, after the optimistic liberal era in social studies came to its point of exhaustion late in the 1960s, the eventual "solution" to the status of the individual amid social things was a somewhat Weberian one—that the individual with her subjective needs for intersubjective adequacy is, when all is said and done, of a different order from the organized spheres of modern society. Thus, in time, came the quite useless canonical distinction between *micro* and *macro* social things. The distinction was, always, a fraud of sorts, a way of organizing the professional world of studies of the social as between those who attend to the smaller and local aspects and those who direct their efforts toward the bigger structural things. This was, and remains, little more than a methodological distinction without any evident empirical or theoretical merit.

The problem is better left to the more modest, if not quite adequate, resolution of the classical period, which was, in effect, the *via negativa* of the missing man. For Marx, the human individual was defined by his estrangement—the one expunged by capitalism's exploitations. For Weber, when he was not troubled by the ethical dilemmas he could not solve, it was the overrationalized subject, a victim of modern methods applied to social life. Even for Freud, hardly a theorist of the individual, the individual was no more than the pathetic solitary ego caught between the forces of nature arising from the id and the social pressures coming down through the superego. In the end, the most mature of the early theories were those that eschewed the micro-macro/subject-object distinctions in favor of sheer description—Simmel's wandering stranger of many minds; or Du Bois's doubly conscious American Negro. The striking thing about the interventions of writers like Simmel and Du Bois early in the twentieth century was that, a full half century before Bourdieu and others began to question the benefits of the subjectivism-objectivism dichotomy, they simply set the formula aside in favor a stark but well-formed descriptive approach.

Still, for me at least, the question remains open and in need of attention. What is one to do about the individual as a theoretical *and* practical aspect of the social? And what might be the meaning of the quandary provoked by personal stories told by the multitudes is that, though many in their details, in the long run there are so few stories to be told. River towns or prairies, the missing man family, the lost boys and girls who do or do not find themselves, their lost parents who do or do not triumph over their doubts, the forbidden but intimate strangers in the family mix, the awkward mix of economic and racial as of sexual and sexed differences, the effects of wars and weakly held peaces, of migrations and fears, and so on and so forth—all, and more, are the dramatic elements of human storytelling. Yet, whatever the source of the stories we hear and tell, it is the details that vary wildly while the plots and themes remain disconcertingly similar and few. This, I now believe, is the real and effective consequence of what we still tend to call social structures. Whether the structures are local or global, earthshaking or long-enduring, good or evil, structures do what they do within a narrow range of possibilities—otherwise they would not be structures and social things would slide into a sea of chaos.

This is a lesson that I, for one, required the better part of a lifetime to learn. Why I took so long, I cannot say. But I can make a good enough guess based on what I now know about the story of a quite undistinguished kid who was caught in a series of dilemmas. None were of his making, as with kids they never are. None were his alone. Many, if not all, of the dilemmas were determining if not determinative. He—which is to say, I—came in time to settle on the racial dilemma as the crucial one. Other kids have parents who are transparently incompetent to their obligations. Others, of the several races, call on colored women for help. Others suffer (or benefit) from the missing man syndrome. But somehow in this case the particular woman, Florence, who joined the aggravated family and the aggrieved boy, found a way to break through the veil without crossing the color line.

One reason she did was her religion. Another was that, as a young girl fresh to the near North, she had faced down the color line in her first factory job and did it with her fists. She loved Jesus and she defended herself against the odds. How she, in this setting, affected me is a matter of other stories. What outs in the end is that she was the one who exposed me, so to speak, to churches, several of which we desegregated in the 1940s. What I took from that other than the idea that church-going was a great way to get out of the house when the white father threw one of his Sunday morning fits is hard to say.

In college I began studying science, thinking I would follow in the path of the doctor. At a decisive moment late in the spring of 1958 I was faced with a choice—either to accept a summer research fellowship at a leading research institute in the East or accept a summer job as counselor at a very liberal church camp. Had I chosen the former, I may not have been a doctor but I probably would have become an embryologist or some other kind of biology person. Academic science was easy to me, then, because success in the classroom required little more than hard work and memorization. I was not, then, or so I now think, very good at the science itself—the creative aspects of the vocation. I chose the church camp for the summer after my junior year in college. My final year in college was my last in the natural sciences.

In 1959, I accepted a generous fellowship designed to seduce science students to the study of theology. I went off to a seminary in Boston in a Chevy not quite packed with my worldly possessions. I had only the haziest idea as to what theology was meant to do but whatever it was I found it a quite remarkable thing—the very idea of attempting to state in so many words the truth behind truths that cannot be stated in so many words was just the sort of mystery work for which I hungered. That hunger is, I now realize, part of the hard work of serious science, which some-how never moved me deeply. Why not? Perhaps, I would suppose, because the facts of my young life were so indefinite. The whole thing was so unmentionable, thus opaque or, better, stupid in the sense of stupor-inducing. Either way, theology led to philosophy and history eventually to social theory and psychoanalysis, the major disciplines of the unthinkable.

After seminary, I started at Harvard in the Study of Religion doctoral program, which meant Social Relations in the Graduate School of Arts and Sciences and social ethics in the Divinity School. These were still the days of systematic theology. At

Harvard, I attended the lectures of Paul Tillich and Talcott Parsons. I read as much of what each wrote as I could follow. I devoured the concepts and theories of these two very systematic thinkers. The difference between their methods was, to me, negligible. Both required, in Parsons's terms, an analytic realism, or, in Tillich's, a method of correlation. Both amounted (or so I then thought) to the same thing—taking analytic concepts and their articulation as real enough in themselves whether aimed at the inscrutable dynamics of social action or the void between God and culture. For Parsons the realism was more or less grounded in a series of second-order historical allusions much like the early pages of Weber's *Protestant Ethic.* As his pupil, and as a student of theology, I then found almost nothing about his writing or lecturing abstract. It all made perfect sense to me for much the same reason that I was moved by Talcott Parsons. I experienced him as modest and unassuming, anything but the kind of abstracting monster others from C. Wright Mills on would turn him into. Nor, again, did I find the ideas anything but enchanting—and this because, much the same as the theologians, and especially Paul Tillich, Parsons's social theory was a bold attempt to write and talk about the mysteries of social action. To me the difference was real but slight.

Like the dark inscrutable place alleged to occupy the space between individuals and structures, the mystery of how and why individuals act as they do—under the guise of freedom, yet within the rules of the game—finds its homologue in the improbabilities of monotheistic religions. Why exactly do people stake their lives on a god who is who he is, nameless and distant? To write or speak of these things, either way, is to engage in a parallel if not identical kind of faith that puts everything at risk. From Søren Kierkegaard I had learned the leap of faith for which the paradigmatic story is that of Abraham, the father of the three monotheistic religions, who proved himself worthy by being willing to sacrifice his beloved son Isaac to the point of raising the knife to the boy's throat. Whether the leap is into the nether space beyond the individual into the dominion of invisible structures or into the between of the believer and her god, the form of the action is much the same.

Harvard to me was not everything, far from it. In 1963, after my first year of graduate study, I decided to leave to pursue a life in the Protestant ministry. I finished the academic year, was ordained in 1964, began service as a sincere if naïve minister to youth in a conservative parish affiliated with the most liberal of Protestant sects. What I did not count on was that my regard for the mysteries of faith would not be shared by those I was meant to serve—and certainly not to the point of social action. There were good people among them but most in that parish were white folk of means, richer than my river town parents could have imagined. They were terrified by changes that were then, in Tillich's phrase, shaking the foundations. Whatever they believed in respect to Christianity, their practical ethical principles did not, for the most, extend to a hearty embrace of the demands of the civil rights movement. Naturally, I threw myself into all that as did most of the young clergy of my acquaintance. To act at such a time was, we believed, the divine imperative. We hardly knew what we were doing. If we thought about it, we thought of ideas like Tillich's: "The courage to be is the courage to accept oneself, in spite of being unacceptable" or of Reinhold Niebuhr's Christian social ethic that, in thought and deed, exemplified Kierkegaard's leap of faith. We leapt. None of us died. A few remained with the church. Most of us fled in due course.

By the end of the decade I was back at Harvard to write my exams, then to accept a fellowship at the Joint Center for Urban Studies, where I would write my doctoral thesis. In the fall of 1969, the Joint Center was, after Nixon's election in 1968, a refuge for Kennedy-Johnson liberals not ready to give up on what they had wrought through the 1960s. We debated urban policy, housing, and poverty with an urgency we thought we had earned the right to (but, also, in order to avoid as long as we could determining what actions were demanded of us in the regard to the war in Vietnam). The center, just off Brattle Street, was as close as we could get to the rumbles of the 1960s—Barney Frank shoeless and brash, talking a mile a minute at the Friday afternoon luncheons, while mayors and former secretaries of HUD looked on knowingly, students doing their best to present themselves as in the know.

Somewhere in that time I took a very small group-reading tutorial with Robert Bellah, who was, I thought, brilliant, genial, and generous. With him I read Weber and Durkheim (who were staples in the Divinity School ethics program) but also Freud for the first time. I remember opening one meeting with a version of "What the hell?" The reading had been, I think, *Moses and Monotheism*. My bewilderment was an academic symptom of the extent to which, all the enchantment with mysteries notwithstanding, I was then ill-prepared to probe below the surface. I was, for the time being, content with the social ethics and applied social theory taught by James Luther Adams and Harvey Cox in the Divinity School. In the wake of the 1960s that was more than enough to handle.

After leaving Harvard for my first job at Southern Illinois University, I soon met Alvin Gouldner, who early in the 1970s had returned from Europe to exile in a tower at nearby Washington University, which could not keep him out but would not let him back in. From Gouldner, I learned Marx, but just as importantly learned the importance of third-way strategies. For him the third way was between Marxism and Sociology. When, about the same time, I began spending time in Paris, I discovered a new kind of Marxism—one beholden to Marx, yes, but also one filtered through Freud and Saussure and much else that for the longest while remained a puzzle of a different kind. Eventually the bifold between individuals and structures folded over again to expose another, more complicated mystery—that of the unknown and unknowable. I read and eventually got the point Foucault was pursuing in the early writings. It took a good long time to come fully to appreciate what he was working toward in his last years, which, we now know, is the vanishing point of articulation with Deleuze's manifold vectors of social actions.

Given the story and its sequelae it should be no surprise—or no particular surprise—that the river town boy would be drawn from the racial dilemma to the mysteries of the betweens of life and faith, to the perversities of the Unconscious wherein is to be found, if at all, the missing man, who, it turns out, was always there, missing only in the sense that the hopes and wishes for the normal were phantasmagoria of raw desire. The missing man is a glass through which we see dimly, never face to face.

The race of time is always about the Dead. Not death, the abstraction, but the Dead within—those aspects of our being that are never fully spoken of, not even in our stories. Our dead are, yes, those we cherish or loathe who have gone on to wherever the Dead go. The race of time leads inexorably to the land of the Dead. Stories are the negotiations with time's dark spaces—the betweens, the hiddens, the mysteries, the absences, the longings, the unknowns, and the unmentionables. Our salvation, so to speak, is in the actions we take, most of which are misdirected or just plain messy. Still, from time to time, they are apt to the point of all social actions. We save ourselves by holding up the community—a maxim that Kant put too abstractly as Giddens put it too technically and Bourdieu put it too thinly. The imperatives, the structurations, the habitus, and all the like fall short of the true ethical imperative that we live by our actions that are irrevocably leaps of faith into an unknown. As Al Gouldner said, we often fall flat on our faces. Fallen, we lift our eyes up to the mountains that, as Braudel and after him Wallerstein taught, endure beyond the time of the local events we try to recover in the stories we tell in order to make sense of what we have done and what has been done to us.

Social studies began as political economy, which is to say as a special brand of philosophical ethics. Social theory, since Marx, has always been a social ethic— that is not so much theory as tellings of what we see through the glass dimly. The glass is really a mirror in which believers imagine they see it all. In fact, we see only what we can say, and that is not so bad, since there are not that many stories to tell or ways to tell them. Everything is in the telling without which we do not negotiate with the Dead without whom we are nothing but idle chatter. Tillich again: "The courage to be is rooted in the God who appears when God has disappeared in the anxiety of doubt."

Books by Charles Lemert

The Structural Lie: Small Clues to a Globalized World (Boulder, CO: Paradigm Publishers, forthcoming)

Globalization: A Reader, edited with Anthony Elliott, Daniel Chaffee, and Eric Hsu (London: Routledge, forthcoming)

Why Niebuhr Matters (New Haven, CT: Yale University Press, 2009)

Social Theory: The Multicultural and Classical Readings, 4th ed. (New York: Basic Books, 2008)

Social Things, 4th ed. (Lanham, MD: Rowman & Littlefield, 2008 [German and Danish editions, 2004])

Thinking the Unthinkable: The Riddles of Classical Social Theories (Paradigm Publishers, 2007)

Durkheim's Ghosts: Cultural Logics and Social Things (Cambridge: Cambridge University Press, 2006 [Turkish edition 2009])

Deadly Worlds: The Emotional Costs of Globalization, with Anthony Elliott (Lanham, MD: Rowman & Littlefield, 2006 [also London: Routledge, 2006, as *The New Individualism* and Italian edition 2008])

The Souls of W. E. B. Du Bois, with Alford A. Young Jr., Manning Marable, Elizabeth Higginbotham, and Jerry G. Watts (Boulder, CO: Paradigm Publishers, 2006)

The Goffman Reader, edited with Ann Branaman, 2nd ed. (London: Blackwell, 2005)

Postmodernism Is Not What You Think, 2nd ed. (Boulder, CO: Paradigm Publishers, 2005 [Portuguese/Brazilian edition, 2001])

Sociology After the Crisis, 2nd ed. (Boulder, CO: Paradigm Publishers, 2004)

Muhammad Ali: Trickster and the Culture of Irony (Cambridge: Polity, 2003 [Japanese translation 2005])

Dark Thoughts: Race and the Eclipse of Society (New York: Routledge, 2002)

Crime and Deviance: Essays and Innovations by Edwin Lemert, edited with Michael Winter (Lanham, MD: Rowman & Littlefield, 2000)

The Voice of Anna Julia Cooper, edited with Esme Bhan (Lanham, MD: Rowman & Littlefield, 1998)

Intellectuals and Politics: Social Theory Beyond the Academy (Thousand Oaks, CA: Sage Publications, 1990)

Michel Foucault: Social Theory and Transgression, with Garth Gillan (New York: Columbia University Press, 1983 [Japanese edition, 1990; Polish edition, 1999])

French Sociology: Rupture and Renewal Since 1968 (New York: Columbia University Press, 1981)
Sociology and the Twilight of Man: Homocentrism and Discourse in Sociological Theory (Carbondale: Southern Illinois University Press, 1979)

Credits

"Cultural Multiplexity and Religious Polytheism," *Social Compass* 21, no. 3 (1974: 241–253.

"Sociological Theory and the Relativistic Paradigm," *Sociological Inquiry* 44, no. 2: 93–104 (originally presented at ASA August 1973).

"Sociology as Theories of Lost Worlds," *Sociology After the Crisis,* 2nd ed. (Boulder, CO: Paradigm Publishers, 2004), 12–31.

"Durkheim's Ghosts in the Culture of Sociologies" *Durkheim's Ghosts*: *Cultural Logics and Social Things* (Cambridge: Cambridge University Press, 2006), 8–28.

"Sociology: Prometheus among the Sciences of Man" *boundary 2* 13, nos. 2–3 (Winter–Spring, 1985): 68–89.

"The Uses of French Structuralisms: Remembering Vietnam," *Postmodernism Is Not What You Think,* 2nd ed. (Boulder, CO: Paradigm Publishers, 2005), 101–120.

"Against Capital-S Sociology," *Sociological Theory 21.1 (2003): 74-83.*

"Dreaming in the Dark, November 26, 1997," in *Dark Thoughts: Race and the Eclipse of Society* (London: Routledge, 2002), 241–250.

"The Race of Time: Deconstruction, Du Bois, and Reconstruction, 1935–1873" in *Dark Thoughts: Race and the Eclipse of Society* (New York: Routledge), 223–246.

"Whose We? Dark Thoughts of the Universal Self, 1998" in *Dark Thoughts: Race and the Eclipse of Society* (London: Routledge, 2002).

"Can Worlds Be Changed? Ethics and the Multicultural Dream," *Thesis Eleven* 78 (2004): 46–60.

"If There Is a Global WE, Might We All Be Dispossessed?" in *Postmodernism Is Not What You Think* (Boulder, CO: Paradigm Publishers, 2005), 151–176.

"Surviving the New Individualism," with Anthony Elliott, in *Deadly Worlds: The Emotional Costs of Globalization* (Lanham, MD: Rowman & Littlefield, 2005). Published in the United Kingdom as *The New Individualism: The Emotional Costs of Globalization* (London: Routledge, 2006).

About the Editors

Daniel Chaffee is an Associate Lecturer and Ph.D. student at the Department of Sociology, Flinders University, Adelaide, Australia.

Samuel Han is Visiting Instructor of Sociology at the College of Staten Island and Ph.D. student in Sociology at the Graduate Center of the City University of New York. He is author of *Navigating Technomedia: Caught in the Web.*

Anthony Elliott is Professor and Chair of Sociology at Flinders University, Australia, and Visiting Research Professor at the Open University, United Kingdom. He is author, with Charles Lemert, of *The New Individualism,* 2nd ed. (2009).